RELIGIOUS CONVICTION IN LIBERAL POLITICS

Is it possible for a deeply religious person to be a good citizen in a liberal democracy? There is room for doubt regarding many religious believers. Why? Many religious people take themselves to be conscience bound to support coercive laws for which they have only religious reasons. But many political theorists claim that such exclusive reliance on religious reasons violates the norms of good citizenship and does so for any of a number of reasons: It grinds to a halt productive conversation on the laws to which we are subject; it injects gratuitously divisive factors in already overheated discussions; it fails to respect the autonomy and personhood of citizens who find religious reasons implausible.

Against this position regarding the proper role of religious convictions in liberal politics, Christopher Eberle argues that citizens can discharge every expectation we reasonably have of them, even if they have only a religious rationale for a favored coercive law. In making his case, Eberle articulates an ideal of citizenship that permits citizens to engage in politics without privatizing their religious commitments and yet does not license a mindless and intransigent sectarianism.

A markedly controversial book that offers a substantial challenge to political liberalism, this work will be read with particular interest by students and professionals in philosophy, political science, law, and religious studies, as well as by general readers who seek insight into the relationship between religious commitments and liberal politics.

Christopher J. Eberle is Assistant Professor of Philosophy at the United States Naval Academy.

D1453565

To my parents
William and Elfriede Eberle
I dedicate this book
in respect and love

RELIGIOUS CONVICTION IN LIBERAL POLITICS

CHRISTOPHER J. EBERLE

United States Naval Academy

CAMBRIDGE
UNIVERSITY PRESS

PUBLISHED BY THE PRESS SYNDICATE OF THE UNIVERSITY OF CAMBRIDGE
The Pitt Building, Trumpington Street, Cambridge, United Kingdom

CAMBRIDGE UNIVERSITY PRESS
The Edinburgh Building, Cambridge CB2 2RU, UK
40 West 20th Street, New York, NY 10011-4211, USA
477 Williamstown Road, Port Melbourne, VIC 3207, Australia
Ruiz de Alarcón 13, 28014 Madrid, Spain
Dock House, The Waterfront, Cape Town 8001, South Africa

http://www.cambridge.org

First published 2002

Printed in the United Kingdom at the University Press, Cambridge

Typeface Meridien 10/13 pt.   *System* LATEX 2$_\varepsilon$ [TB]

A catalog record for this book is available from the British Library.

Library of Congress Cataloging in Publication data
Eberle, Christopher J.
Religious conviction in liberal politics / Christopher J. Eberle.
  p. cm.
Includes bibliographical references and index.
ISBN 0-521-81224-0 – ISBN 0-521-01155-8 (pbk.)
1. Religion and politics. 2. Liberalism – Religious aspects. I. Title.
BL65.P7 .E23 2002
322′.1–dc21   2001043441

ISBN 0 521 81224 0 hardback
ISBN 0 521 01155 8 paperback

CONTENTS

Acknowledgments   *page* ix

PART ONE   RELIGION AND RESTRAINT

1   **Religion and Responsible Citizenship**   3

    1.0 Introduction   3
    1.1 Central Thesis   10
    1.2 Justificatory Liberalism   11
    1.3 Importance of the Issue   13
    1.4 Coming Attractions   17
    1.5 A Final Caveat   21

2   **Pluralism and Religion**   23

    2.0 Introduction   23
    2.1 Secularization, Religion, and Politics   25
    2.2 Liberalism and Pluralism   27
    2.3 The Secularization Thesis   29
    2.4 The Subcultural Identity Theory   35
    2.5 Politically Engaged Religion and Religious Freedom   43
    2.6 Concluding Comments   46

3   **Justificatory Liberalism**   48

    3.0 Introduction   48
    3.1 The Constitutive Commitments of Justificatory
         Liberalism   48
    3.2 The Concept of Public Justification   61
    3.3 Public Justification and Restraint   68

Contents

3.4 Justificatory Liberalism and Religion 71
3.5 Concluding Comments 78

PART TWO   WHY RESTRAINT?

Introduction to Part Two 81

4 What Respect Requires 84

4.0 Introduction 84
4.1 Respect for Persons? 84
4.2 Respect and Rational Justification 88
4.3 Respect and Public Justification 94
4.4 Respect and Mutual Criticism 102
4.5 Respect and Human Dignity 103
4.6 The Ideal of Conscientious Engagement 104

5 What Respect Does Not Require 109

5.0 Introduction 109
5.1 The Intuitive Plausibility of the Claim that Respect
    Requires Restraint 109
5.2 Arguments for Restraint 115
5.3 Rawls on Restraint 140
5.4 Concluding Comments 150

6 Religion, War, and Division 152

6.0 Introduction 152
6.1 The Argument from Bosnia 153
6.2 Criticism of the Argument from Bosnia 158
6.3 The Argument from Divisiveness 166
6.4 Criticism of the Argument from Divisiveness 174
6.5 Concluding Comments 185

**Concluding Comments on the Normative Case
for Restraint** 187

PART THREE   WHAT IS PUBLIC JUSTIFICATION?

Introduction to Part Three 195

7 Populist Conceptions of Public Justification 198

7.0 Introduction 198

Contents

7.1	Enumerative Conceptions of Public Justification	201
7.2	Rationality	202
7.3	Actual Acceptance	203
7.4	Acceptability	207
7.5	Restricting Membership in the Public	209
7.6	Adequate Information	222
7.7	Concluding Comments	232

8 Liberalism and Mysticism — 234

8.0	Introduction	234
8.1	Mystical Perception	239
8.2	A Plethora of Epistemic Conceptions of Public Justification	252
8.3	Intelligibility	252
8.4	Public Accessibility	255
8.5	Replicability	260
8.6	Fallibilism and Inerrancy	263
8.7	External Criticism	267
8.8	Independent Confirmability	278
8.9	Proof of Reliability	286
8.10	A General Objection to Epistemic Conceptions of Public Justification	287

9 A Theistic Case for Restraint — 294

9.0	Introduction	294
9.1	A Theistic Case for Restraint	296
9.2	Is Secular Corroboration to Be Expected?	307
9.3	Should Rational Citizens Doubt Uncorroborated Religious Norms?	322
9.4	Concluding Comments	329

Concluding Comments	331

Notes	334
Index	401

ACKNOWLEDGMENTS

Writing a book encourages one to appreciate a general truth about the human condition, that is, that our successes, modest though they might be, are seldom achieved without the unmerited support of our betters. Without doubt, this work in its current shape would never have seen the light of day absent the kind collaboration of a large number of benefactors. I'd like to thank them, one and all.

My original impetus for this book began when I was a graduate student at the University of Massachusetts at Amherst, while writing a dissertation on religion, politics, and epistemology under Bob Wolff. Although that dissertation didn't turn out as I'd hoped it would, this book more nearly satisfies my original aspirations. My thanks to Bruce Aune and Bob Wolff for their critical judgment and continuing support as I muddled my way through some fairly confusing and complicated philosophical terrain. One can hardly hope for better guides.

Institutional support from various sources was vital. The Pew Evangelical Scholars Program provided much-needed financial support: without a fellowship releasing me from teaching responsibilities in 1999–2000, I'd have been unable to patch together enough time to bring this book to completion. "After Liberalism," a five-week seminar sponsored by Calvin College and directed by Nick Wolterstorff, provided a fruitful environment to explore many of the issues I address herein. My thanks to Susan Felch and Anna Mae Bush for organizing the seminar, to Calvin College and the Pew Charitable Trusts for sponsoring it, to Nick for directing it, and to the other participants for their contributions. Norm Young and Marv Bartell (respectively, Provost and Dean of the College of Arts and Sciences of Concordia University) also provided release time throughout the writing process.

Acknowledgments

The following text raises issues that have required me to venture an opinion on a number of matters about which I am undeniably inexpert. Many people have done their part to ensure that my excursions into unfamiliar waters don't end in egregious and embarrassing error, most particularly Robert Audi, Jon Barz, Kraig Beyerlein, Karen Falcon, Larry Falcon, Marty Freeman, Kent Greenawalt, Dave Jacobson, Philip Quinn, Trevor Rubingh, Chris Smith, Steve Smith, Kurt Stadtwald, Jeffrey Stout, Doug Sweeney, Paul Weithman, Kerry Walters, and Ashley Woodiwiss.

There are several people for whose cooperation and friendship I'm particularly indebted and who I'm therefore delighted to have the opportunity to acknowledge in print. Terence Cuneo and Mickey Mattox read large sections of the manuscript and commented in detail on nearly every major point I address. Michael Perry and Nick Wolterstorff have been unfailing in their support for my work as well as exemplary in their own writing on religion and politics. I have no idea how different this book would be without Terence, Mickey, Michael, and Nick's friendship, but I'm quite certain the product would have been much the poorer (as would I). The scribblings that follow are only a pale reflection of innumerable illuminating and invigorating conversations I've been privileged to have with each.

The debts we owe to those dearest to us are often the hardest to convey. Suffice it to say that my wife Lauren provided more support than a decent spouse would have ventured to request and more joy than a reasonable person could hope to expect. My gratitude, finally, to my parents, whose unconditional acceptance throughout my life is, and has always been, a sign and symbol of unmerited Grace. This book is dedicated to them.

PART ONE

RELIGION AND RESTRAINT

CHAPTER 1

RELIGION AND RESPONSIBLE CITIZENSHIP

1.0 INTRODUCTION

On November 3, 1992, citizens in Colorado voted on a proposed amendment to that state's constitution, "Amendment 2."[1] Had it been successfully enacted, Amendment 2 would have repealed existing laws in Denver, Boulder, and Aspen that prohibit work- and housing-related discrimination against homosexual citizens and would have forbidden the passage of any comparable law elsewhere in the state. Although Amendment 2 was passed by roughly 53 percent of voting citizens, it was eventually struck down by the Supreme Court in 1996 on the grounds that it violated the Equal Protection Clause. The failure of Amendment 2 to pass the scrutiny of Supreme Court has not, of course, quelled any of the controversies regarding the legal status of citizens who adhere to gay, lesbian, and bisexual lifestyles. If anything, we can expect legal and moral issues regarding homosexuality to assume an even more prominent profile in American politics in the near future.[2]

The referendum on Amendment 2 raises all sorts of important questions. Not the least of those questions has to do with the *moral merits* of Amendment 2: are laws that forbid discrimination against gay, lesbian, and bisexual citizens morally appropriate? Is it morally appropriate for the state to force a landlord who believes that homosexuality is an abomination to rent an apartment to homosexual applicants?[3] Or, as advocates of Amendment 2 held, should the state refrain from employing its coercive power to discourage discrimination against homosexual citizens, given that many citizens believe themselves to be morally obliged so to discriminate? These are important and contentious questions and

3

have, as a consequence, been the locus of sustained and acrimonious debate.

There are other important if less obvious questions lurking in the neighborhood. In addition to asking whether Amendment 2 was a morally appropriate policy, we might ask how a responsible citizen may go about *determining* whether the amendment was a morally appropriate policy. That is, instead of asking, "Was it appropriate for citizens in Colorado to have voted for (or against) Amendment 2?" perhaps we should ask, "On what basis would it have been appropriate for citizens in Colorado to have voted for (or against) Amendment 2?" What sort of consideration, what sort of reason may a responsible citizen use in deciding to support (or oppose) Amendment 2? A complementary question would be, "What sort of consideration must a responsible citizen *not* allow to play a role in her decision to support or oppose Amendment 2?"[4]

Such questions are particularly appropriate given the widely recognized and very controversial role that appeal to *religious convictions* played in the furor over Amendment 2.[5] Three activists – David Noebel, Tony Marco, and Kevin Tebedo – were motivated to form Colorado for Family Values, the organization primarily responsible for placing Amendment 2 on the statewide ballot, by their belief that "America has deteriorated because it has turned away from literal interpretations of the Bible, and fundamentalist church teachings must play a bigger role in government."[6] According to Tebedo, "Jesus Christ is the king of kings and lord of lords. That is politics, that is rule, that is authority. So whose authority is going to rule?"[7] A close associate of Colorado for Family Values, Bill McCartney, then head coach of the University of Colorado football team and subsequent founder of "Promise-Keepers," asserted that homosexual lifestyles are an "abomination of almighty God" and urged his fellow Coloradans to support Amendment 2 on that basis.[8]

McCartney's religiously grounded support for Amendment 2 raises the question: was it appropriate for McCartney to vote – not to mention urge others to vote – for Amendment 2 on the basis of his conviction that homosexuality is an abomination to God? As a citizen in a liberal democracy – a democracy pervaded by a diversity of lifestyles and worldviews – was it appropriate for McCartney to support Amendment 2 on the basis of a religious rationale he well knew many of his fellow citizens rejected? Of course, that question arises not just for McCartney but for any citizen: is it morally appropriate for any citizen in a liberal democracy to support a proposed law on the basis of his religious convictions?

We should note immediately that McCartney's willingness to support Amendment 2 on the basis of his religious convictions enjoys long-standing precedent. The history of the United States is pervaded by the actions of citizens who were motivated by their religious convictions to support or oppose proposed laws, many of them extremely controversial. In the antebellum United States, for example, citizens provided explicitly religious reasons in support of proposed legislation that discouraged dueling,[9] in opposition to legislation that mandated agents of the federal government to deliver mail on the Sabbath,[10] and in (futile) opposition to Georgia's expropriation of land granted by treaty to the Cherokee nation.[11] Appeal to religious convictions in political debate over the "twin relics of barbarism – Polygamy and Slavery" was not uncommon.[12] Many abolitionists were moved by their religious convictions to advocate the immediate criminalization of slavery,[13] various pro-slavery "reformers" adduced theological considerations against laws that forbade slave owners to teach slaves to read and in support of laws that prohibited slave owners from separating slave families, and many slaveholders articulated an explicitly theological justification for the existing system of slavery.[14] Mormon polygamists appealed to their Latter-Day revelation as a basis both for supporting laws that legalized polygamy and for disobeying laws that criminalized it,[15] just as antipolygamists adduced theological grounds in support of laws that criminalized polygamy.[16]

The willingness of citizens to support (or oppose) controverted laws on the basis of their religious convictions is not, of course, just a thing of the distant past. Recent examples are easy to identify. Religious citizens played a central role in the civil rights movement: according to Hubert Humphrey, the Civil Rights Act of 1964 "could never have become law" without the support of prominent religious groups (the National Council of Churches, in particular).[17] And, of course, Martin Luther King, Jr., and other members of the Southern Christian Leadership Conference explicitly appealed to their religious convictions in agitating against laws that propped up the system of racial segregation.[18] Religious voices are highly critical of government policy on matters regarding the distribution of wealth. Polygamous marriage remains illegal (although rarely prosecuted) even though there are, in my estimation, no convincing nonreligious arguments in support of a ban on "plural marriages."[19] Citizens in Alabama recently voted to reject "Amendment 1," a proposal to fund various educational initiatives by instituting a state lottery, a result plausibly attributed to the moral suasion and political clout exercised by a broad coalition of Christian churches, clergy, and denominational bodies.[20] Religious citizens and public officials regularly bandy about religious arguments regarding the most divisive issue on the current political docket: abortion. One of the most controversial political movements in recent United States politics, the Christian Right, overtly relies on religious claims to underwrite its political recommendations.[21] The list of examples goes on nearly indefinitely: the political power exercised by religious citizens and religious institutions is pervasive indeed, a situation that can hardly be surprising when a remarkable 63 percent of American citizens believe that religion can answer all or most of today's problems.[22]

Citizens in the past have supported and citizens in the present do support controverted laws on the basis of their religious convictions, and there is every reason to believe that citizens in the future will support their favored laws on religious grounds. As we'll see in detail in the next chapter, the widely held idea, codified in the theory of secularization, that modernizing societies will become progressively irreligious is vulnerable to powerful objections, as is the prediction, also associated with the theory of secularization, that modern citizens will engage in their religious practices *"pianissimo,"* in ever more privatized a fashion.[23] Religion – and specifically, *public* religion – seems here to stay.

The issue I'm interested in pursuing, however, is not a descriptive but a normative one: even though many citizens in the United States support their favored laws on religious grounds, is it *appropriate* for them to do so? When a citizen deliberates about the propriety of a proposed policy, is it *morally proper* for her to decide to support or oppose that policy by relating it to her convictions regarding God's will, her reading of a divinely inspired text, or the dicta of a given religious authority?

It is important to be clear about the issue I broach in this book: I'm interested in determining whether any of the *moral obligations* reasonably associated with the *social role* of citizen in a liberal democracy forbid supporting laws on the basis of religious commitments.[24] A word about social roles and moral obligations will help to clarify this formulation of the issue. Part of the cultural material of any given society is a set of more or less determinate social roles: mother, teacher, soldier, statesman, priest. Attached to each of those roles is a set of obligations, rights, and responsibilities: for example, a person who inhabits the role of "father" in our society thereby incurs a prima facie obligation to provide for his children and thereby enjoys the right to raise his children as he sees fit (within limits, of course). The rights and obligations associated with a given social role constitute an important basis for normative evaluation: that a person inhabits a given social role entitles us to evaluate his actions by reference to the normative standards associated with that role. So if, as is the case in the United States, the role of father is associated with the obligation to provide materially for children, then we regard a father who fails to discharge that obligation as culpable and perhaps as the appropriate object of social stigma. Of course, just as the normative standards associated with some social roles differ from society to society, so also do they change in the course of a given society's development. Clearly, the normative standards associated with a given social role are open to negotiation, criticism, and improvement by those who enter into those social roles: *we* decide which normative standards are to be satisfied by those who enter into some social role.

The issue here has to do with the moral standards we should associate with a social role of central importance in a liberal democracy – that of *citizen.* As with the role of father, the role of citizen is associated with a set of rights, obligations, and responsibilities. For example, each citizen in a liberal democracy enjoys the right to exercise some degree of influence over the laws the state enforces with its coercive power: a citizen exercises that right when he votes for a candidate in a general election or for a particular policy in an initiative. I assume, moreover, that the way citizens may exercise that right is constrained by a set of obligations: in particular, I assume that associated with the social role of citizen is the entirely legitimate expectation that a citizen won't knowingly support laws that further his interests to the detriment of "the common good." Even though a citizen might have a moral *right* to support laws that he realizes are detrimental to the common good, a citizen who knowingly supports such a law violates the moral obligations associated with the role of citizen in a liberal democracy and is thereby open to moral *criticism.*[25]

Assume that the following prohibition is associated with the role of citizen in a liberal democracy: a citizen ought not support any law he conscientiously and sincerely regards as detrimental to the common good. That prohibition, notice, provides no adequate basis for objecting to McCartney's willingness to support Amendment 2 on religious grounds: however we understand the notion of "the common good," we may assume that McCartney conscientiously believed, *on the basis of his religious convictions*, that Amendment 2 furthers the common good. So in voting for and advocating Amendment 2, McCartney can't reasonably be criticized for abusing his moral right to vote as he sees fit – at least, he can't reasonably be criticized on the grounds that he has flouted the prohibition against supporting a law considered detrimental to the common good.[26]

Of course, although McCartney's support for Amendment 2 doesn't violate *that* prohibition, there is still the matter of the overall moral propriety of his willingness to support Amendment 2 on religious grounds. There might, after all, be other normative constraints properly associated with the role of citizen that provide a basis for criticizing him. Are there any other such constraints?

To broach that normative issue in a reasonably sophisticated manner, we need to distinguish between two questions that pertain to the justificatory role that a citizen's religious convictions might play in his political practice. First, is it morally appropriate for a citizen such as McCartney to support his favored laws on the basis of his religious convictions? Second, is it morally appropriate for McCartney to support his favored laws on the basis of his religious convictions *alone*?[27] These two questions are importantly different. It is one thing for McCartney to support Amendment 2 on nonreligious grounds, thereby addressing his nonreligious compatriots, yet *also* to support Amendment 2 on *corroboratory* religious grounds. It is quite another matter – a much more troubling matter, given its sectarian overtones – for McCartney to support Amendment 2 for no reason other than a religious reason.

I believe that the United States' political culture is characterized by an *affirmative* answer to the first question. If a citizen supports or opposes a proposed law on the basis of his religious convictions, then that's just fine. And if he tries to convince other citizens to support or oppose a proposed law by appealing to their religious convictions, that's fine as well. In neither case need he violate any of the obligations attendant to his role as a citizen in a liberal democracy. Indeed, in neither case need he do *anything* that is in the least defective, out of order, less than ideal, or the like. Since there is, I take it, general consensus (though certainly not unanimity) that the first question merits an affirmative answer, and because I believe that that consensus is correct, I'll assume throughout this book that the norms of responsible citizenship permit citizens to support (or oppose) laws on the basis of their religious convictions. For my purposes, the first question is settled.[28]

My sense is, however, that there is no consensus in the United States as to how we ought to answer the second question. Although many a citizen supports (or opposes) a favored policy on the basis of her religious convictions alone, that practice is certainly controversial. The furor over Amendment 2 – and debate over laws that discourage or criminalize homosexual behavior generally – exemplifies our pervasive and contentious disagreement over that practice. In addition to the obvious, I believe that laws discouraging homosexual relations are so controversial because there is no credible nonreligious reason to believe that homosexual behavior is immoral or otherwise aberrant. So anyone who supports a law that discourages homosexual behavior *must* – insofar as she has a clear and sober grasp of the arguments on both sides – be relying on some sort of religious rationale.[29] Because laws that discourage homosexual behavior inevitably depend for their justification on religious claims, the citizens whose behavior is discouraged by such laws naturally regard themselves as subject to religiously grounded impositions – a condition many regard as a repugnant state of affairs indeed.

Many on the other side of the issue reject such protestations out of hand. As they see the matter, a citizen such as McCartney is doing exactly what any other advocate involved in a contentious political dispute does: he supports a law that he conscientiously takes to be morally appropriate given his admittedly fallible and partial understanding of the merits of the issue.[30] The fact that he supports his favored position on the basis of normative commitments he accepts solely on religious grounds is not *relevantly* different from his opponents' supporting the contrary position based on a different but nevertheless partial and fallible normative understanding. Consequently, it is no more objectionable for McCartney to support Amendment 2 on the basis of his religiously grounded normative commitments than it is objectionable for his opponents to reject Amendment 2 on the basis of the parochial moral understanding they bring to the table.

It seems clear that we are divided as to the propriety of a citizen's supporting or opposing a proposed law on the basis of religious convictions alone. Social mores on that issue are unclear, contradictory, and contested. The lack of a settled understanding as to what is required by responsible citizenship regarding the proper role of religious convictions in politics renders that issue a fit topic for investigation. My intention in this book is to contribute to the ongoing discussion of that question and, I hope, to aid in its resolution.

1.1 CENTRAL THESIS

I'll defend the claim that a citizen is morally permitted to support (or oppose) a coercive law even if he has only a religious rationale for that law.[31] So I will defend the claim that a citizen such as McCartney is under no obligation to refrain from supporting Amendment 2 even if he lacks a credible nonreligious rationale in support of that proposal, even if he can't articulate a rationale for Amendment 2 that has a realistic prospect of convincing his compatriots; indeed, even if he realizes that his compatriots are entirely within their epistemic rights in rejecting his religious rationale for Amendment 2. (The same applies, *mutatis mutandis*, to any citizens who *reject* Amendment 2 solely on religious grounds.) The unvarnished truth is that responsible citizenship doesn't require a citizen to restrain his natural and understandable inclination to support a coercive law for which he has a religious rationale, even if he supports that law on the basis of his religious rationale *alone*.[32]

I want to make clear at the outset, however, that I do *not* endorse the position that responsible citizens may support (or oppose) a coercive law without *concern* for whether they can articulate a plausible secular rationale for that law, without even *attempting* to articulate a widely convincing rationale.[33] After all, the claim that a citizen is in no respect morally criticizable for supporting a coercive law solely on religious grounds is entirely consistent with the claim that she has an obligation to do what she can to avoid putting herself in such a condition. And I'll argue that each citizen has just that obligation: each citizen ought sincerely and conscientiously to attempt to articulate a plausible, secular rationale for any coercive law she supports. So, to put my central thesis in summary fashion: *a citizen has an obligation sincerely and conscientiously to pursue a widely convincing secular rationale for her favored coercive laws, but she doesn't have an obligation to withhold support from a coercive law for which she lacks a widely convincing secular rationale.*

1.2 JUSTIFICATORY LIBERALISM

I have no illusions regarding the popularity of this thesis. My defense of the claim that a citizen is in no wise morally criticizable for supporting (or opposing) a coercive law solely on the basis of religious convictions puts me at loggerheads with a number of prominent theorists, including John Rawls, Charles Larmore, Bruce Ackerman, Robert Audi, Amy Gutmann, Thomas Nagel, Lawrence Solum, and Gerald Gaus. Although each of these thinkers differs from the others in significant respects, each adheres to his or her own blend of what I shall call *justificatory liberalism*.[34] And it is because of their adherence to justificatory liberalism that Rawls, Larmore, and others are committed to rejecting my thesis. As a consequence, I'll attempt to establish my thesis by articulating and evaluating the central arguments put forward in support of justificatory liberalism.

What is justificatory liberalism? Although I'll explain that position in more detail in succeeding chapters, a brief characterization here will help to identify the question at issue in this book. Justificatory liberals are committed to liberal principles and practices. For example, they believe that the power of the state over citizens should be severely constrained; that each citizen should enjoy certain familiar rights: freedom of religion, freedom of conscience, freedom of association, the right to own private property, and so on; that laws should be publicly promulgated prior to the state's enforcing those laws; that citizens should be tried in independent courts and accorded due process when defending themselves; that each citizen may participate in selecting his political representatives and thus have some modicum of influence over the laws to which he is subject; and so on. Adherence to such substantive claims is a necessary condition of adherence to justificatory liberalism.[35] (Hence, justificatory *liberalism*.)

But a commitment to liberal practices and principles isn't sufficient for commitment to justificatory liberalism; adherence to such substantive liberal commitments as mentioned earlier doesn't distinguish justificatory liberalism from other species of liberalism. What does? Fundamentally, commitment to the following claim: because each citizen ought to *respect* her compatriots, each citizen ought to pursue *public justification* for her favored coercive laws. According to the justificatory liberal, since each of her compatriots deserves to be treated with respect, a citizen should support only those laws which she sincerely and rationally takes herself to enjoy an appropriate rationale – a rationale in virtue of which her favored laws are *justifiable* to each member of the *public*. The claim that respect requires public justification provides a basis for the central component of the justificatory liberal's ethic of citizenship: *the norm of respect imposes on each citizen an obligation to discipline herself in such a way that she resolutely refrains from supporting any coercive law for which she cannot provide the requisite public justification.* (Hence, *justificatory* liberalism.)

As a consequence of his defining commitments, the justificatory liberal must provide guidance as to the sorts of grounds citizens can appropriately employ as a basis for their favored laws. To provide that guidance, the justificatory liberal must articulate a defensible *conception* of public justification: such a conception should specify both the reasons citizens may use and those they may *not* use in political decision making and advocacy. As should be expected, the common goal of articulating a defensible conception of public justification does not translate into consensus on any particular conception. We will have ample occasion to sample the diverse conceptions now on offer. But the diversity of proposals doesn't obviate the similarity of intent: to articulate concrete, clear guidance as to the sorts of grounds citizens may and may not employ as a basis for supporting (or rejecting) their favored laws.

Just as justificatory liberals disagree over the proper conception of public justification, they also disagree about the sorts of grounds a citizen may and may not employ to support or reject a given coercive law. Nevertheless, the latter disagreement doesn't extend to grounds of every sort. Indeed, justificatory liberals *unanimously* agree that a responsible citizen in a liberal democracy ought not support (or reject) a coercive law on the basis of religious convictions alone.[36] In addition to unanimous agreement on that point, justificatory liberals typically regard a citizen who supports a favored coercive law for which she lacks a nonreligious rationale as exemplifying in a *paradigmatic* way the sort of behavior they intend to discourage. Thus, the justificatory liberal will regard Bill McCartney's support for Amendment 2 as paradigmatically inappropriate and therefore as inconsistent with the requirements of responsible citizenship.[37] (One justificatory liberal, Gerald Gaus, characterizes as "browbeaters" those citizens who support laws that discriminate against homosexual people just on the basis of their religious convictions; according to Gaus, a citizen such as

McCartney browbeats and thereby disrespects his compatriots, not in virtue of the *content* of McCartney's position, but in virtue of his *reasons* for that position – his willingness to support laws regarding homosexuality on the basis of his religious convictions alone.[38]) Of course, because the justificatory liberal is committed to religious freedom, she is committed to allowing McCartney to adhere to his religiously grounded conviction that homosexual behavior is morally wrong as well as to act in accord with that conviction in his private life. The justificatory liberal objects, however, to any attempt by McCartney to impose that conviction on his fellow citizens by supporting (or rejecting) a coercive law for which that conviction is his only basis.

The justificatory liberal, then, assents to the claim that a citizen ought not support (or reject) a coercive law on the basis of religious convictions alone. That claim is a nonnegotiable, constitutive feature of justificatory liberalism – of the commitment to public justification. On the contrary, I believe that a citizen may support (or reject) a coercive law on the basis of his religious convictions alone. That is the crux of the issue between us. My analysis and criticism of the justificatory liberal's position on the role of religious convictions in politics will occupy us for the rest of this book.

1.3 IMPORTANCE OF THE ISSUE

Having identified both the issue that constitutes the primary subject matter of this book and the theorists with whom I will be in dialogue on that issue, the question remains: why is that issue important? There are a number of reasons. The first two are fairly straightforward. First, whether it's appropriate for a citizen to support a coercive law solely on religious grounds is a matter of considerable controversy both within and outside the academy. At least some of the acrimony that characterizes the current political situation in the United States seems to be generated by the willingness of a least a significant minority to support (and reject) coercive laws on the basis of their religious convictions alone. By showing that such religious citizens don't violate any reasonable expectations on the part of their compatriots, we can ameliorate to some degree the resentment that issues from the false impression that such citizens fail to discharge their duties as citizens.

Second, many religious traditions provide their adherents with rich moral resources they can productively employ to evaluate particular laws. In some cases, the moral resources of a given religious tradition can diverge from the commonly held moral wisdom of a hegemonic culture and yet provide a better grasp of the moral truth than is available to those immersed in that culture. And it might very well be that a citizen who adheres to a religious tradition that is thus discrepant from the hegemonic culture can't discern a widely convincing nonreligious rationale for (or against) a given coercive law. It might be quite unfortunate – perhaps catastrophic – for him to refrain from employing the resources of his tradition as a basis for supporting (or opposing) that law. But the strictures on religious convictions to which the justificatory liberal is committed discourage religious citizens from doing so. Hence, it is important to subject those strictures to criticism.[39]

The third reason is a bit more abstruse – although no less important – and so merits explication. *Epistemically* loaded concepts pervade the literature with which I am concerned. One can hardly read an essay about the proper role of religious convictions in liberal politics that doesn't include a healthy dose of references to "rationality," "ideal rationality," "self-critical rationality," "communicative rationality," "reason," "reasonableness," "public reason," "shared reason," "common human reason," "reasonable rejectability," "accessibility," "public accessibility," "in principle public accessibility," "justification," "rational justification," "public justification," "open justification," "closed justification," "mutual acceptability," "criticizability," "intelligibility," "provability," "fallibility," "checkability," "replicability," and so on. To what use does the justificatory liberal put such concepts? She employs them to fashion her favored conception of public justification. The justificatory liberal's appeal to such epistemically loaded concepts as "public accessibility," "criticizability," and "common human reason" putatively provides her with a principled basis for separating the public wheat from the private chaff: citizens may support a given coercive law on grounds that enjoy the epistemic desideratum the justificatory liberal builds into her favored conception of public justification, but they may not support any coercive law solely on grounds that lack that epistemic desideratum.

The justificatory liberal is unavoidably committed to the claim that a citizen in a liberal democracy ought not support (or reject) any coercive law for which she enjoys only a religious justification. As a consequence, one of her central tasks will be to construct and defend a conception of public justification according to which a religious rationale does not constitute a public justification. That task in its turn commits the justificatory liberal to identifying some epistemic desideratum that religious convictions lack: religious convictions must lack some epistemic property in virtue of which they fail to constitute a public justification.[40] As a consequence, the justificatory liberal can't avoid making at least some sort of epistemic evaluation of religious convictions. In many cases, justificatory liberals articulate a conception of public justification that has straightforwardly skeptical implications. In others, they are committed to consigning religious convictions to a decidedly second-class epistemic status – and that is reason enough to scrutinize closely the arguments they present for their position.[41]

But there is a further reason that I, as a citizen committed to the Christian tradition, am concerned with justificatory liberalism. "Reason" is one of the most potent symbols in modern culture. Modernity is characterized, if not defined, by a widely held commitment to the proposition that ordinary people should govern their affairs in accord with the canons of rationality. As a consequence of the widely held cultural norm that actions, norms, worldviews, and institutions should pass rational muster, any of these that is convicted of irrationality carries a debilitating stigma. Religious citizens aren't exempt from the culturally held expectation to govern their affairs rationally. So, given the high regard in which we moderns typically hold rationality, if religion is to thrive, or even survive, in the modern world, its adherents must make good on the claim that their commitment to religion is rational.

That apparently clear directive becomes murkier when we recognize two facts about the concept of rationality. First, there are any number of competing conceptions of rationality.[42] Second, according to some of those conceptions, religious commitment is plausibly regarded as rational; according to others, it is irrational; according to still others, the jury is out. Thus, for example, if we adopt some version of classical foundationalism – for example, the claim that a rational (justified, warranted, entitled) belief is either self-evident or can be inductively or deductively derived from self-evident propositions – it is unlikely that a citizen will be rationally justified in believing, say, that homosexuality is an abomination to God. In fact, given a classically foundationalist construal of rationality, citizens will be rationally justified in assenting to few if any religious propositions.[43] But matters look very different if we adopt a nonclassically foundationalist conception of rationality. For example, if we regard William Alston's doxastic practice approach to epistemology as a credible account of the epistemic criteria we should employ to evaluate a citizen's religious commitments, then we will be much more likely to conclude that fully rational citizens can adhere to religious commitments.[44] Judged with respect to Alston's approach to epistemology, it will be much more plausible for us to regard a citizen such as McCartney as rationally justified in assenting to the claim that homosexual relations are morally abominable. (Of course, I'm not even remotely suggesting that according to Alston's approach, McCartney actually was rationally justified in assenting to the claim that homosexual relations are morally wrong.)

A great deal hinges on the conception of rationality we employ to determine whether a citizen is rationally justified in adhering to some religious commitment. As one factor influencing the ability of religion to thrive in modernity is its perceived rationality (or irrationality), the conception of rationality that enjoys common cultural currency is an important concern for the religiously committed.[45] And given the availability of alternative conceptions of rationality, we should expect that the question of which conception(s) of rationality should enjoy cultural predominance will engender considerable controversy.

Willingly or unwillingly, justificatory liberals often participate in that controversy. After all, the justificatory liberal's express intention is to encode his conception of public justification into the political culture: he articulates a conception of public justification that he builds into an ideal of responsible citizenship and he hopes that most citizens will adhere to that ideal. If the citizens who do so accept his conception of public justification – and why should we doubt that they will? – the success of the justificatory liberal's project will unavoidably affect the culturally predominant understanding of rationality. And if I'm correct that justificatory liberals often build into their conceptions of public justification epistemic claims that consign religious convictions to second-class epistemic status, concern for the ability of religion to thrive in modernity requires that we identify exactly what those epistemic claims are and then determine whether they are defensible. So the attempt to identify and evaluate the epistemic claims the justificatory liberal needs to vindicate will be a central concern of this book.

This last reason for undertaking my inquiry raises two further points. First, my interest in the role of religious convictions in politics, and in justificatory liberalism in particular, has at least as much to do with the effects of politics on religion as it has to do with the effects of religion on politics. Undoubtedly religion and politics exert a mutual influence on one another; also, our understanding of how we ought to conduct ourselves in the political sphere unavoidably affects our understanding of how we ought to conduct ourselves religiously. Although some sort of mutual influence is unavoidable, the *kind* of influence is contingent and contestable. And my intention is to contest a particular understanding of the proper relation between religion and politics, one that I believe has potentially deleterious effects for religion in liberal democracies.

Second, my interest in the role of religious convictions in politics has little to do with resolving disputes over specific laws and more to do with a proper understanding of the place of religion in modernity. I doubt that religious citizens, even the most devout, often support coercive laws on the basis of their religious convictions alone. I surmise that most of the citizens who employ their religious convictions to determine which laws they ought to support have both religious and nonreligious reasons for their favored laws.[46] If that is correct, then the question I raise in this essay doesn't arise for most citizens; at least, it doesn't arise very often. But the frequency with which citizens face the issue I address in this book indicates nothing significant about the importance of that issue: sometimes a problem we rarely face requires us to ask questions of far-reaching importance, and the resolution of these questions requires us significantly to alter our self-understanding – even of how we act in the more familiar cases in which that problem doesn't arise. That is how I regard the issue I broach in this book: what we believe a citizen is morally permitted to do by way of supporting a coercive law for which she enjoys only a religious rationale has far-reaching implications for our understanding of religion, modernity, liberal democracy, and the place of religion in both modernity and liberal democracy.

1.4 COMING ATTRACTIONS

Although I've done my best to focus in this book on the very narrow question of whether a citizen may support his favored coercive laws on religious grounds alone, the ensuing discussion touches on a wide range of issues. As a consequence, it will be helpful to lay out the structure of that discussion.

The next two chapters set the groundwork for the rest of the book. In Chapter 2, I address an objection to one fundamental assumption of my project. It's plausible to suppose that there is an internal relation between *liberalism* and *secularization*. Since liberal societies are irremediably pluralistic, and since pluralism undermines the credibility of religious commitments (or at the very least transforms them into subjective-cum-privatized preferences), we can predict that religion will play an increasingly negligible role in liberal politics. If true, that prediction renders my topic merely academic: I assume that some citizens are willing to support coercive laws on religious grounds alone and my project is of little interest if that assumption is false. Consequently, I endeavor to explain why the putative correlation between pluralization and secularization is specious: I argue both that pluralism doesn't undermine religion and that pluralism invigorates religion. In the course of that discussion, I also provide reason to accept two claims critical to my central thesis: that religious citizens have a deeply vested interest in affirming cultural and religious pluralism and, more particularly, in affirming religious freedom.

Having indicated why we shouldn't expect religion to fade away or to retreat to the private realm, I identify, in Chapter 3, the constitutive commitments of justificatory liberalism and show how they bear on the proper role of religious commitments in a liberal democracy. In this chapter, I articulate the all-important distinction between *pursuing public justification* and *exercising restraint*: between a citizen's attempting to articulate a rationale for her favored coercive laws that is, or can be, convincing to her compatriots and her withholding support from any coercive law for which she cannot discern such a rationale. I understand the justificatory liberal to be committed to both the claim that a citizen ought to pursue public justification and the claim that she ought to exercise restraint. Unlike the former, the latter claim implies that a citizen ought to withhold her support from any coercive law for which she enjoys only a religious rationale, which is flatly inconsistent with my central thesis and is consequently the focus of much of this book.

With these preliminaries as background, I divide my argument and the rest of the book into two parts. That division both in my argument and in the structure of this book corresponds to what I take to be the two central argumentative burdens the justificatory liberal must discharge in order to vindicate his defining commitments.[47] The first burden requires a convincing answer to the question: "Why public justification?" That is, the justificatory liberal must show why a citizen morally ought to commit to a policy of withholding his support from any coercive law for which he lacks a public justification. To discharge this first argumentative burden, the justification liberal must provide *moral* argumentation, and in Part II I evaluate several moral arguments in support of the desired conclusion. The second burden requires a convincing answer to the question: "What is a public justification?" Even if the justificatory liberal vindicates the claim that a citizen ought to withhold his support from any coercive law for which he lacks a public justification, then obviously, he needs to tell us just what public justification is and what counts as a public justification. In Part III, I evaluate various proposed conceptions of public justification.

In Part II, then, I evaluate the central arguments in support of the claim that a citizen morally ought to withhold support from any coercive law for which she lacks a public justification. I address three different categories of argument in support of that claim: the argument from respect, the argument from Bosnia, and the argument from divisiveness. As I see it, an adequate analysis of the arguments from Bosnia and divisiveness presupposes an analysis of the argument from respect, and so I begin my discussion of the normative component of the justificatory liberal's project with an analysis of the argument from respect. In Chapter 4, I discuss the notion of respect for persons and indicate some implications of the claim that a citizen ought to respect her compatriots for the bases on which she may and may not support her favored coercive laws. I argue that respect requires a citizen to adhere to a variety of relevant constraints: she ought to withhold her support from any coercive law for which she lacks a high degree of rational justification; she ought to pursue public justification for any coercive law she supports; she ought to be willing to learn from her compatriots regarding the moral propriety of the coercive laws she supports, and thus must be willing to consider the possibility that her favored coercive laws are in fact morally indefensible. These constraints, and several others as well, jointly constitute what I call the *ideal of conscientious engagement*, an ideal we should encode into the set of normative standards associated with the role of citizen in a liberal democracy.

In Chapter 5, I argue that even though respect requires a citizen to adhere to the ideal of conscientious engagement, respect doesn't oblige a citizen to exercise restraint: she needn't withhold support from any coercive law for which she cannot discern a public justification. In arguing for this conclusion, I begin by explaining why I don't regard as intuitively plausible the claim that respect for her compatriots obliges a citizen to exercise restraint. I then attempt to show that none of the most powerful extant arguments show that respect for her compatriots requires a citizen to exercise restraint. And I conclude by articulating an (ad hominem) argument against the claim that respect requires a citizen to exercise restraint regarding her religious commitments.

In Chapter 6, I address the arguments from Bosnia and divisiveness. The gist of these arguments is that since a widespread refusal of citizens to exercise restraint would result in highly undesirable consequences (civil strife and divisiveness), a responsible citizen will commit himself to exercising restraint. My position is that we have no reason to believe that *so long as citizens adhere to the ideal of conscientious engagement,* their refusal to exercise restraint will have sufficiently dire consequences as to require them to exercise restraint.

In Part III, I address the second argumentative burden the justificatory liberal must discharge – to articulate some defensible conception of public justification and in so doing to provide citizens with principled grounds for determining whether they enjoy an appropriate basis for their favored coercive laws. My intent in this part of the book is to make a consistency argument against the claim that a citizen ought to exercise restraint regarding his religious commitments: there is no principled reason that a citizen ought to exercise restraint regarding his religious commitments but *not* regarding other sorts of grounds that the justificatory liberal regards as entirely appropriate bases for a citizen's favored laws. In particular, I show that justificatory liberals haven't articulated a *defensible* conception of public justification that provides *principled* grounds for the claim that a citizen ought to withhold his support from any coercive law for which he enjoys only a religious rationale.

In Chapter 7, I try to show that various *populist* conceptions of public justification fail to achieve the desired result. Roughly, a populist conception construes a public justification as a rationale that is actually convincing to the citizenry, or that can be convincing to the citizenry without requiring citizens to modify their central commitments too drastically. Such populist conceptions are vitiated by the fact that religious claims, although controversial, are no *more* controversial than are many moral and factual commitments *essential* to healthy political decision making and advocacy. In short, since a responsible citizen in a liberal democracy is unavoidably going to have to support her favored coercive laws on the basis of *some* rationale that many of her compatriots regard as completely unacceptable, then it's arbitrary to forbid a citizen to support her favored coercive laws on religious grounds *for the very reason* that many of her compatriots regard her religious commitments as completely unacceptable.

The demise of populist conceptions of public justification motivates many justificatory liberals to build epistemic claims into their favored conception of public justification. Instead of construing a public justification as a rationale the citizenry actually finds acceptable, the justificatory liberal construes a public justification as a rationale that enjoys certain epistemic desiderata in virtue of which that rationale *merits* the citizenry's approbation. In Chapter 8, I articulate a consistency objection to such epistemically informed conceptions of public justification: focusing on a specific type of religious ground – specifically, mystical perception – I argue that there is no *relevant* epistemic difference between mystical perceptions and grounds that are essential to healthy political decision making and advocacy in virtue of which it is appropriate to mandate restraint with respect to mystical perception but not those other sorts of grounds.

In a concluding chapter, I address an objection to my consistency argument against epistemic conceptions of public justification. The objection is as follows: widely accepted claims about God's nature lead us to expect that God will provide each citizen with adequate *secular* corroboration for any moral truth she accepts on *religious* grounds; hence, any religious citizen who adheres to a moral claim for which she cannot discern an adequate secular rationale ought to *doubt* that moral claim; hence, any citizen who cannot discern an adequate secular rationale for some religiously grounded moral claim ought not be confident enough in that claim to support a coercive law solely on its basis. I respond that when we take seriously the implications of human fallibility and sinfulness, religious citizens need not expect that each religiously grounded moral truth will likely enjoy secular corroboration.

1.5 A FINAL CAVEAT

Let me offer one warning regarding what the reader can expect to find in the following pages. As I've indicated, this book focuses on a very narrow question: does a citizen who supports some coercive law solely on the basis of his religious convictions violate any moral expectations legitimately and reasonably associated with the role of citizen in a liberal democracy? Although very specific, that question has implications for a number of larger matters. But as far as I consistently can, I want to avoid taking a position on those larger matters. Thus, for example, although any reasonably comprehensive answer to the question I address in this book bears on the topic of political legitimacy, I have no intention of committing myself to a general theory of political legitimacy. Although the position I develop in this book is directly relevant to various church-state issues and matters of constitutional interpretation, I steer as far from such matters as I consistently can. Again, although I articulate a position about the sorts of normative expectations we should associate with the role of citizen in a liberal democracy, I provide no account whatsoever as to how we are supposed to encourage and equip citizens to fulfill those expectations. As a consequence, I'm only too aware that the position I develop in this book bears on a number of important issues that I don't adequately address; I leave a large number of important questions unclarified, much less resolved. By way of excuse, this book is already longer than it should be and extending the discussion would do little more than try the reader's patience.

CHAPTER 2

PLURALISM AND RELIGION

2.0 INTRODUCTION

Many citizens of the United States have been raised on a myth. We were raised to believe that our Pilgrim forebears made their way to the New World in order to escape religious persecution, succeeded in setting up a "city on a hill," a polity populated largely by committed Christians, shortly after which there ensued a process of religious decline that has continued to this day (notwithstanding some momentary reversals of fortune). Of course, Americans disagree on their evaluation of that story: some regard the pervasively religious society of early America with nostalgia and pine for a return to that Golden Age; others are more than happy that that Golden Age has, to mix metaphors, ridden off into the sunset. But both those who want America to return to its Christian past and those who want to bury that past accept the same basic story line: the history of America is a history of religious decline.

The story of a decline of religion in America is just one chapter in a much longer narrative, a narrative that, like many a modern myth, enjoys the imprimatur of science and that is codified in the so-called theory of secularization.[1] The theory of secularization, the claim that "modernization necessarily leads to a decline of religion, both in society and in the minds of individuals," has ineradicable narrative elements: once upon a time, people and society were pervasively religious; then society began to change – factories were built, governments refused to impose orthodoxy on their subjects, citizens of different faith traditions lived and worked in the same environments, people got education, science freed itself from the fetters of religious intolerance; and ever since then people and society have become progressively irreligious.[2]

23

The theory of secularization constitutes the primary subject matter of this chapter. I won't articulate a comprehensive evaluation of the current state of debate regarding the theory of secularization; not only would that project require at least one substantial volume, but completing it is far beyond my capacities. Rather, I'll discuss a limited set of claims associated with that theory. Which claims? Put crudely, the theory of secularization, like any scientific theory, has two main components. First, an empirical component: the secularization theorist identifies a range of "facts" about declining religious commitment; any defensible version of the theory of secularization must establish, at the very least, that some sort of decline of "religion" has occurred over the long term. (Debate rages over the sort of decline involved.) Second, an explanatory component: given the relevant facts about religious decline, the secularization theorist must tell a story that "connects" those facts in an empirically adequate and otherwise convincing narrative. Simply put, he must explain why the facts about religious decline are as they are.

Both the factual and the explanatory components of the theory of secularization are hotly debated. With respect to the theory's factual component, it seems that the United States, arguably the most modern of societies, is more religious, even more Christian, than it has ever been in the past. Thus, Jon Butler has argued "that quite contrary to Cotton Mather's well-known (and well-justified) fears, the story of religion in America after 1700 is one of Christian ascension rather than declension – Christianization rather than dechristianization – and of a Christianity so complex and heterogeneous as to baffle observers and adherents alike."[3] The pervasive religiosity in the United States seems to run counter to the predictions of the theory of secularization and elicits from its defenders its fair share of epicycles and deferents.[4]

Although debate about the factual component of the theory of secularization is important and interesting in its own right, I'll be concerned with only the *explanatory* elements of the theory of secularization. More particularly, I'll focus on one very important component of the secularization theorist's explanatory repertoire: the role of *cultural pluralism* in explaining religious decline. Thus, Steve Bruce writes,

> If we are to use differences in degree and extent of religious diversity to explain the degree and extent of popular support for the churches, we have to "unpack" the supposed connection between these two variables

into a story which is plausible and sensible at the level of the individual actor who either stays in a church or leaves it. That is, we have to be able to tell some sensible story about why pluralism might erode or strengthen the religious commitment of an individual actor.[5]

The claim that pluralism undermines the plausibility of religious truth claims is one of the central explanatory components of the theory of secularization. My intention is to articulate, to reconstruct, and to criticize that explanatory component and in so doing achieve clarity on the relations between religion and pluralism.

2.1 SECULARIZATION, RELIGION, AND POLITICS

A natural question arises at this point: of what relevance to my central topic is a discussion of the theory of secularization? Why is it important for my project that we achieve clarity on the relations between religion and pluralism? My discussion of the theory of secularization connects with my treatment of the proper role of religious convictions in politics in the following two respects.

First, I'm interested in setting out a position on the proper role of religious convictions in the political activity of citizens in *liberal democracies*. As we'll soon see, John Rawls has articulated a formidable argument supporting the claim that there is an internal relation between liberalism and *pluralization*. As we'll also see, Peter Berger has articulated an equally formidable argument supporting the claim that there is an internal relation between pluralization and *secularization*. If we accept Rawls's claim, as I believe we should, that liberalism generates pluralism, and we further accept Berger's claim that pluralization generates secularization, then it would appear that over the long term, the chances of religion surviving, much less thriving, in a liberal democracy are quite dim. But that conclusion would render moot the central topic of this book: any discussion of the proper role of religion in liberal politics would be of only academic interest.[6] If the theory of secularization is correct, if religion is doomed to wither away in modern societies, or if "modern" religion is "private" religion, then our topic lacks urgency: why spend time and energy staking out a position on the proper role of religious convictions in liberal politics if one believes, with Steve Bruce, that "the forms in which [religion] is expressed have become so idiosyncratic and so diffuse that there are few specific social consequences"[7] or, with Bryan Turner, that "neither traditional Christianity nor the new religious movements have relevance to public issues of legitimating state activity, welfare distribution or the structure of the economy"?[8]

Second, suppose we can expect, for the foreseeable future, that religion will retain its vitality in liberal democracies. That raises a crucial question: what problems can we realistically expect religion to pose for a liberal democracy? The claim that politically active religion does pose significant problems for a liberal democracy is a staple of the justificatory liberal's diet and often motivates the constraints they intend to impose on religious citizens. So it's obviously crucial for our evaluation of justificatory liberalism that we have a clear understanding of the problems religious advocacy is likely to pose for liberal democracies. My discussion of the theory of secularization will contribute to that understanding by *subtraction*: the following discussion indicates that citizens who rely on their religious convictions to decide which coercive laws merit their support do *not* pose at least two problems popularly attributed to such activity.

A good deal of both the text and subtext of the discussion regarding the role of religious convictions in politics is that pluralism poses a threat to religion and therefore that religion poses a threat to pluralism: because pluralism threatens religion, religious people are regularly tempted to discourage pluralism, even to the point of enlisting state power to quash it.[9] Any such threat would generate obvious problems and appears to motivate some attempts to "privatize" religion. But the claim that pluralism threatens religion is quite dubious. In fact, recent critics of the theory of secularization have argued that pluralism can *vivify* religion – even "conservative" brands of religion. If this is correct, those who wish to privatize religion on account of the danger religion poses to pluralism will find little encouragement from recent discussions of the theory of secularization: the claim that religion ought to be excluded from the political sphere on account of the danger it poses to pluralism founders on the fact that, by and large, pluralism benefits religion.[10]

It isn't uncommon for justificatory liberals to defend constraints on the political activity of religious citizens by appeal to the danger religious groups putatively pose, not to pluralism in general, but to religious freedom.[11] Many seem to fear that even when religious citizens affirm religious freedom, they do so for pragmatic purposes, and that they would flag in their commitment to religious freedom given a "favorable" change of the social and political winds. This concern strikes me as dystopian. Whatever the danger politically active religious people once posed to religious freedom in the bad old days of the Wars of Religion, the following discussion indicates that such concerns are simply out of touch with the current cultural and political conditions in contemporary America. Why?

The very religious groups that putatively pose a threat to religious freedom have a vested interest in supporting the liberal commitment to freedom of religion. If sociologist Christian Smith is correct (and here he rings a theme echoed in many criticisms of the theory of secularization), the establishment of religion *harms* religion and freedom of religion *benefits* religion. Briefly, the idea is this: since the feature of liberalism that generates pluralism is its commitment to freedom of religion, and since pluralism vivifies religion, then religious citizens have a deep and abiding interest in committing themselves to freedom of religion. So politically active religious citizens, and even those willing to support their favored coercive laws on the basis of their parochial religious commitments, have a vested interest in refusing coercively to impose their favored religious orthodoxy on a diverse population.

2.2 LIBERALISM AND PLURALISM

As I have said, I intend to discuss the theory of secularization in order to gain clarity on the relations between pluralism and religion. But that discussion is of central importance to the problem I address in this book *only if* there is an internal relation between liberalism and pluralism. If liberal democracies are inveterately pluralistic, any light our discussion of the theory of secularization sheds on the relation between religion and pluralism will, hopefully, illuminate the relation between religion and liberalism. But are liberal democracies invariably pluralistic? John Rawls has articulated a persuasive reason to believe that they are.

Rawls begins with a point of descriptive epistemology: "Many of our most important judgments are made under conditions where it is not to be expected that conscientious persons with full powers of reason, even after free discussion, will all arrive at the same conclusion."[12] Each citizen is subject to various "burdens of judgment" – factors that give rise to disagreement, even among reasonable people, regarding which religious, moral, and metaphysical claims are true.[13] For example, the evidence that bears on a given issue is "conflicting and complex, and thus hard to assess and evaluate"; it is difficult to determine how much weight we ought to accord to a given consideration, even if we agree that that consideration is germane to the topic; many of the concepts we employ in reflecting on a given issue are "vague and subject to hard cases"; how we assess evidence is shaped by our "total experience," an influence that varies from person to person and is very difficult to detect; and so on.[14]

There are, of course, various nonepistemic factors that affect a citizen's judgments – self-interest, dishonesty, ideological blindness, the oppressive weight of ossified tradition, self-deception. But Rawls's point is that even if we could control for such factors, even if each citizen exercised his cognitive capacities in a flawless manner, the burdens of judgment ensure that large numbers of citizens would reach widely varying conclusions regarding religious, moral, and metaphysical matters.[15] Reason, even if flawlessly executed, leads us not to consensus on ultimate matters, but to considerable dissensus.[16] Charles Larmore echoes that sentiment: "Being reasonable – that is, thinking and conversing in good faith and applying, as best one can, the general capacities of reason that belong to every domain of inquiry – has ceased to seem a guarantee of unanimity. On these matters of supreme importance, the more we talk with one another, the more we disagree."[17]

According to Rawls, "the burdens of judgment" constitute a crucial link between liberal democracy and pluralism. A liberal democracy just is the sort of state that, on principle, provides citizens with considerable leeway to decide for themselves what to believe regarding religious, moral, and metaphysical matters. The commitment to religious freedom is the fundamental charter of the liberal state; no right is more central to a liberal polity than the right to worship as one pleases, or its natural extension, the right to believe in accord with the dictates of conscience. And as long as the state allows each citizen to determine, on the basis of considerations each finds compelling, which religious, moral, and metaphysical commitments each ought to accept, as long as the state doesn't compel citizens to assent to one or another religious, moral, or metaphysical creed, the burdens of judgment ensure that large numbers of citizens will adopt widely varying creeds. As Stark and Finke claim, "Whenever and wherever repression falters, lush pluralism will break through."[18] So the burdens of judgment, in combination with the liberal commitment to freedom of religion and conscience, ensure that liberal democracies will be characterized by pluralism. More precisely, liberal democracies will be characterized by a *reasonable* pluralism: given the burdens of judgment, citizens who exercise their cognitive capacities responsibly and reasonably will nevertheless come to varying conclusions on ultimate matters.[19]

2.3 THE SECULARIZATION THESIS

It's widely believed that pluralism is bad, somehow or other, for religion. In the literature that deals with the proper role of religion in politics, this conviction often manifests itself in the expressed need to contain religion: since pluralism threatens religion, religion threatens pluralism in return, and since the only effective way for religion to quash pluralism is by means of coercion, religion can't be allowed power and thus must be quarantined from politics. In the literature that deals with the theory of secularization, the belief that pluralism is bad for religion manifests itself in the claim that pluralism undermines the plausibility of religion. But why should we believe that pluralism undermines the plausibility of religious commitments?

2.3.1 Pluralism and Secularization

Consider the following thought experiment.[20] Imagine a society – call it Christendom – in which Christianity enjoys an unchallenged and thoroughly dominant monopoly. The denizens of Christendom assume without question that the fundamental tenets of Christianity are true: they are "literal believers, all of the time."[21] Indeed, the truth of Christian tenets is encoded into the very structure of social existence – Christian prayers initiate gatherings of significance, school curricula include intensive study of Christian doctrine, Christian clerics are widely respected as moral authorities, "every significant act of testimony, every contract and every promise [i]s reinforced by oaths sworn on the Bible and before God,"[22] Christian symbols commonly adorn places of power, affirmation of Christian creeds is a condition of holding public office, the state depends for legitimation on a Christian rationale, and "the Christian buildings that loom ... across the countryside proclaim ... Christianity's truth and demand ... adherence with a ubiquity that makes these demands incessant."[23] No dissent is expressed, so there is no need for toleration of non-Christians – much less persecution of heretics. No persuasion is required, since no one needs to be convinced.

Now consider a member of Christendom, Thomas. Imagine that Thomas is an ordinary individual, not more curious than the average chap, but not less, not more critical and reflective, but not less either. In what way should we expect Thomas's immersion in a society so saturated with Christianity to affect his perception of Christianity? We can be reasonably confident that Thomas can resist deference to Christianity only with difficulty – if Thomas can muster the strength and independence of thought to reject Christianity, he'll succeed only with effort and determination. Most likely, however, the massive social confirmation of Christian creeds will have its counterpart in Thomas's subjectivity: Christian tenets will enjoy the maximum plausibility that naturally attends realities that one is fortunate enough to be able to take for granted. As a ubiquitous and firmly entrenched feature of his social environment, Christianity appears to Thomas as a massive reality that imposes itself on his consciousness as ineluctably as do similarly massive features of his natural environment.[24]

What lesson should we draw from this thought experiment? That when a particular religion is socially entrenched, individuals find it easy to regard that religion as true and difficult to regard it as false. Simply put, religious doctrines seem most plausible when a particular religion holds a monopoly on the religious market. Or to put the point in Bergerian terminology, a particular religion thrives when it provides a shared understanding of the meaning of life and life's vicissitudes – a *sacred canopy* under which a critical mass of the members of society can find shelter from anomie.

Let's modify the thought experiment. Suppose, holding steady Thomas's commitment to Christianity, we progressively alter his environment, removing by increments the various Christian trappings that adorn his social landscape. We assume that Christian symbols are removed from places of political power; then that Christian doctrine is excluded from his elementary school education; next that Christian prayers are forbidden from initiating certain sorts of gathering (e.g., judicial ones); and so on. Most important, we assume that dissent from Christian tenets increases: Thomas rubs elbows on a continual basis with Hindus, Buddhists, agnostics, atheists. As the massive social confirmation of Christian creeds in Christendom is slowly whittled away, as competition is introduced into the religious market, what should we expect to be the consequences for Thomas's apprehension of Christianity?

One consequence seems certain: Thomas will no longer be able to take the truth of Christianity for granted. The availability of alternative religious practices in his environment will force Thomas to recognize that he might believe differently than he does in fact. Of course, even in a society characterized by the most massive social confirmation of Christianity, Thomas can recognize the logical possibility of holding different beliefs. But his interaction on a regular basis with respectable, morally upright, and generally intelligent individuals who don't accept his Christian commitments transforms the merely logical possibility of rejecting his Christian commitments into a *living* possibility. His recognition of the living possibility that he might believe differently forces Thomas to *decide* whether he'll believe differently. In the transition from Christendom to a social environment characterized by a pervasive pluralism, an important transformation occurs: Christianity loses its status as a reality Thomas can take for granted and acquires the status of a choice.

It's highly likely to be a precarious choice. Since Thomas chooses to commit to Christian doctrines in a pluralistic environment, the social basis – the "plausibility structure" in Berger's idiolect – of Thomas's Christian commitment is correspondingly weakened. In a highly pluralized culture (such as our own), the best Thomas can reasonably hope for is that his commitment to Christianity will be confirmed by a circle of intimates: his family, friends, members of his church. As a consequence of the erosion of its plausibility structure, the Christian creed seems ever less credible and assent to Christian doctrines requires ever more effort.

What lesson should we draw from this modified thought experiment? That when a particular religion loses its monopoly over the religious market, when that religion must compete with alternatives, when its sacred canopy covers ever fewer members of a given community, individuals find it difficult to regard that religion as true and its competitors as false. Berger and colleagues write,

> In the absence of consistent and general social confirmation, religious definitions of reality have lost their quality of certainty and, instead, have become matters of choice. Faith is no longer socially given, but must be individually achieved – be it by a wrenching act of decision along the lines of Pascal's "wager" or Kierkegaard's "leap" – or more trivially acquired as

31

a "religious preference." Faith, in other words, is much harder to come by in the pluralistic situation.[25]

And if faith is harder to come by in a pluralistic culture, then presumably it will be less common than in a monopolistic culture. Religion declines, then, in the competitive religious economy that characterizes a pluralistic culture. And that is the point of these thought experiments: as a given society moves from a condition in which a particular religion holds a monopoly on the religious market to one characterized by an ever more diverse pluralism, religious commitment declines. That general pattern putatively characterizes the history of both Europe and the United States. After the monopoly of the Catholic Church over the European religious market was successfully challenged by Lutheran, Calvinist, and Anabaptist competitors, the pervasive religiosity of the Middle Ages gave way to the equally pervasive secularity of contemporary Western Europe.[26] After the monopoly of the generic Protestantism that dominated the United States in the nineteenth century was successfully challenged by all manner of upstart sects, cults, covens, Catholics, and others, the pervasively religious culture of early America gave way to the secularized, privatized, and subjective "Sheilaism" of the twentieth century.

2.3.2 Secularization and the Problem of Religious Diversity

Berger sometimes seems to claim that because people must choose their religious commitments, this necessity ipso facto creates a crisis of credibility.[27] But this claim is surely false. If Thomas had at his disposal what he regarded as a compelling argument in support of the truth of central Christian commitments, then the fact that he must choose to adhere to Christian commitments wouldn't necessarily engender a crisis of credibility. It is not that people in pluralistic environments must *choose* their religious commitments that engenders doubt but the *sort* of choice pluralism forces people to make that reduces the credibility of religious creeds. This point requires some explanation.

After the problem of evil, probably the most serious cognitive difficulty any given religious tradition faces is the problem of religious diversity. Simply put, that there are so many different and conflicting religions seems to throw in doubt any particular religious claimant to the truth. At the very least, the multitude of religious options renders acute the problem of distinguishing the true religion from its competitors.

And the apologists for particular religious traditions are notoriously unsuccessful in their ability to produce convincing reasons to adhere to their tradition rather than the alternatives. One doesn't need to be a professional academic for the problem of religious diversity to inject a significant dose of doubt into one's religious commitments.

Pluralism encodes the problem of religious diversity into the very structure of each religious adherent's social existence. In his post-Christian, pluralistic society, the problem of religious diversity is incarnated in Thomas's social life on a regular basis by his daily interaction with respectable citizens who reject his religious commitments. As a consequence of this social incarnation of the problem of religious diversity, Thomas vividly faces a very serious objection to his religious convictions and thus a crisis of credibility that he can overcome only with great difficulty. Given the difficulty of overcoming the problem of religious diversity, we can expect ever fewer people to persist in their religious commitments. In short, as a consequence, not of having to choose religion, but of the conditions in which a pluralistic culture forces people to choose religion, we can expect pluralistic societies to become ever more secular.

This line of argument leads us to expect a considerable decline in religious adherence, at least over the long term. But any such conclusion seems rash. As critics of the theory of secularization have repeatedly pointed out, there is powerful evidence that religious commitment hasn't declined at all in one of the most pluralistic of societies: the United States: "If competition erodes the plausibility of religions, why is the most pluralistic nation on earth among the most religious?"[28] Does the persistence of high levels of religious commitment such as we find in the United States falsify Berger's predictions? Not necessarily. Berger's line of argument can be salvaged by adding a very large and conspicuous epicycle: pluralism might not result in a decline of religion or in a decrease in religious affiliation so much as a transformation of religion.[29] What sort of transformation? Pluralization results in the widespread *privatization* of religion.

Why should we expect pluralism to result in the privatization of religion? I think that my reconstruction of Berger's theory provides an answer. A citizen who decides to commit to one religious tradition out of a set of alternatives but who lacks adequate reason to regard his chosen tradition to be *true* still has to tell himself (and others) a story as to why he commits himself as he does. A natural (if not inevitable) story will accord pride of place to his *preferences* as a basis of selection. The reason Thomas commits to Christianity out of the available alternatives is that he believes Christianity enables him to live a fulfilling and satisfying life, or that it satisfies a deep need, or some similar reason. Given his distinctive psychological profile, Thomas's decision to commit to Christianity makes eminent sense. Deciding to commit to Christianity on that sort of basis comes with a cost, however. Because others have different psychological profiles from Thomas's, Christianity isn't necessarily fulfilling or satisfying for them. They lack, therefore, Thomas's reason for deciding to commit to Christianity. As a consequence, Thomas can't legitimately expect others to choose as he does: for many of his compatriots, given their very different psychological profiles, it makes no sense for them to commit to Christianity.

Thomas's reason for adhering to Christian creeds is based on the fact that such adherence enables him to satisfy his preferences, and this has crucially important implications for its appropriate social location: since Thomas's commitment to Christianity now has the status of a preference, it properly belongs in his private life. More important, it will belong *solely* in his private life: appeal to Christianity in public matters – for example, in public debate regarding some coercive law – will be regarded as outrageously inappropriate by those who realize that his adherence to Christianity is a matter of personal preference. It's no more appropriate for a citizen who merely "prefers" the Christian creed to support coercive policies on the basis of that creed than it is for a person who prefers vanilla ice cream to support a proposed law that forbids other citizens from purchasing and consuming chocolate ice cream.[30]

Berger's argument, then, substantiates the following prediction. Given the highly pluralistic nature of a modern liberal democracy, citizens will find it ever more difficult to regard any particular set of religious commitments as true and competing sets of religious commitments as false. As a consequence, we can expect the following. First, many citizens will find religious commitment incredible and will opt out entirely. (Modern Europe, putatively characterized by a high degree of secularity, is supposed to fall into this category.) Second, many citizens will understand their religious commitments as a set of preferences. (Given that this prediction is consistent with a high degree of religious affiliation, the United States putatively falls into this category.) In either case, the effects we can expect pluralism to have on religion warrant a prediction directly relevant to our topic: "The global tendency seems to be in all cases the emergence of a state emancipated from the sway of either religious institutions or religious rationales of political action."[31] That prediction threatens to render moot my topic, the proper role of religious convictions in liberal politics.

2.4 THE SUBCULTURAL IDENTITY THEORY

I find Berger's version of the theory of secularization quite powerful. But his position has found itself on the receiving end of some fairly trenchant criticism.[32] Christian Smith has recently argued, and quite persuasively, for a conclusion almost exactly the contrary of Berger's – that pluralism encourages religious vitality. More precisely, if Smith is correct, pluralism encourages the vitality of a particular sort of religion, that which adopts values and commitments at *variance* with the dominant culture and yet actively *engages* the dominant culture.[33] Analysis of Smith's criticism of the theory of secularization will aid us in arriving at important conclusions regarding the problems public religion actually poses for a liberal democracy.

2.4.1 Identity Formation in Social Groups

Smith begins with three assumptions.[34] The first is an assumption about human identity. Each person desires to live in a meaningful manner and achieves a meaningful life at least partly by defining herself with respect to her commitment to certain intrinsic moral goods (justice, love, self-sacrifice) and with respect to her rejection of intrinsic moral evils (injustice, hate, self-indulgence).[35] A person who incorporates into her self-understanding a commitment to pursue her favored intrinsic moral goods and to avoid intrinsic moral evils has a *moral identity*. The second is an assumption about the relation of religion to moral identity: in virtue of their content and history, religious traditions provide a particularly rich source of materials a person can employ to construct her moral identity. The third is an assumption about the conditions necessary for a person to acquire and sustain her moral identity. No person acquires or sustains her identity in isolation from other persons. Rather, in the standard case, a person's understanding of who she is and what makes her life worthwhile causally depends on her membership in a social group that confirms her self-understanding. Smith assumes, then, that each person craves a moral identity, that religion is a particularly useful resource for constructing a moral identity, and that a person constructs and maintains her moral identity only as a member of a social group. Thus, Smith writes, "The human drives for meaning and belonging are satisfied primarily by locating human selves within social groups that sustain distinctive, morally orienting collective identities."[36]

These three assumptions lead naturally to the following question: can religious social groups that provide their members with a moral identity survive in a pluralistic environment? Smith's assumptions lead us to ask not whether *individuals* can remain religious in a pluralistic society, but whether individuals *who belong to religious groups* can remain religious in a pluralistic society.[37] If such social groups can survive, then religion can survive as well. And if such social groups can thrive, then religion can thrive as well. Smith's position is that religious social groups can both survive and thrive in a pluralistic environment.

Smith's case for his position begins with the claim that a given social group must establish criteria that determine who is and who isn't a member of that social group. In order for a given social group to exist, that social group must have members. In order to have members, a social group must establish criteria that a person must satisfy to be included in that social group. Thus, to exist, a social group must establish *criteria for inclusion*: a set of rules that identify the characteristics a person must possess to be a member of that group.[38] Thus, for example, inclusion in an evangelical social group requires (a) assent to a set of creeds (e.g., the doctrine of biblical inspiration), (b) rejection of various heterodox commitments (e.g., pantheism), and (c) adoption of a certain ritual vocabulary (e.g., "having a personal relationship with Jesus Christ").[39]

The claim that a social group must enjoy criteria for inclusion has an important implication: criteria for inclusion ipso facto constitute criteria for *exclusion*. If inclusion in a given community is determined by whether a person has a certain set of characteristics, then those who lack that set of characteristics aren't members of that community. If inclusion in a particular neo-Nazi hate group requires a willingness to engage in a racial holy war against Jews, blacks, and Catholics, then those who are unwilling to engage in a racial holy war can't be members of that social group. A given social group, then, is defined by certain characteristics and outgroups are defined as those who lack those characteristics.

The boundaries that define a community typically play a critically important role in the moral identity of the members of that community: the criteria for inclusion/exclusion on which a group's existence depends provide an indispensable resource for identity construction. If inclusion in a given community requires that a person participate in a particular lifestyle, adhere to a set of creeds, engage in a particular ritual, or eat a certain type of food, then the members of that community will likely regard such activities as particularly valuable. Since the members of a community will likely regard the characteristics that determine membership in that community as valuable, and since a person's identity is constructed in light of what he regards as valuable, it's entirely natural for a member of a given community to construct his identity in light of the characteristics that define membership in his community. For the same reason, it's natural for him to define his identity in contradistinction from selected outgroups. If, for example, "living simply" is a condition of membership in a Mennonite community, then members of that community will tend to regard living simply as more valuable or worthwhile than a lifestyle characterized by rampant consumerism. And since the members of that community regard a simple life as more worthwhile than a consumerist lifestyle, they will likely construct their moral identities accordingly: they will be "for" simplicity and "against" consumerism.

2.4.2 Pluralism and Doubt

As we have seen, a person makes use of her social groups' collective identities in constructing her moral identity, and this phenomenon provides Smith with a basis for rejecting Berger's claim that pluralism generates a social environment that inexorably corrodes religious commitment. The fact that a member of a given social group defines her identity by reference both to her own social group and to relevant outgroups indicates that she doesn't form her moral identity by reference to all of those in her social environment, or even to all of those with whom she interacts on a daily basis. Most pertinently, a member of a given social group doesn't seek confirmation for her identity-forming commitments from the members of the various outgroups in reaction to which she constructs her moral identity. It would be unthinkable for a Mennonite to seek social confirmation for her simple lifestyle from those thoroughly committed to consumerism. Rather, a person seeks social confirmation for her moral identity primarily from members of her social group, not from those outside of her social group, and certainly not those who belong to social groups antagonistic to her moral identity. Smith writes:

> We know ... from decades of empirical research that human beings do not care what everyone out there in society may think of them. For "everyone" is too massive and diverse a group to be worrying about their opinions and judgments. Rather, people care what only *certain* other people think of them, those belonging to what sociologists have long called their "reference group." [That set of people whose approval a given person considers when deciding how to act or what to believe.] ... Reference groups serve for people as sources of norms, values and standards of judgment, functioning as informal authorities in the process of evaluation. Thus, people know how to appraise themselves, their own identities, decisions, and actions in large measure by seeing how their reference groups appraise them. And, importantly, what people outside of a reference group think or feel about someone is largely inconsequential for that person's self-evaluation.[40]

Certain individuals, then, will provide social support for a person's moral identity but many others will not, *even if* she interacts with those others on a regular basis. Which individuals provide that social confirmation? The members of the social group(s) to which she belongs. Which individuals don't provide that social confirmation? The members of outgroups, particularly those against whom she defines her moral identity.

This point has direct relevance to Berger's thesis that there is a direct correlation between pluralism and religious decline. If Berger is correct, a person who interacts with those who don't share her religious commitments is thereby faced with the living possibility of rejecting her religious commitments – and can therefore maintain her religious commitments only with great effort. If Smith is correct, however, more is required than mere interaction: those with whom she interacts must play a role in maintaining her self-identity. They must be included in her reference group. But there is no need for a person to include in her reference group those who don't share her religious commitments. After all, each of us maintains a significant degree of control over the membership of our reference group – over those we keep in mind when evaluating the propriety and plausibility of our identity-constitutive commitments. But if "people can simply construct their reference groups to include enough fellow believers so that their faith continues to be affirmed," and if "the views of other people not in their reference group can be, put bluntly, ignored," then "pluralism does not necessarily undermine most people's religious beliefs."[41] Members of religious communities have the resources to quell the doubts engendered by pluralism and thereby to arrest the process of religious decline.

Suppose that we grant Smith's basic point: that the members of a particular religious community *need not* be thrown into a crisis of credibility by the sort of interaction with diverse others that they'll typically experience in a pluralistic social environment. That point raises a further problem. Even if pluralism doesn't necessarily generate a crisis of credibility, it *might* do so. Indeed, it might seem very likely to do so. After all, the problem of religious diversity is a very serious difficulty for any religious tradition, and life in a pluralistic social environment very naturally forces those who adhere to a religious tradition to come to terms with that problem. Adherents to a religious tradition *can* take measures to blunt the corrosive force of pluralism on their religious convictions, but that possibility does not, of course, provide any indication as to what they are *likely* to do. To know that they have an alternative to doubting their religious convictions provides us with no indication as to whether they will pursue that alternative. And of course, how the adherents to a religious tradition will respond to pluralism is a contingent matter, one that will be settled by many decisions made by large numbers of people over extended periods of time. But I think we can make a plausible prediction.

If most people accord overriding weight to arguments that cast doubt on the truth of their identity-constitutive convictions or cease to adhere to these convictions when apprised of an objection to those convictions for which they lack an appropriate response, then Berger's argument would indeed provide us with powerful reason to conclude that pluralism corrodes religious commitment. But it's doubtful that most people do accord overriding weight to arguments that cast doubt on their identity-constitutive convictions. At least as important a factor in determining how most people respond to a putative objection to such convictions is the cost of rejecting or altering them – cost here being a function of the other practices and commitments they must give up as a consequence of altering or rejecting their religious commitments. What are those costs? At the very least, a person in the throes of doubting his religious convictions faces the prospect of losing the moral identity those religious convictions support. (Indeed, he faces the prospect of losing *any* recognizable moral identity. The same considerations that cast in doubt the commitments out of which he constructs his current moral identity will cast doubt on the remaining alternatives, as there is no good reason to believe that the corrosive consequences of pluralism are limited to religious contributions to moral identity.) But the prospect of losing the moral identity that commitment to one's religious tradition affords (and perhaps a moral identity entirely) is a terribly high price to pay. Indeed, if Smith (and Berger) is correct that human beings crave a moral identity, we should expect them to take fairly dramatic measures to protect their moral identities when threatened by doubt. And so we should expect those who have constructed their moral identities on a religious foundation to protect themselves from the threat posed to those identities by their pluralistic environment by ensuring that their reference group includes a sufficient number of those who confirm their religious convictions. In short, not only can religious adherents avoid doubting their religious convictions in a pluralistic environment, but it is also plausible to suppose that most will do what they can to avoid doubt.

My point is not, of course, that a person will (or should, or even can) dismiss any and all evidence that threatens her moral identity, but that such evidence must be particularly powerful in order to overcome a natural and entirely defensible reluctance to revise – or even tenacity in defending – her identity-constitutive commitments. Most people aren't falsificationists regarding the commitments that define their moral identities, if by that one means that they want to challenge their moral commitments, are eager to revise their moral commitments, or are willing to revise their moral commitments when they have some evidence against those commitments. Thus, most citizens, even in a pluralistic environment, don't have what Stephen Macedo calls a peculiarly liberal attitude: "To borrow loosely from Popper, we might say the openness to self-criticism and the 'falsification' of even our basic judgments embodies a peculiarly liberal attitude; this is the way that autonomous liberal citizens ideally support both liberal justice and their personal commitments and values."[42] Most people neither have nor aspire to have what Stanley Fish characterizes as "an open mind, a mind ready at any moment to jettison even its most cherished convictions," an attitude Fish claims "is the very definition of 'reasonable' in a post-Enlightenment liberal culture."[43]

2.4.3 Pluralism and Politically Engaged Religion

The argument in the prior section shows that pluralism need not under-mine the plausibility of religious creeds – indeed, pluralism is unlikely to generate massive defections from religion. That is an important con-clusion. But Smith wants to show that a stronger claim is true – that pluralism can *strengthen* religion.[44] He argues as follows.

When the members of a given social group perceive themselves to be in conflict with the members of other social groups, the boundaries that establish that social group are emphasized, members are more willing to cooperate with one another to combat a common threat, and members are motivated to commit themselves more firmly to that community. (As is frequently noted, the best and surest way for a nation to quell internal dissension is to engage in open conflict with external enemies.) Since conflict fosters group cohesion and commitment, and since com-mitment to a social group and the cohesion between members of a social group are key indices of group strength, opposition and conflict tend to strengthen social groups.

The relation between internal cohesion and external conflict is di-rectly relevant to Berger's theory of secularization: pluralism provides religious groups with a large number of outgroups with which they can enter into the sort of conflict that fosters cohesion and commitment. Pluralism encourages the conflicts that strengthen the boundaries that define the communities that sustain the moral identities that people crave. According to Smith, the

> elementary principle – that out-group conflict typically builds in-group strength – has tremendous relevance for our understanding of the fate of religion in the modern world. We need not assume that conflict with ideo-logical and subcultural competitors and adversaries that religious groups may confront in a pluralistic society will inevitably weaken their beliefs and practices. We have reason to believe that such conflict can strengthen religious beliefs and practices – especially within religious subcultures which can interpret the conflict in a religiously significant framework. Thus, the very kinds of intergroup experiences that a highly pluralistic situation is apt to engender – suspicion, disagreement, friction, conflict – can actually strengthen the groups' subcultural identities and cohesion.[45]

One of Berger's central claims is that a given religion thrives when it enjoys a monopoly on its (local) religious market and declines when its monopoly is broken. Smith argues, however, that a religion that enjoys a monopoly on its market lacks a crucial resource: a plethora of outgroups that serve both to highlight that religion's boundaries and to motivate commitment and cohesion. As a consequence, a pluralistic environment can invigorate and revitalize religious communities in a way unlikely to occur in a monopolistic environment.[46]

From his reflections on the role that membership in social groups plays in the construction of a person's moral identity, Smith articulates what he calls a *subcultural identity theory*. That theory is composed of two theses. The first lays down a criterion for the persistence of religion: *"Religion survives and can thrive in pluralistic, modern society by embedding itself in subcultures that offer satisfying morally orienting collective identities which provide adherents meaning and belonging."*[47] If this first thesis is correct, the religious groups that have the best prospects for thriving in a pluralistic environment are those that clearly maintain the boundaries that distinguish them from other subcultural groups. In the absence of sufficient differentiation from its environment, a given religious group lacks the resources to provide its members with a moral identity and thus lacks the resources to capitalize on the human drive for meaning.

Smith's second thesis lays down a criterion for the relative strength of different religious groups: *"In a pluralistic society, those religious groups will be relatively stronger which better possess and employ the cultural tools needed to create both clear distinction from and significant engagement and tension with other relevant outgroups, short of becoming genuinely countercultural."*[48] If this second thesis is correct, the religious groups that have the best prospects for thriving in a pluralistic environment are those clearly defined groups that nevertheless remain engaged with their cultural, social, and political environment. Mere distinctness, without friction, conflict, and confrontation, denudes a given religious group of a significant cause of vitality, cohesion, and commitment. So religious groups that combine *both* clear differentiation *and* social engagement are more likely to thrive in a pluralistic environment than those that fail clearly to distinguish themselves from other communities or that lack constructive tension with other groups in their environment.

Smith employs his subcultural identity theory to explain why some Christian groups in the United States flourish and others decline. In particular, he uses it to explain why evangelical communities measure higher on key indices of group strength than do other Christian social groups, such as fundamentalist, mainline, and liberal.[49] Evangelical groups have an advantage over liberal and mainline groups because they maintain their distinctness from the dominant culture to a greater degree than do these groups.[50] And evangelical groups fare better than fundamentalist groups since the fundamentalists tend to segregate themselves from the dominant pluralistic culture and thus fail to make use of pluralism to generate tension and conflict.[51] In short, evangelicals maintain the desired balance between differentiation and external tension more effectively than do alternative Christian groups, and their success in maintaining that balance helps to explain their strength. Smith writes,

> Evangelical sensibilities allow neither complete disengagement from [as with fundamentalism] nor total assimilation into [as with mainline and liberal Christianity] the dominant culture. This provokes a situation of sustained dissonance, if not outright conflict, between evangelical believers and the nonevangelical world with which they – with tension – engage. And this fosters religious vitality.[52]

2.5 POLITICALLY ENGAGED RELIGION AND RELIGIOUS FREEDOM

I promised at the outset of this chapter to identify the problems politically active religion poses for liberal democracies and that I would do so by subtraction: by showing that politically active religion doesn't threaten religious freedom. I'll now draw on the preceding discussion to make good on that promise.

José Casanova has suggested that the received theory of secularization has three distinct moments, each of which needs to be evaluated separately.[53] First, the *differentiation thesis* is the claim that various spheres of activity – the state, the economy, science – are functionally differentiated and thus operate according to their own distinctive criteria.[54] Most important for our purposes, the differentiation thesis is a historical claim about the processes by which the state has been removed from ecclesiastical control, has shed its dependence on religion for legitimation, and no longer compels religious observance. The central means by which the modern state has differentiated itself from religion is by disestablishing religion and enforcing the right to religious freedom. Second, the *decline-of-religion thesis* is a claim about the *projected effects* of functional differentiation: the functional differentiation of state, economy, and science will "bring in its wake the progressive shrinkage and decline of religion."[55] Third, the *privatization thesis* is also a claim about the projected effects of functional differentiation: as the state operates under its distinct imperatives, religion will play a progressively less significant role in the state's activities.[56] According to Casanova, only if we distinguish between these three theses can we arrive at a nuanced evaluation of the theory of secularization.

The preceding discussion casts doubt on both the decline-of-religion thesis and the privatization thesis: religious groups can thrive in a pluralistic environment and they will refuse to allow the state to operate with complete autonomy from their religiously grounded moral commitments.[57] But nothing I've argued entails that the differentiation thesis is false.[58] Nothing, for example, in Smith's subcultural identity theory indicates that the modern state (and thus the liberal democratic state) needs religious legitimation or is threatened with transformation into a theocracy. He provides no reason to believe that the modern state will employ its coercive power to eradicate religious heterodoxy among its citizens. The objections to the theory of secularization articulated in this chapter are entirely consistent with the claim that the fundamental charter of the liberal state, religious freedom, is in no danger of being revoked: even though we can expect religious citizens to remain politically active, and even though we can expect them to bring their religious commitments into the political sphere, the very social dynamics that provide a basis for both of those predictions *also* provide a basis for denying that such citizens pose a danger to religious freedom.

Far from it. Since freedom of religion underwrites pluralism, and since pluralism enhances the vitality of religion, members of religious groups have a deep and abiding interest in affirming a political culture that values freedom of religion and a constitutional order that enshrines it. This is a particularly important point for the following reason: many contributors to recent discussions of the proper role of religion in politics seem to assume that allowing religious citizens to support their favored coercive laws solely on religious grounds endangers religious freedom. And many seem to assume that religiously conservative citizens – evangelicals in particular – pose a particularly dangerous threat to religious freedom. But the preceding discussion indicates that such concerns are dystopian. Although it is *possible* that religious citizens will pursue political goals that run counter to their deeply vested interests, it seems very *unlikely* that they will do so: in the end, the benefits of religious pluralism, and thus of the religious freedom that undergirds religious pluralism, will obviate any serious attempts by religious citizens to undermine religious freedom.

I should note that although Smith focuses almost exclusively on the benefits of pluralism to evangelicals, his conclusions are corroborated by theorists whose concerns are not so narrowly focused. For example, Casanova argues that a refusal to resist the differentiation of the state from religion – a differentiation effected most centrally by disestablishment and freedom of religion – is a precondition of the survival of religion in modernity: "In very simple terms, it could be said that the more religions resist the process of modern differentiation, that is, secularization in the first sense, the more they will tend in the long run to suffer religious decline, that is, secularization in the second sense."[59] Another example: Roger Finke and Rodney Stark have argued powerfully that religious establishment – and even more certainly that the denial of religious freedom – undermines competition among religious groups, breeds indifference and lethargy, and thus leads to religious decline.[60] There is a convergence of voices, then, in support of the claim that religious communities benefit from pluralism and thus from a political regime that protects the religious freedom from which pluralism ensues.[61]

We might be skeptical. After all, aren't there all sorts of citizens in the United States who pine for a return to "Christian America"? And wouldn't a return to Christian America require the very denial of religious freedom that I've claimed runs against the vested interests of religious citizens? Indeed, don't we find evangelicals at the forefront of those who advocate a return to Christian America?

Let's continue to focus on evangelicals, since that's the group many regard as posing the greatest danger to religious freedom. There are no doubt *some* citizens associated with evangelical religiosity whose advocacy of a return to Christian America requires a revocation of the right to religious freedom: so-called Christian Reconstructionists explicitly advocate denying to non-Christian citizens any civil liberties (among a number of even more extreme commitments).[62] But that exception proves the rule: Christian Reconstructionists are at the extreme fringe of the evangelical community. Most evangelicals, even given an attraction to the notion of a Christian America, find the Christian Reconstructionist's denial of religious freedom utterly repugnant. Indeed, an analysis of what evangelicals *mean* by the claim that we ought to return to a Christian America indicates that the vast majority are in the business of *legitimation* rather than revolution.

In an extensive set of interviews, Smith and his colleagues queried ordinary evangelicals regarding their understanding of the notion of a Christian America. The results were revealing if only for the various innocuous connotations associated with the evangelical penchant for a Christian America. Indeed, of the evangelicals interviewed, roughly 40 percent understood the claim that the United States is, and should remain, a Christian nation to mean that it "was founded by people who sought religious liberty and worked to establish religious freedom!"[63] Other responses were generally as tame: roughly 35 percent believed that "the majority of Americans of earlier generations were sincere Christians who put their beliefs and morals into practice more faithfully than Americans do today,"[64] roughly 30 percent that "the basic laws and structures of the U.S. government reflect or embody important Christian principles,"[65] slightly less than 30 percent that "most if not all of America's 'founding fathers' were theists who prayed and sought God's will for the nation,"[66] slightly less than 20 percent that vaguely construed Christian "principles and values" were influential in an earlier period of American history,[67] and finally about 12 percent that "in America's past the public expression of religious symbols and customs was deemed normal and acceptable."[68] Although some of these understandings of the notion of Christian America "lend themselves to a justification of Christian cultural hegemony ... it is a mistake ... to presume that all talk of a 'Christian nation' is a sure rhetorical indicator of the desire or intention to reestablish Christian domination of society, culture and politics."[69] To the contrary, most of those who valorize Christian America are engaging in the time-honored practice of providing religious legitimation for the status quo, and in particular, for the current system of government in which the right to religious freedom is deeply ensconced.[70]

2.6 CONCLUDING COMMENTS

Our review of some of the literature on the theory of secularization indicates the following. Religious communities are here to stay; many citizens will make use of the normative resources provided by religious communities to construct their moral identities. The secular state is here to stay as well; barring some demiurgic catastrophe, there is no realistic prospect that the right to religious freedom will be revoked in the contemporary United States. Public, politically engaged religion is also here to stay; religious citizens will not accord the state *complete* autonomy from their normative commitments. Religious citizens will enter the political arena as ordinary participants in the democratic process in order to press their normative claims in concert with and in opposition to other similarly motivated citizens. But, as we've seen, at least some of the religious groups that thrive in a pluralistic environment are likely to be politically active *and* to adhere to distinctive values – values that may very well be deeply discrepant with those to which many of their compatriots adhere.[71]

This last fact undergirds the empirical condition that motivates the central normative question of this book. Given that a pluralistic environment enables politically engaged religious groups that adhere to distinctive normative commitments to thrive, what role may their distinctive commitments play in their political practice? Should citizens whose religiously grounded normative commitments run counter to the normative commitments of their compatriots privatize those commitments? Does appealing to those religiously grounded commitments in "the public square" endanger the common good, say, by threatening to polarize and divide citizens? Does it manifest disrespect for those who reject their religious convictions, thereby generating alienation and resentment? Not a few justificatory liberals have made that case. And it is to justificatory liberalism that I now turn.

CHAPTER 3

JUSTIFICATORY LIBERALISM

3.0 INTRODUCTION

We have good reason to believe that for the foreseeable future, large numbers of citizens will bring their religious commitments into the public square. As a consequence, we face the question: what role may a responsible citizen's religious convictions play in his political practice? The justificatory liberal answers: a responsible citizen may support a coercive law on the basis of his religious convictions, but not on the basis of his religious convictions alone. That answer derives from the justificatory liberal's commitment to *public justification*: the claim that respect for his compatriots forbids a citizen to support a coercive law for which he can't discern a public justification provides a principled basis for the claim that a citizen ought not support a coercive law on the basis of his religious convictions alone.[1] My intention in this chapter is to explicate that principled basis and thereby to explain why, according to justificatory liberals, a citizen ought not support a coercive law on the basis of religious convictions alone.

3.1 THE CONSTITUTIVE COMMITMENTS OF JUSTIFICATORY LIBERALISM

First, a word of caution. My explication of justificatory liberalism distills what I take to be common concerns and commitments from many heterogeneous sources – from a variety of texts that have been published over a number of years, texts that employ widely varying idiolects, that address a multiplicity of problems, that contain ambiguities, inconsistencies, shifts of conviction. Consequently, it's simply impossible to characterize justificatory liberalism in a way that does complete justice to the nuances and qualifications with which each of its adherents formulates his or her favored version of that position. So I don't claim that my characterization of justificatory liberalism captures with complete accuracy the details of each theorist's formulation of the commitments that define that position. Rather, my hope is to articulate a fair and sympathetic representation of a general position, shared by a wide variety of theorists, that, when applied to religious convictions, gives the result that a citizen ought not support any coercive law on religious grounds alone. Inevitably, some will feel that they have been misunderstood, mischaracterized, or falsely assimilated to an alien paradigm. For that, I apologize in advance.

3.1.1 The Problem of Social Harmony

To understand a theoretical position, it is helpful to understand the problems that position is proposed to solve. One problem, which I call the *problem of social harmony*, is mentioned repeatedly in the literature on justificatory liberalism and sheds much light on the justificatory liberal's defining commitments.

Consider the following two facts about a liberal democracy. First, any state – even a liberal democratic state – exercises coercive power over its citizens. Laws are meant to be obeyed, and obedience is secured, in crucial part, by coercion. This is obviously true of laws that prohibit or discourage violent behavior – the state attempts to secure obedience to laws that prohibit murder and assault by authorizing its agents to subdue perpetrators (when necessary) with fists, clubs, and guns. This is also true of many laws that don't restrict or discourage violent behavior – the state employs coercion to ensure that citizens pay taxes, refrain from racial and sex discrimination, obey traffic laws, register for the draft, and so on. Second, liberal democracies are invariably characterized by pluralism. That pluralism inevitably spills into politics: as we saw in the prior chapter, many citizens have a vested interest in bringing their parochial religious commitments into the political arena to lobby for their favored policies. Different citizens, given their distinctive histories, worldviews, and experiences, will rely on their distinctive points of view to determine whether a given law merits their support. The fact that liberal states exercise *power* over a *pluralistically* committed citizenry generates the problem of social harmony.[2]

49

What, exactly, is that problem? If large numbers of citizens will, under conditions of freedom, adopt widely varying worldviews, and if each citizen insists on judging coercive laws from the perspective of her particular worldview, then we can expect a disparity between the coercive laws a given citizen regards as morally appropriate and those her compatriots regard as morally appropriate. As a consequence of the pluralism endemic to liberal democracies and of the willingness of citizens to judge coercive laws from the perspective of their respective worldviews, we should expect irremediable disagreements regarding the true religion and the correct conception of the good to translate into equally irremediable disagreements regarding specific coercive laws. But citizens will still be subject to those laws and the state will continue to enforce those laws with coercion. Typically, citizens who are coerced on the basis of laws that they reject are deeply averse to being so coerced, particularly if they reject those laws on what they consider to be entirely legitimate, reasonable grounds. And treating citizens in ways to which they are deeply averse disturbs the harmony of social relations.

The combination of power and pluralism threatens a liberal democracy with a problem of social harmony. That problem constitutes an essential backdrop to the justificatory liberal's project: he wants to resolve that problem. Of course, justificatory liberals cannot single-handedly solve that problem; whether it is resolved in a given liberal polity depends, in crucial part, on how large numbers of citizens respond to it. But justificatory liberals can *contribute to* a resolution of that problem. How so? Brian Barry argues that "even if people are unhappy with a decision, they are much more likely to accept it if they perceive it as having been taken in a fair way."[3] In a pluralistic society, each citizen is doomed to be subject to coercive laws he finds morally objectionable. And although a citizen naturally regards subjection to such laws as an injury, the *manner* in which a given law is enacted can ameliorate (or exacerbate) his alienation and frustration. And the manner in which a law is enacted depends to a significant extent on the sorts of reasons those who support that law employ as a basis for it.[4]

The justificatory liberal's hope is that if citizens police the reasons on the basis of which they support their favored coercive laws, they make possible consensus on the laws to which they are subject, and even in the absence of consensus, the manner in which citizens decide to support their favored laws can generate mutual trust and respect. Thus, Stephen Macedo writes, "The only way that we can achieve a public moral framework while accepting the deep and permanent fact of diversity is by putting aside not only the personal interests and religious beliefs, but also the many philosophical and moral convictions that reasonable citizens will disagree with."[5] By rigorously disciplining their reasons for supporting their favored policies, diversely committed citizens can commit themselves to a set of commonly shared political practices and contrive to live peaceably even when they cannot agree. And the justificatory liberal contributes to resolving the problem of social harmony by explaining *why* citizens morally ought to police their reasons for coercive laws and by delineating the *sorts* of reasons citizens may and may not employ as a basis for coercive laws.

3.1.2 Public Justification and Respect

Justificatory liberalism is distinguished from other versions of liberalism by two related commitments: to public justification and to respect for persons. Those two commitments constitute the heart of the justificatory liberal's contribution to the resolution of the problem of social harmony and provide a principled basis for the claim that a citizen ought not support her favored coercive laws on the basis of her religious convictions alone. So it's obviously going to be critical that I articulate some reasonably clear understanding of those two commitments.

First, *public justification*. The justificatory liberal intends to contribute to the resolution of the problem of social harmony by articulating an account of the sorts of reasons a citizen may and may not employ as a basis for her favored coercive laws. At the heart of that account is the claim that a responsible citizen ought to ensure that her favored laws are amenable to public justification. Each citizen ought to support only those coercive laws that articulate *in an appropriate way* with the very different points of view of the other members of the public. And what way is that? The reasons on the basis of which a citizen supports her favored laws ought to be convincing, not just to her, given her distinctive point of view, but to other citizens – the members of the public – given their respective points of view. Endorsements of this basic idea are legion. Thus, for example, Stephen Macedo claims that "the moral core of [a liberal] order is a commitment to public justification: the application of power should be accompanied with reasons that all reasonable people should be able to accept."[6] Again, Charles Larmore: "A natural notion to describe the essential character of liberalism is that of *neutrality,*" the pursuit of which expresses a "moral commitment to finding terms of political association that can be the object of reasonable agreement."[7] And like Macedo and Larmore, Amy Gutmann and Dennis Thompson aspire "to a politics in which citizens and their accountable representatives, along with other public officials, are committed to making decisions that they can justify to everyone bound by them."[8] The gist of such statements is clear: each citizen should so discipline herself that she supports only those laws for which she enjoys the appropriate kind of rationale, where what makes a given rationale appropriate is a function, in crucial part, of the acceptability of that rationale to the members of the public. (Exactly what counts as a public justification is a matter of *considerable* dispute among justificatory liberals and will be a topic of great interest throughout this book.) This first defining commitment of justificatory liberalism, then, is a commitment, neither to particular policies, nor to a particular rationale for particular policies, but to a set of normative constraints that govern the sorts of rationale citizens should be able to provide for their favored policies.[9] As Rawls states, "The idea of public reason is not a view about specific political institutions or policies. Rather, it is a view about the kinds of reasons on which citizens are to rest their political cases in making their political justifications to one another when they support laws and policies that invoke the coercive powers of government."[10]

Second, *respect for persons.* Justificatory liberals intend to contribute to the amelioration of social disharmony, not just by articulating a set of constraints on the sorts of reasons a citizen may employ as a basis for his favored coercive laws, but also by explaining why citizens morally ought to adhere to those constraints. Justificatory liberalism is partly constituted by a distinctive *moral rationale* for the commitment to public justification. That rationale depends on an appeal to the norm of respect for persons. Thus, Charles Larmore:

> To respect another person as an end is to insist that coercive or political principles be just as justifiable to that person as they are to us. Equal respect involves treating in this way all persons to which such principles are to apply.[11]

John Rawls:

> Mutual respect is shown in several ways: in our willingness to see the situation of others from their point of view, from the perspective of their

conception of the good; and in our being prepared to give reasons for our actions whenever the interests of others are materially affected.... When called for, reasons are to be addressed to those concerned; they are to be offered in good faith, in the belief that they are sound reasons as defined by a mutually acceptable conception of justice which takes the good of everyone into account. Thus to respect another as a moral person is to try to understand his aims and interests from his standpoint and to present him with considerations that enable him to accept the constraints on his conduct.[12]

Again, Stephen Macedo:

In a liberal society, coercive political arrangements require the support of articulable reasons capable of meeting objections and being fairly applied. This is, in part, because people really do disagree, and because we owe reasonable people the form of respect embodied in public justification.[13]

Paul Weithman:

For the state to base cooperation and exercise power on terms of co-operation that citizens could not reasonably endorse as free equals is to show them a form of disrespect.... Relying on terms that privilege some disregards the interest they have in making only reasonable demands of others. Respect for citizens as such requires recognizing and satisfying this interest. Respect therefore requires that social cooperation be based on terms citizens can accept on the basis of their common reason.[14]

Robert Audi:

I think that sound ethics itself dictates that, out of respect for others as free and dignified individuals, we should always have and be sufficiently motivated by adequate secular reasons for our positions on those matters of law or public policy in which our decisions might significantly restrict human freedom. If you are fully rational and I cannot convince you of my view by arguments framed in the concepts we share as rational beings, then even if mine is the majority view I should not coerce you.[15]

Lawrence Solum:

Respect for the freedom and equality of citizens requires that decisions be made on the basis of public reason.[16]

Respect for his compatriots as persons obliges a citizen to ensure that his favored coercive laws are justifiable from the points of view of those compatriots. When a citizen deploys his modicum of political clout to authorize the state to coerce his compatriots, as he surely may in a liberal democracy, respect for his compatriots requires that he provide them with reasons they can accept in support of the claim that his favored coercive policies are warranted. *Respect for others requires public justification of coercion*: that is the clarion call of justificatory liberalism.

This characterization of justificatory liberalism raises a variety of questions. In the remainder of this section, I will address four. First, to *whom* does the obligation to provide a public justification apply? To citizens, as I have assumed thus far, but to legislators and judges as well? Second, what *sort* of obligation is the obligation to provide public justification? Is that obligation moral in nature or legal as well? And if a moral obligation, what sort of moral obligation? Third, to which *kinds of political commitments* does the obligation to provide a public justification apply? Does it apply only to fundamental constitutional matters, to all coercive laws, or to all political commitments? Fourth, in which *contexts* does the obligation to provide a public justification apply? Does respect for others require a citizen to provide a public justification for his political commitments in any discussion of political matters (a private discussion about Amendment 2 around the dinner table, for example) or only those that most directly impinge on the political process (a speech at a political rally advocating that citizens vote for Amendment 2)?

These questions admit of various reasonable but conflicting answers; consequently, as one might expect, there is no consensus among justificatory liberals as to how they ought to be answered. Nevertheless, in order to streamline my discussion, I'll impute to the justificatory liberal a position on each question and in so doing construct an ideal type of justificatory liberalism. The core of that ideal type is as follows: each *citizen* has a *moral* obligation to provide public justification for any *coercive* law she supports when *deciding* which coercive laws merit her support and when *advocating* her favored coercive laws. Since this formulation carries theoretical weight or narrows the focus of attention in ways that require explanation and, as the case may be, justification, I'll briefly identify my reasons for this formulation.

First, perhaps the most basic question raised by the claim that respect requires public justification is this: to whom does the obligation to provide a public justification apply? It seems to me that the obligation to provide public justification applies most directly and most importantly to *citizens*. In theory at least, the laws that a liberal democratic state enforces with coercion ultimately depend for their authorization on the imprimatur of citizens. After all, if the citizenry of a (suitably functional) liberal democracy finds a given law objectionable enough, they have it within their power to remove or alter that law. And if the justificatory liberal is correct that respect requires public justification of state coercion, presumably any citizen who lends support to state coercion bears a responsibility publicly to justify that law. So, given the influence of citizens over the laws that a democratic state enforces, it seems that citizens ought to ensure that any coercive laws they support are amenable to public justification.

Why focus on citizens rather than legislators or judges? Primarily in the interest of simplicity and ease of exposition: one social role is easier dealt with than two or three. But given that some sort of selection is helpful, why the focus on citizens rather than, say, legislators? Citizens play a fundamental role in a liberal democracy. A legislator's capacity to enact coercive laws depends, in the long run, on support from her constituency; given that legislators are dependent for their capacity to enact coercive laws on their constituency, it makes sense to focus on the constraints on reasons it's appropriate to require of citizens.[17]

Second, if citizens ought to support only those coercive laws that are amenable to public justification, in what sense *ought* a citizen provide a public justification for his favored coercive laws? By common consent, the obligation is not *legal* in nature; I'm not aware of any justificatory liberal who endorses legal constraints on the sorts of reasons a citizen employs as a basis for his favored coercive laws.[18] Again, by common consent among justificatory liberals, the obligation to provide public justification is *moral* in nature. But what sort of moral obligation? To adapt a point made persuasively by Robert Audi, it's plausible to suppose that a citizen who supports his favored coercive laws without a public justification doesn't violate anyone else's *moral rights*.[19] But a citizen who doesn't violate anyone else's rights isn't thereby free from moral criticism: a citizen who refrains from violating the moral rights of his compatriots satisfies the moral minimum, but might very well fail to discharge moral obligations of a higher standard. Thus, for example, even if a citizen who fails to give of his excess to those who lack the basic necessities of life doesn't violate anyone else's moral rights he might nevertheless be morally criticizable for failing to do so. I'll assume that a citizen's putative moral obligation to support only those coercive laws for which he has a public justification falls into this latter category – of moral obligations a citizen must discharge in order to ensure that his actions are free from moral criticism.

Again following Audi, I'll assume that a citizen's putative obligation to ensure that her favored coercive laws are amenable to public justification is a prima facie one – an obligation that can be overridden by countervailing considerations in exceptional circumstances.[20] A citizen's obligation to provide public justification for her favored coercive laws need not take precedence in every case, given that she might have even weightier obligations that excuse her failure to discharge her obligation to provide public justification. But I'll assume that the obligation to provide public justification is particularly important and thus can be overridden only by very powerful considerations, and thus that that obligation in fact constrains the activities of actual citizens in significant respects.[21]

Third, I've assumed thus far that a citizen's obligation to pursue public justification applies to *coercive* laws. (By coercion, I understand both the *actual* employment of punishment and the *threat* of punishment.[22]) But not all justificatory liberals extend their scope that broadly. Some argue that citizens should provide public justification for fundamental matters – constitutional matters and matters of basic justice – but that that requirement may be relaxed for less fundamental matters.[23] I find the wider claim more plausible. As Lawrence Solum has argued, "Most citizens encounter the state most directly and concretely through the coercive exercise of power," as a consequence of which they are most likely to demand justification for ordinary uses of coercive power, even if "the basic structure and constitutional liberties lie behind the scene."[24] And since the justificatory liberal is committed to the proposition that respect for persons requires public justification, that demand for public justification, not just for basic matters but for all state coercion, is legitimate.[25] In short, since citizens are unlikely to limit their demands for public justification to matters of basic justice and constitutional essentials, and since the justificatory liberal can hardly deny the legitimacy of those demands, I'll assume that citizens are expected to pursue public justification with respect to their favored *coercive* policies.

Fourth, if citizens have a moral obligation to provide a public justification for their favored coercive laws, in which *contexts* ought citizens provide a public justification? I take the obligation to provide a public justification to apply most directly to *political decision making*: in the paradigmatic cases, to a citizen's decision to vote for a particular candidate and to her decision to vote for a specific policy. Why? The exercise of power is, we might say, a *transitive* relation: a citizen who employs the modicum of influence at her disposal (e.g., voting) to authorize the state to employ its coercive power exercises coercive power at one remove. Even if *she* doesn't mete out the punishment required by the violation of a law she supports, her support for that law makes it possible for others to inflict the punishment that a violation of that law authorizes. And so, if a citizen decides to vote for some coercive law, then she must be able to provide a public justification for that law.

In addition, I take the obligation to provide a public justification to apply, not just to what occurs in a citizen's interiority, but also to what happens among citizens. A citizen's obligation to provide public justification governs not just political decision making but also *political advocacy*: it governs the reasons a citizen may employ to convince her compatriots that they ought to support her favored coercive laws. When a citizen seeks to convince them, she ought to articulate a public justification for that policy; and if she cannot do so, then she ought to refrain from advocating that law.

I'll assume for the duration that the justificatory liberal's defining claim that respect requires public justification applies most centrally to a citizen when she *supports* a coercive law. And I'll assume that a citizen supports a coercive law, in the paradigmatic case, when she decides to vote for a coercive law directly (say, in an initiative or a referendum) or indirectly (by allowing a prospective legislator's position on some coercive law to influence her decision to vote for that legislator) and when she advocates that others do likewise. An important caveat: although I'll use the language of "support" throughout this book, the obligation to provide a public justification should always be understood to apply to coercive laws a citizen *rejects* as well. I see no compelling reason to believe that, as a general matter, it is morally more desirable for a citizen to support a coercive law on the basis of a publicly justified rationale than it is for her to reject a proposed law on the basis of a publicly justified rationale.[26] Thus, for example, it's no more desirable for Bill McCartney to provide a public justification for Amendment 2 than it is for him to provide a public justification for rejecting laws that protect homosexual citizens from housing and work-related discrimination.

One final point regarding the contexts governed by a citizen's putative obligation to provide a public justification. I've assumed that a citizen's obligation to provide a public justification governs not only her interiority – the bases on which she decides to support a coercive law – but also her interactions with her compatriots – the manner in which she tries to convince others to support a coercive law. But a citizen's obligation to provide a public justification doesn't govern *all* of her interactions with her compatriots. In particular, there's an important distinction between advancing some argument *for purposes of critical discussion* and advancing some argument *for purposes of convincing others to support some law*. I see no reason to ascribe to the justificatory liberal the claim that a citizen ought to restrain herself from articulating only a religious rationale for some coercive policy for purposes of critical discussion. A citizen who articulates a religious argument for purposes of critical discussion without attempting to convince others that they ought to support some coercive law solely on the basis of that argument isn't implicated in the sort of coercion that justificatory liberals regard as requiring public justification. Although there is no doubt some slippage between critical discussion and advocacy, I won't impute to the justificatory liberal the view that a citizen may articulate in 'public' arenas only those arguments she takes to constitute a public justification for a given coercive law.

3.1.3 What Justificatory Liberalism Is Not

At this point it might be helpful to explain justificatory liberalism by distinguishing it from its competitors. I'll do so by identifying three claims that are *not* distinctive to justificatory liberalism. (1) The justificatory liberal is not distinctive in adhering to characteristic liberal commitments. (2) The justificatory liberal is not distinctive in claiming that he enjoys good reason for his liberal commitments. Finally, (3) the justificatory liberal is not distinctive in accepting constraints on the grounds that a citizen may employ in political decision making and advocacy.

Ad (1): The heart of justificatory liberalism, the commitment that distinguishes it from other species of liberalism, is a claim about the kinds of reasons a citizen may employ as a basis for coercive laws. Since what distinguishes the justificatory liberal from other species of liberal is a matter of the sort of justification required for coercive laws, rather than a matter of the specific laws the justificatory liberal affirms, it's possible to *reject* justificatory liberalism without thereby rejecting *any* of the substantive commitments characteristically associated with a liberal polity. It's possible, in short, to reject justificatory liberalism and nevertheless to affirm *mere liberalism*, where a necessary and sufficient condition of commitment to mere liberalism is commitment to a suitable selection of liberal policies. Thus, for example, Elijah can affirm the right to religious freedom, he can affirm that right solely on religious grounds, yet he can deny that he should refrain from supporting that right absent a public justification.[27] In that case, Elijah adheres to a fundamental liberal commitment – to religious freedom – but eschews justificatory liberalism. He is, we may assume, a mere, but not a justificatory, liberal.

To be perfectly clear, let me say that although I find much to dispute with the justificatory liberal, that dispute has *nothing* to do with the sorts of legal rights we should accord to citizens in a liberal democracy. Indeed, I believe, and will assume throughout this book, that a responsible citizen in a liberal democracy adheres to characteristic liberal institutions and practices. Of particular importance, I believe, and will assume throughout this book, that a responsible citizen will affirm the right to religious freedom.[28] But from the fact that a responsible citizen will adhere to liberal commitments, nothing at all follows about his reasons for those commitments and, in particular, whether he has, or needs, a public justification for those commitments.

Ad (2): To repeat: the distinguishing feature of justificatory liberalism is a commitment to a particular constraint on the sort of rationale a citizen should have for his favored coercive laws. The justificatory liberal differs from the mere liberal with respect to the specific sort of justification that we may reasonably require of citizens: the justificatory liberal requires public justification and the mere liberal rejects that requirement. But those who reject justificatory liberalism aren't thereby committed to denying that they have *any* justification for substantive liberal commitments. To the contrary, "mere" liberals are free to believe that they have powerful arguments for the characteristic liberal commitments to freedom of conscience, due process, and so on.[29] How can one believe that one has powerful arguments for liberal commitments and yet deny that one has a public justification for those commitments? Because of the special sort of constraint associated with *public* justification: Elijah can have what he takes to be, and what in fact are, compelling religious reasons to assent to the claim that, for example, each citizen has a right to religious freedom, and at the same time believe that other reasonable and conscientious citizens can have, from their respective points of view, good reason to reject his rationale for that claim. In that case, Elijah's rationale doesn't count as a public justification: his rationale, though compelling from his own point of view, doesn't articulate in the appropriate way with his compatriots' points of view. Having adequate grounds for a given policy is one thing; having grounds that one's compatriots will take to be adequate is another matter altogether.

Ad (3): The justificatory liberal is distinctive in advocating a *particular* constraint on the basis on which it's appropriate for a citizen to support her favored coercive laws. But it isn't the case that those who reject justificatory liberalism are thereby committed to rejecting *all* constraints on the reasons properly employed as a basis for proposed laws. Thus, for example, although I deny that each citizen must be able to provide a public justification for her favored coercive laws, I believe that each citizen ought to be *rationally* justified in adhering to her favored coercive laws.[30] So mere liberals and justificatory liberals differ, not necessarily with respect to whether there are any constraints on political decision making and advocacy, but with respect to what those constraints are.

A specific constraint merits mention at this point. In addition to the claim that each citizen ought to support only those coercive laws for which she enjoys an adequate rational justification, I also believe that each citizen ought to adhere to something like Mill's principle of harm – "that the only purpose for which power can be rightfully exercised over any member of a civilized community, against his will, is to prevent harm to others."[31] But one can consistently endorse the principle of harm without also endorsing the justificatory liberal's commitment to public justification.[32] After all, a citizen can have entirely nonpublic reasons to believe that some action generates the relevant sort of harm, in which case she uses a rationale for proscribing or discouraging that action that satisfies the principle of harm but doesn't constitute a public justification. To take an extreme example, religious opponents of homosexuality sometimes articulate a national defense argument in support of the state's discouraging homosexual relations. This argument satisfies the principle of harm but doesn't thereby constitute a public justification: they claim that if the state permits citizens to engage in homosexual relations, then it risks divine retribution, perhaps even in the form of foreign conquest – a secular harm by any standard, but surely not a public justification![33] Again, a citizen who appeals to the Bible as a basis for the claim that abortion kills a person and who, solely on the basis of that claim advocates that the state prohibit abortion, can't plausibly be supposed to violate the principle of harm – killing a person clearly counts as harm to others – although her appeal to Biblical authority doesn't suffice for a public justification.

3.2 THE CONCEPT OF PUBLIC JUSTIFICATION

Given its obvious centrality to justificatory liberalism, the concept of public justification needs to be explained in more detail. Unfortunately, there is no fully satisfying and efficient way to do that; while there is a rough and ready consensus on the *concept* of public justification, there is no consensus among justificatory liberals on a particular *conception* of public justification. In order to keep my explication of justificatory liberalism to manageable proportions, I'll attempt to characterize only the concept of public justification. A more detailed treatment of various proposed conceptions will have to wait until Part III.

3.2.1 Rational Justification

Perhaps the best way to fix the concept of public justification is to contrast it with a related but importantly distinct concept, that is, rational justification. Here are some truisms about the concept of rational justification that will enable us to explicate the concept of public justification.[34]

First, whether it's rational for a citizen to adhere to a given belief is a function, in part, of the *manner* in which he forms and evaluates that belief.[35] A rational citizen attempts to form his beliefs on the basis of the best available evidence, is willing to pursue evidence when it is not easily available, is willing to subject his own convictions to criticism, and is willing to change his convictions when the evidence seems to point definitively to the contrary. A disposition to decide matters on the basis of evidence, a disposition to subject convictions to criticism when called for, a willingness to change even dearly held convictions in light of critique – those are the sorts of virtues required for, and partly constitutive of, rationality. (I won't even attempt to list in detail the various factors that determine whether a citizen forms his beliefs in an appropriately rational manner.)

Second, a citizen who conscientiously attempts to determine whether a given belief B merits his adherence must rely on a fund of beliefs and experiences he assumes to be true or reliable while evaluating B.

Call that fund of beliefs and experiences his *evidential set*. Whether it's rational for a citizen to assent to B (or accept a given argument for B) depends, in addition to the manner in which he forms his beliefs, on the contents of his evidential set. Thus, for example, assume that Socrates rationally believed in a Ptolemaic understanding of the solar system. I don't share this belief and would be irrational if I denied my neo-Copernican convictions. That difference between what is rational for the two of us to believe has everything to do with correlative differences between the stock of other beliefs on which Socrates relied and the stock on which I rely in deciding which model of the solar system to accept. Given important differences between our respective evidential sets, it was rational for Socrates to accept a model of planetary movement that it isn't rational for me to accept. Moreover, nothing we can reasonably expect Socrates to have done regarding the *manner* in which he arrived at his Ptolemaic commitments would have changed his final conclusion.

Whether a given citizen is rationally justified in adhering to belief B, then, is a function of both his evidential set and the manner in which he employs the evidence available to him. As a consequence, rational justification is a radically *perspectival* phenomenon: whether a citizen is rationally justified in adhering to B depends, at least in part, on his point of view – on the evidence to which he has access by pursuing the appropriate procedures, on the assumptions with which he conducts his inquiry, and so on.

The perspectival nature of rational justification forces us to distinguish between *soundness* and *rationality*. Assume that some version of the problem of evil is sound: there exists a valid argument that takes us from true claims about God's nature and the existence of evil to the conclusion that God doesn't exist. That such an argument exists is, of course, consistent with the existence of fully rational citizens who persist in believing that God exists. Such citizens might assent to false propositions, and they might reject sound argumentation, but they aren't necessarily irrational. Soundness is one thing; rationality quite another. Soundness has to do with the objective adequacy of an argument for a given conclusion; rationality has to do with whether some argument *appears* to be sound given a citizen's evidential set and given that she has gone about evaluating that argument in the appropriate manner.

The perspectival nature of rational justification has another corollary. When *we* attempt to determine whether it's rational for *another* citizen to adhere to a given belief or support a given law, we must do so at least partly on the basis of our knowledge of the content of that citizen's evidential set. We ought *not* determine whether she rationally adheres to belief B on the basis of our evaluation of the *soundness* of the arguments she takes to vindicate B, however obvious it might seem to us that her arguments for B are unsound. Thus, for example, Jack's theistic convictions might seem irrational to Jill, if Jill believes that the logical problem of evil is sound. But Jill should be much less willing to convict Jack of irrationality when she discovers that Jack supports his conviction by relying on a trusted authority, Alvin, whom he rationally believes has engaged in extensive reflection on that problem and concluded, incorrectly by hypothesis, that it can be resolved. Given the other components of Jack's intellectual structure, his theistic convictions are entirely rational and Jill's judgment regarding his rationality should therefore be parasitic, at least in part,[36] on the relation between his theism and the other components of his evidential set.

3.2.2 Rational versus Public Justification

William Alston has emphasized an important distinction that will help fix the content of the notion of public justification. There is, Alston argues, a distinction between being rationally justified in assenting to p and being able rationally to justify p, between the *state* of being justified and the *activity* of justifying.[37] To justify p, a citizen must do something by way of providing some sort of evidential support for p: paradigmatically, she must present some explicitly articulated argument that has p as a conclusion. To be justified in assenting to some proposition a citizen need not show anything: merely seeing a tree, or recalling a past event, or feeling depressed, may suffice to justify her in assenting to p. A citizen need be neither able nor willing explicitly to articulate grounds for p in order to *be* justified in assenting to p; much less need she actually do so.

For a number of reasons, a citizen can find herself in the condition that she is rationally justified in assenting to p but isn't able rationally to justify p. The following condition is particularly worthy of note. Given the contents of Lauren's evidential set, she might assent to a set of premises that, if true, provide fully adequate reason for her to accept p. But her compatriots, who evaluate p on the basis of very different evidential sets, might not assent to the set of premises on the basis of which Lauren assents to p. Moreover, given the peculiarities of their respective evidential sets, Lauren's compatriots might not assent to any claims that, if true, would provide them with adequate reason to assent to p. Consequently, Lauren will be unable to articulate any argument for p that depends for its soundness solely on premises her compatriots regard as true. In virtue, then, of sufficiently wide disparities among evidential sets, Lauren might be unable to articulate any argument for p that her compatriots will regard as sound and thus will be unable to justify p to her compatriots. She will, in short, *be* justified in assenting to p but be unable to *justify p to* her compatriots.

True enough, Lauren might be able to justify p to *some* of her compatriots. For example, the evidential set she relies on to evaluate p might be sufficiently similar to some of her compatriots' respective evidential sets so that Lauren is able to show to those compatriots that p is true. But, pretty obviously, simply because she can rationally justify p to some of her compatriots, it doesn't follow that Lauren can rationally justify p to each of them. Indeed, it seems in all likelihood that in very many cases Lauren will be rationally justified in assenting to p, will be able to justify p to a select few of her compatriots, but will be at a loss to justify p to most, much less each, of her compatriots. But it's only in the latter, very demanding, case, only when Lauren has some rationale that is, or can be, persuasive to *each* of her compatriots, does she have a *public* justification for her favored coercive laws.

Whether a citizen has a public justification for a given coercive law is a function not just of her perspective on the world, not just of whether she is rationally justified in supporting that law, but also of an *appropriate* relation her rationale bears to her compatriots' respective points of view, namely, whether she is able to justify that law to others in a way that *is*, or at least *can be*, convincing to them given their parochial points of view. Note that it is, in principle, possible that a citizen can *be* rationally justified in supporting some coercive law, that she can't rationally justify that law to her compatriots (by presenting some argument that each of her compatriots take to be sound), but that each of her compatriots is also rationally justified in supporting that law. Although a logical possibility, such a fortuitous convergence of conviction would be miraculous. I will assume, then, that a citizen enjoys a public justification for p only if she is able to justify to her compatriots that p merits their support, a process that, in turn, requires her to articulate explicitly some arguments for p that her compatriots *actually* find compelling or, more weakly, that they *can* find compelling in the appropriately specified circumstances.

Although this characterization of public justification is incomplete in numerous important respects, it has enough content to indicate what is required by the obligation to provide a public justification. Since a citizen is publicly justified in supporting a coercive law only if he has a rationale that meshes in an appropriate way with his compatriots' points of view, a citizen's obligation to pursue public justification forbids him to consult *only* his own point of view – his evidential set – in determining whether to support a given law. It enjoins him to look outward, beyond the merely personal, to inhabit the points of view of his fellow citizens, in order to determine whether his compatriots have good reason, from their perspectives, to support a given law. As John Rawls claims: "Public justification is not simply valid reasoning, but argument addressed to others: it proceeds correctly from premises we accept and think others could reasonably accept to conclusions we think they could also reasonably accept."[38] In order to articulate a public justification for a favored law, then, a citizen must connect properly with the content of other citizens' evidential sets: only if he articulates a rationale for his favored policy that draws on premises included in, or that comport with, his fellow citizens' respective evidential sets does he stand a chance of articulating a rationale that will, or can, convince them. In short, "the aim is to search for significant points of convergence between one's own understandings and those of citizens whose positions, taken in their most comprehensive forms, one must reject."[39] (Thus, the importance of public *deliberation* to public *justification*: a citizen can determine whether his rationale articulates in the appropriate manner with his compatriots' distinctive points of view only if he apprises himself of their points of view, and that requires hearing them out.[40])

My explication of the concept of public justification has two important implications for how *we* determine whether a given citizen has a public justification for a given coercive law. First, since public justification is largely a function of factors other than a particular citizen's point of view and her cognitive activities, we can't determine whether she is publicly justified in supporting some coercive law *just by reference to her perspective on the world*. Rather, we can make that determination only if we have recourse to the points of view of her compatriots – to the evidential sets on which her compatriots rely when determining whether a given law merits their support. Second, we can't determine whether a citizen enjoys a public justification for some coercive law *just by determining whether the argument on the basis of which she supports that law is sound.* Just as soundness is insufficient for *rational* justification, so also is soundness insufficient for *public* justification.[41] As a consequence, that a citizen supports a given coercive law on the basis of a sound argument is largely irrelevant to whether she enjoys a public justification for that law.

3.2.3 The Concept versus the Conception of Public Justification

As I've characterized the concept of public justification, a citizen is publicly justified in adhering to some coercive law only if she has a rationale for that law that articulates in the appropriate way with the points of view of her compatriots and thus that enables her to justify that law to her compatriots. Although my characterization of the concept of public justification has enough content to distinguish it from the concept of rational justification, it's of critical importance to the justificatory liberal's project that she specify much more precisely than I have just what constitutes an appropriate articulation. Without specification of what counts as a rationale that articulates appropriately with others' points of view, the sort of rationale a citizen needs will remain mysterious; as a consequence, whether she has a public justification for a favored law will be unclear; and as a further consequence, whether it's appropriate for her to support that law will also be unclear. And that would seem to render the justificatory liberal's advocacy of public justification futile.

Consider two (implausible) conceptions of public justification. Suppose we stipulate that the notion of public justification is to be understood in terms of "beliefs to which all other citizens actually adhere." In that case, we should understand the justificatory liberal as requiring that a citizen articulate a rationale for a given coercive law that is constituted by premises to which each of his fellow citizens actually adhere. So understood, if Bill McCartney's only reason for supporting Amendment 2 is that homosexual relations are an abomination to God, then, since not all citizens regard homosexuality as an abomination, he would lack a public justification for Amendment 2. More generally, since no religious convictions are shared by all of the citizens in a pluralistic, liberal democracy, it follows that no rationale that includes religious premises would constitute a public justification.

But suppose we stipulate that the notion of public justification is to be understood in terms of "beliefs to which it is logically possible for all other citizens actually to adhere." In that case, we should understand the justificatory liberal to require that a citizen articulate a rationale for a given law that is constituted by premises it is logically possible for each of his fellow citizens actually to regard as sound and thus which they *can* find convincing.[42] But since it is logically possible for each of McCartney's fellow citizens to assent to the claim that homosexuality is an abomination to God, it is pretty clear that, on the current conception of public justification, McCartney enjoys a public justification for Amendment 2. And since it's logically possible for the citizens of a liberal democracy to adhere to any given set of religious convictions, it's pretty clear that, interpreted as at present, a citizen who enjoys only a religious rationale for a favored law would nevertheless be publicly justified in supporting that law.

The point of these examples is to emphasize how important it is to the justificatory liberal's project that she articulate a clear and compelling conception of public justification. The justificatory liberal's favored conception of public justification determines the sorts of reasons a citizen may and may not use to support her favored laws. Since different conceptions give different results, the justificatory liberal's commitment to public justification gives determinate guidance only if she specifies a particular conception for citizens to employ. More particularly, since different conceptions give very different results regarding religious convictions, which conception the justificatory liberal adopts has far-reaching implications for the proper role of religious convictions in liberal politics.

There are, of course, a variety of proposed conceptions of public justification, many of which are more plausible than the two I've just mentioned. As I'll explain in Part III, conceptions of public justification fall into two very different categories: *populist* conceptions, according to which a public justification is a rationale that is actually acceptable to the members of the public (suitably construed), and *epistemic* conceptions, according to which a public justification is a rationale that has some epistemic desideratum that facilitates the acceptance or interpersonal evaluation of that rationale. The diversity of available proposals makes it impossible to offer a succinct treatment of *the* conception of public justification to which justificatory liberals are committed: adjudicating between the various proposed conceptions of public justification is obviously going to require quite a bit of explication, reconstruction, and critique. Wisdom counsels that I postpone that task until the matter can be given a sufficiently detailed treatment. As for now, we'll have to understand "public justification" in the vague and amorphous way developed thus far: as a rationale that articulates in some desirable way with the parochial points of view of a citizen's compatriots and thus which she can employ to justify some coercive law to her compatriots.

3.3 PUBLIC JUSTIFICATION AND RESTRAINT

The moral heart of justificatory liberalism is the claim that respect for persons requires public justification. That claim harbors an ambiguity that has far-reaching implications for my argument. Analysis of the justificatory liberal's appeal to public justification reveals that he typically has in mind two distinct claims:

The principle of pursuit: a citizen should pursue public justification for his favored coercive laws.
The doctrine of restraint: a citizen should not support any coercive law for which he lacks a public justification.

In order to distinguish between the principle of pursuit and the doctrine of restraint, it will be helpful to consider a passage that fails to observe that distinction. Consider the following argument pressed by Robert Audi:

> A liberal democracy by its very nature resists using coercion, and prefers persuasion, as a means to achieve cooperation. What we are persuaded to do, by being offered reasons for it, we tend to do autonomously and to identify with; what we are compelled to do, we tend to resent doing. [1]Thus, where there must be coercion, liberal democracies try to justify it in terms of considerations – such as public safety – that any rational adult citizen will find persuasive and can identify with. [2]This is one reason why religious grounds alone are not properly considered a sufficient basis of coercion even if they happen to be shared by virtually all citizens. If fully rational citizens in possession of the relevant facts cannot be persuaded of the necessity of coercion – as is common where that coercion is based on an injunction grounded in someone else's religious scripture or revelation – then from the point of view of liberal democracy, the coercion lacks an adequate basis.[43]

The statement I have marked as [1] is a claim about the pursuit of public justification, about the sorts of grounds – "those that any rational adult citizen will find persuasive" – by appeal to which a responsible

citizen *tries* to justify his favored policies. By contrast, [2] is a claim
about restraint, about a sort of reason – "religious beliefs alone" – by
reliance on a citizen should *not* support a given policy. In the passage
cited, Audi seems to claim that [1] provides reason to adopt [2]; in my
idiolect, he seems to claim that the principle of pursuit constitutes good
reason for the doctrine of restraint. But the fact that citizens in liberal democracies should attempt to articulate grounds for their favored
policies acceptable to "any rational adult citizen" is not a reason *at all*
for the claim that they shouldn't support coercive policies on religious
grounds alone. More generally, the claim that a citizen should pursue
public justification isn't a reason *at all* for the claim that he ought to
exercise restraint. Why?

The doctrine of restraint lays down a constraint on the coercive laws
a citizen is permitted to support: a citizen is permitted to support coercive law L *only if* L is publicly justified. The "only if" provides the
doctrine of restraint with its critical edge: a citizen who lacks public
justification for L *should not* support L. The principle of pursuit, by contrast, enjoins a citizen to do what she can to ensure that each of her
fellow citizens has adequate reason to accept her favored policies; as
Audi says, "Liberal democracies *try* to justify [coercive laws] in terms of
considerations . . . that any rational adult citizen will find persuasive."[44]
It seems entirely possible that a citizen can do everything that can reasonably be expected of her by way of attempting to discern a public
justification, and thus have satisfied her obligation to pursue public
justification, without being successful in the attempt. Pursuits can fail;
we try but do not invariably succeed in our efforts. That a citizen has an
obligation to pursue public justification for a given policy provides her
with no guidance at all as to what she should do in that case: that she
ought to pursue public justification pretty obviously provides her with
no guidance in answering the question, "What should I do in the event
that, *having pursued public justification*, I nevertheless cannot discern the
desired justification?" The justificatory liberal claims that she should
cease and desist from supporting that policy.[45] That is as it may be, but
that claim is distinct from the claim that a citizen ought to pursue public
justification and thus requires additional argumentation.[46]

It might be that, although distinct, the principle of pursuit *entails* the
doctrine of restraint, so that a citizen who has an obligation to adhere
to the principle of pursuit ought thereby to adhere to the doctrine of
restraint. And since, as I'll argue in 4.3, there is more than adequate

reason to accept the principle of pursuit, the distinction I'm attempting to draw might seem purely academic. But this line of argument isn't promising. In fact, I think, this line of argument gets the relations between restraint and public justification exactly backward.

It's plausible to suppose that a citizen who ought to exercise restraint ought also to pursue public justification. If a citizen should do her best *not* to support a coercive law L for which she lacks a public justification, then she *should* seek out public justification for L. Why? If a citizen can discharge some obligation only by pursuing a given course of action, then she is likewise obliged to pursue that course of action. If parents can discharge their obligation to satisfy their child's needs only by holding down a job, then their obligation to provide for that child implies an obligation to pursue gainful employment. As a matter of realistic fact, citizens can discharge their obligation to exercise restraint only by actively seeking out public justification for their favored policies.[47] Pursuit of public justification is an unavoidable means to the end of discharging the obligation to exercise restraint. So the obligation to exercise restraint implies an obligation to pursue public justification.

But an obligation to pursue public justification doesn't imply an obligation to exercise restraint. A citizen can be obliged to pursue public justification for her favored coercive laws without also being committed to withholding support from those laws if public justification isn't in the offing. Why is that the case? A citizen can discharge her obligation to pursue public justification without also exercising restraint. The latter isn't related as means to the former end in the way that the former is related to the latter. That a citizen ought to pursue public justification doesn't require that she withhold support from policies for which she lacks public justification any more than a citizen who has an obligation to seek gainful employment thereby incurs an obligation to support her children. She might have the latter obligation, but she does not have it in virtue of having the obligation to seek employment.

So, then, not only are the obligations to pursue public justification and to exercise restraint distinct, and not only does the obligation to exercise restraint imply an obligation to pursue public justification, but – more important – an obligation to pursue public justification does not imply an obligation to exercise restraint. Thus, it is false that, as Gerald Gaus claims, "the reverse side of our commitment to justify imposing our norms on others is a commitment to refrain from imposing norms that cannot be justified."[48]

have direct implications for my central thesis. What constraints do the principle of pursuit and doctrine of restraint impose on a citizen by way of the proper employment of her religious convictions in political decision making and advocacy?

First, the principle of pursuit. If a citizen enjoys only a religious rationale for a given coercive law L, then she lacks a public justification for L (whatever conception of public justification eventually emerges triumphant). And if she lacks a public justification for L, then the principle of pursuit obliges her sincerely and conscientiously to do what she can to discern some rationale for L that articulates appropriately with her compatriots' distinctive points of view – that will be convincing to them, or that would be convincing to them insofar as they are adequately informed and fully rational, or that they are in a position to criticize, or the like. So the principle of pursuit requires a citizen to do more than stand pat on her religious commitments.

What the principle of pursuit does *not* require of a citizen is just as important as what it does require. Two points are pertinent here. First, the principle of pursuit requires *nothing* more than a sincere and conscientious aspiration to public justification; it is entirely silent regarding what a citizen may or may not do so long as she succeeds in pursuing a public justification for her favored coercive laws. It follows, then, that the principle of pursuit doesn't forbid a citizen to support a coercive law on the basis of her religious convictions. As we have seen, although any religious rationale a citizen enjoys doesn't constitute a public justification for a coercive law, so long as she pursues public justification for that law, she is permitted to support that law on a religious basis as well.

Second, the principle of pursuit is silent regarding whether a citizen may support a given law on the basis of her religious convictions alone. The principle of pursuit mandates that a citizen sincerely and conscientiously attempt to discern a public justification for any law she supports. But, as I argued earlier, it's possible for a citizen sincerely and conscientiously to pursue a public justification for a law yet fail in that attempt. The principle of pursuit tells us exactly nothing about what she ought to do in that sort of case.

What about the doctrine of restraint? As with the principle of pursuit, the doctrine of restraint is consistent with the claim that a citizen may support a coercive law on the basis of her religious convictions: from the fact that a citizen shouldn't support a given law for which she lacks a public justification, it doesn't follow that, if she *possesses* a public justification, she is forbidden from also supporting that law on grounds that don't constitute a public justification. The doctrine of restraint is also consistent with a citizen's being motivated much more by her religious grounds for a given law than by her public justification for that law. Since the doctrine of restraint requires only that a citizen withhold her support from any coercive law for which she lacks a public justification, then, so long as she *does* have public justification for that law, she satisfies the doctrine of restraint even if her public justification is comparatively unimportant to her.[59] Indeed, the doctrine of restraint is consistent with the claim that a citizen may support a coercive law even if the only grounds for that law that *she* regards as compelling are religious. The doctrine of restraint is not consistent, however, with the claim that a citizen may support a coercive law for which she *has* only religious grounds: she must have a rationale that articulates appropriately with the distinctive points of view of her compatriots, even if she doesn't regard that rationale as particularly plausible or sound. If a citizen enjoys only religious grounds for a given coercive law, then, since a religiously grounded norm doesn't suffice for a public justification, the doctrine of restraint enjoins her to withhold support from that law.

It turns out, then, that the justificatory liberal's basis for the claim that a citizen may not support a coercive law on the basis of her religious convictions alone depends on her commitment to the doctrine of restraint. More precisely, the justificatory liberal's basis for that claim depends on two further claims: *both* that a citizen ought not support a coercive law for which she lacks a public justification, *and* that a citizen who enjoys only a religious rationale for a given coercive law lacks a public justification for that law. Accordingly, since my central disagreement with the justificatory liberal is over the propriety of a citizen's supporting a coercive law on the basis of her religious convictions alone, the ensuing discussion will involve a critical analysis of both of those claims.

3.4.4 Privatization and Religion

In order to guard against a possible misunderstanding of justificatory liberalism, I'll explain why I reject a complaint commonly leveled against that position. It's not at all uncommon for critics to claim that justificatory liberalism requires the complete *privatization* of religion.[60] According to such critics, justificatory liberals are committed to the claim that religious convictions may govern a citizen's activities in his private life – how he spends his leisure time, which books he reads, the vocation he chooses, how he will raise his children, whether he'll have any children, and the like. But religion is not welcome in the public world: as a basis for public policy, as a serious contributor to debate about how scarce resources are to be allocated, religious convictions have no legitimate role to play at all. According to such critics, the justificatory liberal shares Rorty's aspiration to make "it seem bad taste to bring religion into discussions of public policy."[61]

As I understand the position, justificatory liberalism requires nothing so draconian as a thoroughgoing privatization of religious convictions. As we've seen, the justificatory liberal claims that a citizen ought not support a coercive law L if he lacks a public justification for L, but that, so long as he enjoys a public justification for L, he is free to support L on religious grounds as well. So the justificatory liberal may admit – indeed, welcome – religious arguments in political decision making and advocacy. Of course, the justificatory liberal *is* committed to the privatization of religious convictions that can't be corroborated by a fully adequate public justification – such religious convictions may guide a citizen's "lifestyle choices," but may not be used as a basis to impose laws on his fellow citizens. But that is a far cry from a thoroughgoing privatization of religious belief – this limited privatization is worlds apart from an *exclusive* version of the doctrine of restraint that forbids a citizen from employing his religious convictions at all in political decision making and advocacy. In short, so long as we adopt an *inclusive* version of justificatory liberalism, one that permits a citizen to support a proposed coercive law on religious grounds *so long as* he also has a public justification for that proposal, the privatization objection to justificatory liberalism evaporates. Robert Audi expresses this inclusive position with admirable clarity: "On my view, it is the advocacy and the support of laws and public policies that are constrained, and the constraint is *inclusive* rather than *exclusive*: the chief point is not that one can't have and be motivated by religious reasons but that one should have and be motivated by one at least set of evidentially adequate secular reasons."[62]

Having said this, I grant that some of those plausibly regarded as justificatory liberals reject the inclusive position I've attributed to justificatory liberalism. So how do I justify my characterization of justificatory liberalism? The exclusive interpretation of the doctrine of restraint is much stronger than the inclusive interpretation: the former forbids a citizen from supporting his favored laws on the basis of any of his religious convictions, whereas the latter requires that he privatize only that subset of his religious convictions constituted by religiously grounded claims for which he lacks a corroboratory public justification. In order to construe justificatory liberalism in the most sympathetic way, I'll saddle it with only the weaker claim. That said, I'll give the exclusivist his day in the sun: in Chapter 6, I'll articulate and evaluate what I take to be the most plausible arguments in support of the exclusive version of the doctrine of restraint.

3.5 CONCLUDING COMMENTS

As we've seen, the justificatory liberal's commitment to the doctrine of restraint provides principled grounds for his position on the proper role of religious convictions in political decision making and advocacy: the doctrine of restraint implies that a citizen ought not support any coercive law for which he enjoys only religious grounds. And not only does it forbid a responsible citizen from supporting any law for which he enjoys only a religious rationale, but, given the paradigmatically nonpublic status of religious convictions, that prohibition is *essential* to justificatory liberalism. Since my central thesis is that it is permissible for a citizen to support his favored laws on the basis of his religious convictions alone, it follows that I must undermine the justificatory liberal's claim that a citizen in a liberal democracy ought to adhere to the doctrine of restraint. I'll attempt to do just that in the remainder of this book.

PART TWO

WHY RESTRAINT?

INTRODUCTION TO PART TWO

My intention in Part II of this book is to answer the question, Is there good reason to believe that a responsible citizen in a liberal democracy morally ought to obey both the principle of pursuit and the doctrine of restraint? The justificatory liberal believes that there is. The "argument from respect" is at the heart of the most promising attempts to articulate a rationale for the claim that each citizen morally ought to pursue public justification and to exercise restraint. In the two immediately succeeding chapters, I will evaluate a number of variations of that argument.

To focus attention on the central issues raised by the argument from respect, I'll adopt the following two assumptions. First, I take for granted the claim that each citizen ought to respect her compatriots. No argument for that claim seems necessary given that the notion of respect enjoys a hallowed place in the pantheon of liberal values. Second, I'll assume for purposes of argument that the justificatory liberal can articulate a defensible conception of public justification. That is, I'll assume that, *if* the justificatory liberal can show that each citizen ought to pursue public justification and exercise restraint, she'll also be able to articulate a defensible criterion that specifies both the grounds a citizen ought to pursue for her favored coercive laws and the grounds on which she may not support her favored coercive laws. (I'll argue that she can't articulate a defensible conception in Part III.) So the question I intend to address in Part II is neither "Why respect others?" nor "What counts as a public justification?" but "Does a citizen's obligation to respect her compatriots require her to pursue public justification for her favored policies?" and "Does a citizen's obligation to respect her compatriots require her to withhold support from any law for which she lacks a public justification?"

I'll argue in support of the following two conclusions. First, a citizen has a moral obligation to obey what I call the *ideal of conscientious engagement*: that ideal is constituted by a number of constraints, one of which is the principle of pursuit. I present my argument for this conclusion in Chapter 4. Second, a citizen doesn't have an obligation to refrain from supporting any coercive law for which he lacks a public justification: even though he has an obligation to respect his compatriots, he doesn't have an obligation to obey the doctrine of restraint. I present an argument for this conclusion in Chapter 5.

I address each conclusion to a specific audience. I direct the first conclusion to those citizens who are content to conduct their political decision making and advocacy entirely within the ambit of their religious convictions. To that audience, I argue that respect for their compatriots as persons morally obliges them to exit their parochial worldviews, to do what is within their power to inhabit the respective points of view of their compatriots, and to attempt to articulate reasons for their favored policies that are convincing to their compatriots. I direct the second conclusion to those who discourage citizens from supporting any coercive law for which the latter cannot discern a public justification. To that audience and to a first approximation, I argue that so long as a religious citizen sincerely and conscientiously attempts to articulate a rationale for his favored coercive policies that will be convincing to his compatriots, then he has thereby discharged his obligation to respect them – even if his attempt ends in failure. In short, both the justificatory liberal and his alter ego, the religious sectarian who supports his political commitments on the basis of his religious convictions alone, misunderstand what respect for others requires and, as a consequence, adhere to a faulty understanding of what makes for responsible citizenship.

In the next two chapters, then, I argue that respect for persons requires a citizen to adhere to an ideal of conscientious engagement but doesn't oblige a citizen to adhere to the doctrine of restraint. Only when I have established both of those conclusions will I be in a position to evaluate another argument for the doctrine of restraint, one very different from the argument from respect. Unlike the argument from respect, which has a decidedly deontological flavor, some justificatory liberals articulate a *historical-consequentialist* case for the doctrine of restraint. They argue as follows: we have learned from past incursions of religion into politics to be extremely wary of mixing religion and politics. As we all know, religious wars and persecution of heretics result when religion and politics commingle. We should take to heart the lessons history teaches us about the past role of religion and politics and apply them to the issue at hand: if large numbers of citizens were to support their favored coercive laws on the basis of their religious convictions alone, they would so divide and disrupt the body politic that they would endanger centrally important political goods. In order to secure those political goods, so the argument goes, we should encode into the role of citizen the expectation that each citizen obey the doctrine of restraint. Restraint, then, is a prophylactic for religiously generated civil strife and polarization. I respond as follows: so long as citizens fully respect their compatriots – which I take to require only that they obey the ideal of conscientious engagement – a widespread refusal on the part of citizens to adhere to the doctrine of restraint need not, and indeed is unlikely to, generate the troubling consequences envisioned by advocates of this argument.

CHAPTER 4

WHAT RESPECT REQUIRES

4.0 INTRODUCTION

One of the fundamental intuitions animating justificatory liberalism strikes me as compelling: that "respect for persons" mandates important constraints on the reasons citizens may employ as a basis for their favored coercive laws. More particularly, the justificatory liberal correctly argues that since each citizen has an obligation to respect her compatriots, she has an obligation to pursue public justification for each of the coercive laws she supports. But that isn't all: a citizen's obligation to respect her compatriots imposes a variety of additional constraints on the reasons she properly employs as a basis for her favored coercive laws. The burden of this chapter is to identify those constraints and to show why each is required by the norm of respect.[1] These constraints combine to form an *ideal of conscientious engagement* that each citizen ought to obey in political decision making and advocacy.

4.1 RESPECT FOR PERSONS?

I begin by explicating the conception of respect implicit in my understanding of respect for persons. I don't have in mind what Stephen Darwall has called *appraisal respect*, that is, the sort of respect that consists in a positive assessment of a person's character or some aspect thereof.[2] The conception of appraisal respect won't do the work I require of it. One of the defining features of appraisal respect is that not every person deserves it. Appraisal respect is a "positive appraisal of an individual made with regard to those features that are excellences of persons. As such, it isn't owed to everyone, for it might or might not be merited."[3] This is an obvious point: since Mother Theresa manifests certain virtues in an exemplary way, we evaluate her character positively, whereas Joseph Stalin, who was beset with a large quantity of despicable character traits, doesn't command our admiration. But the sort of respect I'm interested in must apply to *each* of a citizen's compatriots, whether virtuous or vicious, weak or powerful, wise or foolish, greedy or giving. This is so because the central component of the ideal of conscientious engagement I intend to articulate in this chapter – the obligation to pursue public justification – extends to every one of the citizen's compatriots.[4] The public for whom a citizen ought to attempt to articulate a convincing rationale includes, I believe, each of her compatriots, not just those she likes, or who share her convictions, or who are morally upright, or who are cooperative. Since an argument from appraisal respect to public justification can support only the conclusion that a citizen ought to address a public justification to those compatriots who merit esteem, and since the target conclusion is that a citizen ought to try to justify her favored coercive laws to each of her compatriots, a persuasive argument from respect to public justification won't employ the notion of appraisal respect.[5]

If a citizen has an obligation to respect each of her compatriots, she must have that obligation in a very different sense from that provided by the concept of appraisal respect. A more promising candidate is what Darwall calls *recognition* respect. A citizen has recognition respect for her compatriots as persons just in case she accords due moral weight in her deliberations to the fact that her compatriots are persons. What does it mean for a citizen to accord due moral weight in her deliberations to the fact that her compatriots are persons? At the very least, it is "to regard that fact as itself placing restrictions on what it is [morally] permissible for [her] to do."[6] What is it to allow some fact (such as that one's compatriots are persons) to place restrictions on what it is morally permissible to do? At the very least, it is to recognize that that fact ought to *make a difference* regarding how one ought to act: to accord due weight to some fact is to allow one's understanding of what one ought to do to be *sensitive* to that fact. Thus, for example, to have recognition respect for the fact that Nathaniel is my son is to recognize that his being my son makes a moral difference – other things being equal, the fact that Nathaniel is my son obliges me to treat him differently from other persons: I ought to feed and clothe him but not, ceteris paribus, another person's son. If I deny that I ought to treat Nathaniel differently from any other son, then I fail to accord due weight to the fact that he is my son, and thus lack recognition respect for the fact that he is my son.

In order to respect some fact (such as that one's compatriots are persons) in the recognitional sense, one has to accord *due* weight to that fact. But how does one determine what weight some fact ought to have in one's deliberations? In order to identify the moral constraints imposed on me by the fact that Nathaniel is my son, I must determine which moral truths bear on the fact that Nathaniel is my son. So I must have recourse to moral truths about how parents ought to treat their children, how obligations to persons with whom I have a special relationship articulate with obligations I have toward people in general, and so on. In short, having respect for the fact that Nathaniel is my son forbids me simply to ignore that fact in my deliberations and requires that I advert to whatever moral commitments bear on that fact to determine what weight Nathaniel's being my son ought to have regarding how I ought to act.

On the conception of respect I'll employ in articulating the ideal of conscientious engagement, a citizen respects his compatriots as persons only if he accords due moral weight to the fact that they are persons, which in turn requires this fact to make a moral difference to the way he acts. I'll argue, of course, that the fact that a citizen's compatriots are persons ought to make a difference as to the manner in which he supports his favored coercive laws. But we can determine what difference respect for persons should make for a citizen's behavior only if we know what a person is. So, what feature of a citizen's compatriots is picked out by the fact that they are (properly functioning, adult) persons?[7]

We can begin to answer that question by contrasting persons with inanimate objects. A crucially important difference between a (properly functioning, adult) person and an inanimate object is that a person cares about what happens to him whereas an inanimate object does not.[8] *Mattering* suffices to distinguish a person from, say, a rock. A rock is indifferent (not to say unmoved) as to whether it is crushed to pieces, dropped over a cliff, run over by a truck, or used to landscape a lawn. A person, typically, is not. What accounts for this difference between persons and inanimate objects? In normal cases, a person has a set of concerns and commitments that can be either fulfilled or frustrated. Different outcomes count as better or worse (from his perspective), more or less desirable (from his perspective), as a consequence of whether those outcomes consummate his cares and concerns. A rock, by contrast, lacks a set of concerns and commitments that can be either frustrated or fulfilled. Because a rock lacks cares and concerns, it cannot rank outcomes as better or worse and so nothing that happens matters to it.

Mattering matters. That persons care about the outcomes of our actions makes a moral difference: that people care about what happens to them but that rocks don't care about what happens to them obliges us to treat people differently from rocks.[9] As a consequence, at least one of the facts to which a citizen ought to accord due weight in his deliberations regarding coercive laws is that those laws matter to his compatriots. More particularly, the fact that a citizen's compatriots care about the coercive laws he supports imposes moral constraints on the manner in which he supports his favored laws. The crucial question is, of course, what those constraints are – a topic I'll broach in short order.

Mattering does not, however, identify precisely enough the feature of persons to which I'll appeal in articulating the ideal of conscientious engagement. After all, although the phenomenon of mattering distinguishes persons from inanimate objects, it doesn't distinguish persons from mere animals. Animals, like persons, have a set of cares and concerns in virtue of which different outcomes rank as better and worse, and that can be frustrated, and thus that matter to them. However, persons differ from animals in respects that oblige citizens to treat persons differently from the way they treat animals. What is that relevant difference? A crucial part of that answer is *reflective* mattering.[10] In addition to having a set of cares and commitments in virtue of which things matter to him, a person is also capable of reflecting on his cares and commitments: he can form "higher-level" desires, beliefs, cares, and concerns regarding his "lower-level" desires, beliefs, cares, and concerns. Thus, Elijah can form the higher-level desire that he no longer desires fatty food and can form the higher-level belief that he should believe that fatty foods are unhealthy. In this respect, humans are different from animals: Elijah's dog can desire fatty foods but can't form desires about that desire or commit itself to changing that desire.[11]

A person's capacity to form higher-level cares and commitments has an important consequence: that capacity enables him to exercise some degree of reflective influence over his lower-level cares and commitments. For example, Elijah can come to believe that his uncritical reliance on the testimony of others is misguided and, as a consequence, form the higher-level commitment to be much more reluctant to believe other people just on their say-so. By contrast, Elijah's dog lacks such a capacity to alter, modify, and correct its (lower-level) cares and commitments.

So a person not only has a perspective on the world in virtue of which things matter to him, but he has some degree of reflective control over that perspective: he can modify, alter, and correct it if appropriate.[12] A responsible citizen ought to pay due regard to that fact about his compatriots. If he does, I'll argue, he ought to adhere to at least six distinct constraints on the manner in which he decides to support his favored coercive policies.

4.2 RESPECT AND RATIONAL JUSTIFICATION

As we saw in the prior chapter, rational and public justification are distinct concepts. A citizen is rationally justified in regarding some coercive law as morally appropriate only if she arrives at that conclusion in the appropriate manner (e.g., by discharging the various epistemic obligations that properly govern belief formation in a given case) and only if, as judged from the perspective provided by her evidential set, she enjoys adequate reason to believe that that law is morally appropriate. By contrast, a citizen is publicly justified in supporting some coercive law only if she enjoys a rationale for that law that articulates in the appropriate way with the points of view of other citizens (where the propriety in question can be explicated in various ways). Although I'm concerned primarily with the claims that a citizen ought to pursue public justification for her favored coercive laws and that a citizen ought to refrain from supporting any coercive law for which she can't discern a public justification, comparable claims regarding rational justification are of considerable importance to my central thesis. So in this section, I'll address the topic of the relation between respect and rational justification: I'll argue that a citizen who respects her compatriots as persons ought to pursue a high degree of rational justification for any coercive law she supports and ought to withhold her support from any coercive law for which she lacks a high degree of rational justification.[13] Here is that argument.

(1) *If a citizen ought to respect her compatriots as persons, then she ought to accord due weight, not just to the fact that various states of affair matter to her compatriots, but also to what matters to her compatriots.*

Suppose that, when deliberating about how to treat Jill, Jack intends to accord due weight to the fact that Jill has a set of cares and concerns in virtue of which his actions matter to her. But suppose that Jack knows almost nothing about the specific content of Jill's cares and concerns: he has no idea what, in particular, matters to her. So, for example, Jack surmises that Jill cares about money, but doesn't know whether she wants to accumulate it or give it away. In that case, the fact that Jill cares about money will be deliberatively inert: since he doesn't know whether she wants more money or less money, Jack has no idea whether to give her money or take money away from her. Jack's ignorance of the content of Jill's concerns about money renders him unable reliably to guide his activity by reference to her concerns. Of course, there is nothing special about Jill's concerns about money, and so we may generalize the point: the fact that Jill has cares and concerns in virtue of which various states of affair matter to her will be deliberatively inert unless Jack takes due notice of the content of those cares and concerns. So, since Jack ought to accord due weight to the fact that Jill has cares and concerns, and since he can discharge that obligation only if he accords due weight to the content of her cares and concerns, Jack ought to accord due weight to what Jill cares about.

(2) *If a citizen ought to accord due weight to what matters to her compatriots, then she ought to accord due weight to the fact that her compatriots are legitimately and deeply averse to being coerced.*

Coercion, the reader will recall, is a matter of actual punishment or of the threat of punishment; the state coerces a citizen, for example, when it incarcerates her for committing some crime and when it threatens to incarcerate her if she commits some crime. We – adult citizens in (more rather than less) full possession of our faculties – typically care deeply about coercion; it matters a great deal to us either that we are punished or that we are threatened with punishment. More precisely, we have a profound *aversion* to coercion. We typically resent being forcibly forbidden to act in ways that we wish to act or believe that we ought to act. (This is an empirical judgment about what matters to us, and so might be false, but I assume that it will resonate sufficiently with the reader to render argument superfluous.)

Of course, the mere fact that a citizen is deeply averse to some state of affairs imposes no constraints on how we may act: if that citizen's aversion to some course of action is completely unreasonable, then the fact that she is averse to that course of action needn't make any difference at all regarding the moral propriety of that course of action.

But I'll assume that our aversion to coercion is typically legitimate: as Robert Adams argues, we are legitimately averse to coercion because coercion tends to violate our agency.[14] I will make short work of this step in the argument, then, by assuming the following: because coercion tends to violate our agency, we regard the aversion most feel toward being coerced as entirely legitimate and therefore as a fact that imposes powerful constraints on the way we may treat our compatriots.

(3) *If a citizen ought to accord due weight to the fact that her compatriots are legitimately averse to being coerced, then she has a prima facie moral obligation to refrain from coercing her compatriots.*

As I noted in my explication of the concept of recognition respect, we can determine what sort of weight we ought to accord some fact only if we have recourse to moral truths that bear on that fact. So, in order to determine what follows from a citizen's obligation to accord due weight to the fact that her compatriots are legitimately and deeply averse to being coerced, we must have recourse to whatever moral considerations bear on that fact.

With this in mind, there are certain moral platitudes we can expect any morally decent person to obey, each of which expresses a *presumption*: in almost every circumstance, lying is wrong; in the vast majority of cases, we shouldn't torture others; typically, we ought not steal. There's another claim that although more abstract than the aforementioned is no less platitudinous: when my actions affect another person and that person is legitimately and deeply averse to my actions, then that person's legitimate aversion counts as a presumption against the moral propriety of my course of action. Alternatively put, when some course of action affects another person and that person legitimately resents that course of action, then I have a prima facie obligation to refrain from pursuing that course of action.

The last platitude has a direct bearing on (3). A citizen who accepts the platitude that we have a prima facie obligation not to pursue any course of action that affects others in ways to which they are legitimately and deeply averse, and who wants to accord due weight to the fact that people are legitimately and deeply averse to coercion, will conclude that there is a (moral) presumption against coercion.[15] That citizens are legitimately and deeply averse to some course of action should have the weight of a presumptive moral veto on that course of action. And since a citizen who supports a coercive law engages in an indirect kind of coercion, she ought to recognize that there is a moral presumption against her supporting that law.

(4) *If a citizen has a prima facie obligation to refrain from coercing her compatriots, then she ought not coerce them unless coercing them is morally appropriate, all things considered.*

The platitude that we ought not lie (or steal, or torture) expresses *only* a presumption: there are exceptional circumstances in which we ought to lie (or steal or torture). This is undoubtedly the case with respect to the presumptive moral impropriety of pursuing a course of action to which the affected persons are legitimately and deeply averse. And of course, the prima facie prohibition on coercion is also defeasible: as Michael Perry has argued, "That various considerations counsel against pursuit of coercive political strategies, and that we should therefore be wary, as a general matter, about pursuing such strategies, is not to say that no such strategy should ever be pursued. That position – radical tolerance – would be extreme and extremely silly."[16] If other considerations are such as to outweigh or undermine the presumption against coercion, then it's appropriate, all things considered, for me to pursue a coercive course of action. So, even though respect for other persons requires that I recognize a prima facie obligation not to coerce them, that prima facie obligation can be overridden by countervailing considerations. Of course, if there aren't any sufficiently weighty countervailing considerations, then the prima facie obligation to refrain from coercion counts as a moral obligation, all things considered, in which case I should refrain from coercion.

(5) *If a citizen should not coerce her compatriots unless coercing them is morally appropriate, all things considered, then she ought to pursue rational justification for the claim that her coercive actions are morally appropriate, all things considered.*

Suppose that Elijah is committed to supporting only those laws that are morally appropriate, all things considered. In order for Elijah to make good on that commitment, he must employ the appropriate *means* in pursuing that commitment. One of the things he has to do is to determine whether, in a given case, a coercive law really is morally appropriate. It is no mean task to determine whether, in the case of a given law, the presumption against coercion is overridden. We do not, unfortunately, enjoy cognitive capacities that enable us to intuit, just on considering the matter, whether the presumption against coercion is overridden in a given case: such matters are often opaque on first, and even second and third, reflection. Given the way human beings are put together, we have a realistic prospect of resolving such moral conundrums only if we attempt to resolve them in a rational manner. Hence, Elijah will collect what he takes to be relevant evidence; he'll weigh the moral propriety of alternative courses of action; he'll rely on those he takes to be trustworthy authorities; he'll consult with his compatriots as to the soundness of his arguments for and against alternative courses of action, and so on. And at the end of the process, he'll decide whether he ought to support a given law on the basis of all the reliable evidence he takes to be relevant to the moral propriety of that law. He will, in short, employ his cognitive resources in accord with the canons of rationality to determine whether the coercive laws he supports are morally appropriate, all things considered.

Consider, by contrast, a citizen who is fully committed to supporting only morally appropriate coercive laws but who employs a game of chance to determine whether he ought to support some coercive law. Suppose that Brutus realizes that a law that criminalizes polygamy will authorize the state forcibly to hinder citizens from engaging in polygamy: the state will be authorized to incarcerate recalcitrant polygamists, remove children from the care of their polygamous parents, and the like. And suppose that Brutus resolves that question by the "rock, paper, scissors method." So long as he realizes that his decision-making method doesn't afford him a reliable basis for discerning moral truths, Brutus's basis for resolving his indecision manifests his *disrespect* for his polygamous compatriots. His decision-making "method" – his failure to obey the canons of rationality – manifests a callous indifference to the fact that his compatriots are deeply averse to being forcibly prohibited from pursuing their polygamous lifestyle, and thus that they may be coerced only if coercion is morally appropriate, and therefore that Brutus should do what is within his power to determine whether a ban on polygamy really is morally inappropriate, and therefore that Brutus should pursue rational justification for the claim that coercion is morally appropriate in this case.

(6) *Hence, if a citizen supports a coercive law, she ought to pursue rational justification for the claim that that law is morally appropriate, all things considered.*

Premise (6) follows from (1)–(5) and so is in no need of further justification. Premise (6) is, however, in need of further explication. Although I have no brief and illuminating way to explicate the intuition that some claims enjoy more or a higher degree of rational justification than others, it's clear that that intuition is accurate: my belief that some proof is valid enjoys a higher degree of rational justification, ceteris paribus, when based on an exhaustive analysis of the steps involved than it would were it based on a vague recollection about how that proof goes. Although I won't attempt to explicate the notion of degrees of rational justification, (6) should be read as requiring a *high degree* of rational justification, not just a minimal degree of rational justification. Why?

The more important a decision we face, the more concerned we should be to ensure that our decision is correct. That we should be more concerned to decide important decisions correctly than to decide trivial decisions correctly has epistemic implications: we should do what we can to ensure that, when faced with an important decision, we make that decision on the basis of commensurately reliable grounds. If I'm entrusted to invest my child's college funds, I should base my investment decision on my best analysis of the market rather than on a whim or guesswork. We do not have comparably demanding expectations for the bases on which we make trivial decisions: that I pick a brand of beer for the evening barbecue without accumulating evidence about my guest's preferences generates no (few) cries of condemnation. In short, we should proportion our epistemic expectations for a given decision to the importance of that decision: the more important a decision, the higher our epistemic standards should be for the rationale on which we make that decision.

In many cases people are deeply averse to coercion, rather than just mildly irritated; this renders a citizen's decision to coerce her compatriots particularly important. Given that a responsible citizen should attempt to ensure that very important decisions are decided on highly reliable grounds, and that a decision to coerce another person is extremely important, a respectful citizen should pursue a high degree of rational justification for any coercive policy she supports.

It is, of course, possible that a citizen who pursues rational justification for the overall moral propriety of a coercive law will fail to acquire a sufficiently powerful justification for that law. What then? She ought to be unwilling to support that law. Why? Given the argument up to this point, I can address this question with brevity. As I indicated in

(4), a citizen who respects her compatriots ought not to coerce them unless the presumption against coercion is overridden. Suppose that Elijah, having pursued rational justification for coercive law L, cannot acquire any – so far as he can tell, there is nothing to be said in favor of the moral propriety of L. In that case, Elijah lacks good reason to believe that L is morally appropriate. If Elijah lacks good reason to believe that L is morally appropriate, then all Elijah has to go on in determining whether L is morally appropriate is *guesswork*. But guesswork is no more reliable a way to discern his moral obligations than is Brutus's rock, paper, scissors method. Since, then, Elijah is committed to supporting only those coercive laws that are morally appropriate, and since he can effectively pursue that commitment only if he endeavors to refrain from supporting coercive laws for which he lacks a sufficiently high degree of justification, then Elijah ought to withhold support from any coercive law for which he can't acquire a sufficiently high degree of rational justification.[17]

So the obligation to support only those coercive laws that are morally appropriate, all things considered, imposes on each citizen two further obligations: to pursue rational justification for the claim that a given coercive law is morally appropriate, all things considered, and to withhold support from any coercive law for which she cannot discern the appropriate rational justification. Note that I don't claim that the obligation to withhold support from a given law absent a sufficiently high degree of rational justification *follows from* the obligation to pursue a high degree of rational justification. Rather, there is independent reason to believe both conclusions: both courses of action are essential means to the end of supporting only those coercive laws that are morally appropriate, all things considered.[18]

4.3 RESPECT AND PUBLIC JUSTIFICATION

The argument I articulated in support of the claim that a citizen ought to pursue rational justification for his favored coercive laws depends on the premise that respect for his compatriots requires him to accord due weight to what *matters* to his compatriots. However, a person typically has not only a set of cares and concerns in virtue of which things matter to him, but also the ability to *reflect* upon and *revise* his cares and concerns and thereby to *alter* what matters to him. A citizen who respects his compatriots will accord due weight to that fact when deliberating about how he may treat his compatriots. My intention in this section is to identify the constraints that this imposes on the manner in which a responsible citizen supports his favored coercive policies. In particular, I argue (a) that a citizen ought to communicate to his compatriots his reasons for coercing them and (b) that a citizen ought to attempt to articulate a rationale for the coercive laws he supports that will be convincing to his compatriots.

Ad (a): A citizen's obligation to respect his compatriots imposes on him an obligation to do his best to *address* his compatriots; that is, a citizen who coerces his compatriots ought to *inform* them about his reasons for coercing them. Suppose that Elijah recognizes that some coercive law L – a law that criminalizes polygamous marriages and authorizes the state forcibly to remove children from their polygamous parents' custody – is deeply troubling to some of his compatriots. And suppose that because he realizes how deeply L matters to polygamous parents, Elijah commits himself to pursuing rational justification for L. And stipulate that he's acquired a high degree of rational justification for the claim that L is morally appropriate – he concludes, in good conscience, and after adhering to the appropriate canons of rationality, that the Bible portrays polygamy as unnatural and thus as destructive to self and others. By hypothesis, then, Elijah pursues and achieves rational justification for the claim that L is morally appropriate; moreover, he does so out of respect for his compatriots as persons. And suppose that Elijah decides to support L on that basis. But suppose that Elijah refuses to address his compatriots, not because he is incapable of doing so, nor because he thinks it will do no good, but because he has no desire to do so.

In that case, Elijah fails to respect his compatriots as persons; he treats them not necessarily as objects, but as nonpersons. He doesn't treat them merely as objects since, by hypothesis, he's been motivated to pursue rational justification for the claim that L is morally appropriate by his recognition that his compatriots are deeply averse to being coerced. Clearly, he regards his compatriots very differently from the way he would if he thought they had the moral status of a piece of lint, as if they were mere things to whom his actions don't matter, and thus who may be manipulated at will.

But Elijah treats his compatriots as if they lacked the second component of personhood I identified earlier: as if they were mattering but unreflective beings. Put bluntly, Elijah treats his compatriots as if they were merely animals – dumb brutes. On the one hand, consider that if Elijah is to accord due weight to the fact that his dog, Fido, has cares and concerns in virtue of which things matter to it, he must refrain from frustrating its cares and concerns in a morally inappropriate manner – for example, he ought not to punish it without adequate moral justification. On the other hand, even if it is morally appropriate for Elijah to punish Fido in some situation, he has no obligation to address Fido; Fido's inability to follow a line of argument, and its consequent indifference to Elijah's providing it with a line of argument, absolves Elijah of any obligation to inform Fido of his reasons for coercing it. With respect both to his dog and his polygamous compatriots, Elijah is willing to ensure that his coercive laws are rationally justified but is unwilling to communicate his justifying rationale to those on the receiving end of his coercive ways.

But Elijah's compatriots differ from Fido in such a way that they merit differential treatment: Elijah's compatriots have the ability to understand, reflect upon, and to be moved by Elijah's reasons for coercing them. And because Elijah's compatriots have that capacity, this imposes on Elijah the obligation to inform his compatriots of his reasons for coercing them. Why ought Elijah exit his interiority in order to address the other? There are (at least) two reasons.

First, one of the most valuable features of our compatriots is that they are independent centers of action – each inhabits a perspective on the world that is distinct to each person and that provides each with her own reasons to act as she sees fit. If Elijah is to respect his compatriots as persons, then he must accord due weight to the fact that each of his compatriots has the capacity to inhabit a distinctive point of view and, since the fact that each of his compatriots inhabits a distinctive point of view is particularly valuable, he ought to act accordingly. How ought we treat those who have a valuable capacity? We encourage them to exercise that capacity and to develop and refine it insofar as doing so is feasible. We refrain from undermining it or destroying it insofar as that is possible and appropriate. Thus, for example, if Elijah's child has a special knack for portraiture and has the desire to develop her incipient talent, then Elijah ought, ceteribus paribus, to enable her to develop that capacity. At the very least, Elijah ought not unnecessarily thwart its development.

Exactly the same relation obtains between the way Elijah ought to treat his compatriots and the significant value of his compatriots' capacity to construct a distinctive perspective on the world. He should encourage them to exercise that capacity and, as a consequence, should resist circumventing their efforts to do so. But for Elijah to coerce his fellow citizens without even attempting to communicate to them his reasons for coercing them – although he could easily do so – is unnecessarily to circumvent their capacity to understand the world from their respective points of view and thus is to disrespect them.

Second, Elijah's support for a given coercive law plays a role in bringing distress to his compatriots. Consequently, he ought to do what he feasibly can to ameliorate that distress. He can ameliorate the distress he visits upon his compatriots by attempting to communicate his reasons for coercing them. How so? Elijah's willingness to address his compatriots manifests his recognition that each has her own distinctive point of view and that it is of sufficient value that he is compelled to explain himself. By recognizing that his compatriots have their own points of view and by allowing his recognition of that fact to motivate him to address his compatriots, he communicates to them that he recognizes the very great significance of their ability to form their own opinion regarding his actions – in spite of the fact that he happens to disagree with them in this case – and thus mitigates to some degree the distress generated by his coercive ways.[19] So doing what he can to communicate his reasons for coercing his compatriots not only encourages them to develop capacities that have great value but conveys the high regard in which he holds their agency and so ameliorates the distress he causes by coercing them.

Ad (b): I take it, then, that a citizen who respects his compatriots as persons will accord due weight to their ability to reflect on his actions from their distinctive points of view and will, as a consequence, attempt to address his compatriots. But given that respect for his compatriots as persons requires that Elijah attempt to address them, what form ought that address take? In particular, does Elijah's obligation to respect his compatriots oblige him to pursue public justification for his favored coercive laws? Should Elijah attempt to inhabit the mind-set of his compatriots in order to articulate not just a rationale for a favored law that *he* finds convincing, but also one that he hopes will be convincing to his compatriots? Some deny that he does. Consider William Galston's widely discussed criticism of the argument from respect:

> But while the (general) concept of equal respect may be relatively uncontroversial, the (specific) conception is not. To treat an individual as person

97

rather than object is to offer him an explanation. Fine; but *what kind* of explanation? Larmore seems to suggest that a properly respectful explanation must appeal to beliefs already held by one's interlocutors. . . . This seems arbitrary and implausible. I would suggest, rather, that we show others respect when we offer them, as explanation, what we take to be our true and best reasons for acting as we do.[20]

If Galston is correct, a citizen who respects his compatriots needn't attempt to articulate a public justification for his favored laws (where Galston has in mind a conception of public justification according to which that justification consists only of premises to which all citizens actually adhere). Rather, a citizen who respects his compatriots offers them his true and best reasons for some policy, where "true" and "best" are a function of that citizen's particular point of view – reasons that he takes to be true given his evidential set and that he takes to be superlative given his evidential set.

Galston's proposal is vulnerable to an initial objection that requires emendation. It's possible that Elijah's true and best reasons are miserably inadequate and that he realizes that they are. It might be that Elijah's mother demanded that he support a coercive law L, and that the appeal to his mother's demand is his best reason for supporting L, but that reason doesn't render him rationally justified in supporting L, much less rationally justified to a sufficiently high degree. If Elijah realizes that his true and best reasons fall short of the required degree of rational justification, and nevertheless insists on supporting L – perhaps he doesn't want to disappoint Mother – then he disrespects his compatriots: as I argued earlier, any decision to coerce another person is so important that any such decision must pass a fairly high epistemic threshold.

We need to amend Galston's proposal as follows: a citizen discharges his obligation to respect his compatriots by articulating his best reasons for a favored coercive law, where his best reasons constitute a sufficiently high degree of rational justification for the claim that that law is morally appropriate. I take it that Galston's proposal, as amended, is tantamount to the claim that a citizen who achieves a high degree of rational justification for the claim that a favored coercive law is morally appropriate, and who communicates that rationale to his compatriots, thereby discharges his obligation to respect his compatriots, and therefore has no obligation to do anything more by way of providing a rationale for his favored laws.

Even as amended, however, Galston's proposal strikes me as inadequate. If Galston is correct, a citizen can satisfy his obligation to respect his compatriots without being concerned about articulating a rationale for a favored coercive law that his compatriots will find even remotely convincing. That is, a citizen can articulate his best reasons for a favored coercive law, and thus satisfy Galston's proposal, all the while realizing that his best reasons will be utterly unconvincing to his compatriots. But I believe that a citizen who respects his compatriots should attempt to provide them with reasons they find convincing.

If, as we have seen, Elijah has a prima facie obligation to avoid coercing his compatriots by, say, supporting a law L that criminalizes polygamy, and if the reason he has the prima facie obligation to avoid supporting L is that he has a prima facie obligation to avoid treating his compatriots in ways to which they are deeply averse, then he surely has a prima facie obligation to do what he can to ameliorate the distress caused by his supporting L. If Elijah has a prima facie obligation not to *cause* his compatriots distress, then he must also have a prima facie obligation to *minimize* any distress he causes in cases when that prima facie obligation is overridden.

But there is a simple way for Elijah to ameliorate his compatriots' aversion to L. He can try to convince them that L is morally defensible. Of course, he won't be able to convince them by appealing to his true and best reasons; by hypothesis, those reasons won't be convincing to his compatriots. He has to search for some alternative rationale. If he is to succeed in convincing his compatriots that they should support L, Elijah is going to have to articulate some rationale for L that will be plausible to people with very different evidential sets from his – for example, he'll have to articulate a rationale for criminalizing polygamy that doesn't include the premise that the Bible is divinely inspired. He will have to step out of his worldview, he must inhabit the points of view of his compatriots, in order to determine what would convince them. And then he should endeavor to articulate a rationale for L that will be convincing to them. In short, Elijah ought to pursue public justification for L. Since Galston's position is consistent with Elijah's being utterly indifferent to trying to make sense of L from his compatriots' respective points of view, Galston's position is therefore inadequate. Respect for others does indeed require pursuit of public justification.

Three notes about this conclusion: First, recall that, while there appears to be a stable core to the concept of public justification, there is considerable controversy among justificatory liberals as to the appropriate conception of public justification – although a public justification is a rationale that "articulates appropriately" with the distinctive points of view of a diversely committed citizenry, it's unclear in just what respects a prospective public justification must articulate. The argument I've presented in support of the claim that respect requires public justification does not, so far as I can tell, require that we adopt any particular conception of public justification. Nevertheless, the argument I've presented seems to be better satisfied by some conceptions than by others.[21]

In particular, my argument seems to articulate best with a *populist* conception of public justification, that is, one according to which a rationale counts as a public justification just in case the members of the public find that rationale convincing given their actual epistemic conditions.[22] Ideally, I suppose, Elijah would be able to articulate a classically foundationalist argument in support of a ban on polygamy – that is, in the best of all possible worlds, he'd be able to identify certain indubitable premises from which it deductively follows that polygamy ought to be criminalized. (Presumably, such an argument would be *very* widely convincing.) Since that sort of argument is never available for interesting political claims, Elijah is going to have to lower his expectations: perhaps he ought to pursue a rationale that draws on dubitable premises that his compatriots already accept, or that draws on premises that comport with his compatriots' actual evidential sets. Or, perhaps, given that that sort of argument is also typically unavailable for interesting political commitments, he'll have to lower his expectations even further: he'll have to be satisfied with pursuing some rationale constituted by premises that are *in principle* accessible to his compatriots.[23] Alternatively, Elijah can satisfy his obligation to pursue public justification by articulating a rationale that is constituted solely by premises that are amenable to *external criticism*: even if he can't articulate a rationale that will convince his compatriots that a ban on polygamy is appropriate, he can at least give them the opportunity to play the spoiler by presenting them with an argument that they have a realistic chance of convincing him is unsound. The point is that Elijah's obligation to pursue public justification can be satisfied by his pursuit of arguments that articulate with his compatriots' points of view in a variety of quite disparate respects. Of course, at some point, Elijah might have to conclude that he can't articulate an argument that connects in any meaningful way with his compatriots' points of view, and thus that his pursuit of public justification has ended in failure.

Second, for Elijah to satisfy his obligation to pursue a public justification for his favored coercive laws, he must articulate a rationale that articulates appropriately with the distinctive points of view of *each* of his compatriots. But nothing I've argued supports the conclusion that he must articulate *one* argument that articulates appropriately with the distinctive points of view of each of his compatriots. Although some justificatory liberals adopt that conclusion,[24] it isn't required by my argument: given that Elijah's goal is to ameliorate the distress inevitably generated by his support for the ban on polygamy, and given that Elijah can ameliorate that distress by presenting different arguments to different citizens, Elijah discharges his obligation to ameliorate his compatriots' distress by attempting to articulate a selection of arguments for the ban on polygamy, such that each citizen finds within that selection at least one rationale that articulates in the appropriate way with her distinctive point of view.[25] That said, it seems preferable that Elijah articulate at most a small selection of widely convincing arguments: as a practical matter, that's the only way he'll be able to articulate a rationale that stands a realistic chance of convincing the large number of diversely committed citizens who inhabit a modern liberal democracy.

Third, my argument in support of the claim that a citizen ought to pursue a public justification for his favored coercive laws doesn't require that he pursue a rationale he finds convincing. After all, his goal is to ameliorate the distress he causes to his compatriots as a consequence of his support for coercive laws they find objectionable and he can do this by articulating a rationale that *they* find convincing.[26] As with the prior point, there is a difference between what the argument for public justification requires and what's desirable: it strikes me as morally desirable that Elijah regard as sound at least one of the widely convincing arguments for polygamy he addresses to his compatriots, since it will then be clear that he isn't attempting to *manipulate* his compatriots. So perhaps Elijah should strive to articulate a small selection of widely convincing arguments for his favored coercive laws such that among that selection is at least one argument he regards as providing adequate reason to believe that the relevant coercive law is morally appropriate.[27] That said, the argument I've articulated in support of the claim that Elijah should pursue public justification doesn't strictly require that he pursue a rationale that he finds convincing and thus that might motivate him to support a ban on polygamy.

4.4 RESPECT AND MUTUAL CRITICISM

Up to this point, my analysis of what respect requires focuses too narrowly on what a citizen should do *for* her compatriots; in attempting to determine what respect requires regarding the bases on which a citizen supports her favored coercive laws, I've focused almost entirely on *her* grounds for supporting her favored coercive laws and on the reasons she ought to try to *provide* for her compatriots. But a citizen who fully respects her compatriots ought to be open to movement in the opposite direction. Such a citizen ought to be willing to learn from them, a willingness that requires her to subject her political commitments to her compatriots' scrutiny and to change her commitments if given sufficient reason to do so. A citizen who respects her compatriots as persons attempts, not just to ensure that her own noetic house is in order, and not just to show her compatriots that they should endorse her political commitments, but also to submit her political commitments to their better judgment. She doesn't just teach them the moral truth; she's also willing to learn from them regarding the various possible respects in which her point of view is occluded by self-interest, ideology, prejudice, or self-deception.

Why does respect require a willingness to learn from others? Any minimally reflective citizen will recognize the possibility that a coercive policy she supports is morally inappropriate. Although she ought to withhold support from any coercive law for which she lacks an appropriately high degree of rational justification, and thus should take herself to enjoy a high degree of rational justification for any coercive law she persists in supporting, she'll nevertheless be a *fallibilist* about her political commitments, and in particular, about her conviction that a given coercive policy is morally appropriate.

In a large-scale polity constituted by millions of diversely committed persons, each citizen will be situated in an environment populated by many whose judgments regarding her favored policies merit her admiration. For her to ignore those compatriots, for her to refuse to make use of their capacity to enlighten her about the moral propriety of her favored policies, is to fail to manifest respect for her compatriots as persons. Given that her compatriots are deeply averse to coercion, a citizen should do what is feasibly in her power to ensure that the coercive policies she supports are morally appropriate. Given the availability of fellow citizens whose judgment merits her admiration, it's certainly within her power to rely on those citizens to ferret out coercive laws she mistakenly believes merit her support. She should therefore do so. In short, given that respect requires a citizen to withhold support from morally inappropriate coercive laws, given that a citizen might be wrong about the moral propriety of her favored laws, and given the availability of compatriots who have the capacity to *enlighten* her about the moral impropriety of her favored coercive laws, a citizen ought to be willing to allow her compatriots to aid her in exposing laws she falsely believes are morally appropriate.[28]

Note that I interpret the scope of this fallibility requirement *narrowly*: as applying to a citizen's political commitments and to the grounds that directly bear on her political commitments. A citizen's obligation to respect her compatriots does *not* commit her to fallibilism regarding all of her convictions, or even to all of those convictions that bear on her political commitments: some of the former are sufficiently remote from her political commitments to obviate the need to subject them to criticism.[29] To take a silly example: although Descartes's conviction that he exists clearly has *some* bearing on his political commitments, Descartes need not take seriously the possibility that that conviction is false. To take an example closer to the topic at hand, although Elijah's commitment to the claim that God exists is relevant to his political commitments, Elijah needn't take seriously the possibility that that conviction is false: it seems to me far too onerous a burden to impose on citizens the expectation that they ought to take seriously the possibility that the convictions that define their respective moral identities might be false (whether those commitments are basic *moral* claims, such as that torture is prima facie morally wrong or *theological* claims, such as that God exists). What Elijah needs to do is to take seriously the possibility that political commitments he accepts on the basis of his theistic commitments might be false or misguided and that any theistic convictions directly tied to his political commitments might be false or misguided.[30]

4.5 RESPECT AND HUMAN DIGNITY

The norm of respect for persons imposes on a citizen at least one further constraint. It seems clear that the norm of respect imposes at least some minimal *substantive* constraints on the reasons a citizen may employ as a basis for his favored laws. In particular, a citizen who respects his compatriots ought not support a coercive law on the basis of any reasons that deny their personhood. To take an obvious example, the Nazi who supports a law that obliges Jewish people to live only in ghettos on the basis of the claim that Jewish people are "bacilli" and thus must be quarantined from the rest of humanity *thereby* disrespects his Jewish compatriots. Indeed, he disrespects his compatriots even if he is a "good Nazi" who fulfills each of the constraints to which I've argued respect requires him to adhere: he pursues and achieves rational justification for the claim that Jewish people are bacilli, he attempts to provide a public justification for the claim that Jewish people are bacilli, he's willing to submit his commitment to the claim that Jewish people are subhuman to the critical scrutiny of his compatriots. Commenting on William Galston's criticism of the argument from respect, Michael Perry writes: "It is never to show respect for a human being for one person to offer another – for example, for a Nazi to offer to a Jew – a reason to the effect that 'You are not truly or fully human,' even if the Nazi sincerely takes that to be his best reason for acting as he does."[31] A responsible citizen in a liberal democracy will refuse to support a coercive law on the basis of any claim that denies the personhood and dignity of his compatriots, no matter how he arrives at those claims.

4.6 THE IDEAL OF CONSCIENTIOUS ENGAGEMENT

As I noted at the outset of this chapter, justificatory liberals are correct that reflection on the norm of respect indicates constraints on the manner in which a citizen may support her favored coercive laws. In fact, I believe that a citizen who adheres to the norm of respect will abide by at least six constraints on the reasons she employs in political decision making and advocacy.

(1) She will pursue a high degree of rational justification for the claim that a favored coercive policy is morally appropriate.
(2) She will withhold support from a given coercive policy if she can't acquire a sufficiently high degree of rational justification for the claim that that policy is morally appropriate.
(3) She will attempt to communicate to her compatriots her reasons for coercing them.

(4) She will pursue public justification for her favored coercive policies.
(5) She will listen to her compatriots' evaluation of her reasons for her favored coercive policies with the intention of learning from them about the moral (im)propriety of those policies.
(6) She will not support any policy on the basis of a rationale that denies the dignity of her compatriots.

These six constraints constitute an *ideal of conscientious engagement* that ought, I believe, to govern the way a citizen in a liberal democracy supports her favored coercive laws. As I see the matter, a citizen who satisfies that ideal supports her favored coercive laws in a morally exemplary manner and is, insofar as she satisfies that ideal, free from reasonable moral criticism; correlatively, a citizen who fails to satisfy that ideal is, ceteris paribus, the object of reasonable moral criticism. (It's helpful to recall, at this point, the sort of moral criticism to which a citizen who fails to satisfy the ideal of conscientious engagement is subject: a citizen who fails to satisfy that ideal doesn't necessarily violate any of her compatriots' moral rights. But as Robert Audi has helpfully argued in this context, a citizen who doesn't violate anyone's moral rights might nevertheless be morally criticizable.)

Adopting a label for the six constraints that follow from the norm of respect for persons gives us a convenient way to refer to those constraints. But I haven't adopted that label solely to evade tiresome circumlocution: referring to these six constraints as an ideal of conscientious engagement indicates that the constraints each citizen should strive to satisfy share a deeper unity: each falls into either of two complementary categories.

First, each citizen ought to arrive at conclusions of *conscience* in a *conscientious* manner. A citizen who respects her compatriots won't be satisfied with supporting coercive laws that she merely *takes* to be morally appropriate. She'll do her level best to ensure that the coercive laws she supports *really are* morally appropriate. She can best determine this by obeying her epistemic obligations insofar as they bear on the claim that a favored coercive law is morally appropriate. Thus, she ought to obey constraint (1): she ought to evaluate her favored political commitments in accord with the canons of rational belief formation. And she ought to obey constraint (2) as well: if she concludes, after she has discharged the relevant epistemic obligations, that some coercive law she supports lacks moral legitimacy, then she ought to withdraw her support from that law. In short, epistemic conscientiousness in the way a citizen supports her favored coercive laws is essential to her arriving at conclusions of conscience that manifest respect for her compatriots.

But a citizen who conscientiously arrives at conclusions of conscience by no means satisfies her obligation to respect her compatriots: she must supplement her conscientious pursuit of rational justification with a commitment to *engaging* her compatriots. The sort of engagement we can legitimately expect of a citizen requires, as I've noted above, a movement in two different directions. First, she must articulate her reasons for her favored coercive laws to her compatriots and in so doing put her compatriots in a position to object to those reasons – constraints (3) and (5). In so doing, she puts her compatriots in a position to change her mind as to the soundness of her rationale for her favored coercive laws. And this is as it should be: a citizen who coerces her compatriots engages in too serious a matter to do so without due regard for her fallibility and thus without the benefit of her compatriots' critical insights. Second, assuming that her compatriots are *unable* to convince her to withdraw her support from a favored coercive law, and assuming that she is rationally justified in *persisting* in her belief that that coercive law is morally appropriate, she ought to do what is within her power to identify a rationale that is, or can be, convincing to her compatriots. So a citizen must engage her compatriots in the sense that she must exit her own parochial point of view and attempt to inhabit the points of view of her compatriots in order to put herself in a position to provide them with reasons for her favored coercive laws that they regard as compelling – constraint (4). In short, deliberative and persuasive engagement with others regarding the coercive laws a citizen supports is essential to her manifesting the appropriate respect for her compatriots.

A final point about the internal structure of the ideal of conscientious engagement: Referring to the six constraints as a unified ideal indicates that those constraints bear some important relation to one another. Most fundamentally, constraint (6) constitutes that unifying role: a responsible citizen will adhere to each of the components of the ideal of conscientious engagement out of respect for the dignity of her compatriots.

The ideal of conscientious engagement, it seems to me, provides citizens with the sort of guidance they need to do their part in ameliorating the social disharmony generated by the application of power in a pluralistic society. If citizens genuinely and sincerely adhere to the normative constraints on political decision making and advocacy that follow from the norm of respect, they considerably reduce the resentment that others naturally feel as a consequence of being subject to coercive laws they reject. After all, if each citizen adheres to the ideal of conscientious engagement, and makes it clear that she does so out of respect for her compatriots as persons, when citizens are coerced on the basis of laws they reject, they need not feel disrespected and thus will find it easier to acquiesce to those laws.

This last point merits further explication. Nicholas Rescher has recently argued that we ought to take due notice of the distinction between *consensus* and *acquiescence*. Consensus regarding some coercive law denotes a collective agreement regarding the propriety of that law: if each citizen subject to a given coercive law affirms the propriety of that law, then there is consensus regarding that law. "Consensus by its very nature is a condition of intellectual uniformity, a homogeneity of thought and opinion."[32] Acquiescence denotes a collective willingness to endure certain objectionable conditions: even if many citizens subject to some law deny that that law is morally appropriate, they need not thereby find it so objectionable as to be unwilling to obey it. Acquiescence "is not a matter of *approbation*, but rather one of a mutual restraint which, even when disapproving and disagreeing, is willing (no doubt reluctantly) to 'let things be,' because the alternative – actual conflict or warfare – will lead to a situation that is still worse."[33]

There is no doubt that consensus regarding coercive laws is *desirable*: no morally responsible citizen *wants* to support coercive laws that her compatriots find deeply objectionable. But consensus on coercive laws is seldom *achievable*: each citizen must be willing to acquiesce to many coercive laws that she regards as morally inappropriate. The fact that each of us must be willing to acquiesce to such laws renders particularly important the constraints on reasons that the norm of respect imposes on each citizen in a liberal democracy, it seems obvious that we'll be much more willing to acquiesce to coercive laws we regard as morally objectionable if the imposition of those laws is achieved in such a way as to affirm our value and in full recognition of the burden placed on us. If our concerns are simply discounted, if we aren't consulted, if our compatriots impose their will on us in whimsical fashion, if our compatriots don't even attempt to discern some rationale that might convince us that some coercive law is morally appropriate, then we'll find it much more difficult to acquiesce than if our compatriots hear our concerns, consider our objections on their merits, make a good faith effort to explain why that coercive law is in fact morally defensible, and, throughout the process, make clear that they are willing to abide by such constraints out of respect for our dignity as persons. So long as our compatriots affirm our dignity as persons and manifest that affirmation by committing themselves to the ideal of conscientious engagement, they have done all we can reasonably ask of them to ameliorate the tensions and frustrations inevitably generated by our disagreement regarding the coercive laws to which we are subject.

CHAPTER 5

WHAT RESPECT DOES NOT REQUIRE

5.0 INTRODUCTION

If the line of thought I pursued in the prior chapter is convincing, justificatory liberals correctly focus on the norm of respect in order to identify (at least some of) the constraints a responsible citizen obeys in deciding whether to support a given coercive law and in advocating that others support that law. As I argued, since a citizen ought to respect his compatriots, he ought to adhere to the ideal of conscientious engagement. But the justificatory liberal wants to show a great deal more than that a citizen ought to adhere to that ideal. He also wants to show that respect for persons requires a citizen to adhere to the doctrine of restraint. And his commitment to the doctrine of restraint is, arguably, his central commitment. Indeed, it's because of its commitment to the doctrine of restraint that justificatory liberalism looms so large in my argument: the justificatory liberal's commitment to this doctrine provides him with principled grounds for the claim that a citizen ought not support any coercive law on the basis of his religious convictions alone. So the question I address in this chapter is as follows: given that a citizen ought to respect his compatriots, does he have an obligation, not only to abide by the ideal of conscientious engagement, but also to obey the doctrine of restraint?

5.1 THE INTUITIVE PLAUSIBILITY OF THE CLAIM
THAT RESPECT REQUIRES RESTRAINT

It isn't uncommon for a claim C to grip us, to strike us as having the "ring of truth," independent of our ability explicitly to articulate reasons to accept C. Indeed, it isn't uncommon for our intuitive conviction that

C is true to motivate us to pursue a rationale for C so that our attempt to substantiate C is a *consequence*, rather than a *cause*, of our conviction that C is true. In that case, the arguments we present for C reinforce our commitment to C, a commitment that might persist even if we realize that each of the explicitly articulated arguments we have for C is unsound. The intuitive attractiveness of C can operate at a deeper and arguably more important level than any argument we might construct to vindicate C.

I believe the claim that respect requires restraint strikes many justificatory liberals as deeply plausible in that way: the *intuition* that respect requires restraint drives the various attempts to articulate *arguments* in support of that claim and persists even when one or another of those arguments is shown to be fallacious.[1] But I think the intuitive plausibility of that claim is illusory; more particularly, I think its initial plausibility is a consequence of the *rhetoric* that often accompanies affirmations of the doctrine of restraint rather than the inherent plausibility of the claim that respect requires restraint. Once we pierce through the rhetoric, I'm hopeful that the claim that respect requires restraint will lose its intuitive luster.

The justificatory liberal's characterization of those who refuse to exercise restraint is a crucial component of the rhetorical aspect of the case for restraint. In fact, I believe that the regular and consistent practice among justificatory liberals of exemplifying the refusal to exercise restraint by reference to folks like Bill McCartney (or Jerry Falwell or Pat Robertson) plays a crucial role in eliciting the intuitive feeling that there is some important relation between respect for persons and obedience to the doctrine of restraint. Recall our opening exhibit, that is, Bill McCartney's willingness to support Amendment 2 solely on the basis of the claim that homosexuality is an abomination to God. As long as McCartney constitutes a paradigm of the sort of citizen who refuses to exercise restraint, we can quite naturally take a refusal to exercise restraint as a manifestation of disrespect and, correlatively, take advocacy of restraint as a necessary and effective means of discouraging other citizens from emulating McCartney's behavior. But it isn't at all clear that it is McCartney's refusal to exercise restraint that merits the judgment that he disrespects his compatriots. There are various other possibilities: our sense that McCartney disrespects his compatriots might be evoked by a number of factors that are distinct from, but that are easily confused with, his refusal to exercise restraint. I list three, although there are no doubt more.

First, McCartney's support for Amendment 2 involves an emotionally charged issue – homosexuality – about which many feel deeply and about which many have strongly held convictions. Since it's easy for revulsion at the *substantive injustice* of Amendment 2 to elide into revulsion at McCartney's unwillingness to exercise restraint regarding Amendment 2, it will be easy for us to attribute our sense of moral impropriety, not to its proper object – the injustice of Amendment 2 – but to McCartney's unwillingness to exercise restraint. The same elision is a danger when the justificatory liberal uses citizens who advocate laws that criminalize abortion, ban or severely restrict the dissemination of pornography, ban or restrict the dissemination of birth control, and so on as examples of the refusal to exercise restraint.[2]

Second, McCartney belongs to a movement that is very unpopular among academics – evangelicalism – about which those familiar with the literature on restraint – academics – are likely to harbor invidious stereotypes. If an evangelical, particularly one who fulminates about abominations to God, constitutes our paradigm of the refusal to exercise restraint, it's no wonder that we have an allergic reaction to the refusal to exercise restraint; it's very easy for a distaste for *those who refuse to exercise restraint* to elide into a distaste for their refusal to exercise restraint. I don't think it an exaggeration to claim that the evangelical or fundamentalist, particularly one who advocates policies that are unpopular among academics, serves as the most common whipping boy for the justificatory liberal.[3] And I surmise that a great deal of the intuitive plausibility of the doctrine of restraint is a consequence of the subterranean association of religious "fanatics" such as McCartney with the refusal to exercise restraint.

Third, the most likely confusion that elicits our sense that McCartney's refusal to exercise restraint is ipso facto disrespectful is an elision from his unwillingness to exercise restraint to his unwillingness to obey the constraints constitutive of the ideal of conscientious engagement – most particularly, the principle of pursuit. As we've seen in 4.3, a citizen who refuses to pursue public justification exhibits a callous indifference to the fact that his compatriots are deeply averse to coercion. As a consequence, we have legitimate grounds for imputing disrespect to McCartney if, as I've assumed is the case, he refuses to pursue public justification for Amendment 2. But if we fail to distinguish between public justification and restraint, then we'll naturally impute to those who refuse to exercise restraint the sort of indifference we legitimately impute to those who refuse to pursue public justification. How would we react if presented with a citizen who assiduously pursues public justification for his favored coercive laws (and who satisfies the various other constraints constitutive of the ideal of conscientious engagement) yet refuses to exercise restraint? So far as I am aware, justificatory liberals don't consider that possibility.[4]

To avoid being misled by obfuscatory rhetoric, we should test the intuitive judgment that respect requires restraint by portraying a citizen who refuses to exercise restraint but who is admirable in other respects – she supports the "right" policies, she doesn't belong to a religious group burdened with a variety of invidious stereotypes, she strives to fulfill the ideal of conscientious engagement. If – once we've bracketed extraneous factors – the citizen we portray doesn't evoke in us the sense that she disrespects her compatriots, then we ought to conclude that the intuitive appeal of the claim that respect requires restraint is due to the rhetoric that accompanies admonitions to exercise restraint, rather than the actual propriety of the doctrine of restraint.

With this is mind, consider the following portrait. Elijah believes that the wide and ever-widening disparities in wealth between rich and poor both within his country and between rich countries and poor countries is morally repugnant. As a consequence, Elijah advocates quite a radical redistribution of wealth. Although Elijah's condemnation of the disparity between rich and poor is based partly on moral commitments he believes his fellow citizens have good reason to accept from their respective points of view, the radicalism of his proposed redistribution has a peculiarly religious rationale: Elijah has acquainted himself with Liberation Theology, come to believe that God has a preference for the poor, and concluded that God's preference for the poor obliges us to take quite drastic measures in narrowing the disparities in life opportunities between rich and poor. Stipulate that given his evidential set, Elijah enjoys a high degree of rational justification for the claim that radical measures to redistribute wealth are morally obligatory.

Given his conviction that existing disparities between rich and poor are morally repugnant, Elijah rationally regards himself as morally obliged to support a whole bevy of proposed laws that will, he believes, effect the desired radical redistribution. But Elijah wants to avoid cramming his favored policies down his compatriots' respective throats. So Elijah pursues public justification for his favored policies, because he recognizes that many of his compatriots will find his favored policies misguided, dangerous, or even morally offensive. Unfortunately, even though Elijah is fully committed to public justification and articulates such nonparochial arguments as he can find, he takes his pursuit of public justification to have ended in failure: his radicalism turns out to be uneliminably dependent on his theological commitments – commitments many of his compatriots have no good reason to accept (given their evidential sets). He comes to that conclusion as a consequence of long hours of serious deliberation and vigorous argument with his compatriots, in which it becomes clear that many of them, given their respective evidential sets, have no good reason to accord the needs of the poor – particularly those who live in distant lands – the weight that he believes their needs deserve.[5]

Given the importance of the issues involved, however, Elijah persists in supporting the drastic measures he believes will alleviate the conditions of the poor, even though he can't convince his compatriots that he is correct. He regards his situation as *tragic* – doubly so. First, the destitute are in desperate need of aid and his compatriots' refusal to redistribute wealth costs lives, perpetuates suffering, and sustains injustice. Second, he is conscience bound to impose his religiously grounded norms on citizens who, he realizes, nonculpably lack what they take to be compelling reasons to accept those norms.

Does Elijah disrespect his compatriots? I can't see that he does. He takes no joy in imposing his conviction that God has a preference for the poor on his compatriots; his support for a radical redistribution of wealth is motivated, not by a gleeful imposition of power and not by indifference to his compatriots' cares and concerns, but by his commitment to act in accord with moral convictions for which he has, by hypothesis, a high degree of rational justification. In short, he acts in accord with the dictates of his conscience, dictates he has arrived at in a fully conscientious manner. Moreover, he has done what is within his power, by virtue of his genuine and sincere pursuit of public justification and his willingness to engage in long hours of sustained dialogue with his compatriots, to avoid simply imposing his religiously grounded moral norms on his compatriots. In short, Elijah doesn't aspire to support his favored policies on the basis of his religious convictions alone; he has done what is within his power to avoid doing that, but he is conscience bound to act in accord with what he rationally believes to be the dictates of justice.

I see no basis for imputing disrespect to Elijah. Indeed, I see no basis for criticizing Elijah in any respect whatsoever. Our reaction to Elijah, however, in all likelihood differs from our reaction to McCartney: many will regard McCartney's advocacy of Amendment 2 as obviously disrespectful and many others will regard it as deeply problematic. What accounts for that difference (assuming that there is one)? Each of the factors I mentioned above might have a role to play.[6] Part of the explanation for our differential evaluation of Elijah and McCartney is, perhaps, a consequence of the differential attractiveness of their respective political commitments – at least among academics, it is much more popular to advocate assistance for the poor than to militate against the homosexual. Part of the explanation is, perhaps, that Elijah belongs to a religious group about which we lack invidious stereotypes: academics are much more likely to warm to the liberation theologian than to the evangelical. Part of the explanation is, perhaps, that McCartney's manner of advocacy is gratuitously inflammatory and thus offensive, whereas Elijah's is cooperative and deliberative.[7] Who can deny that, at the subterranean level at which we make our judgments of intuitive plausibility, those sorts of factors, rather than McCartney's refusal to exercise restraint, might generate the intuition that McCartney acts disrespectfully?

I surmise, however, that the most important factor in explaining why McCartney strikes us as disrespectful whereas Elijah does not is that unlike McCartney, Elijah is attuned to the distinctiveness of his compatriots' points of view and desires to communicate with his compatriots so they can see that they should support his favored laws. Elijah *pursues* public justification for his favored policies and *thereby* exhibits respect for his compatriots. In this, he is crucially different from citizens such as McCartney who aren't interested in public justification at all: such citizens, I think, disrespect their compatriots. But not Elijah.

The contrast I've drawn between McCartney and Elijah should attune us to the critical distinction between pursuing public justification and exercising restraint. As long as we fail to abide by that distinction, we'll be inclined to assimilate Elijah into the ranks of those who, quite obviously, aren't interested in communicating at all with their compatriots: since Elijah refuses to exercise restraint, he *mustn't* give a whit about pursuing public justification, and since Elijah doesn't care to pursue public justification, he ipso facto disrespects his compatriots. But when we make the required distinction, we should see that we lack adequate reason to impute disrespect to those who, like Elijah, refuse to exercise restraint but pursue public justification. Not only, then, does distinguishing between public justification and restraint enable us to arrive at a nuanced evaluation of Elijah's manner of political decision making and advocacy, but it gives us insight into why we might have been inclined to accuse him of disrespect in the first place.

5.2 ARGUMENTS FOR RESTRAINT

Once we remove the rhetorical clutter that accompanies many discussions of the doctrine of restraint, I believe that it's quite implausible to impute disrespect to a citizen just on account of her unwillingness to exercise restraint. Such judgments of plausibility are, of course, irreducibly subjective and person-relative: what we take to have the "ring of truth" varies in accord with our different interests, background commitments, individual experience, and other qualities. So it's entirely possible that I've accomplished little by way of injecting doubt into the claim that respect requires restraint; perhaps that claim will persist in appearing intuitively obvious to the reader. That is as it may be. Given this clash between intuitions, it seems that the only way to resolve the issue is to determine whether there are any *arguments* that settle the matter. If the justificatory liberal can construct some argument in support of the claim that respect requires restraint, then it doesn't matter very much that that claim, when pared down to its essential content, seems highly implausible. After all, plenty of initially implausible claims turn out to be true. And so it's to an analysis and critique of several arguments in support of the doctrine of restraint that I now turn.

Before I do that I'll confess that I'm in a somewhat awkward position. Although the argument from respect to restraint is central to justificatory liberalism, and although references to some such argument pervade the literature, it's quite difficult to discern in the literature explicit and detailed formulations of that argument. Very often, formulations of the argument from respect have the feel of an incantation: the justificatory liberal attempts to beguile the reader into endorsing the doctrine of restraint without specifying exactly what understanding of respect she employs or without identifying exactly why one who accepts the obligation to respect others ought thereby to exercise restraint.

Perhaps the paucity of detailed argument is to be explained by the (illusory) intuitive power of the claim that respect requires restraint. I don't know. The fact is, however, that there is little clear and compelling argumentation in the literature. That said, I'll articulate and evaluate the versions of that argument that I've found to be either instructive in their inadequacy or plausible on their merits (even if unsound).

5.2.1 Solum on Respect and Restraint

Lawrence Solum has articulated the following argument, which I quote fully.[8] (Note that although Solum presents his argument so that it applies to judges, the application to citizens is fairly straightforward.)

> The first argument for the requirement of public reason can be called the argument from respect for citizens as free and equal. The premise for this argument is that society should respect the freedom and equality of citizens.... My argument is that judicial decisions made or justified on the basis of reasons that are not publicly accessible, for example, on the basis of sectarian religious premises, would be disrespectful of the freedom and equality of citizens. I will begin by discussing justification. Imagine that a public official justifies a political decision with her own religious beliefs. Perhaps she appeals to a passage in the New Testament and to her belief that Jesus of Nazareth was the son of God, or perhaps a passage in the Koran and to her belief that Mohammed is the true prophet of God. Such reasons could not be accepted by citizens that did not share her religious beliefs. One aspect of respect for fellow citizens as free and equal is the giving of reasons that allow one's fellows to accept the government action as reasonable.[9]

As I read this passage, Solum's argument has two premises and a conclusion. His first premise is that "society should respect the freedom and equality of citizens." His second premise is that respecting the freedom and equality of others requires "the giving of reasons that allow one's fellows to accept the government action as reasonable." Solum's conclusion, I gather, is that a necessary condition of a judge's (or, henceforward, a citizen's) respecting her compatriots is that she justify a decision on the basis of publicly accessible reasons.[10] Solum's argument, then, moves from the claim that each citizen ought to *respect* her compatriots, to the claim that each citizen ought to give her compatriots reasons that enable them to *accept* her favored coercive laws as reasonable, to the conclusion that each citizen ought to articulate *publicly accessible* reasons in support of her favored coercive laws.[11] The conclusion of the argument is, of course, directly applicable to religious beliefs such as that the Bible is the word of God (or that homosexuality is an abomination to God, or that God has a preference for the poor): since such "reasons could not be accepted by citizens that do not share those religious beliefs," then an argument that included any such claim wouldn't enable a citizen's compatriots to see that a given law is reasonable, and thus wouldn't constitute a public justification, and thus ought not be employed as the sole basis for a given coercive law.[12]

What should we make of Solum's argument? The notion that there are people who *can't* accept the claim that the Bible is the word of God (or that homosexuality is an abomination or that God has a preference for the poor) is, if not simply false, then more than a little mysterious, given that, over roughly the past 1,500 years, large sums of diversely committed people have passed from a state of disbelieving that the Bible is the word of God to believing that it is. It isn't obvious, therefore, that Solum's argument has the implications he thinks it has, that a citizen ought not support a coercive law solely on the basis of her religious convictions. Since, however, a discussion of this point will play a central role in my analysis of the notion of public accessibility (in 8.4), I'll postpone pursuing it for the moment.

More important, it seems that Solum's argument begs the question. Note that Solum's second premise is substantially equivalent to his conclusion. Since the second premise is that respect requires a citizen to articulate reasons that enable her compatriots to regard the government's actions as reasonable, and since such a reason is a publicly accessible reason, the second premise is equivalent to Solum's conclusion – that respect requires a citizen to articulate publicly accessible reasons. So what seems at first blush to be an argument with two premises collapses into an argument with one premise: from the fact that a citizen ought to respect the freedom and equality of her compatriots, a citizen ought to provide her compatriots with publicly accessible reasons for her favored coercive policies. But if that is how we are to understand Solum's argument, then his argument begs the question: the question at issue is whether a citizen's obligation to respect her compatriots as free and equal persons imposes on her the further obligation to provide her compatriots with a public justification for any coercive law she supports.

Although I regard Solum's argument as vitiated by a fairly straightforward flaw, it affords us an opportunity to explicate further the centrally important distinction between pursuing public justification and exercising restraint. Notice that Solum doesn't formulate his argument by employing locutions such as that a citizen should *pursue* public justification. Rather, he states that a citizen should *provide* public justification. His second premise isn't that respect obliges a citizen conscientiously to *aspire* to provide reasons that enable her compatriots to accept the government's actions as reasonable, but that respect obliges her to *give* those reasons. His conclusion isn't that respect obliges a citizen to *try* to provide publicly accessible reasons for her favored coercive laws, but that she *succeed* in giving publicly accessible reasons. But the language of success is very different from the language of aspiration, and both are in turn very different from the language of restraint.[13]

It is essential to my argument that we abide by a threefold distinction: between the claims (1) that a citizen ought to pursue public justification for her favored coercive laws, (2) that a citizen ought to restrain herself from supporting any law for which she lacks a public justification, and (3) that a citizen ought to provide a public justification for her favored coercive laws. Why?

I've already argued that (1) doesn't entail (2): the claim that a citizen ought to pursue public justification doesn't entail that she ought to exercise restraint and so a citizen may be committed to pursuing public justification without thereby being committed to exercising restraint. The same relation does not, however, obtain between (3) and (2): if a citizen has an obligation to *provide* a public justification for any coercive law she supports, then any citizen who lacks a public justification for a given coercive law ought to withhold her support from that law. Consider the following analogy. The obligation to provide a public justification isn't an obligation to attempt to actualize a certain state of affairs; rather, it is an obligation to actualize that state of affairs. In this respect the obligation to provide a public justification is comparable to the obligation to provide a ticket upon entering a theater: a patron has an obligation, not just to attempt to purchase a ticket, but actually to produce the ticket on entering the theater. If a patron genuinely and sincerely attempts to procure the required ticket, but fails in her attempt, she knows that, given her inability to bring about the appropriate state of affairs, she would be culpable were she to enter the theater. Without a ticket, she should stay out. The obligation to provide a public justification and the obligation to purchase a ticket are exactly analogous in that both obligations require those bound by them to succeed in bringing about the appropriate state of affairs and, in case of failure, entail restrictions on permissible actions. In short, (3) entails (2).

Distinguishing between public justification as aspiration (1) and public justification as success (3) provides us with fair warning against one way in which the justificatory liberal can smuggle the doctrine of restraint under cover of the claim that "respect requires public justification." How might that occur? The justificatory liberal presents an argument in support of the claim that respect requires public justification, but this claim is ambiguous between (1) and (3). As we have seen, there are good reasons to believe that respect requires that a citizen pursue public justification, so the justificatory liberal has no problem establishing (1). But since (1) doesn't entail (2), showing that (1) is true won't achieve the goal of showing that (2) is true; (3), however, does entail (2). Since the claim that "respect requires public justification" is ambiguous as between (1) and (3), there is a temptation to elide from (1) to (3). Once (3) has been "established," it is no difficult matter to show (2). (It seems to me that we can explain whatever plausibility Solum's argument might have by reference to this sort of elision: his second premise is plausible when read as requiring the pursuit of public justification, whereas he applies his conclusion to religious convictions as if he had shown that citizens have an obligation to provide public justification.)

But once we duly note the distinction between (1) and (3), we are no closer to resolution on the issue of restraint. Up to this point I've claimed that the justificatory liberal can't show that respect requires a citizen not just to pursue public justification but also to exercise restraint. In light of the distinction I've drawn in this section, we can reformulate that claim as follows: the justificatory liberal can't show that respect requires a citizen, not just to pursue public justification, but also to provide a public justification. The central difficulty in meeting this objection is as follows: more than one claim about political decision making and advocacy is putatively derivable from the norm of respect – (1) the claim that respect requires pursuit of public justification and (3) the claim that respect requires successful public justification. The latter claim is *much* more powerful than the former and so requires a commensurately more compelling argument. Given that the norm of respect requires *something* by way of public justification, the justificatory liberal must provide some argument for adopting the *stronger* understanding of what respect requires. But so long as we're willing to grant the weaker claim, as we should, the stronger claim seems gratuitously strong.[14]

5.2.2 Larmore on Respect

Charles Larmore has articulated a well-regarded version of the argument from respect to restraint. His argument moves from *respect*, to *rationality*, to *public justification* (in Larmore's idiolect, to *neutrality*). More formally:

(1) A citizen ought to respect each of his compatriots as a person, and in particular each one's ability to construct a coherent understanding of how she should live her life.

(2) Since a citizen ought to respect each compatriot's ability to construct a coherent understanding of how she should live her life, then he ought to decide which laws to support on the basis of the outcome of a rational discourse with his compatriots.

(3) Since a citizen ought to decide which laws to support on the basis of the outcome of a rational discourse with his compatriots, then he ought to justify those laws on the basis of "neutral ground."[15]

Ad (1): According to Larmore, each person inhabits his own point of view on the world; Jack's ability to form and revise his own point of view on the world is of great value and significance; as a consequence, if Jill respects Jack as a person, she'll accord due weight to the very great value of Jack's capacity to form his own perspective on the world. In short, for Larmore, the sense of respect that is relevant to the doctrine of restraint is of the recognitional, not the appraisal, sort: even if Jill thinks that Jack is a despicable person or that he adheres to abhorrent personal ideals, she ought to accord due weight to the fact that, as a person, "whatever [Jill] do[es] that affects [Jack] is something with which he must deal from within his own perspective."[16]

Ad (2): Given the value of Jack's capacity to form his own view of the world, Jill ought not treat Jack merely as an object to be manipulated; she ought not treat Jack just as a means to her ends but also as an end in himself. Treating Jack as an end in himself forbids Jill merely to coerce him. Larmore writes:

> Now forcing people to comply with principles of conduct is to treat them as means: their compliance is seen as conducive to public order or perhaps

to their own reformation. In itself the use or threat of force cannot be wrong, for otherwise political association would be impossible. What is prohibited by the norm of respect is resting compliance only on force. For the distinctive feature of persons is that they are beings capable of thinking and acting on the basis of reasons. If we try to bring about conformity to some political principle simply by threat, we will be treating people solely as means, as objects of coercion. We will not be treating them as ends, engaging directly their distinctive capacity as persons.[17]

The fact that Jack is a person requires that Jill treat him not just as a mean to her own ends but also as end in himself; more precisely, she needs to treat him as an end in virtue of his capacity to form his own point of view on the world. And what does treating Jack as an end in himself require of Jill? That Jill commit herself to resolving their differences on the basis of "the unforced force of rational argumentation" (to use Habermas's phraseology), not just on the basis of power. Only by way of a rational discourse about how to resolve those differences does Jill accord due weight to the fact that Jack is capable and desirous of being moved by reasons. In short, Jack's capacity to be moved by reasons, in combination with Jill's obligation to treat Jack as an end in himself, obliges Jill and Jack to resolve their differences by means of rational discourse.

Ad (3): Suppose that Jill supports some coercive law L that affects Jack, that Jack lacks reason to support L, and that both Jack and Jill are committed to resolving their disagreement over L in accord with the canons of rational discourse. Such canons require that Jill attempt to articulate some argument for L that Jack, given his evidential set, has good reason to accept. (And vice versa, of course.) And this requires that Jill articulate some argument that employs premises both of them accept: if Jack and Jill disagree about some claim, and both are committed to a rational resolution of their disagreement, then they ought to retreat to *neutral ground*. Jill ought not repeatedly reassert in mantra-like fashion arguments for L that contain premises Jack rejects; that would be irrational. Larmore writes,

> In discussing how to resolve some problem (for example, what principles of political association they should adopt), people should respond to points of disagreement by retreating to neutral ground, to the beliefs they still share in order either to (a) resolve the disagreement and vindicate one of the disputed positions by means of arguments that proceed from

this common ground, or (b) bypass the disagreement and seek a solution of the problem on the basis simply of this common ground.[18]

If Larmore is correct, to resolve a given disagreement rationally, Jack and Jill must rely on shared convictions, premises contained in both of their evidential sets, that enable them to agree on a resolution of their disagreement. Note, however, that Jack and Jill can arrive at the appropriate resolution in either of two ways.

First, suppose that Jack and Jill disagree about the propriety of a particular coercive law L, such as a constitutional ban on polygamy. They can achieve a resolution of their disagreement by bracketing the claims that give rise to their differential resolutions of L, identifying other claims contained in both of their evidential sets, and showing that those shared claims entail some position on L. Thus, suppose that Jack, as a Mormon, believes that polygamy is essential to salvation, that Jill, as a Catholic, believes that polygamy is sinful, and that both arrive at their respective evaluations of L on the basis of their parochial religious commitments. To resolve their disagreement over L rationally, Jack and Jill mustn't repeatedly reassert their parochial religious claims; they must lay those claims to the side in order to discern some common ground that will enable them to resolve their disagreement. So, suppose that both are fully committed to limiting the state's power, as much as is feasible, to regulate the sexual practices and child-rearing commitments of the citizenry: on the basis of that shared commitment, they might be able to agree that the ban on polygamy is misguided.

Second, perhaps Jack and Jill don't share commitments that are sufficiently rich to allow them to reach an agreement on L. In that case, Larmore proposes a fallback position: if Jack and Jill lack common ground that is sufficient to resolve their disagreement over L, they should retreat to whatever common ground there is in order to forge a mutually acceptable agreement as to how they ought to act, given their continuing disagreement over L. Jack and Jill must now decide what to do in cases of irreconcilable disagreement, and to do that rationally, they need to arrive at common ground regarding what to do about laws about which they have irreconcilable disagreements. So, perhaps both Jack and Jill are direct democrats and on the basis of their commitment to allowing citizens to decide important political questions as directly as possible, both agree to resolve the issue by initiative.

5.2.2.1 Critique of Larmore's Argument. If Larmore is correct, each citizen has an obligation to resolve disagreements over coercive laws in accord with the norms of rational discussion. To do that, according to Larmore, the parties to a given disagreement must retreat to common, neutral, or public ground – premises to which all parties adhere and that make possible a mutually agreeable resolution of their dispute. But it's a contingent matter whether there actually is common ground to which the parties can retreat. As Larmore notes, whether Jack and Jill can resolve their disagreement over coercive law L on the basis of common ground is a contingent matter, one that (often?) fails to obtain. That is why, of course, Larmore proposes his fallback position: since it might very well be the case that Jack and Jill lack common ground on the basis of which they can agree on the moral propriety of L, they must retreat to some further common ground that will enable them to determine what to do given their inability to resolve their disagreement over L. But the existence of common ground that is sufficiently rich as to allow them to determine what to do given their inability to resolve their disagreement over L is no less contingent a state of affairs than is the existence of common ground that enables them to agree on the moral propriety of L. In both cases, with respect to L, and with respect to what to do given their interminable disagreement over L, it's possible that Jack and Jill will lack the requisite common ground. It's therefore possible that Jack and Jill will be unable to forge a publicly justifiable resolution of their disagreement.

It seems that many citizens will find themselves in exactly this condition with respect to the issue of abortion. Not only is it possible (indeed, likely) that there is insufficient common ground among advocates of a pro-life position and advocates of a pro-choice position on the basis of which they are able to forge a public justification for any particular position on abortion, it's possible (again, likely) that there is insufficient ground on which they can agree about what to do given their irremediable disagreement about the moral and legal propriety of abortion.[19] Is the fact that we can come to no agreement about the moral and legal propriety of abortion best dealt with by allowing individual women to decide whether they will have an abortion? Should we decide by majority vote? Should the United States Supreme Court decide? Should State Supreme Courts decide, each for its own state? I see no reason to believe that we're any more likely to arrive at a publicly justifiable resolution of how to deal with our disagreement on abortion as we are to agree on the propriety of abortion itself. At the very least, there is a real possibility that we lack the requisite common ground required to enable all parties to reach a mutually agreeable resolution.

Given that there might be no common ground to which Jack and Jill can repair in order to reach a publicly justifiable resolution of their continuing disagreement over a given issue, it seems to me quite misleading to claim that the norms of rational discourse oblige Jack and Jill to retreat to common ground. That claim assumes that there will be common ground to which they can retreat. Since, however, there might be none, it would seem more accurate to claim that Jack and Jill have an obligation to retreat to common ground *as long as common ground is available*. After all, the norms of rational discourse can't require Jack and Jill to do the impossible: to retreat to a place that doesn't exist.

So suppose we reformulate Larmore's conclusion accordingly: Jack and Jill ought to retreat to such common ground as is available in order to resolve their disagreement over a given issue. That conclusion has important implications. It requires Jack and Jill to do their level best to determine whether they have common ground: they ought to be willing to criticize their prejudices, alter indefensible commitments, scrutinize hitherto unquestioned assumptions. It obliges each to be open to persuasion by the other in order to establish new ground which, they hope, they now share in common. It obliges them to probe one another's evidential sets in order to guard against prematurely concluding that they lack common ground. In short, it entails that Jack and Jill ought sincerely and genuinely to pursue common ground on the basis of which to resolve their disagreement over the issue that divides them.

Each of these claims is of capital importance, but none of them provides adequate reason to conclude that a citizen ought to obey the doctrine of restraint. As the reader will recall, the doctrine of restraint tells a citizen what to do when he has discharged his obligation to pursue public justification but can't discern a public justification. Since, according to the doctrine of restraint, a citizen may support a given coercive law L only if he has a public justification for L, then, if he has pursued but can't discern a public justification, he ought to withhold support from L. Larmore shows, however, only that a citizen has an obligation to pursue a public justification – to retreat to common ground insofar as common ground is available. His version of the argument from respect provides a citizen with no guidance at all as to what to do in case his pursuit of public justification fails.

124

One further point about Larmore's argument. I've objected to Larmore's third premise by focusing on the claim that the norms of rational discourse require a citizen only to pursue public justification, not to provide a public justification, nor to exercise restraint in case he can't provide a public justification. Suppose that I'm correct about that. It might still seem that Larmore's argument has some life in it. After all, it might seem that a citizen who can't provide a successful public justification for a given coercive law, but who persists in supporting that law, fails to treat his compatriots as ends in themselves. After all, he coerces his compatriots against their will, without being able to provide them with reasons that are convincing to them given their points of view.

This response strikes me as inadequate. A citizen who respects his compatriots is forbidden to treat them as means *only*, but he isn't forbidden from treating them as means *at all*. But a citizen who pursues public justification for his favored laws doesn't treat his compatriots *only* as a means: he attempts to address them on the basis of their respective capacities to form their own points of view regarding his actions. He attempts to reason with them, to convince them that his favored policies are appropriate. That he doesn't meet with success, and thus regards himself as conscience bound to support coercive laws absent a public justification, doesn't obviate his according significant weight to the fact that his compatriots are persons and allowing that fact to constrain the manner in which he supports his favored laws. Pretty clearly, a citizen who is committed to pursuing public justification but not exercising restraint treats his compatriots *both* as means *and* as ends in themselves.

As I see it, the claim that a citizen who refuses to exercise restraint treats his compatriots solely as means and not as ends at all is plausible only if we fail to distinguish between pursuing public justification and exercising restraint. If we fail to make that distinction, then we might assume that a citizen has two basic options: (a) he is willing *neither* to pursue public justification *nor* to exercise restraint or (b) he is willing *both* to pursue public justification *and* to exercise restraint. That is, if we assume that pursuing public justification and exercising restraint are all of a piece, then we'll assume that a citizen must choose between both or neither. And if a citizen chooses neither to pursue public justification nor to exercise restraint, then it's plausible to claim that he treats his compatriots as means only. But if we distinguish between public justification and restraint, it's clear that there are not two but three options: (a) a citizen is willing neither to pursue public justification nor to exercise restraint; (b) a citizen is willing both to pursue public justification and to exercise restraint; and (c) a citizen is willing to pursue public justification *but not* to exercise restraint. Only with respect to (a) is it plausible to suppose that a citizen treats his compatriots as means only. So it's possible for a citizen to reject the doctrine of restraint but still treat his compatriots as ends in themselves.

5.2.2.2 Respect and Accommodation. It's possible that I've mistaken Larmore's intentions: that Larmore doesn't intend to establish the doctrine of restraint. Indeed, there is some indication that Larmore intends to show that each citizen need only to pursue public justification *so long as* she's also willing to *accommodate* those for whom she can't provide a successful public justification. Thus, having laid out his version of the argument from respect, Larmore considers the objection that his conclusion is utopian:

> There remains, however, one final objection to this argument for the distinctive feature of a liberal political order. Even if this argument is faultless, some will complain, the obvious fact is that "neutral ground" offers too weak a basis for deriving any political principles that assign basic liberties and distribute wealth. Neutrality is powerless, the objection claims, as a method for solving the fundamental problem of politics. As a result, actual political systems that call themselves liberal must be either confused or disingenuous.[20]

How does Larmore respond to this argument? He doesn't dispute the claim that "full neutrality in a modern society may prove too empty to generate any substantive political principles."[21] But that would be a problem only if neutrality (public justification) were "the [justificatory] liberal's only desideratum."[22] In fact, however, justificatory liberals are also committed to an effective political order and thus realize the need to decide on and implement political principles. So the justificatory liberal should be willing to consider trade-offs between these goals. More particularly, the need to decide on and implement political principles warrants us, in some cases, in implementing political principles we can't establish by relying on common ground and thus for which we lack a public justification. Nevertheless, Larmore argues, a citizen's decision to support a coercive policy for which she lacks a public justification ought to be consistent with the *spirit* of public justification: she should accommodate her compatriots by supporting her favored policies on the basis of the *least controversial* rationale available. Larmore writes: "The important point for the liberal is that such tradeoffs [between public justification and practicality] can still be devised in the spirit of neutrality. Guiding them will be a principle embodying a higher neutrality; namely, that one should institute only the least abridgement of neutrality necessary for making a decision possible."[23] (Larmore here advocates what Amy Gutmann and Dennis Thompson call "an economy of moral disagreement": "in justifying policies on moral grounds, citizens should seek the rationale that minimizes rejection of the position they oppose."[24])

As I see it, Larmore's claim that a citizen has an obligation to support her favored laws in the spirit of public justification is an important one. A citizen who realizes that she can't provide a public justification for a favored law ought to accommodate her compatriots by attempting to articulate some rationale for that law that isn't gratuitously objectionable. She ought not provoke her compatriots needlessly; she ought to make it as easy as is feasible for her compatriots to *acquiesce* to her favored laws. Perhaps Bill McCartney strikes us as disrespectful because he fails to accommodate his compatriots in this way. His rhetoric about abominations is unnecessarily provocative – McCartney could have articulated a rationale for Amendment 2 that was less provocative to his homosexual compatriots, even though it is highly unlikely that he could articulate a rationale for Amendment 2 that his homosexual compatriots would find plausible, much less convincing.

That noted, it strikes me that Larmore concedes the essential point. It isn't the case, as he claims more than once, that "the liberal state can intervene in an area of social life only if the state has a neutrally justifiable goal that requires that intervention."[25] That claim involves the language of success, not the language of aspiration; it requires more than that we attempt to articulate a public justification for our favored coercive laws, and accommodate our compatriots if our attempt fails. It requires us to have a public justification in order to be permitted to support our favored coercive laws, and implies that we disrespect our compatriots if we persist in supporting a coercive law for which we realize that we lack a public justification. It implies that Bill McCartney disrespects his compatriots by his willingness to support Amendment 2 solely on the basis of his conviction that homosexuality is an abomination to God and, as a consequence, that McCartney should cease and desist from supporting Amendment 2 on that basis. But Larmore's concessions to practicality undermine that evaluation of McCartney's behavior: McCartney might be guilty for failing to pursue public justification, he might be guilty of failing to accommodate his compatriots, but he isn't guilty for failing to exercise restraint, for it might be that there simply is not the common ground between McCartney and his compatriots that would enable them to achieve a mutually agreeable resolution of their dispute over Amendment 2.

As I noted above, perhaps Larmore never intended to establish the doctrine of restraint. Perhaps he would be satisfied to show only that a responsible citizen in a liberal democracy ought to pursue public justification and to accommodate when public justification is unavailable. That is fine: I'm not interested in scoring debater's points. But in that case, perhaps it would be less misleading to tone down the restraint-like language: not "a citizen may support some coercive law only if she has a public justification for that law," but "when a citizen supports some coercive law, she should do her level best to articulate a public justification for that law." Not the language of success, but the language of aspiration. Not, "you don't have the ticket, so stay out," but, "thanks for trying."

5.2.3 Gaus on Respect

Gerald Gaus has articulated an argument in support of the doctrine of restraint that differs in significant respects from the versions of the argument from respect I have discussed thus far. Most important, Gaus's argument is not vitiated by a failure to distinguish between pursuing public justification, exercising restraint, and providing public justification. Nevertheless, I argue that Gaus's argument is flawed by a faulty understanding of the relations between a citizen's imposing some moral claim on his compatriots and a citizen's regarding those who violate that moral claim as blameworthy.

5.2.3.1 Explication of Gaus's Argument. Gaus's argument in support of the claim that citizens should exercise restraint moves from a claim about *moral impositions*, through a claim about *culpability*, to a conclusion about *restraint*.

(1) Responsible citizenship requires that a citizen impose moral convictions on his compatriots.
(2) It is reasonable for a citizen to impose a given moral conviction on his compatriots only if he regards them as culpable in the event that they violate that conviction.

(3) A citizen who regards his compatriots as culpable for violating a given moral conviction respects them only if he can provide them with adequate reason for that conviction as judged from their respective points of view.

Running the argument in the other direction, if a citizen's compatriots lack what they take to be good reason to adhere to a given moral norm, then it's disrespectful for him to regard them as culpable for violating that norm; and if it's disrespectful for a citizen to regard his compatriots as culpable for violating a given norm, then he ought not impose that norm on them.

Ad (1): A citizen in a democratic regime has a modicum of power over his compatriots: by electing candidates and more rarely by selecting policies via referendum, he plays some role in constraining the activities open to his fellow citizens. Given the importance of such constraints, a responsible citizen should support only those coercive policies that pass deliberative muster. Responsible deliberation requires a citizen to accord significant weight to moral considerations, and these considerations will often constitute decisive grounds for a given policy. And for a citizen to support a policy on moral grounds is to impose his moral norms on his compatriots. Responsible citizenship thus commits a citizen to imposing his moral convictions on his compatriots.

Ad (2): According to Gaus, for Jack to make moral demands on Jill is for Jack to be rationally committed to holding her *culpable* if Jill fails to adhere to those demands: "When [Jack] makes a moral demand on [Jill], he not only seeks to impose on her but, in the event of her ignoring his demand, he appropriately can blame her, resent her, feel indignation, and so on."[26] Suppose Jack supports a ban on nuclear weapons on the ground that, since the normal and expected use of a nuclear weapon has the likely consequence of annihilating numerous innocent civilians, to disseminate nuclear weapons is to collude in genocide. Given this ground, if Jill provides underdeveloped countries with the technological wherewithal to deliver nuclear weapons, Jack is committed to regarding her as blameworthy for violating the obligation not to collude in genocide.

Ad (3): In order for Jack reasonably to hold Jill blameworthy for violating some norm, Jack must accept claims about Jill's epistemic condition vis-à-vis that norm. For example, if Jack blames Jill for colluding in genocide, he is committed to the claim that Jill *could have known* that she ought not collude in genocide. Gaus writes: "Blaming another or feeling resentment that your moral demand has been ignored are only appropriate when someone has ignored moral demands when, as we say, she should have known better. These reactions are thus not appropriate toward babies or those who could not possibly have known about the relevant norm, rule, or principle."[27] Suppose Jill is an engineering genius whose talents are employed by nefarious elements to develop delivery systems capable of long-range nuclear strikes. Suppose further that, although an engineering genius, Jill is a moral dolt and lacks the moral-conceptual apparatus required to appreciate that colluding in genocide is morally repugnant. Given Jill's desperate state of moral ignorance, it hardly makes sense to blame her for complicity in genocide: since she is incapable of forming the concept of "genocide" and thus *couldn't* have known that collusion in genocide is morally wrong, Jack can't reasonably regard Jill as culpable for violating the norm that prohibits collusion with genocide. A necessary condition, then, of Jack's reasonably blaming Jill for violating some obligation is that he justifiably believes that she could have known that she had that obligation.

Suppose Jack blames her anyway. In that case – and in any case in which Jack demands that Jill perform an action that she couldn't know she should perform – we have a case of *browbeating*: "a very firm insistence [devoid of rationale] that you must believe what I believe, or act as I would have you act."[28] For Jack to browbeat Jill – to insist (perhaps very loudly) that she obey a moral demand that she has no reason to accept other than his insistence that she should – constitutes mere bullying and is a manifestation of disrespect.[29]

For Jack appropriately to regard Jill as blameworthy, he must not only accept the claim that Jill could have known better than to act as she did; he must also accept additional claims about Jill's epistemic condition. Suppose that Jack votes in an initiative to ban same-sex marriages because he believes God has informed humanity in the Bible that homosexual relations are unnatural and therefore that homosexual relations are destructive of both self and others. Suppose further that Jill is aware both of Jack's moral conviction regarding homosexual relations and its basis, but that Jill lacks any evidence that the Bible is a reliable indicator of moral truths. Now in a reasonably straightforward sense, Jill *could have known* that same-sex relations are morally wrong: she can make a leap of faith and convert. Surely such a scenario is possible both logically and psychologically: it is possible because it has already happened in any number of cases in various cultures to individuals of vastly different psychological profiles.

Even though Jill could, in some sense, have known about the moral impropriety of pursuing her sexual inclinations, Jack would nevertheless browbeat her were he to blame Jill for flouting his demand that she cease engaging in same-sex relations. Even though it is logically and psychologically possible for her to have known better, nothing in Jill's ken indicates that there is anything wrong with same-sex relations. That a leap of faith could land her in a position to discern a moral obligation doesn't license Jack to blame her for violating that obligation. Rather, something accessible to Jill given her extant perspective on the world, given her existing system of beliefs and fund of experiences, must indicate that she has that moral obligation. Thus, Gaus writes: "To make genuine moral demands on others, and not browbeat them or simply insist that they do or believe what you want, you must show that, somehow, their system [of beliefs] yields reasons to embrace your demand. Morality, then, requires that we reason from the standpoint of others."[30]

That Jill's system of beliefs must provide her with adequate reason to believe that she has a given obligation in order for her to be blameworthy for failing to discharge that obligation is essential to Gaus's claim that a citizen has an obligation to adhere to the doctrine of restraint. It implies that in order for Jack reasonably to hold Jill accountable for failing to discharge some obligation, he is committed to the claim that she has good reason to believe that she has that obligation, where a "good" reason is determined (at least in part) by Jill's evidential set. And since Jill's evidential set will very likely differ from Jack's, it isn't sufficient for Jack to have good reason *from his perspective* to believe that Jill has violated some obligation. Rather, for Jack to avoid browbeating Jill, and thus to avoid disrespecting her, he must show that his moral demands are justifiable to her given her evidential set. And since there is nothing special about Jack and Jill's situation, we may generalize: in order for Jack to respect his fellow citizens, he must show that each citizen subject to laws he supports on the basis of his moral convictions has good reason from within each's system of beliefs to accept those moral convictions. If he can't do that, if he can't publicly justify the moral demands he imposes on them, then he browbeats his compatriots and thereby disrespects them. In short, respect requires that Jack support only those laws that each member of the public has good reason to accept and thus that Jack refuse to support any law for which he lacks the requisite justification.[31]

5.2.3.2 Critique of Gaus's Argument. I believe that (2) is false: it isn't the case that if a citizen imposes some moral norm on his compatriots, then he must regard them as culpable for violating that norm. Rather, if a citizen demands that his compatriots adhere to some norm, *and* if they have good reason to do so, *then* he must regard them as culpable for violating that norm. Actually, this is a bit too simple. At the very least one further condition must obtain: his fellow citizens must *be able* to adhere to the moral norms imposed on them. By common consent, it's appropriate for a citizen to blame his compatriots for violating some moral norm only if they have the capacity to adhere to that norm. It seems plausible to suppose, roughly, that a citizen who imposes some moral norm on his compatriots is rationally committed to regarding them as culpable in the event they violate that norm if and only if (a) they have good reason to believe that they should adhere to that norm and (b) they can adhere to that norm.

My understanding of the proper relations between moral impositions, culpability, and justification is very different from Gaus's understanding. If Gaus is correct, for a citizen to impose a given moral norm on his compatriots by itself rationally obliges him to regard them as culpable, which in turn rationally commits him to regarding them as having good reason to obey that norm. If I'm correct, a citizen may impose a moral demand on his compatriots but realize that because his compatriots lack what they take to be good reason to adhere to that demand, they should not be held culpable. In fact, in my view, a citizen can impose some moral norm on his compatriots but realize that they lack what they take to be good reason to obey that norm, in which case he may *excuse* them if they violate that norm. Far from being committed to the claim that his compatriots are rationally justified in adhering to a given norm, a citizen who imposes that norm on his compatriots may claim that his fellows aren't rationally justified in adhering to that norm as sufficient reason to absolve them of culpability for failing to act in accord with (what in fact are) their obligations.

The difference between Gaus's and my understanding of the relations between moral impositions, culpability, and justification should be clear. How do we resolve this difference? Perhaps we can get a clearer view of the matter by considering a structurally similar situation. The relations between moral impositions, culpability, and justification are structurally the same as the relations between moral impositions, culpability, and having a capacity to obey a given moral norm. So let's focus on the latter set of relations. Suppose Jeffrey so lacks control over his baser instincts that he is incapable of controlling his urge to torture his fellow human beings. Although, by hypothesis, Jeffrey is justified in believing that torturing people is wrong, he finds himself incapable of resisting his inclination to inflict pain on others. Now, since we're assuming that Jeffrey really can't resist his inclination to torture, it hardly makes sense to blame him for torturing his victims. But should we impose on him our conviction that torture is wrong? It's important to recall what Gaus regards as a moral imposition. A citizen imposes a moral demand on his compatriots if that moral demand counts as a decisive reason for him to support a given policy, particularly a coercive one. So the question is, should we support, on moral grounds, coercive laws that constrain the dysfunctional proclivities of citizens like Jeffrey? I think it's obvious that we should. We should impose on Jeffrey and others like him our moral demand that citizens not be tortured. But we should also withhold our blame. Imposing our moral norms is one thing; blaming Jeffrey is quite another.

If it's appropriate for us to impose moral demands on those who can't adhere to those demands, I see no reason that we may not impose moral demands on those who lack what they take to be good reason to adhere to our moral demands. Although it's fairly obvious that we shouldn't aspire to or take joy in imposing our moral demands on those who lack good reason (given their respective evidential sets) to accede to those demands, I can see nothing morally criticizable in so doing and much that is morally desirable. In this regard, recall the morally obtuse engineer from the beginning of this section. Although an ordinary moral agent in most respects, Jill has a most serious moral blind spot: she is incapable of forming the concept of genocide and therefore can't appreciate our objection to collusion in genocide. Given the grave risk she poses to millions of innocent civilians, we should impose our moral norms on her, and others like her, as effectively as we can. Of course, because we know that she isn't justified in adhering to the norm prohibiting collusion in genocide, and because we know that, in order reasonably to regard her as culpable, she must have good reason to adhere to that norm, we must refrain from regarding her as culpable. If anything, we should regard her with pity and compassion rather than condemnation, resentment, and blame. But impose on her we will and should.

It seems clear, then, that a citizen who imposes his moral demands on his compatriots isn't thereby committed to regarding them as culpable; consequently, it isn't the case that a citizen who supports some coercive law on the basis of some moral demand is committed to the proposition that each of his compatriots is rationally justified in adhering to that moral demand. As a consequence, Gaus's argument fails to show that respect for others requires a citizen to restrain himself from supporting coercive laws for which he lacks a public justification.

5.2.4 Audi on Restraint

Robert Audi has also presented an argument that it's plausible to construe as moving from the claim that a citizen ought to respect her compatriots to the claim that a citizen ought to exercise restraint. Audi's argument begins with the claim that a citizen ought to respect her compatriots as her equals, moves to the claim that she ought to be willing to reverse roles with them, and concludes with the claim that she ought not support any coercive policy on the basis of her religious convictions alone.

5.2.4.1 Audi's Role-Reversal Argument for Restraint. According to Audi, each citizen ought to obey what he calls *the principle of secular rationale*: a citizen "has a prima facie obligation not to advocate or support any law or public policy that restricts human conduct, unless [she] has, and is willing to offer, adequate secular reason for this advocacy or support (say for [her] vote)."[32] Pretty obviously, the principle of secular rationale is a very specific formulation of the doctrine of restraint: it's a version of the doctrine of restraint that applies specifically to religious convictions. (I'll maintain that narrow focus throughout my discussion of Audi's argument.)

What argument does Audi present in support of the claim that a citizen ought to obey the principle of secular rationale? I'll set aside until the next chapter an argument that Audi articulates quite often and that sets the tone for his discussion, namely, that the intrusion of religion into politics generates all sorts of problems that can be ameliorated if citizens adhere to the principle of secular rationale. I'm now interested in only those arguments that move from the claim that a citizen has an obligation to respect her compatriots to the conclusion that a citizen has an obligation to exercise restraint. So why, according to Audi, does respect require a citizen to obey the principle of secular rationale and thus exercise restraint with respect to her religious commitments? Audi argues as follows.

(1) Jack can't respect Jill and also adhere to a policy of deciding which coercive laws merit his support if he would resent Jill's adhering to a relevantly similar policy in deciding which policies merit her support.

(2) Jack's supporting coercive laws whose justification relies solely on a religious rationale would be to adhere to a policy he would resent were Jill to adhere to a relevantly similar policy.

(3) Therefore, Jack ought not support those laws whose justification relies solely on a religious rationale.

Ad (1): One of a citizen's fundamental moral obligations is to treat her compatriots as persons who enjoy a dignity and value that is *equal* to her dignity and value. A necessary condition of a citizen's treating other persons as equally valuable is that she is willing to *reverse roles* with them: because Jack and Jill have equal value as persons, it's inappropriate for Jack to pursue practices he's unwilling to allow a similarly circumstanced Jill to pursue as well.[33] This constraint ought to govern not just the coercive laws Jack supports, but also Jack's reasons for supporting them. Most important, for our purposes, the role-reversal constraint applies to Jack's practice of supporting his favored coercive policies on the basis of his religious convictions alone. Thus, Audi writes: "If the only reasons that move me are religious, and if I would not want to be coerced on the basis of religious reasons playing a like role in someone with a conflicting religious perspective, I would want to abstain from coercion."[34]

Ad (2): Audi is confident that religious citizens will be unwilling to generalize the policy of supporting coercive laws solely on the basis of their religious convictions. If Audi is correct, nearly everyone regards as reprehensible the prospect of being coerced solely on religious grounds they reject:

> There is something repugnant about being convicted (or having one's liberty restricted) on the basis of someone else's religious attitudes or views, even if they are only a significant part and not the whole of the ground of the ... coercer's ... case; or at least, this is a feeling that tends to be shared both by those who are religious – especially if they are in a religious minority in their society – and those who simply respect liberty, whether or not they are religious.[35]

If Audi is correct about the intuitive repugnance most citizens feel toward the prospect of being coerced on another citizen's religious grounds, it would seem that such citizens would be unwilling to accept a generalized policy permitting *any* citizen to support her favored coercive laws solely on religious grounds. In short, rejection of Audi's principle of secular rationale does not pass the role-reversal test. (And insofar as unwillingness to obey only those principles that pass a role-reversal test is indicative of a citizen's having respect for her compatriots as her equals, then a citizen who rejects the principle of secular rationale seems to disrespect her compatriots.)

Audi's argument is most convincing, it seems to me, when formulated concretely. Audi confronts the religious adherent who considers rejecting his principle of secular rationale with a specific law that depends solely on religious grounds for its justification and asks whether she would be willing to allow others to violate his principle of secular rationale in that case. Addressing a hypothetical citizen who decides solely on religious grounds to support a law that restricts meat consumption, Audi writes:

> Suppose, however, that much money must be spent in enforcement and that many jobs are lost through changes in the food sector of the economy, so that human conduct is significantly restricted, even if meat consumption remains legal. Then one might ask the religious voters in question whether they would accept comparable restrictions of their conduct, as well as similar job losses or mandatory shifts, on the basis of coercive legislation protecting the dandelion as a sacred species or prohibiting miniskirts and brief bathing suits as irreverent.[36]

According to Audi, any citizen who decides to support, on the basis of her religious convictions alone, a coercive law that restricts the consumption of animal meat must be willing for her compatriots to adhere to a relevantly similar policy: she must be willing to allow her compatriots to support, solely on the basis of *their* (religious) conviction that the dandelion is sacred, a coercive law that forbids her to engage in the wanton destruction of dandelions and thus, say, that forbids her to mow her lawn. If, of course, she's unwilling for others to do so, then she ought to be unwilling to support any coercive law on the basis of *her* religious convictions alone.

5.2.4.2 Criticism of Audi's Role-Reversal Argument. What should we make of Audi's case for (his version of) the doctrine of restraint? Audi's argument hinges on the bet that his audience will balk at the prospect of being coerced on the basis of religious convictions they reject. Thus, for example, Audi is confident that the members of his audience will resent being forbidden to mow their respective lawns solely on the ground that dandelions are sacred. I think that Audi's confidence is well justified. Or perhaps I should speak only for myself: I would resent any such law. But what follows from that? In order to answer that question, it's essential to specify exactly *why* I would resent being subject to a law that forbids me to kill dandelions. Only if we can identify my reasons for that reaction is it possible to determine the respects in which I am and am not willing to reverse roles with my compatriots. (It is to reasons for reactions, rather than reactions, that the role-reversal test applies.)

As I reflect on Audi's scenario, I find that the following is the case: I find it hard to believe that a citizen who genuinely and sincerely pursues *rational* justification for the claim that dandelions are sacred would conclude that dandelions are in fact sacred and, furthermore, would be willing to coerce me on that basis. The claim that dandelions are sacred and thus that killing them is morally objectionable is so absurd that it's hard to imagine that a rational citizen could, in good conscience, support a coercive law on its basis. But as I argued in the previous chapter, I have a legitimate expectation that my compatriots will withhold their support from any coercive law that lacks, from the perspective of their respective evidential sets, the requisite rational justification. If my compatriots persist in supporting a coercive law that lacks the requisite rational justification, then I may legitimately resent their support for that law.

It seems to me that my resentment at being subject to a law that forbids me to kill dandelions is a function not at all of the fact that my compatriots have only a religious reason for that law, but of (what I naturally assume to be) the fact that they lack the requisite rational justification for that law. Since it's unlikely that my compatriots are rationally justified in believing that dandelions are sacred, it's plausible to suppose that my resentment results from my reasonable belief that either my compatriots have failed to pursue rational justification or they are willing to coerce me without having achieved the requisite rational justification. Consequently, the resentment I feel *need not* be attributable to my compatriots' willingness to support that law on the basis of their religious beliefs alone.

Of course, I don't deny that it's possible for my compatriots to be rationally justified in believing that dandelions are sacred. So it's easy to reformulate Audi's scenario. Without taking the time to fill in all of the details, assume that a majority of citizens have genuinely and sincerely pursued rational justification for the claim that dandelions are sacred, assume further that they are willing to withhold their support from a law that prohibits massacring dandelions if they lack adequate reason to support that law, and suppose that they take themselves to have acquired the requisite rational justification. Suppose finally that each member of the majority has satisfied each of the other constraints that constitute the ideal of conscientious engagement.

How do I react to Audi's scenario thus reconstructed? Would I resent being coerced by a law that forbids me to kill dandelions if my compatriots are rationally justified in believing that the dandelion is sacred, have attempted publicly to justify that law, are willing to accommodate me, take seriously my objections to that law, and so on? It's hard to tell, since the possible world we're now discussing isn't particularly close to the actual one (and as R. M. Hare has persuasively argued, our "intuitive" reactions and emotional responses are designed to provide accurate moral guidance in the actual world and nearby possible worlds and might very well be highly unreliable moral guides in distant possible worlds).[37] Nevertheless, it seems worthwhile to make the effort. So here is my best estimate of the situation.

Although it's less clear to me that I would resent being subject to a law that forbids me to kill dandelions in the case under consideration, it seems, on introspection, that I nevertheless would experience some degree of resentment. At the very least, I would experience frustration and anger at being subject to that law. I very much want to mow my lawn and would do so were I not discouraged from doing so by the state. The fact that I'm forcibly inhibited from achieving my aims is a natural source of frustration, anger, and perhaps even resentment.[38]

Does this provide the advocate of restraint with the opening necessary to drive home the essential point? I don't believe it does. The frustration, anger, and resentment I'd feel if subject to a law that forbids me to kill dandelions seems to me a consequence not of the fact that my compatriots support that law on the basis of their religious convictions alone, but of the *content* of that law (as well as of the coercion employed to secure my obedience to that law). It's the coercive law itself that frustrates and infuriates me, not my compatriots' reasons for supporting that law. The imposition of that law inhibits me from attaining ends I very much want to pursue; as a consequence, it's entirely natural and appropriate for me to feel frustration and anger at being so constrained. But I don't see that my reaction has anything in particular to do with my compatriots' willingness to support that law solely on religious grounds. *Whatever* their reasons for supporting that law, then, so long as I persist in my desire to mow my lawn and thus to kill dandelions, that law would frustrate my desires, and thus lead to the anger and frustration I feel at being subject to that law.

We can see that the religious basis of a law forbidding the killing of dandelions has nothing to do with the frustration I feel at being subject to that law by replacing that religious basis with a secular basis. Suppose that an environmentalist group has successfully lobbied to have a law enacted that forbids me to mow my law on the basis that dandelions are an endangered species. Suppose, however, that I reject that rationale – I don't believe that dandelions are endangered. (At the very least, they seem to be thriving in my corner of reality.) Keeping my desire to mow my lawn constant, I see no reason to believe that I would feel any less resentment or frustration at being subject to that law given that it has an entirely secular basis than I would feel were it to enjoy an entirely religious basis. So long as the content of the law is sufficiently objectionable, my allergic reaction to that law persists, whatever its rationale. Thus, the cause of my resentment is not that the law has only a religious rationale. But in that case, I'll have no problem reversing roles with those who support their favored coercive laws solely on religious grounds.

The strength of the argument under discussion is that it provides a simple and straightforward way to get at the heart of the issue of the proper role of religious convictions in political decision making and advocacy: are those who reject the doctrine of restraint, as I do, prepared to apply their refusal to exercise restraint impartially, such that they are willing to permit each citizen to support her favored coercive laws on the basis of her religious convictions alone, whatever those religious convictions might be? The weakness of Audi's version of the argument is that it depends entirely on what the audience is willing to allow others to do.[39] And I find that I have no hesitation in allowing others to decide whether a coercive law merits their support on the basis of their religious convictions alone. More precisely, I have no hesitation allowing my compatriots to decide whether a coercive law merits their support on the basis of their religious convictions alone, *so long as* each of my fellow citizens adheres to the constraints constitutive of the ideal of conscientious engagement. Indeed, I can't imagine discouraging others from supporting whatever coercive laws that they take in good conscience to be morally obligatory, whatever the content of their reasons (with one important exception: so long as those reasons do not deny my dignity as a person).

5.3 RAWLS ON RESTRAINT

Up to this point in my discussion of the claim that respect requires restraint, I've attempted to indicate why that claim is intuitively implausible and I've evaluated several arguments intended to overcome the intuitive implausibility of that claim. In this section, I articulate an (admittedly ad hominem) argument against the doctrine of restraint. I'll do so by availing myself of some of the machinery John Rawls employs in arguing that respect *requires* restraint.

5.3.1 The Strains of Commitment

The following principle – Rawls calls it the *liberal principle of legitimacy* – lies at the center stage of Rawls's Political Liberalism and is closely associated with the norm of respect (for citizens as free and equal):

> Our exercise of political power is fully proper only when it is exercised in accordance with a constitution the essentials of which all citizens as free and equal may reasonably be expected to endorse in the light of principles and ideals acceptable to their common human reason.[40]

The liberal principle of legitimacy has direct implications for our topic, for it entails what Rawls calls the *duty of civility*. Rawls continues:

> And since the exercise of political power must be legitimate, the ideal of citizenship imposes a moral, not a legal, duty – the duty of civility – to be able to explain to one another on those fundamental questions how the principles and policies they advocate and vote for can be supported by the political values of public reason. . . . [All citizens] should be ready to explain the basis of their actions to one another in terms each could reasonably expect that others might endorse as consistent with their freedom and equality.[41]

140

So, on Rawls's accounting, the liberal principle of legitimacy entails a duty of civility and the duty of civility obliges a citizen to explain to his compatriots just how his favored political policies enjoy public justification. Rawls is clear, moreover, that he understands the duty of civility to oblige a citizen to refrain from supporting political policies for which he can't provide the requisite public justification, not just that he should attempt to provide public justification: when a citizen who attempts to articulate a public justification for a favored coercive law finds himself at a "standoff," then he ought not have recourse to his nonpublic grounds.[42]

If the move from the liberal principle of legitimacy to the duty of civility exhausted Rawls's argument, it seems to me that his argument would be of little interest. For as Michael Perry has argued, the liberal principle of legitimacy and the duty of civility are substantially *equivalent.*[43] But perhaps Rawls's argument can be taken a bit further. Suppose we ask: what is the status of the liberal principle of legitimacy? What does Rawls have to say in favor of that principle? Unfortunately, very little. He does, however, allude to one such argument: Rawls suggests that we may vindicate the liberal principle of legitimacy by means of the same sort of argument he has articulated for his two principles of justice.

> In justice as fairness ... the guidelines of inquiry of public reason, as well as its principle of legitimacy, have the same basis as the substantive principles of justice. This means in justice as fairness that the parties in the original position, in adopting principles of justice for the basic structure, must also adopt guidelines and criteria of public reason for applying those norms. The argument for those guidelines, and for the principle of legitimacy, is much the same as, and as strong as, the argument for the principles of justice themselves. In securing the interests of the persons they represent, the parties insist that the application of substantive principles be guided by judgment and inference, reasons and evidence that the persons they represent can reasonably be expected to endorse. ... Thus we have the principle of legitimacy.[44]

So, Rawls says, the argument for the liberal principle of legitimacy is "much the same as, and as strong as, the argument for the principles of justice." That is also to say, I suppose, that the argument for the liberal principle of legitimacy is going to be *extremely* complicated: much ink has been spilled exegeting Rawls's argument for his two principles, and

I can't imagine that the argument he has in mind for the liberal principle of legitimacy will be any easier to explicate (particularly since, so far as I'm aware, Rawls doesn't develop that argument in detail anywhere in his corpus). I certainly don't intend to spill much more ink over the original position and what can be derived from that construction. Nevertheless, I'm interested in one argument, namely Rawls's "strains of commitment" argument for his two principles, and will explicate just enough of his machinery to get the gist of that argument across.[45] My intention is to show that Rawls's liberal principle of legitimacy doesn't satisfy his strains of commitment test and thus to show that the liberal principle of legitimacy violates the norm of respect for persons (insofar as Rawls's machinery adequately models the norm of respect for persons).

As I assume the reader is aware, Rawls attempts to vindicate his two principles of justice by showing that those two principles would be chosen by suitably construed parties in a suitably construed choice situation: the original position. At the heart of his construal of the original position is "the veil of ignorance": the parties in the original position must choose the principles of justice that will unalterably govern the society in which they live without being able to rely on any information that enables them to predict their specific life prospects in that society. In particular, the parties in the original position are unaware of their economic status, race, gender, and most important for our purposes, their religious convictions. The veil of ignorance is not complete, of course; there are plenty of things the parties in the original position do know. For example, they have a general knowledge of human psychology. Indeed, they must have a general knowledge of human psychology if the strains of commitment argument is to succeed: that the parties in the original position have a general knowledge of human psychology enables them to determine which conception of justice "involves the greater stress" and thus whether they will be able to abide by the conception chosen in the original position when they find themselves permanently and unalterably ensconced in a society governed by that conception.[46]

In choosing a conception of justice, the parties are to abide by a number of constraints, of which one is critical to Rawls's strains of commitment argument. Rawls endorses the moral claim that "when we enter an agreement, we must be able to honor it even should the worst possibilities prove to be the case. Otherwise we have not acted in good faith."[47] As a consequence, Rawls argues that the parties in the original position must select a conception of justice in accord with the following constraint: they must be able to "honor [the conception they agree to] under all relevant and foreseeable circumstances"[48] and will therefore refuse to "enter into agreements that may have consequences they cannot accept."[49] Given this constraint, Rawls argues that "the two principles of justice seem distinctly superior" to the principle of utility: "should a person gamble with his liberties and substantive interests hoping that the application of the principle of utility might secure him a greater well-being, he may have difficulty abiding by his undertaking. [If the gamble fails, h]e is bound to remind himself that he had the two principles of justice as an alternative."[50]

Although Rawls articulates a number of arguments in support of his two principles, the strains of commitment argument plays a central role. Indeed, if Brian Barry is correct, the strains of commitment argument is *essential* to Rawls's case against the average principle of utility.[51] The importance of that argument to his case for the two principles would lead one to expect the strains of commitment to play a commensurately central role in vindicating the liberal principle of legitimacy. Consequently, if we can show that the liberal principle of legitimacy would impose too great a strain on the parties in the original position, we would thereby have a powerful argument against that principle (and thus the duty of civility, and thus against the doctrine of restraint).[52] And it does seem plausible to suppose that the parties to the original position would reject that principle, as explained in the next section.

5.3.2 A Strains of Commitment Argument against Restraint

Although the parties to the original position lack any knowledge of their particular religious commitments, they know that many citizens in the society governed by the agreement they reach in the original position will be theists. They will therefore be aware that *they* might be theists. So they have to determine whether the liberal principle of legitimacy is *acceptable* to theists. In particular, they have to determine whether they can, if they turn out to be theists, commit in good faith to abide by the liberal principle of legitimacy in "relevant and foreseeable" circumstances. And in order to make that determination, they will have to apprise themselves of at least two things. First, they must determine what the liberal principle might require of them under foreseeable circumstances. Second, with that determination in mind and armed with a general knowledge of human psychology, they must decide whether theists will be able to abide by those requirements.

The first determination is fairly easy. According to the liberal principle, if a citizen is unable to explain to his compatriots "how the principles and policies" he advocates and votes for "can be supported by the political values of public reason," he ought to withhold his support from those principles and policies. Since Rawls is clear that the values a citizen adheres to solely on the basis of his theistic convictions don't count as components of public reason,[53] it's possible that he'll find himself circumstanced in the following way: he genuinely and sincerely believes that some policy is mandated by his religious convictions, but he can't provide a public justification for that policy. In such circumstances, the implications of the liberal principle of legitimacy are clear and unambiguous: he must withhold his support from that policy.

The second determination is more complicated. Will a theist be able to withhold his support from political commitments he takes to be mandated by God in cases when he lacks a public justification for those political commitments? It seems to me quite doubtful that he will: given a general knowledge of human psychology and an understanding of a common sort of theism, the parties in the original position should conclude that a theist can't abide by the liberal principle of legitimacy (and its associated duty of civility). In support of this claim, I'll briefly describe a common sort of theism, explain why citizens who adhere to that sort of theism will find the liberal principle intolerable, and thus vindicate the claim that the parties in the original position would reject the liberal principle of legitimacy.

First, it's absolutely critical not to be misled by a common misconception about religious commitment. As we've seen, some of the social dynamics internal to any modern liberal democracy "encourage" citizens to transform their religious commitments into privatized preferences or lifestyle choices. When citizens regard their religious commitments as preferences on the order of a desire for a particular flavor of ice cream, it seems not just unreasonable but perverse for them to insist on supporting their favored coercive laws on the basis of their religious commitments. But many theists regard the transformation of religious commitment into personal preference as an abdication of their religious commitments: they take their religious commitments to involve *obligations* to which they are subject irrespective of their feelings, desires, or thoughts *about* those obligations.

Second, many theists will regard their obligation to obey God as far and away their most important obligation, such that in case of conflict between that obligation and some other (to race, family, state, ethnic group) they must opt in favor of obedience to God. That is, they'll regard their obligation to obey God as *overriding*. The challenge by Martin Luther King, Jr., to American Christians to oppose racial segregation aptly expresses the priority many theists accord to their obligation to obey God.

> You have a dual citizenry. You live both in time and eternity. Your highest loyalty is to God, and not to the mores or the folkways, the state or the nation, or any man-made institution. If any earthly institution or custom conflicts with God's will, it is your Christian duty to oppose it. You must never allow the transitory, evanescent demands of man-made institutions to take precedence over the eternal demands of the mighty God.[54]

Distinct from the overriding obligation to obey God held by many theists, many will also regard their obligation to obey God as *totalizing*: that is, they will take the scope of their obligation to obey God to extend to whatever they do, wherever they are, and in whatever institutional setting they find themselves. A fortiori, they'll take their obligation to obey God to extend into the political realm. Nicholas Wolterstorff is particularly eloquent on this point:

> It belongs to the *religious convictions* of a good many religious people in our society that *they ought to base* their decisions concerning fundamental issues of justice *on* their religious convictions. They do not view it as an option whether or not to do so. It is their conviction that they ought to strive for wholeness, integrity, integration, in their lives: that they ought to allow the Word of God, the teachings of the Torah, the command and example of Jesus, or whatever, to shape their existence as a whole, including, then, their social and political existence. Their religion is not, for them, about *something other* than their social and political existence; it is *also* about their social and political existence.[55]

To this we might add that many theists who take their obligation to obey God into the political realm will regard *that* obligation as overriding: they will resist dividing their lives into a private realm governed by a set of overriding obligations to God and a public realm in which they accord their divinely imposed obligations some lesser weight.

Finally, as the reader will recall, a citizen's moral identity is constituted by his commitment to certain intrinsic goods and by his avoidance
of certain intrinsic evils.[56] Given the content of the sort of theistic
commitment under consideration, a citizen's theistic commitments will
likely constitute an essential component of his moral identity. And since
a citizen's moral identity contributes in crucial respects to what gives
his life meaning, it's clear that the theist's pursuit of his totalizing and
overriding obligation to obey God will be essential to his living a meaningful life. Consequently, a theist's pursuit of the social and political
implications of his religious commitments will be essential to his living
a meaningful life. Michael Perry expresses the relation between moral
identity, religious commitment, and political participation with admirable clarity:

> One's basic moral/religious convictions are (partly) self-constitutive and
> are therefore a principal ground – indeed, the principal ground – of polit-
> ical deliberation and choice. To "bracket" such convictions is therefore to
> bracket – to annihilate – essential aspects of one's very self. To participate
> in politics and law – in particular to make law, to break law, or to interpret
> law – with such convictions bracketed is not to participate as the self one
> is but as some one – or rather some thing – else.[57]

A common sort of theism, then, involves what the theist takes to be
an overriding and totalizing obligation to obey God, pursuit of which is
essential to the theist's living a meaningful life. The question is, given
that the parties in the original position might turn out to be theists,
and given that they might take themselves to have an overriding and
totalizing obligation to obey God, can they commit themselves in good
faith to the liberal principle of legitimacy? Whether they will depends
in crucial part on the alternatives. Fortunately, there is one alternative
to the liberal principle of legitimacy ready at hand: the ideal of conscientious engagement. So, when the parties in the original position
consider the liberal principle of legitimacy and the ideal of conscientious engagement in light of the fact that they might turn out to be
theists, which constraint would they choose?

It seems to me that they will choose the ideal of conscientious engagement for two reasons.[58] First, abiding by the liberal principle might
require the theist to disobey obligations he takes to be imposed on him
by God. But a theist will regard as anathema his failure to act in accord with what he takes to be God's mandates. Given their knowledge

of the general facts of psychology, the parties in the original position will know that people will find extremely burdensome any constraint that requires them to violate their most important normative commitments. Hence, the parties in the original position will know that theists will find the liberal principle of legitimacy extremely burdensome. Consequently, given that they might be theists, the parties in the original position will avoid choosing the liberal principle if there is a more acceptable alternative. And there is a more acceptable alternative: the ideal of conscientious engagement imposes no such requirement on the theist.

Second, the parties in the original position will realize that the theist's pursuit of obedience to God is essential to his moral identity; they will be aware of the general psychological fact that acting in accord with the commitments constitutive of a person's moral identity is essential to his living a meaningful life, and thus they will know that the theist's pursuit of obedience to God is essential to his living a meaningful life. Since abiding by the liberal principle of legitimacy may very well commit the theist to refrain from pursuing the commitments constitutive of his moral identity, and thus inhibit him from living what he takes to be a meaningful life, and since the parties in the original position will also know the general psychological fact that living a meaningful life is a crucially important desideratum for the vast majority of people, they will avoid committing themselves to the liberal principle if there is a better alternative. And there is a better alternative: the ideal of conscientious engagement permits a citizen to support coercive laws he conscientiously takes to be mandated by God, even if he lacks a public justification for those laws.

We can combine these two points in the following way. If the parties in the original position choose the liberal principle of legitimacy, they take a gamble of considerable magnitude: committing to the liberal principle might require them to violate their deepest and most important commitments. They have every reason to avoid taking that gamble, particularly since there is a more attractive alternative: the ideal of conscientious engagement. In fact, the parties in the original position seem to be in much the same position with respect to the liberal principle of legitimacy as they are, on Rawls's accounting, with respect to the principle of utility. Just as the person who gambles that the principle of utility will leave him better off than Rawls's two principles and who loses that gamble "may have difficulty abiding by his undertaking" and "is bound to remind himself that he had the two principles as an alternative," the person who gambles that the liberal principle of legitimacy will not require him to violate his overriding commitment to God and who loses that gamble "may have difficulty abiding by his undertaking" and "is bound to remind himself that he had [the ideal of conscientious engagement] as an alternative."[59]

It seems reasonably clear that if we attempt to vindicate the liberal principle of legitimacy by determining whether parties in the original position would accept that principle, and if the parties in the original position have to take seriously the possibility that they might turn out to be theists, then the parties in the original position will reject the liberal principle of legitimacy and choose the ideal of conscientious engagement instead. If this conclusion stands, it has important implications for the issue at hand. The device of the original position and its associated machinery provide an intuitively powerful test of the fairness of different political principles. If the liberal principle of legitimacy, and therefore the duty of civility and doctrine of restraint, fail to pass muster before that test, then we have powerful reason to reject that principle. And it seems that the liberal principle of legitimacy is unfair even on the justificatory liberal's terms – or at least, on the terms articulated by a very prominent and widely regarded version of justificatory liberalism.

5.3.3 Can Theists Be Reasonable?

All is not lost, however, for the liberal principle of legitimacy. There is in fact an easy response to my use of the strains of commitment argument against the liberal principle, that is, to show that the parties in the original position need not take seriously the possibility that they might turn out to be theists. This seems to be Rawls's working assumption: as Robert Paul Wolff has suggested, it's "obvious that the parties in the original position are rational, secular, scientific men and women."[60] But what principled reason do we have to think that the parties in the original position are rational, secular, and scientific and thus don't have to take seriously the prospect that they might turn out to be theists?

It might seem that my characterization of what I've called a common sort of theism is in fact a characterization of a disagreeable and intransigent kind of theism: I've confused theism with *fundamentalism*. After all, "some members of certain fundamentalist sects . . . ascribe overriding weight to the belief that God's will should dominate human political relations."[61] Fundamentalists are, as everyone knows, unreasonable, in that they are unwilling "to submit matters of justice to consideration in terms that are reasonable to other reasonable people."[62] And the parties in the original position don't need to take seriously the stresses imposed by the liberal principle of legitimacy on unreasonable people any more than they need to take seriously the stresses imposed on thoroughly irrational or insane people.[63]

This kind of response, which is common enough, strikes me as problematic on at least two counts. First, the claim that a theist has an overriding and totalizing obligation to obey God is hardly the personal property of "certain fundamentalist sects": it is an ecumenical claim, endorsed by theologically liberal Catholics, Orthodox Jews, politically liberal evangelicals, Eastern Orthodox Christians, and adherents to almost any other theistic perspective. Although there will no doubt be very great differences between a liberal Catholic, a fundamentalist Muslim, and an evangelical Protestant regarding the *content* of the theist's putative obligation to obey God, the epistemic *sources* they employ to identify what God requires of them, and the *language* they use to describe their obligation to obey God, one thing they are *unlikely* to disagree about is the overridingness of their obligation to obey God. Moreover, the vast majority of Americans are theists and given the ecumenical nature of my characterization of theism, it's likely that very many, perhaps most, citizens in the United States understand their commitment to obey God in roughly the way I have described.[64] Given the pervasiveness of the commitment to theism as I've described it, it strikes me as disastrous for the justificatory liberal to portray the theist as "unreasonable": that move would require him to dismiss from consideration in the original position many, perhaps most, of the citizens who actually inhabit the United States. But that is just the sort of consequence Rawls, at least in his recent work, wants to avoid.

Second, there is no good reason to deny that theists *are* reasonable, at least as that term is understood by Rawls, that is, as denoting a willingness to propose and abide by fair terms of social cooperation. Their conviction that they have an overriding and totalizing obligation to obey God is in no wise inconsistent with a willingness to propose and abide by political principles acceptable to all similarly motivated citizens. In fact, the theist may very well propose the ideal of conscientious engagement and be willing to abide by it with the hope that it will be acceptable to other citizens of goodwill. But the theist will certainly not agree to political principles that oblige him to violate his deepest convictions or that impede him from living a meaningful life. No one is willing to do that, and so the theist shouldn't be expected to either. Indeed, to stigmatize the theist for refusing to violate his deepest convictions strikes me as a particularly egregious instance of unreasonableness.

5.4 CONCLUDING COMMENTS

I mentioned earlier that the distinction between pursuing public justification and exercising restraint is critical to my argument. The prior discussion bears that judgment out. The justificatory liberal's valorization of public justification is most plausible, even platitudinous, when he advocates pursuing public justification: who really disagrees, for example, with the claim that "it is worth striving for" a "reasonable consensus and trust among those who might be otherwise . . . deeply opposed."[65] Who would object to trying to resolve political disagreements by focusing "on values such as peace and freedom that can be shared by reasonable people?"[66] If such constraints on political decision making and advocacy exhausted the justificatory liberal's arsenal, then there would be precious little to disagree with.[67] All would be sweetness and light. But of course, the justificatory liberal wants to press for much more than such platitudes: he also wants to make a claim about what a citizen should do when he has made the necessary effort to support some favored coercive law on the basis of appeals to "peace and freedom" but that effort fails: if, at the end of the day, he enjoys only a religious rationale for that coercive law, then, according to the justificatory liberal, he should withhold his support from that coercive law. It's that latter claim that is highly contentious, that many religious citizens find quite burdensome, and for which they'll require some compelling rationale. And as I see the matter, the justificatory liberal hasn't provided that compelling rationale. Although each citizen ought to adhere to the various constraints constitutive of the ideal of conscientious agreement, and in particular the principle of pursuit, I know of no compelling argument in support of the claim that he ought also adhere to the doctrine of restraint. In that light, it's plausible to suppose that imposing the doctrine of restraint on religious citizens is itself a violation of the norm of respect: given the lack of anything like an adequate justification for the doctrine of restraint, and given that the doctrine of restraint would require of many theists an extremely burdensome willingness to violate their most fundamental commitments, advocacy of the doctrine of restraint might very well constitute the kind of browbeating associated in some of the literature with those who refuse to exercise restraint.

CHAPTER 6

RELIGION, WAR, AND DIVISION

6.0 INTRODUCTION

The argument from respect has a decidedly deontological tone: although the justificatory liberal expects obedience to the doctrine of restraint to have all manner of salutary effects – facilitating harmonious relations among diversely committed citizens, for example – the argument from respect doesn't depend for its soundness on any such claim about consequences. Given the demise of the argument from respect, then, perhaps a *consequentialist* rationale for the doctrine of restraint has a better chance of carrying the day. More particularly, perhaps the justificatory liberal would do well to articulate a consequentialist argument in support of the claim that citizens should exercise restraint with respect to their religious commitments.

In fact, some justificatory liberals take just that tack. An important argument for the doctrine of restraint, as Rorty puts it, is "historical, not philosophical."[1] Rather than adverting to abstract analyses of what respect requires, the justificatory liberal appeals to certain salient facts from the history of religion. History teaches us that when religion intrudes upon politics all manner of calamities ensue: the Crusades, the Wars of the Schmalkaldic League, the French Civil Wars – most particularly the St. Bartholomew's Day Massacre, the Swedish Civil War, the Thirty Years' War, the English Civil War, the Inquisition, the Conquest of the Aztecs and Incas, the Salem Witch Trials, the Bosnia conflict, perhaps even the Second World War.[2] Appeal to the consequences of admixing religion and politics putatively succeeds where the argument from respect fails: because the intrusion of religion into politics has had such baleful consequences in other times and in other places, we ought to quarantine religion from politics in the contemporary United States. In short, the lesson *history* has to teach us about the *consequences* of commingling religion and politics is that religious citizens ought to *privatize* religion. (Note that, for the duration of this chapter, I'll assume that justificatory liberals are committed to establishing the claim that citizens should privatize their religious commitments, that is, adhere to the exclusive, rather than just the inclusive, version of the doctrine of restraint.[3] In order to mark this transition, I'll dispense in this chapter with the language of restraint and employ only the language of privatization.)

My intention in this chapter is to articulate and criticize two versions of this historical-consequentialist argument for privatizing religion. Both versions depend crucially on claims about what happens when large numbers of citizens refuse to privatize religion but differ as to what we can expect to happen in that case. The first argument, which I'll call the *argument from Bosnia*, predicts quite dire consequences.[4] According to that argument, religion ought to be relegated to the private realm in order to inhibit religious disagreement from escalating into *religious strife, religious persecution,* and *even religious warfare.* The second argument, which I'll call the *argument from divisiveness*, predicts considerably less dire consequences. According to that argument, religion ought to be relegated to the private realm in order to avoid *disruption* and *disharmony* among citizens. I conclude that neither argument vindicates the privatization claim.

6.1 THE ARGUMENT FROM BOSNIA

Justificatory liberals often begin their case for the privatization of religion with a historical preamble: a narrative relating the conditions under which liberal democracies first arose. Most particularly, they remind us – a salutary reminder – that the liberal commitment to freedom of religion was formulated and defended in direct reaction to an extreme and appalling series of events: a century and a half of wars fought to "resolve" religious disagreements (the French Civil Wars, the Thirty Years' War, the English Civil War, and others). That preamble colors the ensuing discussion: the impression left on the reader is that the privatization of religion serves as a prophylactic for religious conflict, and that those who refuse to privatize their religious convictions undermine a crucially important bulwark protecting us from clerical tyranny, confessional authoritarianism, and religious persecution. In short, the message – sometimes explicitly stated, more often subtly implied – is that those who reject the privatization claim exhibit a "disdain for the lessons of history," of which a central lesson is that a widespread refusal to privatize religion might result in religious conflict.[5]

Anyone even passingly familiar with the relevant literature will have run across some variation on this theme. Mary Ann Glendon might very well be correct that "the most commonly *stated* reasons for drawing a *cordon sanitaire* around legal political discourse ... are ... that religion has often been a source of civil strife, and that particularistic religious groups are often intolerant and 'illiberal.'"[6] Here are some representative (and easily multiplied) examples.

> The central task of liberalism is to guard against the irresolvable political differences generated by diverging religious views. Now I know one should never claim anything is the central task of anything, especially liberalism, but we do seek a political world that would avoid such things as the Thirty Years' War in Europe, the Bosnia conflict, and other disastrous and intractable occasions of violent group collision. I worry that by inviting religion into the public square we risk just such battles, and battles in which force is the only likely result if religious language permeates public debate. (Martha Minow)[7]

> Religion has its dark side. This dark side, moreover, has the potential to be a powerfully destructive political force. It may, for example, harm the process of political decision-making. A believer who sees those who oppose or question her beliefs as aligned with the "powers of chaos" is likely to treat the public square as a battleground rather than as a forum for debate. Religion, if unleashed as a political force, may also lead to a particularly acrimonious divisiveness among different religions. Those religions that are accused of representing the powers of chaos are likely to react with similar vehemence in denouncing their attackers. Finally, and most problematically, religion's participation in the political process can produce dangerous results: Fervent beliefs fueled by suppressed fear are easily transformed into movements of intolerance, repression, hate, and persecution. There are, in short, substantial reasons for exercising caution with respect to religious involvement in the public square. (William Marshall)[8]

> When a religious person chooses, or chooses to remain in, a particular group, she makes an implicit statement about that group's relationship

with ultimate reality. At a rational level, it necessarily claims a special status for the individual believer and her fellow congregants. On this assessment, when one couples this unavoidable consequence of choice with a natural penchant for absolutizing, arrogance and its twin, authoritarianism, become built in, if latent, components of religious belief and commitment, if not faith. It is a short step from latency to an outright claim of superiority to an assertion of hegemony. (It is worth recalling that the Nazis did claim to have God on their side.) (Theodore Blumoff)[9]

And if religious considerations are not appropriately balanced with secular ones in matters of coercion, there is a special problem: a clash of Gods vying for social control. Such uncompromising absolutes easily lead to destruction and death. (Robert Audi)[10]

Just as the affirmative right to practice a specific religion implies the negative right to practice none, so the negative bar against establishment of religion implies the affirmative "establishment" of a civil order for the resolution of public moral disputes. Agreement on such a secular mechanism was the price of ending the war of all sects against all. Establishment of a public civil order was the social contract produced by religious truce. Religious teachings as expressed in public debate may influence the civil public order but public moral disputes may be resolved only on grounds articulable in secular terms. Religious grounds for resolving public moral disputes would rekindle inter-denominational strife that the Establishment Clause extinguished. (Kathleen Sullivan)[11]

A possible result of explicitly religious political competition might be the undermining of religious toleration, which in turn might engender further religious divisiveness. How far might political stability be undermined? It might be contended that the risk of major instability generated by religious conflict is minimal. Conditions in modern democracies may be so far from the conditions that gave rise to the religious wars of the sixteenth century that we no longer need worry about religious divisiveness as a source of substantial conflict. But I think that we cannot be confident about these optimistic possibilities. A survey of world history and contemporary experience reveals that seemingly unshakable stability can rapidly degenerate into strife and even chaos. (Lawrence Solum)[12]

The theme rung by each of these passages is quite clear: there is a *dark side* to religion. That dark side is exceedingly *dangerous*. Religion is particularly dangerous when allowed *political power*: give religious believers unconstrained access to the power of the state and their authoritarian proclivities will surely out – they will grasp for "hegemony" in Nazified fashion, "collide violently" with other religious groups, institute a reign of "intolerance, repression, hate, and persecution," precipitate a "war of all sects against all," initiate "strife and even chaos," "destruction and death." As a consequence, so the argument goes, we need to impose constraints on religious citizens so as to inhibit them from employing state power for religious ends. In particular, by encoding into the social role of citizen informal, moral constraints that prohibit citizens from employing their religious convictions to direct state coercion, we forestall religious believers from imposing their favored orthodoxy on an unwilling population and thus inhibit religion from playing its customary role in causing confessional warfare and generating religious strife.

The gist of the foregoing is fairly straightforward: certain states of affair are morally abhorrent; certain courses of action might result in those states of affair; consequently, we ought not pursue those courses of action. A bit more formally:

(1) It is always and everywhere immoral to engage in conflict over religious matters.
(2) The refusal of large numbers of citizens to privatize their religious convictions might result in conflict over those religious convictions.
(3) Hence, religious citizens morally ought to privatize their religious convictions.[13]

Three initial points about this argument. First a note about its conclusion: as I've indicated, I take it that the argument from Bosnia most naturally articulates with the *exclusive* version of the doctrine of restraint. The combination of politics and religion is so toxic that the two must be *completely* segregated. And the toxicity of that combination is by no means neutralized by its accompaniment with public justification, much less the mere pursuit of public justification. (If anything, correlation of public justification with religious argumentation provides ample opportunity for rationalization, self-deception, and subterfuge.) So the argument from Bosnia has as a conclusion that religious citizens ought not support their favored coercive laws on religious grounds *even if* they also enjoy a public justification for those laws.[14]

Second, (1) contains an implicit claim that conflict over religious matters is so morally repugnant as to outweigh any morally desirable consequences (if any) that might ensue from religious conflict. Too briefly, the claim is that, even if some conflicts are morally justified (the Second World War, for example), those conflicts pursued solely or predominantly for religious purposes are never morally justified. I endorse that evaluation. We don't need to engage in an elaborate consequentialist calculation; I grant from the outset that the morally negative consequences of religious conflict far outweigh the morally positive consequences (if any).

Third, granted that religious war is immoral, the crucial premise of the argument from Bosnia must be (2). But how should we understand the modal term embedded in (2)? We can't understand (2) as claiming merely that there is a *logical possibility* that a widespread refusal to privatize religion will generate religious strife. There are, no doubt, possible worlds in which some regard "public" religion as so absolutely intolerable that a widespread refusal to privatize would touch off a bloodbath. But simply because such a scenario is logically possible has little bearing on whether a citizen in the contemporary United States ought to privatize her religious convictions: she can't determine how she ought to act in the actual world by avoiding actions that eventuate in dire consequences in some distant possible world. The advocate of privatization is well advised to avoid the other extreme, however: it's clearly not the case that a widespread refusal to privatize religion would *necessarily* result in religious conflict, whether the sort of necessity involved is of the logical, metaphysical, or causal sort. Neither is it plausible to suppose that a widespread refusal to privatize religion is *likely* to generate religious conflict – I judge that that claim is too strong as well.

Fortunately, there is a more attractive candidate: the justificatory liberal should, in my estimation, claim that a widespread rejection of privatization has a *realistic prospect* of generating religious conflict in the contemporary United States. If we imagine a continuum that stretches from logical possibility through various shades of probability to necessity, the realistic prospect node of the continuum lies somewhere between logical possibility and likelihood. This (2) is best understood – or, more cautiously, I shall understand (2) – as the claim that a widespread refusal to privatize religion has a realistic prospect of eventuating in religious conflict in the contemporary United States, even if that result is not terribly likely. (This is more than a little vague, I realize, but sufficient for our purposes.)

6.2 CRITICISM OF THE ARGUMENT FROM BOSNIA

So much for explication of the argument from Bosnia. What of evaluation? In particular, what should we make of (2)? If large numbers of citizens refuse to privatize their religious commitments, do we face a realistic prospect of "strife and even chaos,"[15] death and destruction?"[16] Is it reasonable to "worry that by inviting religion into the public square we risk just such battles [as the Thirty Years' War and the Bosnia conflict]?"[17]

Well, what must the justificatory liberal do in order to vindicate (2)? That question is more complicated than it might seem at first blush. Indeed, it seems to me that the justificatory liberal must discharge at least two argumentative burdens.

(A) Let me make one point at the outset. I certainly don't deny that there have been times in the past (say, late sixteenth-century France or mid-seventeenth-century England) when the widespread refusal to privatize religion was so explosive that citizens of good conscience should have been willing to abide by "gag rules" regarding their religious commitments.[18] And perhaps there are now some societies in which the intrusion of religion into the political sphere is so inflammatory as to have a realistic prospect of generating religious persecution, strife, and even warfare (say, Bosnia or Palestine). For citizens in those societies, the argument from Bosnia would be compelling: in their context, privatization is essential to securing the political good of peaceful coexistence and avoiding the political evil of violent conflict for religious aims. None of this, however, is to the point.

What we need to know is whether the dreary record of religious interventions into the political provides us with the basis for an application to our present circumstances: the justificatory liberal must show that, given that religious involvement in politics has resulted in religious strife *then* (e.g., the Thirty Years' War) and *there* (e.g., Bosnia), we have reason to be concerned that religious involvement in politics has a realistic prospect of generating comparable consequences in the *here and now* (the contemporary United States). After all, even if religion played a role in generating the Thirty Years' War or the Bosnia conflict, those facts provide citizens in the United States with *no* reason to privatize *unless* religion has a realistic prospect of playing a similar role *in the United States today*. And to determine if this is the case, we must determine *under what conditions* it is feasible for religion to play a role in generating conflict in the contemporary United States: what is it about the United States that renders religious conflict a realistic prospect here and now?

(B) In addition to showing that conditions as they exist in the United States are amenable to religiously generated conflict, the justificatory liberal must show that, given those conditions, a widespread refusal to *privatize religion* has a realistic prospect of initiating conflict. We are, after all, interested in the argument from Bosnia only insofar as it provides support for the claim that religion should be privatized; as a consequence, only if a widespread refusal to privatize religion has a realistic prospect of generating conflict in the contemporary United States do citizens in the here and now have reason to privatize religion. By contrast, even if religion does have a realistic prospect of generating conflict in the United States, so long as we have no reason to believe that a widespread refusal to privatize religion holds out that prospect, then citizens in the United States have no reason to privatize their religious convictions.

So, are conditions in the United States ripe for religious warfare? And if they are, is there a realistic prospect that a widespread refusal to privatize religion can bring that potential to fruition? I doubt that the justificatory liberal can discharge either of the burdens she must in order to vindicate (2).

Ad (A): To discharge her first argumentative burden, it seems to me that the justificatory liberal must articulate some general account as to the role or roles religion plays in generating conflict. Appeal to some such general account seems necessary to bridge the gap between the "then and there" and the "here and now," as it would provide the requisite basis for inferring from other cases in which religion plays a role in generating conflict to our own case. With that account in hand, we'll be able to determine whether current conditions in the United States allow religion to play that role. But without some such account, claims to the effect that religion causes war and that refusing to privatize religion risks interdenominational conflict count as mere hand-waving.[19]

Pretty obviously, providing the requisite account is going to be a monumental task. In order to articulate a general account of the causal role(s) religion plays in generating conflict, the justificatory liberal must identify a range of such cases from which to generalize. That in turn requires the justificatory liberal to produce a bevy of historical and sociological evidence. But, to put the matter bluntly, no justificatory liberal has presented anything like the kind of empirical argument needed to make the required case.[20] At least, I'm unaware of any sustained attempt to make that case. And that means we find ourselves somewhat at an impasse: without some reasonably accurate understanding of the conditions in which the admixing of religion and politics generates civil conflict, we cannot reasonably reach any definitive evaluation of (2).

I don't feel comfortable leaving matters at this impasse. In spite of a serious empirical deficit, given my own lack of mastery of the historical and sociological materials relevant to the issue at hand, I feel the need to address the central concerns raised by the argument from Bosnia more directly than making the debater's point that its advocates have yet to make their case, particularly since that argument draws on convictions regarding religion and conflict that have considerable play in popular culture. As a consequence, I have little choice but to meet speculation with speculation. I'll suggest what I take to be a plausible generalization regarding the conditions in which religion has played a role in generating civil strife and use that generalization as a basis for evaluating the claim that there is a realistic prospect that a widespread refusal to privatize religion will generate conflict in the contemporary United States. I want to emphasize, however, the speculative nature of what follows: I suggest the following *in lieu of* the necessary empirical analysis and submit it to the evaluation of those better able to judge the issue.

First, then, a suggestion as to the causal role religion plays in generating conflict (when it does play a role): I suggest that this occurs when some agency – I focus exclusively on the state, although that is a significant simplification – employs coercion to compel citizens to worship in accord with a religious creed they reject, punishes citizens for heterodox religious practices – in short, when the state employs coercion to achieve religious ends. *That* use of the state's coercive power naturally results in resistance: coerced religious communities might very well defend themselves – by force of arms if necessary.[21] Locke seems to have accepted a roughly similar view of the relation between religion and the "bustles" and "wars" afflicting the Europe of his day. He writes, for example, that "it is not the diversity of Opinions (which cannot be avoided) but the refusal of Toleration to those that are of different Opinions (which might have been granted) that has produced all the Bustles and Wars, that have been in the Christian World, upon account of Religion."[22] According to Locke, it is the forcible compulsion to assent to orthodoxy, the use of coercion to achieve religious uniformity, that causes religious war. Again,

> No body, therefore, in fine, neither single Persons, nor Churches, nay, nor even Commonwealths, have any just Title to invade the Civil Rights and Worldly Goods of each other, upon pretence of Religion. Those that are of another Opinion, would do well to consider with themselves how pernicious a Seed of Discord and War, how powerful a provocation to endless Hatreds, Rapines, and Slaughters, they thereby furnish unto Mankind. No Peace and Security, no not so much as Common Friendship, can ever be established, so long as this Opinion prevails, That *Dominion is founded in Grace*, and that Religion is to be propagated by force of Arms.[23]

So here's my working hypothesis: insofar as religion plays a role in generating strife and conflict, it does so when the state employs its coercive apparatus in order to secure such religious aims as conversion, suppression of dissent from the reigning orthodoxy, participation in religious rituals, and so on.

Assuming this hypothesis about the causal role religion has typically played in generating conflict, note a second point: liberals have already taken measures to inhibit religion from playing that role again. Liberals learned a crucially important lesson from the many decades of warfare that afflicted and exhausted early modern Europe: they learned that the state must leave whatever religious convictions a citizen accepts and whatever religious practices he pursues entirely "to the Conscience of every particular man."[24] The lesson liberals should learn, and did learn, from the wars of religion was that the state ought to accord each citizen a right to worship as he sees fit without being subject to punishment for the way he exercises that right.

It seems that the measures liberals have taken to inhibit religious disagreement from escalating into civil strife are sufficient to the task: *so long as* religious freedom is adequately protected, religious disagreements don't escalate into conflict for religious ends. I know of no case in which a regime that successfully protects religious freedom is also plagued by religiously generated destruction, death, strife, or chaos.[25] So the proper prophylactic for religiously generated strife is a legal and constitutional one: effective protection of religious freedom.[26] Thus, John Noonan: "That religion has caused many acts of violence and perpetuated many hatreds is a datum of history. . . . For the evils, at least for most of the evils that religion brings, a sovereign remedy exists – free exercise!"[27]

The implications of this second point for (2) are direct. If, to simplify, religion generates conflict only when the state attempts coercively to impose some religious orthodoxy, and if the state coercively imposes religious orthodoxy only if it violates religious freedom, then religion can generate conflict in the United States only if our government, somehow or other, commits itself to violating the religious freedom of its citizens. In short, if the justificatory liberal is to show that there is a realistic prospect of religious warfare in the United States, then she must show that there is a realistic prospect that the United States' long-standing commitment to freedom of religion stands in danger of dissipation. She must construct a plausible scenario in which the United States' commitment to freedom of religion lacks widespread support from its citizenry. Of course, it is easy to show that it is *possible* that citizens will flag in their commitment to freedom of religion. But that's not the question. The justificatory liberal must articulate a plausible story that takes us from our current state to some condition in which large numbers of citizens are intent on employing state power to compel others to adhere to some religious creed or participate in some religious practice. Can the advocate of the argument from Bosnia identify some "social subject" that has a realistic prospect of taking us from here to there?

I see no reason to think so. First, citizens in the United States are firmly committed to religious freedom and indicate no inclination to renege on that commitment. As Michael Perry says, "The proposition that neither the national government nor state government constitutionally may establish religion [or] prohibit the free exercise thereof . . . has come to be a virtual axiom of American political-moral culture. The proposition is so deeply embedded in the American way of life that, as a practical matter, it is irreversible."[28] Second, religious citizens in the United States have a vested interest in continuing to affirm the right of their compatriots to worship freely. I have discussed one such reason in 2.0: freedom of religion benefits religious citizens by fostering a pluralistic environment that provides religious groups with a variety of outgroups against which they can define their respective collective identities and in so doing define the moral commitments that sustain the respective moral identities of their members. There are, of course, any number of additional respects in which religious citizens have a vested interest in freedom of religion. Religious citizens – even those who refuse to privatize – benefit from a political order that secures freedom of religion as they are thereby protected from persecution for *their* religious commitments and practices. The pluralistic social milieu fostered in a political order that effectively protects freedom of religion encourages competition between religious entrepreneurs (so long as the state does not interfere with the "religious market" by *establishing* any particular religious tradition), thus stimulating innovation, which improves the religious product offered, which in turn translates into vibrant and vivified religion.[29] For these reasons, and for a variety of others, religious citizens have a vested interest in according their compatriots freedom of religion.

In light of those facts, the argument from Bosnia seems *dystopian*. It recommends that we take seriously in our practical deliberations a possibility that has no realistic prospect of actualization under current or foreseeable conditions. That is, it counsels religious citizens to privatize their religious commitments because the alternative risks societal dysfunctions that have only the *remotest* prospect of occurring. Although it is no doubt logically possible that a widespread refusal to privatize will result in religious warfare, conditions in a contemporary liberal democracy such as the United States render that possibility too remote to vindicate the privatization claim. Why is the prospect of religious warfare so remote? What is it about the early twenty-first-century United States that allows us to safely dismiss the prospect that we will be engulfed by a religiously generated war like that which afflicted, say, mid-seventeenth-century England? What's changed in the meantime? Simply put, we now have in place measures that effectively insulate us from religious warfare – the constitutional and legal protection of religious freedom.

Ad (B): Not only must the justificatory liberal show that conditions in the United States hold out a realistic prospect of religious conflict, but she must also show that it's a refusal to privatize religion on the part of the citizens of the United States that holds out that prospect.

After all, if the conclusion of the argument from Bosnia is that citizens ought to privatize their religious convictions, and if, according to that argument, citizens ought to privatize their religious convictions to avoid religious conflict, then we need some reason to believe that, somehow or other, a widespread refusal to privatize religion poses a danger of religious conflict. But given the argument up to this point, a state that protects each citizen's right to religious freedom does all that is necessary to inhibit religious disagreement from escalating into religious strife. If that argument is plausible, then the remaining move open to the justificatory liberal is to argue that a refusal to privatize religion, somehow or other, is inimical to a commitment to religious freedom.[30] But by what alchemy should we expect a widespread refusal to privatize religion to transmute into an antipathy to religious freedom?

I know of no plausible story. Three factors, in particular, provide reason for skepticism. First, my claim that a citizen need not privatize her religious convictions is just a part of a broader understanding of what responsible citizenship requires: even though a citizen needn't privatize her religious convictions, she does have an obligation to adhere to the ideal of conscientious engagement. That understanding of responsible citizenship ought to be evaluated as a whole. So in determining whether large numbers of citizens who refuse to privatize their religious commitments would also flag in their support for freedom of religion, the justificatory liberal must assume that those who refuse to privatize adhere to my understanding of responsible citizenship in toto. Most pertinently, she must show that citizens who assiduously and sincerely pursue rational justification for their favored political commitments and who are genuinely desirous of learning from their compatriots regarding the moral propriety of their favored political commitments have a realistic prospect of flagging in their commitment to religious freedom. But what reason is there to think that there is any such prospect? Given their experience of a regime that protects religious freedom, how many citizens in the United States who genuinely and sincerely attempt to evaluate in a rational manner the considerations for and against religious freedom will conclude that they ought not support religious freedom?

Second, since we can assume that the citizens who refuse to privatize religion nevertheless pursue rational justification for their favored political commitments, we can assume that most of them won't confuse the claim that they may refuse to privatize religion with the entirely distinct claim that they may reject the right to religious freedom. These two claims, the reader will recall, have to do with entirely distinct levels of discourse (3.1). The claim that each citizen ought to privatize her religious convictions imposes a constraint on the *reasons* a citizen may employ as a basis for her political commitments. The claim that each citizen has a right to religious freedom is a *substantive political commitment* for which a citizen might or might not take herself to have sufficient reason. Given that the privatization claim imposes a constraint on the reasons a citizen employs as a basis for her political commitments, but not on the political commitments she ought to support, it's entirely possible for a citizen to reject the privatization claim but to commit herself to religious freedom. In fact, it's possible – indeed likely for members of the dominant faith traditions in the United States – that citizens will commit to religious freedom *for* religious reasons. (Indeed, it's possible for a citizen to commit herself to religious freedom *solely* for religious reasons, thereby violating not just the exclusive version of the doctrine of restraint now under discussion, but also the weaker inclusive version.[31])

Third, not only is the claim that religion ought to be privatized distinct from the claim that each citizen has a right to freedom of worship; citizens who reject the privatization claim have special reason to commit themselves to religious freedom. Why? Freedom of religion provides a political framework in which religious citizens can "crusade" to transform the laws that govern the United States without thereby initiating the sort of religious strife that bedeviled the sixteenth and seventeenth centuries. Public affirmation of the right to worship freely, and, more important, zealous defense of the right to worship freely, exhibits a commitment to refrain from pursuing that (sometimes) religiously motivated practice that has proved so destructive in the past: the forcible imposition of orthodoxy. This commitment to religious freedom allows citizens who refuse to privatize their religious convictions to employ the moral resources of their respective religious traditions to mold and shape the laws that govern the United States free from the stigma that rightly attaches to those who would attempt to employ the power of the state to punish heretics or impose religious orthodoxy. Her commitment to religious freedom frees the citizen who refuses to privatize her religious convictions to engage in the democratic process on equal footing with her compatriots: by supporting her favored coercive policies on the basis of whatever grounds she rationally regards as most compelling.[32]

As I see it, then, the argument from Bosnia founders on the fact that there are crucially important differences between the conditions that obtain in a contemporary liberal democracy such as the United States and the conditions that obtained in the confessional states party to the wars of religion. In particular, the confessional states' denial of religious freedom gave to religion an incendiary potential it lacks when citizens are free from the threat of persecution for their religious commitments and practices. But liberal democracies such as the United States have implemented the required constitutional protections. Religious citizens in the United States have benefited directly from those protections. Religious believers, including those who refuse to privatize their religious convictions, have benefited from religious freedom. In the vast majority of cases, they enthusiastically endorse religious freedom. Affirmation of that right frees them to engage in religiously grounded advocacy, even advocacy based solely on religious grounds. There is, therefore, no reason to believe that religious citizens will somehow come to the conclusion that they should no longer support a constitutionally protected right to freedom of religion. And since that is what would need to happen for a widespread refusal to privatize religion to have a realistic prospect of generating religious conflict, there is no reason to believe that, under current conditions, a refusal to privatize religion has a realistic prospect of causing conflict. To gloss H. L. A. Hart, the argument from Bosnia "hover[s] in the air above the *terra firma* of contemporary social reality."[33]

6.3 THE ARGUMENT FROM DIVISIVENESS

The argument from Bosnia associates a widespread refusal to privatize religion with quite debilitating social and political dysfunctions: that argument succeeds only if a widespread refusal to privatize religion has a realistic prospect of embroiling us in conflicts on the order of the Crusades, the English Civil War, and others. The gravity of these consequences lends that argument its rhetorical punch: since such religious conflicts are morally abhorrent, the justificatory liberal can safely assume that, *if* a widespread refusal to privatize religion has a realistic prospect of generating civil conflict, that constitutes powerful, even conclusive, reason to privatize. But the source of the argument from Bosnia's rhetorical power is at the same time a crucial weakness: the possibility of religious conflict has no realistic prospect of actualization in the United States. These two points are, of course, closely related. Religious conflict has no realistic prospect of actualizing in the contemporary United States in part *because* religious conflict is so abhorrent: citizens – not least *religious* citizens – in liberal democracies have, thankfully, learned from the tragedies of the past and have taken measures to ensure that they don't occur again. The high level of differentiation that characterizes liberal regimes such as the contemporary United States curtails religious strife; more particularly, insofar as such regimes succeed in protecting each citizen's right to religious freedom, they inhibit the religious disagreement endemic to liberal democracies from escalating into religious conflict.

The defect I've pointed out with the argument from Bosnia suggests a natural modification: the justificatory liberal must identify prospective consequences of refusing to privatize religion that, although of lesser gravity than religious conflict, are nevertheless more likely to occur in a political framework that protects each citizen's right to religious freedom. The justificatory liberal can articulate a more plausible version of the historical-consequentialist argument for privatization by showing that a widespread refusal to privatize is likely – even in a highly differentiated society such as the United States – to generate social and political maladies that lack the severity of religious conflict, but are serious nonetheless. What sorts of maladies might those be? The following list is representative.

> When legislation is expressly based on religious arguments, the legislation takes on a religious character, to the frustration of those who don't share the relevant religious faith and who therefore lack access to the normative predicate behind the law. (Abner Greene)[34]

> Why isn't it all right to advocate political positions in terms of narrower religious convictions? After all, a public speech relying heavily on religious arguments might be expected to reach some coreligionists and others of like view. In a very religious but extremely tolerant society, public airing of particular religious views might work well, but in actuality such discourse promotes a sense of separation between the speaker and those who do not share his religious convictions and is likely to produce both religious and political divisiveness. If public argument is seen to turn on which interpretation of the Christian tradition is sounder, non-Christians may feel left out and resentful. (Kent Greenawalt)[35]

My own history as a Mid-Western non-Christian who has spent the past several years in the Baptist heart of Georgia suggests that it is not accidental that Perry and Greenawalt [both of whom, Blumoff claims, deny that religiously based arguments for political commitments are any more divisive than secular arguments] share a common Christian heritage. The indisputable fact is that neither has participated in public debate as one standing outside the predominant public religious experience; neither has felt the profoundly alienating ordeal of listening to a public debate in which the speakers simply assume that all members of the audience share Christo-centric beliefs. (Theodore Blumoff)[36]

Religious people often tend to be, in a way that is rare in secular matters, highly and stubbornly passionate about the importance of everyone's acting in accordance with religious reasons, and non-religious people often tend to be highly and stubbornly passionate about not being coerced to do so. If many who are religious are vehemently opposed to the sins of a multitude outside of their fold, many who are not religious are incensed at the thought of manipulation in the name of someone else's non-existent deity. (Robert Audi)[37]

The gist of these passages is clear: the practice of supporting coercive laws on religious grounds generates various undesirable consequences – frustration (Greene), separation, divisiveness, and resentment (Greenawalt), profound alienation (Blumoff), and extreme anger (Audi). These consequences are, of course, undesirable: we should aspire to a society in which none are excluded or alienated from the process by which we select the laws to which all of us are subject. Therefore, each citizen should privatize her religious convictions: in order to forestall alienation, frustration, anger, and resentment, each citizen ought to refrain from supporting her favored coercive laws on religious grounds.[38]

The basic intuition animating the argument under consideration should be clear. Consider, then, an initial, quite simplistic, version of the argument from divisiveness:

(1) A morally responsible citizen won't engage in divisive activity.
(2) A widespread refusal to privatize religion is divisive.
(3) Hence, a morally responsible citizen will privatize her religious convictions.[39]

Note that the *structure* of this argument is identical to that of the argument from Bosnia: both advocate privatization on the basis of the moral undesirability of the (putative) consequences of refusing to privatize. The central difference between the two arguments is, of course, a matter of *content*: each argument predicts different results from a widespread refusal to privatize. The argument from Bosnia predicts the most extreme consequences: religious conflict. The argument from divisiveness predicts considerably less dire, although by no means insignificant, consequences: alienation, frustration, exclusion – in short, divisiveness. Appreciating that central difference enables us to see why the argument from divisiveness significantly improves over the argument from Bosnia. The argument from divisiveness, as formulated, is quite plausible at exactly the point at which the argument from Bosnia is implausible: unlike the consequences predicted by the latter argument, those predicted by the former are all too familiar to us. As a matter of empirical fact, a fact that we can verify just by heeding the concerns expressed both in popular culture and in academic writing on the proper role of religion in politics, some citizens feel excluded, alienated, and frustrated when their compatriots support their favored laws on the basis of their religious commitments. (This fact should not be at all surprising to us, given that, as Christian Smith argues, religious communities have a vested interest in "symbolic conflict" with "outgroups," conflict that we can expect to be manifest in the public arena, and which undoubtedly generates division and alienation in members of outgroups.) Clearly, the sort of objection I pressed against the argument from Bosnia won't work against the consequentialist argument now under discussion. The bone of contention won't be (2) – whose correlate in the argument from Bosnia I provided reason to doubt – but (1).

And (1), stated thus baldly, is obviously false: it isn't the case that a responsible citizen will refrain from engaging in divisive activity. Far from it. In some cases, a citizen is morally permitted, and even morally obliged, to engage in divisive behavior. Examples abound. The system of racial segregation in the South was unjust. Many of those implicated in that system refused to dismantle racial segregation, in spite of its injustice. Many citizens responded by engaging in divisive activities. They drank water from fountains they were legally proscribed from using. They sat in bus seats that were reserved, by law, for their white compatriots. They picketed and boycotted department stores complicit in the system of racial segregation. Each of these activities was divisive, and some intentionally so.[40] But they were not thereby morally inappropriate. In fact, they were morally admirable actions, for which those who carried them out are rightly commended. It follows, then, that a responsible citizen sometimes engages in divisive activity. And if a responsible citizen sometimes engages in divisive activity, it might be the case that she'll rightly refuse to privatize her religious commitments, even though doing so is indisputably divisive.

This obvious point is by no means the end of the argument from divisiveness. It shows only that the advocate of privatization can't establish that a responsible citizen will privatize her religious commitments just because the alternative generates division. Although the prospects for a convincing historical-consequentialist case for privatization are greatly improved by altering the predicted consequences of refusing to privatize from religious conflict to division, matters are not so simple as showing merely that the appeal to religious convictions generates alienation, frustration, division, or resentment.

The argument from divisiveness is easily modified. The justificatory liberal might be able to capitalize on the fact that refusing to privatize religion is *very* controversial, at least in some quarters. Since some citizens take considerable umbrage at "public" religion, he might articulate the following (rather mechanical) alteration: in order to render the argument from divisiveness consistent with the obvious truth that a responsible citizen is permitted to engage in activities that generate *some* division, he might argue that citizens should avoid engaging in practices that generate *a great deal* of division.[41] Thus, he might argue as follows:

(1*) A morally responsible citizen won't engage in activity that generates a great deal of division.

(2*) A widespread refusal to privatize religion generates a great deal of division.

(3) Hence, a morally responsible citizen will privatize his religious convictions.

This version of the argument from divisiveness isn't much more convincing than its predecessor. The problem is not, as I see it, that the quantitative standard expressed in (1*) is too vague – we're used to vagueness in such matters. The problem is that the argument is vulnerable to a simple consistency response. I see no reason to believe that reliance on religious convictions in support of coercive laws necessarily, or even probably, generates more division than does reliance on secular considerations. For example, perhaps many moral-political issues are so controversial that the quantity of division associated with those issues is relatively unaffected by the sorts of reasons citizens employ to resolve them. Thus, Michael Perry writes:

> American history does not suggest that religious debates about controversial issues – racial discrimination, for example, or war – are invariably more divisive than secular debates about those or other issues. Some issues are so controversial that debate about them is inevitably divisive without regard to whether the debate is partly religious or, instead, only secular.[42]

If appealing to secular considerations generates just as much division as does appealing to religious convictions, then the argument under discussion falters. Since it advocates privatization just in virtue of the fact that supporting coercive laws on religious grounds generates a great deal of division, and since there is no reason to believe that such reliance on religious commitments is necessarily, or likely to be, any more divisive than reliance on secular considerations, the justificatory liberal can require the privatization of religious convictions but not secular considerations only on pain of arbitrariness.

This consistency objection shows that the formulation of the argument from divisiveness under discussion is unsound. But it does not show *why*, and thus provides us with little guidance as to how best to reformulate that argument. To determine how to modify the argument in such a way as to avoid this consistency objection, we need to identify much more precisely than I have the conditions in which it is morally inappropriate for a citizen to engage in divisive activity.

Recall, then, the sort of stylized moral lesson commonly employed in introductory discussions of moral theory. It's morally desirable that each of us refrain from knowingly and willingly causing pain to other people. Since punishing my child causes him pain, it would seem that there is at least a moral presumption against punishing my child. But the overall consequences of refraining from punishing my child are morally quite problematic – by refusing to punish my child at all, I inhibit him from obtaining great good that would otherwise be attainable to him, and I fail to deter him from causing considerable pain and suffering both to himself and others. When I survey my child's future life as likely to unfold with punishment and without punishment, I find that his life prospects are far better, morally speaking, with punishment than without. Stylized examples like this make the obvious point: the mere fact that a given activity has a certain set of morally undesirable consequences (such as generating pain in a child) doesn't thereby render that activity morally inappropriate. Rather, in order to determine whether punishing my child is morally appropriate, we must take into consideration *all* of the morally relevant factors associated with punishing my child and with refraining from punishing my child and then we must determine which of those alternatives is morally superior on balance.

The application of this point to the argument from divisiveness is straightforward. Given that refusing to privatize religion generates *some* division, even *considerable* division, it by no means follows that a responsible citizen ought to privatize his religious commitments. Although the justificatory liberal would have a much easier time making his case if he needed to show only that a widespread refusal to privatize religion generates a great deal of division, it's clear that his task is quite a bit more complicated than showing that.[43] Rather, he must show that what is *true* of the pain parents inflict on their children is *false* regarding the division generated by religious political advocacy, namely, that the division associated with religious political advocacy, *unlike* the pain associated with punishing children, is morally undesirable on balance. In particular, the justificatory liberal must show something like the following: if we take into consideration all of the morally relevant consequences of both privatizing and refusing to privatize religion, the United States is better off, morally speaking, when citizens privatize their religious commitments than when they refuse to do so.

Return now to the arbitrariness objection I just noted. Even if appeal to secular commitments generates a much larger quantity of division than does appeal to religious commitments, the justificatory liberal can nonarbitrarily advocate the privatization of religious convictions. After all, undoubtedly the appeal to secular considerations in political decision making and advocacy has a number of consequences of such moral importance that we are properly willing to put up with the considerable amount of division generated by appeal to secular considerations. Thus, for example, since vibrant and healthy public dialogue regarding the coercive laws to which we are subject is a great political good, and since it's hard to imagine this kind of dialogue in a pluralistic democracy such as the United States that doesn't contain considerable reliance on secular grounds, we should allow citizens to support their favored coercive laws on secular grounds even though doing so inevitably generates considerable division.

So it seems that, if the justificatory liberal is to formulate a plausible version of the argument from divisiveness, he must establish the following: that appeal to religious considerations in political decision making and advocacy doesn't contribute to moral goods that are sufficiently weighty as to override the divisiveness that such appeals invariably generate. Appeal to religious commitments, even if it generates considerably less division than appeal to secular considerations, doesn't make a liberal democracy morally better off, all things considered. So the morally relevant difference between appealing to religious commitments and appealing to secular commitments in virtue of which we ought to privatize the former but not the latter is *not* that the appealing to religious commitments generates *more* division than appealing to secular commitments, but that appealing to religious commitments makes a liberal democracy morally worse off, on balance, than does appealing to secular considerations. With this in mind, here is a third formulation of the argument from divisiveness:

(1**) Given two alternative activities, a responsible citizen will engage in the alternative that renders the political community morally better off, all things considered.

(2**) A widespread privatization of religion will render the political community morally better off, all things considered, than a refusal to privatize.

(3) Hence, a morally responsible citizen will privatize his religious convictions.

I take this third and final formulation of the argument from divisiveness to be much more promising than the previous two formulations. But it also *significantly* complicates the case for privatization. In order to establish (2**), the justificatory liberal must accomplish two tasks. First, he must identify *all* of the morally relevant consequences likely to ensue both from a widespread refusal to privatize religion and from a widespread willingness to privatize religion. Second, he must determine whether, given those consequences, the United States is morally better off, all things considered, when citizens privatize religion than when they don't. That is, he must engage in that complex weighing process characteristic of consequentialist arguments of the sort under discussion: he must identify the morally desirable and morally undesirable consequences that would result were either of the two alternatives to

materialize, add up the morally desirable consequences of both alternatives, subtract from each sum the morally undesirable consequences of
each alternative, and then determine on the basis of those calculations
which of the two alternatives is morally preferable on balance – a tall
order, to say the least!

6.4 CRITICISM OF THE ARGUMENT FROM DIVISIVENESS

Like many others, I'm skeptical as to our ability to arrive at morally
illuminating conclusions by this means. In particular, I doubt that the
weighing process whereby we add, subtract, and then compare the
morally relevant consequences of our actions is distinct from an appeal
to the moral intuitions that we bring to that weighing process, that
guide that process throughout, and that emerge from our calculations
more or less unchanged by that process. I doubt, moreover, that we're
able to acquire reliable information regarding the consequences that
would ensue from a widespread refusal to privatize religion and from
a widespread privatization of religion: in both cases, the evidence to
which we appeal to justify claims about those consequences is likely
to be little more than an appeal to idiosyncratic experience and thus
doesn't constitute anything more than anecdotal – and likely highly
subjective – evidence.

In spite of these doubts, I don't object to the argument from divisiveness on either score. As with my analysis of the argument from Bosnia,
I set aside such epistemic scruples and address the substantive concerns
expressed in the argument from divisiveness by relying on what I admit
to be a considerable amount of conjecture. (Hopefully, that conjecture
will be plausible.) In particular, I argue both that a widespread refusal
to privatize religion would *not* have the dire consequences the justificatory liberal predicts and that a widespread privatization of religion
would have worse consequences than the justificatory liberal envisions.
Establishing these two points will render implausible the claim that privatizing religion would make the United States better off, all things considered, than refusing to privatize. (In the nature of the case, though,
it would be rash to draw that conclusion with complete confidence:
there are undoubtedly many factors relevant to the required calculation that the ensuing discussion ignores. As with the argument from
Bosnia, I make no pretense of a definitive evaluation of the argument
from divisiveness.)

6.4.1 Some Initial Criticisms of the Argument from Divisiveness

Before I explain why I take the argument from divisiveness to fail, I'll address several objections that seem to me to have some weight, but that are, I think, vulnerable to counterargument. The first objection I'll discuss is straightforward. The United States has witnessed a number of what John Noonan characterizes as "crusades" – "campaigns to change the laws of the country and thereby to change the conduct of the people of the country; campaigns waged with intense and explicit religious conviction, with the use of religious categories and symbols, citing sacred scripture; campaigns led by churchmen and organized by churches, employing prayer in their support and contending that the crusaders seek to enact the will of God."[44] Noonan mentions four such crusades: the "paradigmatic crusade" for the abolition of slavery, against polygamy, for prohibition, and for civil rights.[45] Two of those crusades, the abolitionist crusade and the civil rights movement, have powerfully shaped the political and legal framework of the United States and the consensus is that their role was of first moral importance. In light of the exemplary contributions of those two crusades to the moral reform of the United States, we might argue that imposing on citizens an expectation that they privatize their religious commitments denudes the United States of one of its most powerful forces for moral good. After all, had our predecessors privatized their religious commitments, so the argument goes, the United States might very well never have benefited from arguably the two most important movements for political reform in its history. As a consequence, the moral cost of privatizing religion is too high: since the United States would be *worse* off, morally speaking, were our predecessors to have privatized their religious commitments, there is no reason to believe that the United States would be *better* off, morally speaking, in both present and future if citizens adopt a policy of privatizing their religious commitments.

What should we make of this objection? First, a point about consistency. If a citizen is permitted to rely on her religious convictions in political decision making and advocacy, then she must be permitted to rely on "bad" as well as "good" religion. If we reject privatization in order to allow for the abolitionist and civil rights crusades, then we must also allow for crusades about which we are, or should be, considerably more ambivalent. If rejecting privatization makes possible a crusade to ensure that the state protects African-Americans' civil rights, it also makes possible a crusade to enslave black people, expropriate the land of Native Americans, colonize distant lands, deny homosexual citizens their civil rights, and so on.

Whether we reject privatization or we embrace it, then, consistency requires that we take good religion with the bad. As a consequence, the appropriate response to the objection under discussion depends crucially on an evaluation of the moral successes and failures of crusades (as well as other manifestations of public religion). *If* it were invariably the case that crusades effect morally desirable political reform, then this objection to the argument from divisiveness would be quite powerful. By contrast, *if* it were invariably the case that crusades effect morally undesirable political reform, then this objection would be quite weak.

I take it to be fairly obvious, however, that neither of these extremes is plausible. The truth lies somewhere in the middle: the intervention of religion into politics is neither invariably conducive nor diabolically inimical to the achievement of justice and the common good. In my estimation, the mixed record of religiously inspired movements for political change considerably weakens any response to the argument from divisiveness that appeals to the moral achievements of crusades (and suchlike phenomena). Why?

There is, in the vast majority of cases, no uncontroversial way to determine where on the continuum that ranges between angelic good and demonic evil we ought to place a given crusade. Not only does the truth lie somewhere between the extremes, but where one places a given crusade on that continuum unavoidably depends on a complicated moral evaluation that is (typically) going to be at least as controversial as the argument from divisiveness itself. To take an obvious example, suppose that one attempts to factor the various crusades associated with the Christian Right (regarding homosexuality, prayer in public schools, abortion) into one's determination as to the moral contributions effected by crusades. Any such determination will depend on an evaluation of the specific goals pursued by that movement and as such will be eminently controversial: there are, after all, few claims more controversial than that the Christian Right is a force for moral good rather than a force for moral evil. Similar comments will apply to most of the crusades that have occurred in the United States. But it's polemically useless to object to the argument from divisiveness by appealing to considerations that are so controversial: even if one believes that the contribution of religion to the pursuit of justice and the common good lies somewhere close to the positive end of the continuum, any such judgment will be eminently disputable. As a consequence, it seems the better part of argumentative wisdom not to object to the argument from divisiveness on this basis. (And vice versa, of course: it would be unwise for the justificatory liberal to rest her case for privatization on the claim that religiously inspired movements tend to pursue morally undesirable political goals.)

It might seem that I've missed the point of this objection to (2**). The point isn't that religion provides a powerful force for good as opposed to evil, but that religion provides a powerful counterweight to the state. Public religion, so this response goes, constitutes a crucially important moral contribution to a liberal democracy *irrespective* of the overall moral propriety of the specific policies pursued. Thus, Stephen Carter writes, "Religions that command the devotion of their members actually promote freedom and reduce the likelihood of democratic tyranny by splitting the allegiance of citizens and pressing on their members points of view that are often radically different from the preferences of the state."[46] We might fill in some of the detail of this objection as follows. In spite of the fact that liberals have historically been suspicious of state power, and thus have attempted to impose considerable limits on the state, the power of even liberal governments over the lives and activities of citizens has increased considerably in the recent past. Given that increase, we need to foster communities that can serve as counterweights to state power: any community that equips its members with a moral identity that enables them critically to analyze the state's activities, and does so without being beholden to the state, is a highly desirable commodity in the current institutional configuration. Thus, Jacques Ellul writes:

> We must try to create positions in which we reject and struggle with the state, *not* in order to modify some element of the regime or force it to make some decision, but, much more fundamentally, in order to permit the emergence of social, political, intellectual, or artistic bodies, associations, interest groups or economic or Christian groups totally independent of the state, yet capable of opposing it, able to reject its pressures as well as its controls and even its gifts. These organizations must be completely independent, not only materially but also intellectually and morally, i. e., able to deny that the nation is the supreme value and that the state is the incarnation of the nation.[47]

Religious communities have a significant potential to perform this oppositional role. But a widespread privatization of religion would inhibit religious citizens from doing so: privatizing religion would inhibit citizens, not from forming effective religiously grounded moral identities that could serve as a basis for criticizing the state but from bringing their religiously grounded moral commitments to bear in criticizing the state. As a consequence, the privatization of religion is exactly the wrong prescription for current maladies: the divisiveness of religion pales in moral importance to the capacity of religious communities to serve as critical counterweights to the ever-increasing power of the state.[48]

I am entirely sympathetic to the claim that religious communities can and ought to serve as moral counterweights to the state but, as with the prior objection, we must take into consideration *all* of the expected consequences of the refusal to privatize. More particularly, consistency requires that we take into consideration in the calculation required by (2**) that citizens will employ their religious commitments *both* to oppose *and* to legitimate the state.

And we have good reason to believe that religion will *very often* legitimate the state and its policies. In general terms, the relation of religion to the social and political order is fundamentally ambiguous. Religion does not invariably – or even typically – provide a moral counterweight to the state's activity. Indeed, religion is a powerful source of integration and legitimation. The primary function of religion in society, at least as portrayed by such luminaries as Marx, Durkheim, Parsons, Berger, and Habermas, is not to serve as a source of opposition to the state, but to ensure obedience to the state, to effect integration into society, to serve as the social cement that binds citizens into a more or less unified whole, to function as an opiate that deadens people to the misery and suffering generated by their existence in this vale of tears.[49] Thus, Bryan Turner summarizes the dominant trend in the sociological tradition as follows: "In conceptualising the social functions of religion in human societies, sociologists of religion have either approached religion as a form of social cement that creates a bond between potentially antagonistic individuals or as a form of social opium that suppresses the conflict of interests between antagonistic social groups. On both accounts, religion functions to preserve social cohesion."[50] I don't by any means endorse the position that this is the whole story: the notion that religion is a social cement, legitimates the social-political order, or functions as an opiate hardly captures the full complexity of the social functions performed by religion. It fails, in particular, to capture the *disruptive* side of religion: the history of religion is replete with religiously inspired movements that challenge a social-political order, whether the state, or some dominant ideology, or a widely accepted practice.[51] Religion isn't just an opiate, it's also an "amphetamine."[52]

But the fact that religion serves both to legitimate and to de-legitimate weakens considerably the objection to (2**) now under discussion: although privatizing religion would inhibit religion from providing a source of moral criticism of the state, privatizing religion would also inhibit religion from legitimating the state. Given the ambiguous relation between religion and the social-political order, it seems to me quite difficult to draw the conclusion that privatizing religion would denude liberal democracies of a moral source that, on balance, provides effective opposition to the existing social-political order.

Michael Perry has articulated another objection to the argument from divisiveness that deserves scrutiny. Perry argues as follows. Even if we succeed in encoding in the political culture of the United States an expectation that citizens ought to privatize their religious commitments, religious citizens will invariably and unavoidably employ their religious convictions as a basis for their favored coercive laws: "It is inevitable that some . . . citizens . . . will rely on – will put at least some weight on – religious arguments in voting for political choices about the morality of human conduct."[53] In many cases, requiring citizens to privatize their religious convictions will discourage them from appealing to their religious convictions in public debate, but it won't discourage them from employing their religious convictions to decide whether a given coercive law merits their support. But that state of affairs is highly undesirable: doing so, in effect, shields a citizen's religious rationale from the public scrutiny it would otherwise receive were she to articulate her religious rationale in public. As a consequence, we should encourage religious citizens to articulate in public their religious reasons for whatever coercive laws they support, even if doing so would generate considerable division in the political community. Perry concludes, "Because of the role that religiously based moral arguments inevitably play in the political process, then, it is important that such arguments, no less than secular moral arguments, be presented in, so that they can be tested in, public political debate."[54]

Perry's point seems to me to be a valuable one. But it seems consistent with justificatory liberalism as most plausibly construed. As the reader will recall, I've characterized justificatory liberalism as imposing constraints on religious reasons that apply only to *political decision making* and *advocacy*: the justificatory liberal wants to discourage a citizen from relying on her religious commitments either to decide whether a given coercive law merits her support or to convince other citizens that they ought to support it.[55] But the claim that a citizen should privatize her religious convictions doesn't forbid a citizen from articulating her religious rationale for a given coercive law L *in the appropriate settings*, for example, in contexts in which it's clear that she is *not* advocating that others support L on the basis of that rationale. So the justificatory liberal is willing to allow, and is free to encourage, a citizen to engage in public discussion as to the plausibility of her favored religious rationale. So long as she refrains from supporting state coercion on religious grounds, she's free to discuss with her compatriots the respective merits and demerits of whatever religious arguments – even those that endorse state coercion – she finds worthy of analysis. As a consequence, the privatization of religious belief needn't shield from public scrutiny any of a citizen's religious reasons and a fortiori whatever religious reasons she might be inclined to employ as a basis for her favored coercive laws.

6.4.2 Why the Argument from Divisiveness Fails

It seems to me that the last two objections to the argument from divisiveness I've considered have some weight. The considerable control the modern state currently exercises over the lives and activities of its citizens renders vitally important the existence of moral and religious communities willing to and capable of engaging in effective criticism of the state's activities; and the more powerful the state, the more pressing the need for counterweights to state power. And I believe that the privatization of religion would insulate religious reasons from critical scrutiny to some degree – though perhaps not to the degree envisioned by Perry. But I believe that the force of each of these objections is blunted by powerful counterarguments. So what else can be said by way of critical analysis of the argument from divisiveness?

The first and probably most important point I want to make is the following: we must ensure that the division adduced in favor of privatization is properly attributed to a refusal to privatize religion rather than to disregard for the various constraints constitutive of the ideal of conscientious engagement.[56] In particular, we must differentiate between the consequences of refusing to pursue public justification and the consequences of refusing to privatize religion. Much alienation and frustration, I think, would be generated by a widespread refusal to pursue public justification. If large numbers of citizens supported their favored coercive laws on religious grounds and didn't even attempt to articulate reasons for their favored coercive laws that are convincing to those who reject their religious commitments, then they would thereby disrespect their compatriots – and that seems a recipe for a large quantity of division. But, as I have argued *ad nauseam*, a citizen can wholeheartedly pursue public justification and be equally resolute in refusing to privatize his religious convictions. As a consequence, *none* of the division that results from the refusal to pursue public justification may be adduced in support of the claim that citizens ought to privatize their religious convictions.

We ought, in addition, to differentiate between the consequences of refusing to privatize religion and the consequences of refusing to adhere to the various other constraints constitutive of the ideal of conscientious engagement. For example, no doubt some of the divisiveness generated by the political employment of religious commitments in the United States is a consequence of the inflammatory rhetoric some religious citizens employ – it's no surprise that religious advocacy is divisive when citizens identify their political competitors as agents of the devil, when they accuse their compatriots of committing moral abominations, and the like. But such consequences ought not be attributed to a refusal to privatize religion: a citizen who refuses to privatize his religious commitments isn't thereby committed to employing inflammatory rhetoric to make his case. He can be wholeheartedly committed to accommodating his compatriots and therefore to abstaining from character assassination or vicious stereotyping. As a consequence, none of the division generated by a citizen's unwillingness to accommodate his compatriots may be weighed in the balance against the refusal to privatize religion.

As with the argument from respect, I believe that making the distinction in question takes the argumentative wind out of the rhetorical sails of the argument from divisiveness. More particularly, if we observe the distinction between the pursuit of public justification and the privatization of religion, we'll see that the argument from divisiveness is much weaker than it seems at first blush: the quantity of division that weighs in favor of privatization and against the refusal to privatize is much lower than might at first seem to be the case. Recall, for example, the "profoundly alienating ordeal" to which Blumoff refers in the passage cited earlier. The alienation he experienced on participating in a political dialogue conducted exclusively in sectarian religious terms would be significantly ameliorated, I believe, had his interlocutors genuinely and sincerely attempted to articulate reasons that were convincing to him. The alienating condition in which he found himself was a consequence, most likely, of his interlocutors' failure to think they had an obligation to pursue a nonsectarian rationale and therefore to make the attempt, rather than because, having made the attempt, they couldn't discern a nonsectarian rationale and thus could do nothing else but appeal to sectarian grounds. Only in the latter case would the ordeal to which Blumoff was subjected be attributable to a refusal to privatize. (Of course, as this last point indicates, the pursuit of public justification doesn't entirely eradicate exclusion and alienation, as it will sometimes be the case that the pursuit of public justification ends in failure, to the understandable frustration and alienation of those to whom no such justification is available.)

A first and very significant point is that as long as we fail to bear in mind the distinction between privatizing religion and pursuing public justification, we're likely to overestimate considerably the morally undesirable consequences of a widespread refusal to privatize religion – by counting the divisiveness generated by the refusal to pursue public justification in favor of privatization. But keeping that distinction in mind *reduces* the amount of division to which the justificatory liberal may appeal in his attempt to show that a refusal to privatize religion makes a liberal democracy morally worse off, all things considered, than does privatizing religion. This is important since the argument from divisiveness, in accord with its consequentialist nature, unavoidably involves us in a numbers game: given that the central question raised by that argument is whether refusing to privatize religion puts us further in the "moral black" than the alternatives, anything that dramatically reduces the debit side of the ledger is obviously of crucial importance.

Of course, this first point doesn't imply that refusing to privatize religion generates *no* division. Indeed, the contrary is clearly the case: if some citizens refuse to privatize their religious convictions, others will take considerable umbrage and feel alienation no matter how conscientiously in other respects the citizens who reject privatization conduct themselves. As a consequence, it's important to identify morally undesirable consequences of *obedience to* the privatization claim of such magnitude that they can outweigh the division generated by repudiation of the privatization claim. And it isn't difficult to identify the ill consequences that might result from the effective enforcement, by means of social stigma, of the expectation that citizens privatize their religious convictions. It seems to me that those consequences fall into two general categories.

First, as I've already argued, many citizens don't regard their religious commitments as a set of preferences on the order of a taste for schnapps or a desire to live in the suburbs. Rather, they regard themselves as bound to obey a set of overriding and totalizing obligations imposed on them by their Creator. They regard their failure to discharge those obligations as anathema.[57] If we impose on such citizens the expectation that they ought to privatize their religious commitments, we thereby impose on them the expectation that they be willing to violate their fundamental commitments. We ask them to commit to a policy that might require them knowingly and willingly to disobey God. In so doing, we also ask them to act in a way that would inhibit them from living their lives in a meaningful way. Pretty obviously such expectations, enforced by social stigma as they must be in order to be effective, would generate considerable alienation and frustration in religious citizens.

Second, we have every reason to believe that religious citizens will associate the alienation and frustration they experience as a consequence of having to privatize their religious commitments with its source: the requirements of citizenship in a liberal democracy and the informal pressures by which citizens are encouraged to abide by those requirements. If religious citizens in the United States are to be stigmatized for refusing to privatize their religious commitments, if citizenship in the United States imposes on citizens an obligation to violate the commitments that define their respective moral identities, then it should come as no surprise that religious citizens will want to have as little to do with liberal politics as they can. This might involve a withdrawal from active political engagement – a disinclination to vote or an unwillingness to keep up with important political issues. At the limit, alienated citizens might exit the liberal camp altogether. Since we can assume that a well-functioning liberal democracy is a great moral good, and since it's safe to assume that participation in and loyalty to any given liberal democracy on the part of its citizens is an important factor in the stability of that liberal democracy, then the

alienation of religious citizens from liberal democracy is a *highly* undesirable consequence of requiring religious citizens to privatize their
religious commitments.

Thus are the two kinds of consequences likely to result from encoding the obligation to privatize religion into the role of citizen in a liberal
democracy. One final point is essential: as I've noted, the argument from
divisiveness is a consequentialist argument and therefore depends on
the exact quantities of morally good and morally bad consequences
we can expect to be generated by the relevant alternatives. Successful
prosecution of the argument from divisiveness depends on a numbers
game: *How much* alienation is likely to be generated by the refusal to
privatize? *How many* citizens will be alienated from the liberal state?
How many citizens will find privatization objectionable? In light of this
aspect of the argument from divisiveness, the following seems directly
relevant to our discussion. The vast majority of the citizens in the United
States are theists, a condition that will likely persist into the foreseeable
future. And many, I surmise, understand their religious commitments
in the way I've described: it is, after all, a fairly ecumenical view. Given
the large number of citizens affected by the justificatory liberal's favored
constraints on religious convictions, it seems very doubtful that we'll
find ourselves further in the moral black by imposing on citizens the
expectation that they privatize their religious convictions than by imposing on them a much weaker and commensurately less objectionable
set of constraints – that they genuinely and sincerely pursue public justification for their favored coercive laws but that they needn't privatize
their religious convictions.

There's a better way than the path the justificatory liberal wants us
to tread. We shouldn't impose on religious citizens the constraint that
they'll regard as most intolerable: to privatize their religious commitments and thus to be willing to disobey God. Thus, we shouldn't give the
justificatory liberal what he most wants. But religious citizens should do
what they can to ameliorate the alienation, frustration, and resentment
that their appeal to religious commitments generates in their compatriots. In particular, they must pursue public justification and in so doing
aspire to avoid imposing coercive laws for which their compatriots lack
what they take to be a convincing rationale. That we expect religious
citizens to satisfy the ideal of conscientious engagement, but that we
don't expect religious citizens to refrain from supporting coercive laws

on religious grounds – that seems the policy most likely to reduce the amount of division associated with the appeal to religious convictions in political decision making and advocacy.

6.5 CONCLUDING COMMENTS

I hope that two facts are apparent about my analysis of the historical-consequentialist case for privatization. First, my analysis presupposes in important ways the conclusions for which I argued in my treatment of what respect does and does not require regarding the proper use of religious convictions. (I hope it's therefore obvious why I discussed the arguments from Bosnia and divisiveness *after* I addressed the argument from respect.) A central part of my objection to the argument from Bosnia is that even if a citizen refuses to privatize his religious convictions, he ought to withhold his support from any coercive law for which he lacks *rational* justification, and that for the vast majority of United States citizens, it will seem irrational to deny their compatriots religious freedom and thus it will be improper for them to support the sorts of coercive policies that engender religious strife. A central part of my objection to the argument from divisiveness is that even though a citizen needn't privatize his religious convictions, each citizen ought to pursue public justification for his favored coercive laws; religious citizens manifest their respect for their compatriots by sincerely pursuing public justification; consequently, refusing to privatize religion isn't nearly as divisive as the justificatory liberal predicts. In both cases, my analysis of what respect does and doesn't require plays a crucial role in my vindication of the claim that a religious citizen may without any moral impropriety support his favored coercive laws on the basis of his religious convictions (alone).

Second, I hope it's clear that my objections to the argument from Bosnia and my objections to the argument from divisiveness are mutually supportive. As I noted in my treatment of the argument from Bosnia, if it were the case that a widespread refusal to privatize religion has a realistic prospect of generating religious strife in the United States, then that would constitute compelling support for the privatization claim. The moral horror of religious strife obviates the need for the balancing of moral considerations required to vindicate the argument from divisiveness. But if we dismiss the appeal to religious strife as an appeal to dystopia, then the justificatory liberal is required to retreat to much less stable ground – he must identify less dire consequences of refusing to privatize. But the justificatory liberal's retreat from religious strife to division lands him in a complicated and inherently contentious weighing of disparate factors – a weighing process vitiated by the anecdotal nature of the evidence available for the relevant considerations – which stands little chance of carrying the day.

CONCLUDING COMMENTS ON
THE NORMATIVE CASE FOR RESTRAINT

The central question I address in this book is the following: What is the proper role of religious convictions in political decision making and advocacy? The most contentious issue associated with that question is whether it's morally appropriate for a citizen to support a coercive law L even if he enjoys only a religious rationale for L. My central thesis addresses that issue directly: as the reader will recall, I claim that a citizen has no obligation to withhold support from L even if he possesses only a religious rationale for L. This thesis is inconsistent with a defining commitment of justificatory liberalism, according to which each citizen morally ought to adhere to the doctrine of restraint – he ought to withhold support from any coercive law for which he can't discern a public justification. And since a religious rationale doesn't suffice for a public justification, the justificatory liberal is committed to denying that a citizen may support L if he enjoys only a religious rationale for L. Thus is the justificatory liberal committed to denying my central thesis. In order to vindicate my thesis, I've attempted to determine whether justificatory liberals have articulated compelling reason for the doctrine of restraint.

Although I have, for obvious reasons, focused my discussion on justificatory liberalism, recall that my stated intention is to address *two* audiences: the justificatory liberal, to be sure, but also his alter-ego: the *religious sectarian* who intends to conduct his political decision making and advocacy entirely within the ambit of his theological commitments. As anxious as I am to reject the justificatory liberal's constraints on the role religious convictions may play in political decision making and advocacy, I have no interest in providing aid and comfort for a mindless or intransigent sectarianism. There is certainly more to be said regarding the appropriate role of religious convictions in the political arena than that religious citizens needn't exercise restraint regarding their religious commitments. Most important, even though justificatory liberals haven't shown that citizens ought to adhere to the doctrine of restraint, it doesn't follow that "anything goes" by way of the political uses to which citizens may put their religious commitments. Even if religious citizens have no moral obligation to adhere to the doctrine of restraint, they're still morally obliged to obey the ideal of conscientious engagement.

To dispel the impression that my rejection of the doctrine of restraint commits me to a thoroughly antinomian position on the proper political role of religious convictions, we must distinguish the doctrine of restraint from several other claims that I heartily endorse. Note, in particular, that my rejection of this doctrine in no way commits me to rejecting any of the commitments constitutive of what I earlier called mere liberalism. Nothing I have shown in the previous three chapters implies that any of the substantive political commitments associated with the liberal tradition are false, irrational, or the like. No conclusion I've drawn or argument I've articulated commits me to denying that there are powerful reasons for central liberal commitments, particularly for the claim that each citizen ought to enjoy a fully adequate scheme of rights. Of course, my argument does show that it's morally permissible for a citizen to be so committed solely on the basis of his religious commitments. And it also shows that it's morally permissible for him to resolve any of the political controversies currently at play in contemporary United States' politics (abortion, death penalty, homosexuality, etc.) solely on the basis of his religious commitments.

Neither does my rejection of the doctrine of restraint militate against the claim that there is a general presumption against coercion. Again to the contrary, religious citizens, even those who reject the doctrine of restraint, ought to be extremely reticent to impose coercive laws on their compatriots. As I've argued, since people are legitimately and deeply averse to coercion, there is a moral presumption against coercing them. And, as is obvious, that presumption can be overridden. About both of these claims, the justificatory liberal and I are (or at least can be) in agreement. We part ways, however, with respect to the sorts of grounds a citizen must enjoy in order for him properly to believe that the presumption against coercion is overridden. According to the justificatory liberal, a citizen must withhold support from a given coercive law if he lacks a public justification for the claim that the presumption against coercion is overridden in a given case.

I believe the justificatory liberal is wrong about that. Although I endorse the claim that a citizen ought to be extremely reticent in supporting a given coercive law L, I don't believe that he must be able publicly to justify L in order properly to overcome his reticence. As a consequence, I don't believe that because a citizen enjoys only a religious rationale for L, this implies that he ought to be any more reticent to support L than he is already, considering that L involves coercion. So I differ from the justificatory liberal only with respect to what a citizen requires in order to overcome a morally obligatory presumption against coercion, not with respect to whether there is a presumption against coercion.

Again, that I reject the doctrine of restraint in no way commits me to rejecting the principle of pursuit. It doesn't commit me to rejecting the claim that public justification is a highly desirable political commodity. It doesn't commit me to a tepid endorsement of the practice of public justification. Each of these to the contrary: each citizen – a fortiori, each religious citizen – ought to be fully committed to pursuing public justification for his favored coercive laws. Even if he wholeheartedly rejects the doctrine of restraint, he may just as wholeheartedly endorse the project of pursuing public justification. And he *should* endorse that project: as long as he can achieve public justification for his favored coercive policies, it would be perverse for him not even to attempt to acquire that justification, and it would be even more perverse not to articulate that justification if he has one. So citizens have every reason to participate, and no reason to avoid participating, in what Perry calls "ecumenical political dialogue," that is, to aspire "to discern or achieve, in a religiously/morally pluralistic context, a common ground that transcends 'local' or 'sectarian' differences."[1] Again, there is powerful reason to endorse Robert Audi's claim that "morally conscientious citizens will seek grounds that include reasons of a kind that any rational adult citizen can endorse as sufficient for that purpose"[2] and to answer in the affirmative Stephen Macedo's rhetorical question: "Should we not try and offer our fellow citizens reasons that they ought to accept without making the absurdly unreasonable demand that they first accept our convictions about the ultimate ends of human life?"[3]

A citizen ought to do so, moreover, out of respect for his compatriots: his moral obligation to respect them imposes on him a moral obligation to pursue public justification. And each religious citizen has a moral obligation to pursue public justification, a point of central importance. Why?

Recall the problem that motivates justificatory liberalism: the problem of social harmony. Since liberal democracies are inveterately pluralistic, and since even liberal states coerce citizens, it's important that citizens do what is within their power to build up relations of mutual trust and respect among one another, so that when citizens find themselves subject to coercive laws they regard as morally inappropriate – as each of us unavoidably will, so long as we live "east of Eden" – they remain confident that those laws aren't designed to degrade or humiliate them. Whether citizens trust and respect one another depends on the moral tenor of their relations, and this depends not just on how citizens treat one another, but also on the reasons they treat one another as they do. If religious citizens are morally committed to pursuing public justification, and publicly acknowledge that they are thus committed, this should generate the desired trust and mutual respect. (Of course, the justificatory liberal is also committed to this hope.)

It's important to insist that religious citizens have a moral obligation to pursue public justification. It is *not* important to insist on that claim because citizens who recognize that they have that obligation will be forced to change the way they make political decisions or encourage support for their favored laws. After all, we have no reason to impute pragmatic ineptitude to the religious sectarian: he is well aware that in order to achieve his political aims, he must be willing to convince his nonreligious compatriots to support them.[4] And to convince these nonreligious compatriots, he must, as a matter of pragmatic fact, appeal to them on the basis of nonreligious, widely convincing considerations; pursuing public justification is the only effective means to achieve his political aims. So religious citizens will most likely pursue public justification regardless of whether they have an obligation to do so.

But if religious citizens pursue public justification solely for instrumental purposes, they fail to generate the bonds of trust and comradery that are so important to harmonious relations between citizens in a pluralistic culture. If religious citizens pursue public justification only so long as they are pragmatically required to do so, but are willing to break off this pursuit when doing so is no longer pragmatically necessary, then, even when they do pursue public justification, their nonreligious compatriots rightly resent them. By contrast, if citizens are confident that their compatriots are committed to the pursuit of public justification even when such pursuit is no longer instrumentally required, they can trust fellow citizens to relate to them, not merely by employing naked force, but, so far as is feasible, by means of persuasion. That citizens – and a fortiori religious citizens – are *morally committed* to pursuing public justification for their favored coercive laws is one important way citizens can ameliorate the disharmony that naturally results from the imposition of coercive laws in a pluralistic society.

If we need to note the salutary consequences that, we hope, results from the moral commitment to pursue public justification, we also need to be clear about the limitations that attend this pursuit. Even though each citizen has a moral obligation to pursue common ground that will enable the diversely committed citizens of a modern liberal democracy to agree on the moral propriety of the coercive laws to which they are subject, and even if each citizen conscientiously and assiduously pursues public justification for his favored coercive laws, we have no reason to expect that we'll achieve consensus on the laws to which we're subject. Disagreement is an ineradicable feature of a well-ordered liberal democracy, as Rawls argues, and while there is some slight hope that the pursuit of public justification will narrow the scope of disagreement somewhat, at least about some issues and over the long run, the salutary effects of the pursuit of public justification don't consist in its ability to generate consensus. Rather, it is primarily valuable as a means of reinforcing the bonds of the political community.[5] Or, to refer to a previous discussion, if citizens are morally committed to pursuing public justification, to pursuing rational justification, to accommodating one another, to learning from one another, then it will be much easier for each of us to *acquiesce* to coercive laws with which we disagree.

One final point. As I've noted, I direct my central thesis both to justificatory liberals and to religious sectarians. In spite of these divergent audiences, it's important to notice that the arguments I address to a particular audience enhance the plausibility of the arguments I address to the other. On the one hand, that religious citizens morally ought to abide by the ideal of conscientious engagement ought to make more palatable to justificatory liberals the claim that religious citizens need not exercise restraint. On the other hand, that religious citizens have no obligation to adhere to the constraint they are most likely to regard as objectionably intrusive ought to make more palatable to religious citizens the claim that they are nevertheless morally obliged to adhere to the ideal of conscientious engagement. My strategy, then, for defending my central thesis – that a citizen has an obligation sincerely and conscientiously to pursue a nonreligious, widely convincing rationale for his favored coercive laws, but that he doesn't have an obligation to withhold support from them if he cannot discern a widely convincing, nonreligious rationale for those policies – is to grant to the justificatory liberal much of what he wants, save what he wants most (restraint), and to impose on the religious sectarian a variety of constraints, save that which he finds most objectionable. This seems to be a suitably accommodating result.

PART THREE

WHAT IS PUBLIC JUSTIFICATION?

INTRODUCTION TO PART THREE

In order to vindicate justificatory liberalism, its advocates must discharge two argumentative burdens. First, they need to show that citizens ought to adhere to the doctrine of restraint. Discharging this first burden requires *moral* argumentation. As we have seen, the heart of the justificatory liberal's normative case for restraint involves an appeal to respect: a citizen ought to obey the doctrine of restraint in virtue of her obligation to respect her compatriots as persons. I believe I've shown that respect doesn't require that a citizen obey the doctrine of restraint and thus that advocates of justificatory liberalism haven't discharged their first argumentative burden.

Second, advocates of justificatory liberalism must articulate a defensible distinction between the grounds on the basis of which it is, and the grounds on the basis of which it isn't, appropriate for a citizen to support her favored coercive laws. That is, even if justificatory liberals *could* show that respect requires restraint, their work wouldn't be complete: they must also provide some clear guidance as to the *sorts* of grounds regarding which citizens ought to exercise restraint. Failure on this score would scuttle the justificatory liberal's project: absent a clear understanding of the sorts of grounds regarding which they ought to exercise restraint, citizens can't determine how to discharge their obligation to exercise restraint, in which case they can hardly be expected to try to fulfill that obligation. To provide the requisite guidance, justificatory liberals have articulated various conceptions of public justification. In Part III, I'll attempt to show that justificatory liberals haven't articulated a *defensible* conception of public justification and that there is no reason to expect that justificatory liberals will succeed in the future when they have failed so often in the past.

This task is greatly complicated by the absence of consensus among justificatory liberals regarding the appropriate conception of public justification. There is, I think, agreement on a core concept of public justification: a citizen enjoys a public justification for coercive law L only if she enjoys a rationale that articulates in some appropriate way with the distinctive and divergent points of view of her compatriots. But agreement on that core concept is riven with disagreement as to the way a public justification articulates appropriately with other citizens' points of view; agreement on the core concept of public justification coexists with considerable disagreement regarding the preferred conception of public justification. This disagreement greatly complicates my evaluation of justificatory liberalism: there is no alternative but to articulate the dominant conceptions of public justification and then to evaluate each conception on its merits.

The focus of my attention in the ensuing discussion will, of course, be on *religious grounds*: justificatory liberalism is of interest to me only insofar as it endorses the claim that a citizen ought not support her favored coercive laws solely on the basis of her religious commitments. According to the justificatory liberal, the reader will recall (3.4.2), religious grounds have the status of being a *paradigm* of the sort of grounds regarding which a citizen ought to exercise restraint. Given that privileged status, an adequate conception of public justification *must* have the result that a religious rationale is not sufficient for a public justification: any conception according to which a religious rationale is sufficient for a public justification is too weak to do the exclusionary work required of it. This constraint on what counts as a public justification will provide some discipline to the ensuing discussion: I'll fairly regularly rule a proposed conception of public justification out of bounds just because it's too weak to support the claim that a citizen should exercise restraint regarding her religious convictions.

One of my central claims in the following discussion is that the justificatory liberal is eventually forced to articulate her favored conception of public justification in *epistemic* terms: the inevitable demise of so-called populist conceptions of public justification forces the justificatory liberal to have recourse to so-called epistemic conceptions of public justification. The crucial question then becomes: can the justificatory liberal articulate an epistemic conception of public justification (1) that constitutes a principled basis for prohibiting a citizen from supporting her favored coercive laws on the basis of religious grounds alone and

(2) that satisfies various other constraints it's reasonable to impose on an adequate conception of public justification? Otherwise put, can the justificatory liberal articulate an epistemic conception of public justification that *requires* a citizen to exercise restraint regarding her religious convictions but that does *not require* a citizen to exercise restraint regarding grounds that are essential to healthy political decision making and advocacy?[1] The burden of my argument in Part III of this book is that she cannot.

CHAPTER 7

POPULIST CONCEPTIONS OF PUBLIC JUSTIFICATION

7.0 INTRODUCTION

Recall the distinction between a rational justification and a public justification. As I noted (3.2.1), rational justification is a function, in crucial part, of evidential set: whether Elijah is rationally justified in assenting to p is a function, in crucial part, of the evidence Elijah has to go on, of the other beliefs and experiences Elijah brings to bear in determining whether p merits his assent. But the dependence of rational justification on evidential set has the following implication: Elijah can be rationally justified in assenting to p even if none of his compatriots are rationally justified in assenting to p. Indeed, since Elijah's compatriots no doubt have very different evidential sets, Elijah's compatriots might very well be rationally justified in finding p completely unacceptable.

The unavoidably perspectival or person-relative nature of rational justification opens up space for the concept of public justification: if a rational justification is a rationale a citizen regards as providing adequate support for a certain coercive law given her distinctive evidential set, a *public* justification is a rationale *other people* regard as providing adequate support for that law given *their* respective evidential sets. If we define "the public" as the set of "other people" who must find a given rationale R adequate,[1] and if the public can be construed in various different ways, then a public justification is a rationale that the members of the public, suitably construed, find adequate given their respective evidential sets. So a rationale counts as a *public* justification in virtue of the fact that the members of the public (suitably construed) find that rationale adequate, whereas a rationale counts as a public *justification* in virtue of the fact that the public finds that rationale *adequate.* Adequate for what? Adequate as a basis for supporting some coercive law (and more particularly, for believing that a given coercive law is morally appropriate). This intuitive understanding of what counts as a public justification raises two questions on which I'll focus in this chapter, both of which admit of various importantly different answers.

First, who is a member of the public? Who plays a role in determining what counts as a public justification? A natural answer is the citizens who inhabit a given liberal democracy. In order for a citizen's rationale to count as a public justification for some coercive law, her compatriots must find that rationale an adequate basis for supporting that law. But which of her fellow citizens? All of them? Some subset? If a subset, which one? And if a particular subset, why that one and not another? A first question we may put to a given conception of public justification is, who constitutes the public?

Second, in light of which commitments may the members of the public (however construed) evaluate a citizen's rationale? If a public justification is a rationale the members of the public regard as providing an adequate basis for a coercive law, they will evaluate that rationale from various specific perspectives: each citizen will evaluate it from the perspective afforded by her parochial evidential set. But what of the character and quality of a given citizen's evidential set? Must a prospective public justification gain the imprimatur of the members of the public even if they are ignorant, prejudiced, uncooperative, or dull-witted? Or may we *idealize* the members of the public, for example, by imputing to them information they do not in fact have? So here is a second question raised by the core concept of public justification: on what sort of *basis* do the members of the public evaluate a prospective public justification?

The core concept of a public justification, then, raises at least two importantly distinct questions, each of which admits of a number of different answers, and different answers that give rise to different conceptions of public justification. *Different* characterizations of the public (who they are and what they know) give rise to *different* conceptions of public justification. And, of course, this variation among conceptions of public justification is critical to the issue at hand. Exactly which construal of the public a given justificatory liberal adopts can have profoundly important implications for the sorts of grounds regarding which citizens ought to exercise restraint: differing conceptions of public justification, one would assume, will require citizens to exercise restraint regarding different sorts of grounds.

In this chapter, my intention is to articulate and evaluate a representative sampling of *populist* conceptions of public justification.[2] Populist conceptions of public justification have two defining characteristics. First, populist conceptions involve an *inclusive* construal of the public: the default populist position is that *each* citizen in a given liberal democracy counts as a member of the public and therefore plays a role in determining whether some rationale counts as a public justification. Deviations from that default position require argument: if some of the citizens who actually inhabit a liberal democracy don't play a role in determining whether some rationale counts as a public justification, the justificatory liberal must provide some principled reason in support of the claim that those citizens don't count as members of the public. Second, populist conceptions of public justification also *take citizens as they are*: the default populist position is that a rationale R counts as a public justification only if the members of the public find R acceptable in light of their existing evidential sets, irrespective of their epistemic pockmarks and doxastic defects. Thus Joseph Raz: "Political principles must be accessible to people as they are. It is not enough that . . . those who are totally rational and open to rational conversation will be persuaded, and be radically changed. Politics must take people as they come and be accessible to them, capable of commanding their consent without expecting them to change in any radical way."[3] That is, populist conceptions of public justification resist *idealizing* the members of the public: they resist identifying a public justification with what citizens *could* or *would* accept if they were to enjoy certain moral or epistemic desiderata, that is, if they found themselves circumstanced very differently from the way they do in fact.

So, on a pure and unsullied populist conception of public justification, a rationale R counts as a public justification for some coercive law only if each of the citizens who inhabit a given liberal democracy regard R as a sufficient basis for that law and each citizen does so in light of her own actual convictions and experiences. Of course, populist conceptions of public justification come in various degrees: a recognizably populist conception of public justification needn't include *all* citizens in the public and needn't require that the members of the public, taken *exactly* as they are, must regard some rationale as a sufficient basis for coercion. Membership in the public can be more or less inclusive;

members of the public can be construed more or less as they actually are. But as I understand them, populist conceptions of public justification incline strongly in the direction of identifying the public with the actual citizenry of a given liberal democracy and tend to require of a given rationale that the members of the public regard that rationale as adequate in their actual epistemic conditions.

7.1 ENUMERATIVE CONCEPTIONS OF PUBLIC JUSTIFICATION

Before we examine specific populist proposals, we need to establish a baseline for the ensuing discussion. To establish that baseline, consider what we might call an *enumerative* conception of public justification: a conception constituted by a *list* of the sorts of rationale that putatively don't constitute a public justification (and thus regarding which a citizen ought to exercise restraint). Moreover, consider an enumerative conception that goes right to the heart of my concerns, one that applies to religious grounds in particular:

(1) In order for a citizen's rationale R to count as a public justification for some coercive law, R must not be essentially dependent on religious considerations.[4]

Alternatively, consider an enumerative conception of public justification that lists *all* the kinds of ground regarding which we (without getting too particular about who "we" are) believe that a responsible citizen ought to exercise restraint:

(2) In order for a citizen's rationale R for some coercive law to count as a public justification, R must not be essentially dependent on religious considerations, a controversial conception of the good, a comprehensive doctrine, and so on.

What should we make of (1) and (2), and indeed, of any enumerative conception of public justification?

A conception of public justification constituted by a laundry list of unacceptable grounds leaves us entirely in the dark as to why a citizen ought to exercise restraint with respect to the kinds of rationale included on that list but not with respect to the kinds of rationale that haven't been included on that list. This has as a consequence that we are unable to determine whether that conception is arbitrary. Since, for example, (1) forbids a citizen to support a given coercive law solely on religious grounds but doesn't articulate a principled justification for that prohibition, we have no way of determining whether there are relevantly similar nonreligious kinds of rationale that the justificatory liberal can't afford to exclude from political decision making and advocacy. But we must be able to do so if we are to determine whether the prohibition on religious grounds is arbitrary; the justificatory liberal must do so in order to defend herself from the (inevitable) charge of unwarranted partiality.

I'll assume, therefore, that any adequate conception of public justification will include some *principled* basis a citizen can employ to distinguish between the sorts of grounds regarding which she ought to exercise restraint and those regarding which she needn't exercise restraint.

7.2 RATIONALITY

A populist conception of public justification assumes as a default position that each citizen in a given liberal democracy enjoys membership in the public. Thus, the default position associated with a populist conception of public justification is something like the following:

(3) In order for a citizen's rationale R to count as a public justification for some coercive law, each of his fellow citizens must accept R.

So far as I am aware, no justificatory liberal endorses (3). Membership in the public, on any defensible conception of public justification, is limited to a *subset* of the citizens who actually inhabit a given liberal democracy. In particular, *any* defensible conception of public justification must limit membership in the public to those citizens who satisfy at least very minimal standards of rationality. The citizens who constitute the public, for example, must be able to understand an argument and to alter their convictions as a consequence of their understanding of that argument. Thus, madmen and infants are excluded from the public. What warrants this exclusion? Since a public justification is a rationale that must articulate appropriately with the distinctive points of view of the members of the public, then citizens who can't engage in rational evaluation at all have no position to be taken into account, and therefore *can't* play a role in determining whether a given rationale counts as a public justification. It seems entirely appropriate, then, to restrict membership in the public to citizens to whom a rationale can be addressed with the expectation that those citizens can accept or reject that rationale on the basis of what they take to be good reason.

It's important to enter two caveats here. First, the kind of rational competence required for membership in the public mustn't be too *demanding*. Consider an understanding of rationality that requires competence in modal logic. Since only a small minority of citizens are competent in modal logic, any conception of public justification that includes in the public only those adept at modal logic would exclude all but a few citizens from membership in the public: no doubt the proponent of that conception and perhaps a few of his logic-chopping friends. But if the justificatory liberal is to articulate a *populist* conception of public justification, he'll want membership in the public to include as many of the citizens who actually inhabit a given liberal democracy as is feasible. So he'll reject the "modal logic" conception of public justification.

Second, the kind of rational competence required for membership in the public mustn't *prejudge* live moral or political disputes. That is, the justificatory liberal mustn't build into her conception of rationality the claim that rational citizens will assent to one or another moral or political position. In particular, the justificatory liberal mustn't define the notion of rationality in such a way as to ensure that all rational citizens adhere to characteristic liberal commitments. Such a prescriptive conception of rationality would render the obligation to provide a public justification of liberal commitments redundant: if the justificatory liberal defines rationality so that rational citizens assent to characteristic liberal commitments, and if he limits membership in the public so as to include only rational citizens, then liberal commitments will, by definition, enjoy public justification. But in that case, the justificatory liberal can dispense with the requirement of public justification. Of course, he'll also face an entirely new and intractable set of difficulties: he'll have to defend his stipulation that rationality requires adherence to such and such liberal commitments even though many citizens of good faith and cognitive competence reject those commitments.

7.3 ACTUAL ACCEPTANCE

I'll assume, to be brief, that any defensible conception of public justification will limit membership in the public to rational citizens, where the sort of rationality required is roughly equivalent to a citizen's being able to understand and be moved by argument. A further question: what stance must the members of the public take with respect to a citizen's rationale if that rationale is to count as a public justification? It seems to me that justificatory liberalism articulates most naturally with the claim that the appropriate stance is *actual acceptance*. That is, it seems to me that justificatory liberalism naturally gravitates toward something like the following populist conception of public justification:

(4) In order for a citizen's rationale R to count as a public justification for some coercive law, each of his rational compatriots must regard R as an adequate basis for supporting that law.[5]

Under what conditions does a citizen actually accept a given rationale? The first and most obvious condition is that he already adheres to each of R's premises, is aware that he adheres to each of R's premises, and draws the desired conclusion regarding the relevant coercive law. Other possibilities are somewhat less demanding. For example, a citizen might tacitly assent to each of R's premises and might even act in such a way as to indicate that he has drawn the desired conclusion, although he is unaware that he assents to R and doesn't realize that he is acting on the assumption that R establishes the desired conclusion. Again, a citizen accepts R in the relevant sense if he *would* regard R as compelling just on reflection about R although he might not, as of yet, have done so and therefore might not already accept R. Other possibilities abound. But each possibility satisfies a common constraint: in each case, whether a given rationale counts as public justification is severely constrained by how the members of the public regard that rationale from the perspective provided by their actual evidential sets.

As I said, I think that justificatory liberalism articulates most naturally with populist proposals such as (4) because populist formulations of justificatory liberalism comport exceptionally well with the argument from respect.[6] If Elijah is to respect his compatriots, he must respect them *in their particularity*, as they actually are, rather than as he wishes them to be, as they ought to be, or as they could be under different circumstances.[7] Consequently, Elijah most naturally satisfies his obligation to respect his compatriots by articulating reasons that his compatriots accept given their actual points of view. The most direct way for Elijah to discharge that obligation is to articulate an argument that employs only premises to which his compatriots actually assent – as (4) requires. Of course, in order to articulate some such argument, Elijah won't be able to appeal just to premises that *he* finds convincing. Rather, he will have to undergo a "purging operation": he'll have to survey his noetic endowment, identify those grounds in his noetic endowment that his compatriots find deeply objectionable, and voluntarily refuse to support any policy that depends essentially on such grounds.[8] The hope is that once each citizen excludes from political decision making and advocacy any and all grounds others in fact find deeply objectionable – once each citizen exercises restraint with respect to significantly controverted grounds – we'll have left over a pool of shared convictions from which we may draw to justify the coercive laws to which we are subject.[9]

In addition to the fact that (4) comports particularly well with the argument from respect, (4) is attractive for two further reasons. First, (4) provides us with a principled basis for determining whether a citizen ought to exercise restraint regarding a given rationale: for any rationale R, if other rational citizens – even a minority of citizens – regard R as unacceptable, then R doesn't constitute a public justification and therefore doesn't constitute a sufficient basis for coercion. Second, (4) gets the right results in a central range of cases. Most important for our purposes, it gets the right results regarding religious grounds. As I noted earlier, a necessary condition of the adequacy of any conception of public justification is that it gives the result that a religious rationale is insufficient for a public justification; (4) satisfies that constraint in spades: it's safe to say that there is no religious rationale for any coercive law of moment that all of the rational citizens in a liberal democracy such as the United States actually accept.[10]

In spite of its attractive features, (4) is a complete, albeit instructive, failure. It violates a condition that any defensible conception of public justification must satisfy, namely, a *sufficiency condition*. A defensible conception of public justification must permit each citizen to rely on considerations that are sufficiently rich as to enable him to articulate a public justification for characteristic liberal commitments. Why must an acceptable conception of public justification satisfy the sufficiency condition? Justificatory liberals are *liberals*: they are committed, for example, to the claim that the state ought to protect each citizen's right to religious freedom. If some conception of public justification sets so high a standard that such liberal commitments stand no chance of enjoying public justification, and therefore forbids citizens from supporting those commitments, then the justificatory liberal's commitment to restraint undermines his commitment to liberalism. Since that is a condition justificatory liberals will, no doubt, avoid at considerable cost, we may assume that any acceptable formulation of the doctrine of restraint will employ a conception of public justification that satisfies the sufficiency condition.[11]

It seems to me, although nothing essential to my argument depends on this, that we should broaden the scope of the sufficiency condition: a defensible conception of public justification must permit each citizen to rely on a fund of considerations that is sufficiently rich as to enable him not only to articulate a public justification for characteristic liberal commitments, but also to arrive at a publicly justifiable resolution of a wide range of the important political decisions he faces.[12] Only then will a citizen be able to satisfy his obligation to provide a public justification for his favored coercive laws: if each citizen has an obligation to articulate a public justification for his favored coercive laws, then he must be *able* to articulate some such public justification, and that requires a sufficiently permissive conception of public justification. In general, then, although the main thrust of the doctrine of restraint is to place constraints on the grounds a citizen may employ in political decision making and advocacy, those constraints mustn't be so demanding that citizens lack access to a set of considerations sufficiently rich as to enable them to reach a publicly justified resolution of the most important, if not all, of the political quandaries they face.

Thesis (4) violates the sufficiency condition. If we take the (rational) citizens of the United States *as they are*, given their actual personality dispositions, levels of education, access to information, prejudices, and cognitive skills, those citizens will exhibit a wide and ever-widening diversity of religious, moral, and political commitments. Consequently, the set of claims to which each rational citizen actually assents will be meager indeed.[13] Although we can grant that all rational citizens will accept certain platitudes – for example, that rape is morally wrong and that torture ought to be legally proscribed – the set of those platitudes will be so meager as to enable citizens to arrive at a publicly justified resolution of only a tiny proportion of the political quandaries they face and, no doubt, for *none* of the live political quandaries they encounter.[14] Actual unanimity is too demanding an ideal to govern the activities of the fractious and fallible mortals who inhabit actual liberal democracies.

I conclude, then, that the distinction between the grounds a citizen may and may not employ in support of his favored coercive laws differs from the distinction between the grounds his rational compatriots accept and those they reject. More precisely, a rationale R's being accepted by the rational citizens who inhabit a given liberal democracy isn't a necessary condition of R's counting as a public justification. This conclusion has an important implication: since R's being accepted by rational citizens isn't a necessary condition of R's counting as a public justification, it is *not* the case that a citizen ought to exercise restraint regarding his *religious convictions* just in virtue of the fact that many of his rational compatriots reject his religious convictions.

7.4 ACCEPTABILITY

Thesis (4) founders on the fact that the rational citizens who inhabit a liberal democracy disagree with one another to such an extent that the set of claims to which each actually assents is quite small. A natural response to this predicament is to weaken the condition (4) lays down on the stance the members of the public must take regarding a prospective public justification. In particular, a natural response is to weaken (4) so that it requires only that rational citizens find a given rationale accept*able*. That is, instead of requiring that rational citizens must actually assent to rationale R's premises in order for R to count as a public justification, the justificatory liberal might require only that rational citizens *can* assent to R's premises.[15]

(5) In order for a citizen's rationale R for some coercive law to count as a public justification, each of his rational compatriots must find R acceptable.

The move from actual acceptance to acceptability significantly weakens the constraints on what counts as a public justification imposed by (4) and consequently enriches the pool of claims from which a citizen may draw to formulate a public justification. After all, the members of the public are no doubt *able* to accept many more claims than they *actually* accept.

Just how permissive (5) is depends entirely on how the justificatory liberal construes the modal claim implicit in (5). If a public justification is a rationale that the members of the public find acceptable, and if a rationale is acceptable just in case the relevant parties *can* accept that rationale, under what conditions can the members of the public accept some rationale? We may eliminate one option from the start. It's obvious that *logical* possibility is a nonstarter. After all, it's clearly logically possible for a normal, adult citizen to accept any given religious claim – even an explicitly self-contradictory one! It is, in fact, logically possible for even the most hard-bitten atheist to accept any given religious claim. Consequently, if we understand acceptability as merely logical possibility, (5) wouldn't preclude a citizen from supporting his favored coercive laws solely on the basis of his religious commitments. And so interpreted, (5) would be unable to fulfil the exclusionary role designed for it.

Clearly, the sense in which some rationale must be acceptable to the members of the public must be considerably more demanding than that of logical possibility. There are numerous options – metaphysical possibility, causal possibility, psychological possibility, and so on. Instead of cycling through a tiresome selection of unsuccessful proposals, I'll discuss the proposal I find most plausible: a citizen can accept rationale R only if accepting R wouldn't rationally require him drastically to revise his evidential set.[16] I have no simple formula for determining what counts as a drastic revision, but the basic idea is easily conveyed by example. Consider Bill McCartney's religious rationale for Amendment 2: if an atheist actually assented to McCartney's rationale, he'd be rationally compelled to revise his noetic structure so as to render his occurrent commitments consistent with theism, and the implications of such a revision would no doubt be quite extensive – they would require an overhaul of his metaphysics, would likely require a radical revision of his moral priorities, and other drastic measures.

Although (5) significantly weakens (4), (5) still seems much too strong. After all, there are any number of rational citizens who not only reject liberal commitments, but find those commitments at such variance with their fundamental convictions that to accept them would require them to revise *their* noetic structures in quite radical respects. For example, some citizens are "Christian Reconstructionists." Here is Clyde Wilcox's description of the Christian Reconstructionist creed:

> At the fringe of the Christian Right is a group of theorists who adhere to the doctrine of *Christian reconstructionism....* These reconstructionists are post-millennialists who believe that Christians must work to recover control of America from the forces of Satan in order to establish the millennium and allow Christ to come again. To do this requires that society be reconstructed from the ground up, generally in keeping with Mosaic

law (the laws of Moses) as detailed in the first five books of the Bible. Rousas John Rushdoony, the most influential reconstructionist thinker, has said that a reconstructed America would have no room for Jews, Buddhists, Muslims, Hindus, Bahais or humanists. There might not even be room for unreconstructed Christians.[17]

That some citizens in the United States are Christian Reconstructionists undermines the adequacy of (5). So long as Christian Reconstructionists rationally adhere to their illiberal creed, and there is no reason to deny that they do,[18] then there are some citizens whose fundamental commitments are so unalterably opposed to the liberal commitment to religious freedom that inclusion of that commitment in their evidential set would require drastic revisions in their respective noetic structures. And since, according to (5), in order for a citizen's rationale R to count as a public justification, his compatriots must be able to incorporate R into their respective evidential sets without being rationally compelled drastically to revise their evidential sets, it follows that (5) would render the liberal commitment to religious freedom publicly unjustifiable.[19] Consequently, (5) violates the sufficiency condition and thus is indefensible.

7.5 RESTRICTING MEMBERSHIP IN THE PUBLIC

A natural strategy for amending (5) is to further restrict membership in the public: instead of including all rational citizens in the public, membership in the public must be limited to a subset of rational citizens. The motivation for doing so is straightforward. Most obviously, we can rid ourselves of those pesky Christian Reconstructionists: if we limit membership in the public to a subset of citizens, and if that subset doesn't include any Christian Reconstructionists, then the mere existence of a fringe group that rejects religious freedom needn't scuttle (5). And more generally, if we limit membership in the public to only *some* of the rational citizens who inhabit an actual liberal democracy, rather than including *all* rational citizens, then we can safely assume that the convictions the public shares will increase in both number and richness. And if the convictions the public shares increases in both of those respects, then a suitably modified populist conception of public justification might satisfy the sufficiency condition. Consider in this regard the following.

7.5.1 Most Citizens

If the justificatory liberal is going to limit membership in the public to only a subset of rational citizens, then why not just incorporate that limitation, in unadulterated fashion, into her favored conception of public justification? Why not require that, in order for a citizen's rationale R to count as a public justification, *most* of that citizen's compatriots must find R acceptable? In that case, even if *some* rational members of the public regard R as unacceptable, R might nevertheless count as a public justification. The move here is to weaken the notion of public justification so that it requires *wide agreement* rather than *unanimity*.[20] Thus, the following conception of public justification might seem promising:

(6) In order for a citizen's rationale R for some coercive law to count as a public justification, most of her rational compatriots must find R acceptable.

Thesis (6) strikes me as ill suited to the justificatory liberal's purposes. As I see it, justificatory liberalism is unabashedly and unavoidably *universalistic*: its central claim is that *each* citizen deserves to be respected by her compatriots and thus that *each* citizen has a right to demand a public justification for the coercive laws to which she is subject, where a public justification is a sort of rationale that articulates appropriately with *each* citizen's distinctive point of view.[21] The universality of the obligation to respect others translates directly into a *universality condition* on an adequate conception of public justification. Why?

On a conception of public justification that requires only wide agreement, it might be that any number of coercive laws count as publicly justified even though many rational citizens of good faith – just *how* many depends on how wide an agreement the conception of public justification under consideration requires – lack any reason whatsoever from their point of view to accept that coercive law. But I fail to see any *morally relevant* difference between a citizen who refuses to adhere to the doctrine of restraint, and who is thus willing to support a coercive law solely on the basis of a rationale that *most* of her rational compatriots find deeply objectionable, and one who adheres to the weakened version of the doctrine of restraint under consideration, and who is thus willing to support coercive laws solely on the basis of a rationale that *some* of her rational compatriots find deeply unacceptable. Both citizens are willing to coerce many – no doubt thousands and possibly millions in a society as populous as the United States – of their compatriots on the basis of a rationale those compatriots regard as unacceptable. In that case, I should think the justificatory liberal would claim that *neither* citizen has treated her compatriots with the respect that is their due. Both citizens violate the norm of respect, do so for the same reason, and do so to the same degree: after all, surely a citizen's manifesting or failing to manifest the relevant sort of respect isn't a function of the *number* of people she's willing to coerce absent a rationale they find acceptable.

7.5.2 Reasonable Citizens

The justificatory liberal is not without recourse here. The problem with construing a public justification as a rationale that elicits wide agreement is not that it restricts membership in the public, but that it does so in the wrong way. Instead of straightforwardly abandoning the universalistic commitments of justificatory liberalism, the justificatory liberal needs to articulate *principled* grounds for taking into consideration the commitments of only some rational citizens in determining whether some coercive law enjoys public justification. There is a crucial difference between the claim that only those rational citizens who satisfy a reasonable set of conditions enjoy membership in the public and the claim that only those rational citizens who adhere to a widely prevailing view enjoy membership in the public.[22] In the first case, we can provide a principled reason for excluding some citizens from membership in the public, whereas in the second case, we can provide no such reason – the excluded citizens are simply unfortunate enough to accept a minority position.

Nothing is ever simple in Rawls's exegesis, and I have no intention of pursuing an extensive excursus on his conception of public justification, but as I read him, Rawls takes this tack in developing his conception of public justification.[23] Three brief points by way of explication. First, Rawls is clearly committed to a populist conception of public justification of some sort: the basic components of public reason are to be located in the stock of commitments shared by the members of a liberal political culture. Rawls writes:

> How might political philosophy find a shared basis for settling such a fundamental question as that of the most appropriate family of institutions to secure democratic liberty and equality? . . . We collect such settled

convictions as the belief in religious toleration and the rejection of slavery and try to organize the basic ideas and principles implicit in these convictions into a coherent political conception of justice. These convictions are provisional fixed points that it seems any reasonable conception must account for. We start, then, by looking to the public culture itself as the shared fund of implicitly recognized basic ideas and principles. We hope to formulate these ideas and principles clearly enough to be combined into a political conception of justice congenial to our most firmly held convictions. We express this by saying that a political conception of justice, to be acceptable, must accord with our considered convictions, at all levels of generality, on due reflection.[24]

In order to articulate a conception of justice that enjoys the imprimatur of public reason, we must ensure that that conception of justice accords with "our most firmly held convictions." But *whose* firmly held convictions does Rawls have in mind here? Surely not *each* citizen's firmly held convictions: as we have seen, Christian Reconstructionists rationally reject the liberal commitment to religious freedom. If Rawls intended us to consult the convictions of Christian Reconstructionists, his position would fare no better than (4) and (5): although slavery and religious persecution are quite unpopular nowadays, there are no doubt many citizens who find themselves out of step with the regnant liberal culture on those points.

Second, the citizens whose firmly held convictions we must take into consideration are, Rawls claims, "reasonable" citizens; according to Rawls, the target group that determines what counts as a public justification is limited to reasonable persons.[25] For Rawls, the "reasonable" is, most fundamentally, a moral concept. In Rawls's idiolect, a citizen is reasonable only if she satisfies at least two conditions. First, she's willing to seek out and obey fair principles of social cooperation.[26] Second, she recognizes the burdens of judgment and their implications; in particular, she recognizes that persons of good faith and cognitive competence can assent to any number of conflicting religious, moral, and metaphysical worldviews.[27] Rawls's restriction of the public to reasonable citizens explains why he can claim that among "our" firmly held convictions are the claims that slavery is wrong and that religious persecution is unjust: what he means is that "reasonable" citizens adhere to those claims.[28]

Why is Rawls so confident that reasonable citizens affirm religious freedom and reject slavery? Those values are, of course, deeply embedded in the political culture of the United States. But the fact that some value is deeply embedded in a given political culture isn't nearly sufficient for its being affirmed by reasonable citizens. Rawls answers as follows: reasonable citizens are committed to searching for fair terms of social cooperation, and "for these terms to be fair terms, citizens offering them must reasonably think that those citizens to whom such terms are offered might also reasonably accept them."[29] But it's obvious that we can't expect each of our compatriots to accede to religious persecution or slavery: for example, even if *most* citizens were to adhere to some religious orthodoxy, there will always be, in a liberal democracy such as the United States, *some* citizens who reject that prevailing orthodoxy. Consequently, a *reasonable* citizen won't support any policy that authorizes the persecution of those who reject that orthodoxy: no one could, with a straight face, claim that each of her compatriots might accept that policy as a basis for social cooperation and therefore that that policy counts as fair in the relevant sense.[30] Thus, Christian Reconstructionists are unreasonable just because they intend to impose on their compatriots a regime that requires the stoning of heretics even though they realize that at least some of their rational and reasonable compatriots will find any such regime utterly repugnant.

As I understand his position, Rawls circumscribes membership in the public by drawing moral lines in the sand. It is from among the commitments shared by rational and reasonable citizens – those willing, among other things, to seek out and abide by fair terms of social cooperation – that we draw the considerations out of which we fashion a public justification for the coercive laws to which we're subject.[31] Only if a citizen can articulate some rationale for her favored coercive laws by drawing on claims shared by the set of rational and reasonable citizens does that citizen enjoys a public justification for those laws. And if she can't articulate some such rationale, then she ought to withhold support from those laws. Suppose, then, that we reformulate (6) in a Rawlsian spirit:

(7) In order for a citizen's rationale R for some coercive law to count as a public justification, each reasonable and rational citizen must find R acceptable.[32]

Note that, although Rawls argues that the materials out of which we construct a public justification must be shared by reasonable and rational citizens, he does *not* claim that publicly justifying a given law will elicit consensus on that law, even among reasonable and rational citizens.[33] The point is to articulate some rationale that *begins* from common ground, even if the position that that rationale supports is highly controversial and therefore is rejected by even entirely rational and reasonable citizens.[34] So we move *from* but not invariably *to* common ground.

Third, Rawls's restriction of the target group to reasonable persons seems defensible. Just as there is little point in allowing infants and madmen to count as members of the public, and just as it's appropriate to restrict membership in the public to rational citizens, so also is there little point in allowing unreasonable citizens to count as members of the public. After all, a citizen's commitment to public justification just is a commitment to seek out fair terms of social cooperation for the members of a highly pluralistic society. A citizen who rejects public justification entirely can hardly complain if those who affirm public justification don't concern themselves with her protestations when the latter determine whether they enjoy a public justification in a given case. In short, a citizen who doesn't value public justification forfeits her right to play a role in determining what counts as a public justification.[35]

7.5.3 The Implications of the Burdens of Judgment

What should we make of (7)? I don't think that (7) holds out any brighter prospects than previous populist proposals. Rawls wants to take to heart the fact that a modern liberal democracy such as the United States is characterized by an irremediable and pervasive pluralism. The move to public justification, according to Rawls, is a consequence of the need to respond in a morally responsible way to the fact that, in a free society, rational citizens will invariably and reasonably disagree among themselves regarding which way of life is most meaningful, which religion is true, what counts as beautiful, and so on. I concur entirely in that judgment: when repression fails, pluralism prevails. But Rawls's populist conception of public justification commits him to the claim that the pluralism endemic to a free society has its limits: Rawls's, and indeed *any* populist, conception of public justification is an obvious nonstarter unless there is a set of claims that rational and reasonable citizens find acceptable. Although the reasonable pluralism endemic to a liberal democracy is pervasive and extensive, it must nevertheless be *partial*: there are some things about which those among us who are rational and reasonable concur. And not only is pluralism partial, but it is partial in just the right way: the things we rational and reasonable people find acceptable must be sufficiently rich, such that by relying on that common ground, we are able to articulate a rationale that provides a determinate resolution for the political quandaries we face.

I see no reason that we should expect a modern liberal democracy to exhibit the partial consensus that must obtain if Rawls's conception of public justification is to avoid violating the sufficiency condition. I admit that the state of affairs that must obtain for Rawls's populist conception of public justification to work is *logically* possible. And I fully admit that rational and reasonable citizens will share a fund of platitudes; they will agree that rape and gratuitous torture are morally wrong and ought to be legally prohibited. But I see no reason to think that the partial consensus that must obtain in order for (7) to satisfy the sufficiency condition is *actual* or even *likely*. After all, why should the burdens of judgment give rise to an irremediable pluralism regarding Rawls's favored targets (conceptions of the good, metaphysical claims, comprehensive doctrines, religious traditions, etc.) and *not* give rise to a similarly extensive divergence of conviction regarding all but the most platitudinous claims? Why shouldn't we expect that the very factors Rawls seizes upon to explain the reasonable pluralism endemic to a free society result in dissensus not just regarding conceptions of the good and religious commitments but regarding all but the most vapid commonplaces?[36]

As I see it, Rawls's account of the burdens of judgment provides us with good reason to doubt that the required partial consensus has a realistic prospect of obtaining in a modern liberal democracy such as the United States. On Rawls's account, disagreements regarding conceptions of the good and religious commitments, comprehensive doctrines don't arise primarily, or even typically, from a deficit of reasonableness. Much to the contrary, Rawls is at pains to point out that dissensus regarding conceptions of the good and religious commitments will persist among reasonable people. For that dissensus is to be explained by the fact that even fully reasonable and rational citizens are beset by a number of factors that render quite hazardous the judgments required to evaluate religious commitments, conceptions of the good, and so on: for example, the difficulty of ranking disparate values given our different personal histories as well as the complexity and inconsistency of the empirical evidence that bears on a given issue.[37] But if the disagreement that scuttles the preceding populist proposals isn't *generated* by the unreasonableness of citizens, then we need some explanation as to why *limiting* membership in the public to only reasonable citizens will *eliminate* (or even significantly mitigate) that disagreement. Absent such an explanation, we should expect that the disagreement among reasonable citizens will be just about as extensive as the disagreement among reasonable and unreasonable citizens – which is to say that it will extend to all but the most platitudinous claims. And that disagreement, it is plausible to suppose, is sufficiently extensive as to ensure that a citizen who intends to conduct her political decision making and advocacy solely on the basis of grounds she shares with her rational and reasonable compatriots will have no chance of providing a public justification for many, if not all, of the commitments at the heart of the liberal tradition. Moreover, she'll have no chance of providing a publicly justified resolution of many, if not all, of the live political quandaries she faces. As with (4) and (5), (7) violates the sufficiency condition; moreover, we have the same reason to believe that (7) violates the sufficiency condition that we have to believe that (4) and (5) violate that condition. In light of the burdens of judgment, then, Gerald Gaus's evaluation of Rawls's version of justificatory populism seems compelling:

> Rawls' theory ... is indicative of the problems of embracing the commitment to justify while at the same time forgoing epistemological commitments. Political liberalism is driven to a sort of populist consensualism because it deprives itself of the resources on which to ground the claim that liberal principles are justified in the face of sustained dissent by reasonable people. Any reasonable person who does not accept its claims becomes a counter-example. Pushed by its populism, [Rawls's theory] moves to modify and weaken its liberal commitments in search of an ever wider and thinner consensus. Ultimately, I think, it loses its character as a liberal doctrine, for little, if anything, is the object of consensus among reasonable people. ... The project of securing a consensus of all reasonable people leads to the undermining of [Rawls's] liberalism, which is to say that it leads to self-destruction.[38]

My central objection to (7) is that the burdens of judgment render utopian the hope that the many tens of millions of rational and reasonable citizens who inhabit the United States will be able to agree on a sufficiently rich set of claims as to enable them to articulate a public justification for characteristic liberal commitments. In the next two subsections, I'll illustrate how two of the burdens of judgment Rawls enumerates – the difficulty of weighing disparate moral values and the complexity of politically relevant empirical information – renders it possible for entirely rational and reasonable citizens to find themselves at loggerheads over two issues: abortion and religious freedom. I'll argue that, given those two burdens of judgment, citizens we have no reason to believe are either irrational or unreasonable can reject the positions regarding abortion and religious freedom that, according to Rawls, reasonable and rational citizens will accept.

7.5.3.1 Abortion. Assume for purposes of argument, Rawls suggests, that the abortion question implicates three political values: to due respect for human beings, to the ordered reproduction of society, and to the equality of women as equal citizens.[39] In order to count as publicly justified, any political resolution of the abortion controversy must be supported by a rationale that involves a "reasonable" balance of these three values.[40] According to Rawls, "any reasonable balance of these three values will give a woman a duly qualified right to decide whether or not to end her pregnancy during the first trimester."[41] By contrast, "any [rationale] that leads to a balance of political values excluding that duly qualified right in the first trimester is to that extent unreasonable."[42] Indeed, according to Rawls, a rationale that denies that right even excepting the cases of rape and incest might be "cruel and oppressive."[43] So Rawls claims that one position on the issue of abortion enjoys public justification, namely, that the state ought to grant each woman a duly qualified right to abortion during her first trimester, and that another position on the issue of abortion lacks public justification, namely, that the state ought to prohibit a woman from having an abortion even in cases of rape and incest. And given Rawls's conception of public justification, it follows that the policy granting each woman a duly qualified right to abortion in the first trimester enjoys some rationale that relies solely on claims that rational and reasonable citizens find acceptable and it also follows that the policy denying each woman a duly qualified right to abortion in the first trimester doesn't enjoy some rationale that relies solely on claims that rational and reasonable citizens find acceptable.

Assume for purposes of argument that the vast majority of citizens are committed to the three political values that are, as Rawls constructs his illustration, implicated in the abortion question: they count as *platitudes* for citizens of the United States. Do we have reason to believe

217

that there is some way to fashion those platitudes into an argument in support of one or another position on abortion that includes among its essential premises only those claims which rational and reasonable citizens in the United States find acceptable? I doubt it.

First, a mere laundry list of the values implicated in the abortion controversy won't provide, by itself, an adequate basis for any particular position on abortion. Appeal to those values, even if they are platitudinous, requires *supplementation*: as Rawls acknowledges, the values implicated in his formulation of the abortion controversy will support a given position only if we accord them a particular weighting. (Rawls is explicit about how "reasonable" people weigh the relevant values: "at this early stage of pregnancy the political value of the equality of women is overriding."[44])

Second, any rationale that counts as a public justification must contain *only* those premises that rational and reasonable citizens find acceptable. After all, it's trivially easy to articulate an argument in support of one or another position on abortion that incorporates *some* premises reasonable citizens find acceptable and *some* premises they do not. All we need to do, for example, is to claim that God has revealed that the various platitudes implicated in the abortion issue are to be given such and such a weight: for example, that the equality of women ought to override due respect for human life in the first trimester. Any such argument would, of course, appeal to platitudes, but not *only* to platitudes. But it wouldn't be any better a candidate for public justification than a rationale that appealed to no platitudes at all, since the *crucial* premise – the premise that instructs us as to how we ought to weigh the relevant values – is as controversial as a premise can get.

Third, given that a laundry list of the platitudes implicated in the abortion issue requires supplementation by some ranking of those values, given that each of the premises of a putative public justification must be acceptable to rational and reasonable citizens, and given, more particularly, that the premise that *ranks* the values implicated in the abortion issue must be acceptable to rational and reasonable citizens, it's clear that Rawls can't articulate a public justification for the claim that the state ought to grant each woman a right to have an abortion in the first trimester. Any supplementary ranking of the implicated political values that gets the desired result will be anything but platitudinous: claims about platitudes are not *typically* platitudes themselves, and claims that rank the platitudes implicated in the abortion issue will *invariably* be controverted by fully rational and reasonable citizens. Nearly any ranking of the platitudes implicated in the abortion controversy, including Rawls's claim that "at this early stage of pregnancy the political value of the equality of women is overriding" will be contested by reasonable citizens.[45]

This should be anything from surprising. Among the factors included in Rawls's account of the burdens of judgment that should lead us to expect disagreement among reasonable people regarding religious convictions, comprehensive doctrines, and so on, is the fact that

> to some extent (how great we cannot tell) the way we assess evidence and weigh moral and political values is shaped by our total experience, our whole course of life up to now; and our total experiences must always differ. Thus, in a modern society with its numerous offices and positions, its various divisions of labor, its many social groups and their ethnic variety, citizens' total experiences are disparate enough for their judgments to diverge, at least to some degree, on many if not most of the cases of any significant complexity.[46]

It seems pretty clear that this particular "burden of judgment" will preclude agreement among even rational and reasonable citizens as to how we ought to weigh due respect for human beings and the equality of women. In fact, few claims – even few religious claims – will be as controverted as are claims that purport to provide a fair weighing of such values as the equality of women and due respect for human beings.[47] Consequently, we should expect that even the most plausible arguments in support of a given position on abortion will include premises to which any number of rational and reasonable citizens will vociferously object. We have no reason to expect, given the burdens of judgment, that any rationale regarding abortion will move from common ground among reasonable and rational citizens; any such rationale begins from contested ground and never leaves it.

There is no reason to believe that the abortion controversy is distinctive in this respect: issues of economic fairness, pornography, welfare reform, sex education, and others require us to engage in an eminently controversial process of weighing values – values that are, in the best case, platitudinous, but in the typical case, are both contested and highly ambiguous. Consequently, for any number of live political disputes, we can expect that large numbers of rational and reasonable citizens will reject any proposed balance of the values implicated in those disputes.

And in that case, a citizen who attempts to resolve some political dispute by relying solely on claims each of her reasonable compatriots finds acceptable – who exercises restraint in accord with (7) – will find herself without any way of resolving that dispute. Even if *some* or even *many* of the claims on which a citizen relies will enjoy the imprimatur of each of her reasonable and rational compatriots, any argument she articulates in support of a live political dispute will employ as least *one* premise which *some* of her reasonable and rational compatriots find deeply objectionable. It seems reasonable to suppose, therefore, that (7) violates the sufficiency condition.

7.5.3.2 Religious Freedom. Rawls claims, as we have seen, that a reasonable citizen will commit himself to religious freedom. To deny another citizen freedom to worship as he pleases is to refuse to offer him fair terms of social cooperation – terms he can reasonably accept – and is thereby unreasonable.[48] Suppose, for the sake of argument, that Calvin is reasonable in Rawls's sense. Suppose, further, that Calvin has good reason, given *his* evidential set, to believe that Servetus is a heretic. As a reasonable person, Calvin will respect the burdens of judgment in his practical deliberations and realize that Servetus, given *Servetus'* evidential set, will properly reject Calvin's belief that Servetus is a heretic. Consequently, Servetus will reject any proposal that the state may employ its coercive power to burn folks who adhere to Servetus' "heretical" creed. That Servetus properly rejects any law that authorizes the state to burn those who adhere to his religious creed entails that any such law doesn't count as generally acceptable: at the very least, Servetus and his co-religionists will refuse to accept any such law. Given this state of affairs, Calvin will refrain from trying to induce the city fathers at Geneva to burn Servetus: so refraining is required by Calvin's commitment to seek out and obey fair terms of social cooperation. Since exactly the same argument would apply to Servetus, were he to propose burning heretics of the Calvinist persuasion, it seems that "the only generally acceptable basis for freedom of worship is equal freedom for everybody."[49]

Rawls's argument seems to me to provide compelling reason to believe that Calvin's support for burning heretics isn't the sort of rationale required by (7). But is it really true that according religious freedom to everyone is *generally* acceptable? Is it true that a policy that grants Servetus and his co-religionists religious freedom constitutes a fair basis for social cooperation? That seems unlikely. In fact, it seems likely that there is *no* generally acceptable resolution of the dispute between

Calvin and Servetus. After all, it seems just as unreasonable (in Rawls's sense) for Servetus to affirm religious freedom, and thus authorize the state to employ its coercive power to protect religious freedom, as it was unreasonable for Calvin to reject religious freedom. Why? Calvin might very well find Servetus' affirmation of religious freedom just as objectionable as Servetus finds Calvin's denial of religious freedom, in which case *Servetus* lacks the sort of rationale required by (7) and thus lacks a public justification for religious freedom. That is, Servetus finds himself in exactly the same condition with respect to the propriety of his commitment to religious freedom as Calvin finds himself with respect to his commitment to burning heretics. How so? Surely Calvin cannot *reasonably* reject religious freedom.

It seems, to the contrary, that he can: Calvin can be fully reasonable, and thus genuinely and sincerely committed to seeking out and obeying fair terms of social cooperation, but he rationally believes that to accord religious freedom to Servetus would be to court truly debilitating societal dysfunctions. Let's assume that Calvin accepted a commonplace of premodern and early modern political theory: that agreement on fundamentals is essential to social order.[50] Many of Calvin's contemporaries believed that a necessary condition of social stability is that the population, by and large, commits itself to the same set of moral and religious creeds; correlatively, many of Calvin's compatriots adopted the "commonsense" dictum that deviation from the hegemonic creed was a threat to social order. Heresy, on this way of thinking, is tantamount to treason: the heretic endangers society simply in virtue of rejecting the commitments that provide society with the social glue necessary to avoid anarchy and the many societal dysfunctions that ensue from anarchy.

If, as we are assuming, Calvin genuinely and rationally believes that social order requires agreement on fundamentals, then surely Servetus cannot propose as a basis for social cooperation a policy that accords heretics such as Servetus religious freedom: he would, in effect, be proposing as a basis for social *cooperation* a policy that Calvin rationally takes to be a recipe for social *chaos*! But in that case Servetus lacks a public justification for his commitment to religious freedom: given Rawls's understanding of reasonableness, it would have been just as unreasonable for Servetus to support a law mandating that the state protect religious freedom as it was for Calvin to support a law that mandates the burning of Servetus and his co-religionists.

It seems that Calvin and Servetus' disagreement over whether Servetus should be burned need have *nothing* to do with the reasonableness of either party and have everything to do with their differential convictions as to the likely consequences of allowing people with Servetus' convictions to ply their heretical trade unhindered by government censure. That is, even if we assume that both Calvin and Servetus fully commit to seek out and obey fair terms of social cooperation, and that both fully recognize the implications of the burdens of judgment, it's possible for both of them to arrive at diametrically opposed positions on the issue of religious freedom. Their disagreement is a consequence, not of unreasonableness on the part of one or the other party, but of their differential convictions regarding the causal *consequences* of according religious freedom to folks such as Servetus: Calvin thinks that, as a matter of fact, religious freedom results in anarchy; Servetus thinks that it does not.

But *that* sort of difference is exactly what we should expect if we accept Rawls's account of the burdens of judgment. After all, to gloss Rawls, "the evidence – empirical and scientific – bearing on the [issue of religious freedom] is conflicting and complex, and thus hard to assess and evaluate."[51] Given Rawls's account of the burdens of judgment, we can expect citizens to arrive at very different but rationally defensible conclusions regarding all manner of factual claims, many of those claims will bear directly on the propriety and impropriety of characteristic liberal commitments and, as a consequence, some citizens will find unacceptable many liberal commitments even though they are fully committed to proposing and supporting generally acceptable terms of social cooperation.

It seems, then, that what a citizen will take to be fair terms of social cooperation depends on the evidential set he relies on to evaluate the various contenders. Given the variation we can expect in the evidential sets different citizens will employ to evaluate one or another proposal, it seems highly likely that only a very few proposals will enjoy the imprimatur of reasonable and rational citizens, in which case it seems that (7) violates the sufficiency condition.

7.6 ADEQUATE INFORMATION

As I noted at the outset of this chapter, populist conceptions of public justification tend to include in the public as many citizens as is feasible and they tend to require that the members of the public regard some rationale as an adequate basis for a given coercive law *from the perspective constituted by each citizen's actual evidential set.* But my discussion of Calvin's objection to the liberal commitment to religious freedom suggests that the justificatory liberal would be well advised to moderate the latter tendency. That is, the justificatory liberal should require, not that a rationale be acceptable to citizens given their actual evidential sets, but that a rationale be acceptable to citizens given suitably *idealized* evidential sets. After all, we *know*, given the past several hundred years of history, that the empirical claim that motivated many premodern objections to religious freedom is *false*. It is *not* the case that religious freedom is a recipe for social anarchy. Consequently, even if Calvin or his modern descendants, the Christian Reconstructionists, *think* that social order requires agreement on fundamentals, and even if they are *rationally justified* in thinking that social order requires agreement on fundamentals, we are entitled to take into consideration the fact that that claim is false in determining whether we enjoy a public justification for religious freedom. After all, it seems unduly constraining to require that, in order for some rationale to count as a public justification, that rationale must be convincing to the members of the public, *no matter how* uninformed or benighted (some of) the members of the public might be. Surely, a successful public justification must be convincing only to *adequately informed* citizens – that is, to rational and reasonable citizens who evaluate a given rationale in light of reasonably reliable information. (Thus, Brian Barry: "What cannot be accepted is that agreement should be stymied by objections based on misinformation."[52])

Our discussion of Calvin, then, suggests that the justificatory liberal should require that a citizen attribute *adequate* information to his compatriots and then determine whether his compatriots, so idealized, would find some rationale R acceptable. If a citizen's compatriots, suitably idealized, wouldn't find R acceptable, then R doesn't count as a public justification and he ought not support a coercive law solely on the basis of R. It is natural, therefore, for the justificatory liberal to endorse the following conception of public justification:

(8) A citizen's rationale R counts as a public justification for some coercive law only if R would be acceptable to his reasonable, rational, and adequately informed compatriots.[53]

A crucial question: under what conditions are a citizen's compatriots adequately informed? This seems to me to be an exceedingly difficult question (although not one on which advocates of this kind of idealizing conception of public justification spend much time).[54] The information (8) allows a citizen to impute to his compatriots can't be constrained by what his compatriots are rationally justified in believing: Calvin is, by hypothesis, rationally justified in believing the falsehood that social order requires agreement in fundamentals and so an understanding of "adequate information" that is too weak to allow a citizen to impute information to his compatriots that they explicitly and rationally reject won't have the desired consequences. On the other hand, it seems utterly pointless to adopt some radically objective interpretation of adequate information, such that a citizen is adequately informed about some coercive law only if he is *omniscient*: since none of us has any idea as to the sort of information an omniscient being has regarding a given coercive law, such an interpretation would render (8) otiose.

An appropriate interpretation of adequate information will lie somewhere between these extremes; the following seems a natural interpretation – although by no means the only one. A citizen is adequately informed with respect to R only if he evaluates R in light of whatever socially available and reliable information bears on the soundness of R.[55] Thus, suppose Elijah supports some law designed to reduce the rate of global warming. Suppose Elijah supports that law on the basis of some rationale that depends essentially on a reputable scientific theory T. But suppose many of his compatriots are *ignorant* of T and as a consequence refuse to accept his rationale. In that case, (8) allows Elijah to impute to his compatriots knowledge of T and to determine whether they would find his rationale acceptable once their evidential sets have been modified in light of the new information about T.

Thesis (8), however, allows Elijah even more latitude than permitting him to impute to his compatriots information of which they are ignorant. It also allows him to impute to his compatriots information of which they are aware but reject.[56] Thus, for example, suppose Elijah's compatriots know of T, reject T, and are rationally justified in doing so. On the understanding of adequate information embedded in (8), (8) still allows Elijah to impute knowledge of T to his compatriots. In short, the understanding of *adequate* information embedded in (8) is not constrained by what other citizens take to be adequate information. Of course, that the understanding of adequate information in (8) is not thus constrained is why it's plausible to suppose that other citizens would find a given rationale acceptable if they were better informed than they are in fact. The less "adequate information" is constrained by other citizens' actual convictions, then, presumably, the more likely they – or, more precisely, their counterfactual counterparts – will be able to agree on the propriety of the coercive laws to which they are subject.

What should we make of (8)? Three objections to (8) seem to me to be telling and, moreover, indicate that the idealizing strategy as a whole can't be worked out in a satisfactory manner.

First, (8) is too weak to forbid a citizen from supporting his favored coercive policies solely on religious grounds and can't thereby do the exclusionary work required of it. Suppose that Bill McCartney is fully committed to obeying (8) and wants to determine whether he enjoys a public justification for Amendment 2. Does the claim that homosexuality is an abomination to God afford McCartney the desired public justification? Well, many of McCartney's rational and reasonable compatriots *disagree* with his rationale for Amendment 2. But, pretty obviously, that they disagree with his rationale doesn't settle the issue. What would settle the issue is the following: that his rational, reasonable, *and* adequately informed compatriots would find his rationale for Amendment 2 unacceptable. In that case, (8) would forbid McCartney from supporting Amendment 2 solely on the basis of his conviction that homosexuality is a moral abomination.

So, what would McCartney's reasonable and rational compatriots make of his rationale if they were adequately informed about the considerations relevant to Amendment 2?[57] McCartney believes that homosexuality is an abomination to God on the basis of his belief that the Bible is divinely inspired: the Bible is a source of information – not *just* a source of information, but *at least* a source of information – that McCartney takes to contain information that is highly relevant to Amendment 2. So would his compatriots be aware that the Bible is divinely inspired? If adequately informed, would his compatriots be aware of and make use of the Bible in determining whether to support Amendment 2? What should *McCartney* think about that counterfactual? (He is, after all, the person the justificatory liberal is expecting to apply (8).)

It seems eminently reasonable for McCartney to conclude that his compatriots would be aware that the Bible is divinely inspired. The following argument in support of that conclusion seems to me to be compelling.

(1) If it is appropriate for McCartney to determine, by employing his religious convictions, what adequately informed citizens would find acceptable, then it is appropriate for McCartney to conclude that adequately informed citizens would regard the Bible as inspired.

(2) It is appropriate for McCartney to determine, by employing his religious convictions, what adequately informed citizens would find acceptable.

(3) Hence, it is appropriate for McCartney to conclude that adequately informed citizens would regard the Bible as inspired.

Ad (1): Thesis (8) requires that a citizen who intends to exercise restraint must determine the truth of a particular counterfactual claim C: if his compatriots were adequately informed, would they find his rationale for a given coercive law acceptable? Presumably, each citizen ought to make that determination *rationally*. Whether it's rational for a citizen to accept C is determined, in crucial part, by the total set of evidence in light of which he evaluates C. Since different citizens will invariably evaluate C in light of different evidential sets, it will often be rational for different citizens to reach differing and incompatible conclusions regarding C. There is every reason to believe that the conclusions citizens reach regarding the relevant counterfactual claim will vary in the expected way: since different citizens rely on different evidential sets, they will rationally arrive at different conclusions regarding what suitably idealized citizens would find acceptable. And the conclusions a given citizen reaches regarding what his appropriately idealized compatriots would find acceptable will vary in accord with differences in the evidential set he employs in arriving at these conclusions. Otherwise put, the conclusions that a citizen draws regarding what his adequately informed compatriots would find acceptable are a function of the information he relies on in making that determination.

Thus, for example, justificatory liberals typically claim that citizens who are adequately informed about some coercive law would evaluate that law in light of whatever well-established scientific theories bear on that law. Their confidence in the reliability of science is not imposed by transcendental necessity. Rather, it is based on what they take to be adequate evidence that science provides us with an accurate understanding of reality. Those who lack that evidence, of course, won't be so willing to impute awareness of well-established scientific theories to adequately informed citizens. A primitive tribesman, if the justificatory liberal could induce him to adhere to (8), would reasonably conclude that adequately informed citizens are aware, say, that the reading of chicken entrails is a reliable way of forming beliefs. The tribesman wouldn't, we may assume, impute awareness of well-corroborated scientific theories to adequately informed citizens. The difference in the convictions the justificatory liberal and the tribesman impute to idealized citizens is a function of differences between the parochial convictions on the basis of which they attempt to determine what the appropriately idealized citizens would believe.

Similarly for religious citizens such as McCartney. Since McCartney believes that the Bible is a reliable source of information about God's will and nature, it's natural for him to conclude that an adequately informed citizen would be aware of that fact. He has the same reason to impute the conviction that the Bible is divinely inspired to adequately informed citizens that the justificatory liberal has to impute the conviction that science is reliable to adequately informed citizens. After all, how could McCartney's compatriots be adequately informed about homosexuality if they are ignorant of one of the most important facts about homosexuality, namely, that God – an omniscient moral authority – has expressly condemned homosexual behavior?[58] McCartney claims that nonbelievers think otherwise because they are *inadequately informed*, just as justificatory liberals are committed to the claim that a primitive tribesman who immigrates to the United States and who rejects the claim that science is reliable is inadequately informed.[59]

Ad (2): It seems clear that *if* McCartney is permitted to employ his religious convictions to determine what adequately informed citizens would believe, he will quite properly read his parochial religious convictions into his understanding of what such idealized citizens would believe. So, if the justificatory liberal who advocates (8) is to achieve his exclusionary purposes – to articulate a principle of restraint powerful enough to exclude religious convictions as a basis for political decision making and advocacy – he must show that it's inappropriate for McCartney to employ his religious convictions to determine what adequately informed citizens would believe. That is, he must articulate some principled reason why McCartney may not employ his religious commitments in determining whether adequately informed citizens would realize that the Bible is divinely inspired. But there is no such principled reason, so far as I am aware.

Note first that the justificatory liberal has no option but to permit McCartney to determine what adequately informed citizens have good reason to believe *by relying on his own parochial commitments*. The argument in support of this claim takes the form of a dilemma. Either McCartney may determine what idealized citizens would find acceptable by relying on some rendering of what idealized citizens would find acceptable or it is not the case that he may determine what idealized citizens would find acceptable by relying on some rendering of what idealized citizens would find acceptable. By hypothesis, McCartney doesn't yet know what an adequately informed citizen would believe about the Bible: we are imagining him in the throes of determining what the appropriately idealized citizens would find acceptable. Hence, he can't determine what such citizens would find acceptable by relying on some rendering of what idealized citizens find acceptable. Consequently, in determining what an adequately informed person would believe, McCartney must rely on *someone's* parochial convictions regarding reliable belief-forming practices, well-corroborated scientific theories, moral truths, and the like. He could, of course, rely on someone *else's* convictions in determining what idealized citizens would find acceptable, but that seems arbitrary: given that the content of "adequate information" is going to be filled out by *someone's* parochial convictions, why someone else's and not his own? It seems, then, that if McCartney is actually going to apply (8) in his actual circumstances, he has no option but to rely on *his own* parochial commitments. As is the case with every one of us, McCartney's judgment regarding what *ideally circumstanced* citizens would believe about the reliability of the Bible is unavoidably parasitic on judgments he has formed in his own circumstances.

Of course, that McCartney may rely on his parochial commitments in determining what suitably idealized citizens would believe doesn't imply that he may rely on *all* of his parochial commitments. Certainly, he may rely on some – otherwise he has no basis on which to make the relevant determination. But perhaps not all. And if not all, then perhaps *none* of his religious commitments. So here is the question: if McCartney is permitted to rely on *some* of his parochial commitments in determining what adequately informed citizens would find acceptable, then why can't he rely on his religious convictions in making that determination? If he can rely on his scientific, perceptual, moral, and introspective commitments in determining what adequately informed citizens would find acceptable, then why not his religious commitments as well? We need some reason to single out religious commitments for special treatment.

Religious commitments are, of course, widely contested. But dissensus regarding religious convictions provides no good reason to prohibit McCartney from employing his religious commitments to determine what adequately informed citizens would find acceptable. After all, the move *to* an idealizing conception of public justification is motivated by the reality that fully reasonable and rational citizens in modern, pluralistic democracies disagree with one another about so much; more particularly, just as many citizens will reject the claim that an adequately informed citizen would be aware that the Bible is reliable, many will reject the claim that an adequately informed citizen would be *un*aware that the Bible is reliable. Since it seems likely that citizens in modern liberal democracies will disagree with one another about reliable sources of information just about as violently as they will disagree about anything else, to repair back to populism at this point would be to admit defeat. But in that case, what other options are open to the advocate of (8)?

So long as McCartney's goal is to determine what adequately informed citizens would find acceptable, it seems to me that there is no plausible alternative open to the justificatory liberal other than the following: McCartney should make his determination on the basis of whatever information he rationally and conscientiously regards as reliable. Since McCartney, we may assume, rationally and conscientiously regards the Bible as reliable, it seems appropriate for him to conclude that adequately informed citizens would be aware that the Bible is reliable. It follows, further, that (8) provides no basis for the conclusion that citizens should withhold support from any policy for which they enjoy only a religious rationale. But this renders (8) unacceptable because it is insufficiently exclusionary.

My second objection addresses the relation between the argument from respect and (8). As I noted at the outset of this chapter, it seems to me that the argument from respect articulates most naturally with a populist conception of public justification. Since each citizen has an obligation to respect her compatriots as they are, rather than as she wishes they were or as she thinks they ought to be, and if respect for her compatriots requires a citizen to provide something by way of public justification, then it would seem most natural to claim that she ought to provide them with some rationale for her favored coercive laws that they find acceptable more or less as they are. That is, it would seem most natural that a citizen who respects her compatriots ought to provide them with some sort of populist public justification.

By contrast, it strikes me as utterly unnatural for the justificatory liberal to claim that respect for her compatriots requires a citizen to articulate a rationale that satisfies (only) an idealizing conception of public justification. Consider that if a citizen's rationale R for some coercive law satisfies an idealizing conception of public justification, R will be acceptable to her compatriots' counterfactual counterparts, but R might very well be deeply objectionable to the actual citizens who would be subject to that coercive law. That her counterpart in some – perhaps very distant – possible world would find R acceptable is cold comfort to the flesh and blood citizen who isn't so favorably circumstanced with respect to R and thus finds R deeply objectionable.[60]

It might seem that the justificatory liberal can avoid this objection by articulating an even more moderate version of (8) – one that imposes populist constraints on what counts as adequate information. Gerald Gaus has developed a conception of public justification of this sort. Gaus's position, in brief, is as follows. Suppose we distinguish between commitments at the core of a citizen's noetic structure and those at the periphery of her noetic structure. A citizen's core commitments are her convictions as to what counts as genuine or reliable evidence: say, her belief that sense perception provides humans with reliable access to the natural world. A citizen's peripheral commitments are her particular sense-perceptual beliefs: say, her belief that there is a bluebird on the nearby birch tree. And suppose we employ that distinction between core and peripheral commitments to impose constraints on the sorts of information a citizen may impute to her compatriots: the only information she may impute to her compatriots is information that is of a kind they regard as reliable – that their respective systems of belief "acknowledge as relevant."[61] So if Jill takes sense perception to be a reliable source of information, then we may impute to her any reliable sense-perceptual information that bears on a given coercive law. If, by contrast, Jill does not regard telepathy as reliable, then we may not impute to her any information generated by telepathic means, even if we take telepathy to be a highly reliable source of information. So, on Gaus's moderately idealizing understanding of what counts as adequate information, other citizens' commitments impose *some* constraints on the sort of information we impute to them, although we are free to impute information to them that they in fact reject. Thus, to gloss Gaus, a genuine public justification "genuinely addresses [Jill], and genuinely shows that *[Jill] has reason* to embrace B. On the other hand, [a genuine public] justification does not hold [Jack] hostage to [Jill's] current errors, *so long as they are errors from the perspective of [Jill's] system of beliefs.*"[62]

Even though Gaus imposes populist constraints on the sort of information we may impute to our compatriots, and he does so in order to ensure that a citizen who publicly justifies her favored coercive law to her compatriots genuinely respects *them*, it's clear that the sense in which a citizen must address her compatriots is very thin indeed. After all, so long as Jill is willing to grant that a certain kind of information is reliable, Gaus's moderately idealizing conception of public justification allows Jack to idealize away from all of the particular bits of information that Jill actually regards as reliable. If Jill believes that sense perception is reliable, then, according to Gaus, Jack is free to support laws on the basis of a set of sense-perceptual claims *all* of which Jill vociferously rejects. But in that case, it is entirely unclear that Jack is really addressing *Jill*. Granted that Jack articulates a rationale for his favored coercive laws that connects in some tenuous way with the contents of Jill's evidential set, surely the connection is far too weak: after all, Jack can satisfy the constraints Gaus imposes on an adequate public justification without articulating a rationale that includes *any* premises Jill finds *remotely* plausible (even though they are of a *kind* that Jill is prepared to admit as having evidential weight).

Gaus's moderately idealizing conception of public justification at least attempts to ensure that there is some connection between a genuine public justification and the commitments of the actual citizens who inhabit a liberal democracy. Other idealizing conceptions of public justification require an even more tenuous connection between the citizens who actually inhabit a liberal democracy and a public justification. And to the degree that they do so, it seems to me that they fail ever more clearly to ensure that there is some intelligible and important connection between respect and public justification.

One final objection to (8): it is *suspicious*. The appeal to what adequately informed citizens would find acceptable turns out to be an indirect way of expressing one's conviction that some policy is, well, the correct policy. Since any claim about what idealized citizens would find acceptable depends for its justification on one or another less than fully idealized person's evidential set, for any person to claim that adequately informed citizens would find rationale R acceptable is just another way of expressing her conviction that others ought to find R acceptable. Those who disagree with her will, of course, avail themselves of the parallel claim: citizens in ideal circumstances – differently construed, of course – would find R unacceptable. Nothing is really excluded by the appeal to what adequately informed citizens would believe; such appeals are, when all is said and done, merely self-congratulatory. Indeed, (8) seems to license a dangerous and suspicious trumping of the citizenry's parochial and fallible political commitments by an appeal to some less cluttered view of the political landscape to which they, unfortunately, aren't privy. How is the appeal to adequate information any less suspicious than the appeals to false consciousness and ideological blindness that have been so often abused by those unable to gain the *actual* assent of those on the receiving end of state coercion? (Just as one can imagine Stalin assuring the kulaks whose meager property he is in the process of expropriating that they would find his quite brutal methods acceptable if they weren't so stricken with false consciousness, one can also imagine the justificatory liberal assuring the fundamentalist parent that she'd find acceptable a policy that "encourages" her school-age children to be more open-minded about other religions if only she were slightly better informed about what's good for her children.)

7.7 CONCLUDING COMMENTS

As I noted at the outset, populist conceptions of public justification articulate most naturally with the central argument for the doctrine of restraint, that is, the argument from respect. But the actual disagreement among the citizens who inhabit large-scale liberal democracies requires the justificatory liberal to tinker with the most straightforward populist conceptions: only by weakening the most demanding and intuitively appealing populist conceptions is it feasible to suppose that central liberal commitments are amenable to public justification. The justificatory liberal weakens such populist conceptions in two central respects: by limiting membership in the public and by idealizing the public. Limiting membership in the public has limited effectiveness, as I see it, and so the justificatory liberal has little option but to salvage the populist impulse by recourse to idealization. But the move to idealization has entirely disastrous implications. As the justificatory liberal idealizes the members of the public, as she "purifies" the evidential sets the members of the public employ to evaluate a given coercive law, she must vindicate her particular conception of the respects in which the evidential sets of the members of the public must be purified. And I see no nonarbitrary way to do that: any claim about what idealized citizens would believe is uneliminably dependent on an implicit appeal to what those in much less than ideal conditions would believe, and any such appeal can – and will – be met by competing claims about what idealized citizens would believe, which are in turn dependent on an implicit appeal to a different set of claims formed in less than ideal conditions. The appeal to what idealized citizens would believe is, in short, a circuitous way for nonidealized citizens to express their disagreements with one another.

The conclusion we should draw from this, I think, is that populist conceptions are most likely indefensible and that a natural strategy for modifying of populist conceptions – idealization – holds out little hope of addressing the objections to which populist conceptions are vulnerable.

CHAPTER 8

LIBERALISM AND MYSTICISM

8.0 INTRODUCTION

Imagine Bill McCartney in the throes of deciding whether Amendment 2 merits his support. He is, we may assume, rationally justified in believing that same-sex relations are an abomination to God and in believing that, if the state forces a landlord to rent to homosexual persons, then the state forces that landlord to allow her tenants to use her property to engage in what she rationally regards as morally abominable activity. Assume further that McCartney is rationally justified in adhering to the time-honored claim stating that to violate divine law is to risk divine retribution[1] and in applying that claim to the present case: McCartney rationally believes that for the state to employ its coercive power in such an irresponsible way is to risk divine retribution. On the basis of some such "National Defense Argument for Amendment 2," McCartney is strongly inclined to support Amendment 2 and in so doing, to put it a bit melodramatically, to use his modicum of power with the aim of averting a national tragedy.

Suppose, however, that McCartney is convinced by the argument from respect and believes that he ought not support his favored coercive laws if he lacks a public justification for those laws.[2] To determine whether he may support Amendment 2, McCartney must determine whether his rationale for Amendment 2 counts as a public justification. The justificatory liberal will advise him that it isn't, but he is surely not going to take the justificatory liberal's word on the matter. Rather, he'll demand, and rightfully so, that the justificatory liberal provide him with principled grounds for the claim that his religious rationale doesn't constitute a public justification.

234

So imagine McCartney casting about for the target conception of public justification. There are, of course, a multitude of proposals and he decides to cycle through as many as he has time to consider. He realizes that his rationale can't be disqualified simply because many of his cognitively competent compatriots find it utterly implausible: as we have seen, a necessary condition of a rationale's counting as a public justification is not that other citizens in fact accept that rationale. Nor, McCartney realizes, is it necessary that each of his cognitively competent compatriots be able to accept that rationale without too much tinkering to their evidential sets. After all, even though all of the extant justifications for the right to religious freedom are utterly foreign to McCartney's Christian Reconstructionist brethren, none of the justificatory liberals he knows is willing to conclude that, as a consequence, the right to religious freedom lacks public justification. Nor is it necessary for a rationale to count as a public justification that each of the rational and reasonable citizens who inhabit a liberal democracy find that rationale acceptable. Although some of McCartney's Christian Reconstructionist friends are irrational, unreasonable, or both, some are not: their rejection of religious freedom hinges not on an unwillingness to seek out and obey fair terms of social cooperation, but on their conviction that tolerating heretics elicits divine displeasure – displeasure that manifests itself in ways that *all* would regard as significant social dysfunctions. McCartney is himself attracted to a conception according to which a rationale counts as a public justification only if each of his rational, reasonable, and adequately informed compatriots finds it acceptable: given *that* conception, McCartney is sure that his rationale for Amendment 2 counts as a public justification, since it seems obvious to him that any adequately informed person knows that God punishes nations that persecute the righteous. However, once McCartney puts this line of thought to justificatory liberals, they tend to withdraw their support from that conception or they impose various arbitrary constraints on what counts as an adequately informed citizen.

After concluding his preliminary survey of some popular conceptions of public justification, McCartney is inclined to conclude that the justificatory liberal lacks principled grounds for the claim that his rationale for Amendment 2 doesn't constitute a public justification. Even though it's highly controversial and notwithstanding that many of his compatriots reject his rationale even though they've understood it and given it a fair hearing, McCartney concludes that his rationale for Amendment 2 isn't relevantly different from the kinds of rationale that his compatriots will eventually have to employ as a basis for their favored political commitments – perhaps for their position on Amendment 2. (After all, McCartney will, given *his* evidential set, likely find his compatriots' reasons for rejecting Amendment 2 just as controversial as they find his rationale for supporting Amendment 2.) He concludes, moreover, that populist conceptions of public justification hold out little hope of providing him with principled grounds for the claim that his rationale doesn't constitute a public justification: whatever a public justification turns out to be, it needn't be a rationale that his reasonable and rational compatriots regard as acceptable given their actual epistemic circumstances.

The case is, however, by no means closed on the status of McCartney's rationale. Clearly, the justificatory liberal must articulate some *weaker* condition than acceptability to the public: she must articulate some conception of public justification according to which McCartney's rationale is disqualified from counting as a public justification on grounds other than its being the object of sustained dissent from his rational and reasonable compatriots. But the appropriate condition on what counts as a public justification must be sufficiently *strong* to mandate that McCartney refrain from supporting Amendment 2 solely on the basis of his religious rationale. For the justificatory liberal to articulate some such nonpopulist conception of public justification, I see no option open to her other than the following: she must construe a public justification as a rationale that enjoys some *normative* desideratum and thus that *merits* the status of a public justification *in spite of* the fact that many citizens of good faith and cognitive competence are aware of that rationale, understand it perfectly well, and nevertheless reject it. Gerald Gaus expresses this claim with admirable clarity:

> Given the actual disagreement in our Western societies over liberal ideals, it is manifest that justificatory liberalism cannot explicate "publicly acceptable" principles as those to which each and every member of our actual societies, in their actual positions, actually assent. If that is the test of public justification, justificatory liberalism is most unlikely to vindicate substantive liberal principles. Justificatory liberals require a *normative theory of justification* – a theory that allows them to claim that some set of principles is publicly justified, even given the fact that they are contested by some.[3]

Not only must the justificatory liberal defend some normative conception of public justification, the promising options seem limited to a particular sort of normative conception, namely, a conception that requires of any prospective public justification that it enjoy an *epistemic* desideratum of some sort or other. So far as I can see, the justificatory liberal has no option but to articulate an *epistemic* conception of public justification. I have no idea how to defend that claim; I can only plead ignorance of a plausible alternative. I'm encouraged, however, that this is the tack justificatory liberals typically take in articulating their favored (nonpopulist) conceptions of public justification: much more often than not, justificatory liberals help themselves quite "liberally" to epistemic claims in sifting the public wheat from the private chaff. As Nicholas Wolterstorff writes, "All versions of the liberal position, with the exception of the clear-and-present-danger version, make crucial use of epistemological assumptions in what they say about acceptable versus non-acceptable reasons."[4] Kent Greenawalt echoes Wolterstorff's generalization: "For this book, how far liberal democracy is committed to some form of rationalism is more critical than the place for individualist premises. The centrality of this problem is evident once one understands that the argument against reliance on religious convictions often comes down to an argument *for* reliance on premises that are deemed rational in some way that excludes religious convictions."[5] I'll assume for the duration of this discussion, admittedly without a conclusive showing, that the cut between the grounds regarding which a citizen ought to exercise restraint and those regarding which she need not exercise restraint is parasitic on a correlative distinction between grounds that enjoy some epistemic desideratum and those that lack that epistemic desideratum.

Of course, not just any such epistemic criterion will do. A defensible proposal will have to satisfy at least two constraints. First, a proposal mustn't imply *skepticism* about religious convictions. Why? Most of the citizens in the United States are religious; many of those citizens are politically active; and undoubtedly, many of them decide political issues on the basis of their religious convictions. These facts are among the familiar features of our political terrain and, as we've seen, we have no reason to believe that they will change any time in the near future. But it's highly undesirable for a justificatory liberal to endorse a conception of *public* justification that would itself be rejected by a substantial proportion of the public.[6] After all, if many members of the public reasonably reject the doctrine of restraint, then the justificatory liberal seems at the very least to violate the spirit of her project. Granted that advocacy of the doctrine of restraint is not tantamount to support for a coercive policy, it should be more than a little unsettling if the best justificatory liberals can do is to articulate a highly sectarian argument in support of the claim that citizens have a moral obligation not to coerce others on entirely sectarian grounds.[7] Rather, the justificatory liberal should endeavor to articulate a conception of public justification acceptable to the public that is to obey the doctrine of restraint, and thus must also be acceptable to the religious citizens who constitute a substantial component of that public and thus mustn't imply that a religious citizen's most cherished commitments – her religious commitments – are epistemically defective.[8]

Second, there are constraints on the sorts of epistemic desiderata a justificatory liberal may usefully employ to articulate her favored epistemic conception of public justification. What kinds of constraints? A set of constraints imposed by the *concept* of public justification. A conception just is a specification of a more general concept; so a conception of public justification just is a specification of a more general concept of public justification. As I've already noted, there is a stable core to the concept of public justification: a citizen enjoys a public justification only if she enjoys a rationale, not just that *she* finds plausible given her evidential set, but that articulates in some *appropriate* way with other citizens' distinctive points of view. Given that core concept, any *conception* of public justification must provide some specification of just in what an appropriate articulation consists.

Populist conceptions provide a natural specification: each of the premises that constitute a given rationale must be included in other (reasonable, rational, etc.) citizens' evidential sets, or at least can be so included without drastic revision. But since populist conceptions are untenable, the justificatory liberal must identify some other, perhaps less natural but nevertheless meaningful, specification of the respect in which a citizen's rationale must articulate with her compatriots' respective points of view. And that goal imposes constraints on the sorts of epistemic desiderata the justificatory liberal may employ to articulate her favored epistemic conception. The sort of epistemic desideratum she'll appropriately employ will be the sort that constitutes some desirable epistemic relation *among* citizens. As I see it, the feature that unifies each of the epistemic desiderata I discuss in this chapter – intelligibility, in principle accessibility, criticizability, independent checkability – is that each desideratum facilitates *interpersonal evaluation*: the fact that a citizen's rationale possesses such and such an epistemic desideratum ensures that her compatriots will be in a position to understand, acquire, criticize, or confirm that rationale. So even if a public justification need not be convincing to the public, it's nevertheless amenable to meaningful evaluation by the public.

These two constraints on an epistemic conception of public justification give the justificatory liberal considerable latitude: there are any number of epistemic desiderata that facilitate interpersonal evaluation and thus that the justificatory liberal may require in order for some rationale to count as a public justification. Consequently, there is a number of epistemic conceptions of public justification the justificatory liberal might endorse. My intention in this chapter is to articulate and evaluate a representative selection of epistemic conceptions. My guiding aim, of course, is to determine whether there is an epistemic conception that provides principled grounds for the claim that a citizen ought to exercise restraint regarding her religious commitments and that also satisfies various other conditions on an adequate conception of public justification. I'll argue that there is no such conception: justificatory liberals are unable to articulate an epistemic conception that is sufficiently *powerful* to mandate restraint regarding religious grounds, but is sufficiently *weak* to allow citizens to rely on other sorts of grounds that are essential to healthy political decision making and advocacy.

8.1 MYSTICAL PERCEPTION

Justificatory liberals often operate with an unappealing and sometimes even implicitly skeptical analysis of the epistemic credentials of religious convictions. Consequently, they often have no difficulty showing – to their satisfaction – that religious grounds lack the sort of epistemic desiderata de jure for a public justification. But once the justificatory liberal takes her argument into epistemic terrain, the case for restraint regarding religious convictions is by no means easily vindicated. I will argue that a sympathetic – although not pollyannaish – rendering of the epistemic status of religious grounds reveals that religious grounds aren't nearly as easily dealt with as justificatory liberals often suppose. Given this sympathetic rendering, if the justificatory liberal is to get the desired results regarding religious convictions, she'll have to impose fairly demanding epistemic constraints on what counts as a public justification. But this need to impose ever more demanding constraints on what counts as a public justification has entirely untoward consequences for the justificatory liberal's project: epistemic constraints that are sufficiently powerful to rule out reliance on religious grounds *also* rule out reliance on grounds that are essential to healthy political decision making and advocacy. At least, that is what I shall argue.

To press this objection, I have no alternative but to foray into the complex and contentious field of religious epistemology: if the case for restraint regarding religious grounds is to hinge on the claim that religious grounds lack some epistemic desideratum, then there is no alternative but to determine whether religious grounds do lack that epistemic desideratum and that requires recourse to the voluminous literature on the epistemology of religious belief. That the case for restraint regarding religious grounds comes to this poses considerable problems of explication. First, there is, to put it mildly, no settled agreement as to the epistemic status of religious grounds. Second, to speak so generally of the epistemic status of "religious grounds" covers too much territory: religious grounds come in all shapes and sizes and no doubt enjoy a variety of epistemic virtues and vices. It seems that adequately to address the epistemic claims to which justificatory liberals so often avail themselves would send us careening off on a book-length lemma.

I'll cut the Gordian knot in the following way: I'll use as a test case *one* kind of religious ground, will focus on the kind of religious ground I regard as most congenial to the justificatory liberal's case, and will articulate a sympathetic account of the epistemic status of that kind of religious ground. I assume that the sort of religious ground most congenial to the justificatory liberal's case is *mystical perception*. For sympathetic and compelling treatments of the epistemic status of mystical perception, there is none better than the analysis William Alston has developed over the past two decades or so. So I provide a brief overview of Alston's description and defense of the positive epistemic status of mystical perception and then use Alston's position as a test case for various epistemic conceptions of public justification.[9]

8.1.1 A Doxastic Practice Approach to Epistemology

At least some citizens undergo religious experiences; they seem to come into contact with a supernatural reality and thereby to gain information about that reality. Some of those citizens seem to *perceive* God and as a consequence form beliefs about God: they take themselves to perceive God as having certain characteristics (compassion, justice, etc.) and as performing certain sorts of actions (commanding, forgiving, informing, etc.). Alston is serious about the *perceptual* nature of mystical experience. According to Alston, some citizens perceive God in generically the same way that they perceive physical objects: "The experience, or, as I shall say, the perception, of God plays an epistemic role with respect to beliefs about God importantly analogous to that played by sense perception with respect to beliefs about the physical world."[10] Alston calls the beliefs formed on the basis of putative perceptions of God *Manifestation-beliefs* or *M-beliefs* for short.[11]

For clarity's sake, let's have before us an example of the phenomenon Alston has in mind. In his biography of Martin Luther King, Jr., David Garrow recounts an experience King had during a particularly difficult period in the boycott on the Montgomery City Lines bus company.

"I sat there and thought about a beautiful little daughter who had just been born. . . . She was the darling of my life. I'd come in night after night and see that little gentle smile. And I sat at that table thinking about that little girl and thinking about the fact that she could be taken from me at any moment.

"And I started thinking about a dedicated, devoted and loyal wife, who was over there asleep. And she could be taken from me, or I could be taken from her. And I got to the point where I couldn't take it any longer. I was weak. Something said to me, you can't call on Daddy now, he's up in Atlanta a hundred and seventy miles away. You can't even call on Mama now. You've got to call on that something in that person that your Daddy used to tell you about, that power that can make a way out of no way.

"And I discovered then that religion had to become real to me, and I had to know God for myself. And I bowed down over that cup of coffee. I will never forget it . . . I prayed a prayer, and I prayed out loud that night. I said, 'Lord, I'm down here trying to do what's right. I think I'm right. I think the cause we represent is right. But Lord, I must confess that I'm weak now. I'm faltering. I'm losing my courage. And I can't let the people see me like this because if they see me weak and losing my courage, they will begin to get weak."
Then it happened.

"And it seemed at that moment that I could hear an inner voice saying to me, 'Martin Luther, stand up for righteousness. Stand up for justice.

Stand up for truth. And lo I will be with you, even until the end of the world.' ... I heard the voice of Jesus saying still to fight on. He promised never to leave me, never to leave me alone. No never alone. No never alone. He promised never to leave me, never to leave me alone."[12]

As with King, most of those who form M-beliefs adhere to a specific religious tradition. Those who take themselves to perceive God typically take themselves to perceive God as construed by Jews or Christians or Muslims, or some other religious tradition. Alston focuses, as shall I, on those who adhere to the Christian tradition. Those who fit in the last category participate in what Alston calls the *Christian Mystical Practice* (CMP),[13] which has correlates in each relevantly different religious tradition.

CMP is a *doxastic practice*, that is, a socially established way of forming and evaluating beliefs. A doxastic practice is constituted by (1) a family of dispositions to form beliefs with a certain content when an agent is in a certain kind of mental state, and (2) a matrix of beliefs and procedures by which members of a given doxastic practice can determine whether the beliefs they are disposed to form deserve continued adherence.[14] This second feature of a doxastic practice is very important and hence has a title: Alston calls it an *overrider system*. What is an overrider system? Alston is a thoroughgoing fallibilist; no matter how subjectively confident we are that a given belief is true, there is always the possibility that it isn't. As responsible epistemic agents, we should do the best we can to check whether beliefs that appear to be true are in fact true. A doxastic practice's overrider system provides participants with the wherewithal to do so. Roughly put, a doxastic practice's overrider system is constituted by beliefs and procedures that enable its participants to determine whether what seems to them to be the case is in fact the case: "attached to each practice is an 'overrider system' of beliefs and procedures that the subject can use in subjecting prima facie justified beliefs to further tests when that is called for."[15]

Since discussion of CMP's overrider system will play a central role in the ensuing argument, I'll say a bit more about it. I do so by contrasting it with the overrider system we employ in sense perception (SP). Suppose some agent claims to have seen a snark but that we dispute her claim. We have ready to hand a variety of tests by which to check whether what she claims to have experienced in fact occurred. We ask her where she saw the snark, return to that location, and cast about for signs of its whereabouts. We look for tell-tale indications of the past or present presence of the elusive snark: spoor, cigarette butts, stool, broken twigs, footprints. If her story fails to check out after the appropriate kind of investigation, then we regard her assertion as false, and conclude that she is deceptive, deluded, mistaken, credulous. That others can employ the same effective procedures for confirming and disconfirming an agent's sense perceptual beliefs is crucial to our confidence in SP. [16]

Participants in CMP enjoy a set of tests they can employ to distinguish between veridical and nonveridical mystical perceptions, but they are very different from the tests we employ in SP. The tests CMP affords to its participants are *consistency* tests. When evaluating some putative perception of God, whether our own or that of another participant in CMP, we check that putative perception by determining whether it comports with the understanding of God's nature and past activities as that understanding has developed in the history of CMP, with the depiction of God in other sources of information about God such as a sacred writing or natural theology, and with our understanding of the world as developed in other nonreligious doxastic practices. Thus, for example, if a citizen claims to have experienced God as telling her to kill all of the phenomenologists she can find, participants in CMP have good reason to reject her claim: God, as a wholly good being, would not have issued such a command and so she must either have failed to perceive God or have misinterpreted a genuine perception of God. In this case, we employ beliefs we have formed by engaging in some other doxastic practice – say Biblical interpretation or moral reflection – to show that some putative mystical perception is illusory even though it might seem to be reliable at first blush. Simply put, even if CMP's overrider system includes no procedures for *confirming* beliefs,[17] it is constituted by a set of beliefs about God's character and past activities with which a citizen's M-beliefs must cohere and which enable a citizen to *disconfirm* M-beliefs.

8.1.2 Criteria for Evaluating Doxastic Practices

So far, this is all descriptive epistemology; but Alston is interested in evaluation – in articulating general criteria for evaluating doxastic practices. More particularly, he is interested in determining whether, according to our best account of such criteria, a citizen can be rationally justified in engaging in CMP and in trusting the information gained by engaging in CMP. I turn now to the evaluative component of Alston's project.

Alston articulates the following general criteria for evaluating doxastic practices:

(I) A necessary condition of the positive epistemic status of a given doxastic practice is that it generates a sufficiently high ratio of true to false beliefs. That is, it is reliable.

(II) We are in no position to show that any of our basic doxastic practices are reliable. That is, we have available to us no noncircular and otherwise acceptable arguments in support of the claim that the components of the *standard package* of doxastic practices – sense perception, memory, introspection, inductive inference, and deductive inference – are reliable.

(III) In spite of our inability to show that those practices are reliable, we remain confident that the beliefs we form by engaging in the standard package are generally true. Hence, we would be guilty of employing a double standard were we to require that nonstandard practices enjoy discursive redemption. Consistency requires, then, that we regard any given doxastic practice as presumptively innocent.[18]

(IV) Presumptive innocence does not render a given practice immune from external critique; if we have good reason to believe that a given practice is unreliable, than we should cease engaging in it. A given practice forfeits its presumptive innocence if it generates a high ratio of inconsistent beliefs or if it generates a high ratio of beliefs which are inconsistent with the beliefs generated by more reputable practices.[19]

According to Alston, doxastic practices such as SP are "innocent until proven guilty"[20]; although we can provide no noncircular justification for our conviction that SP is reliable, we aren't epistemically remiss in believing that it is reliable. But that a given doxastic practice is presumptively reliable doesn't grant it "diplomatic immunity" from imputations of guilt; that would be unduly conservative. So, in order to counterbalance the conservative "presumptively innocent" end of the dictum, Alston adds an "until proven guilty" rider. Hence, even though epistemically upstanding agents need not show that SP is reliable, they need to respond to arguments to the conclusion that SP is unreliable.[21]

The innocent until proven guilty dictum applies forthwith to religious doxastic practices such as CMP. According to Alston, consistency requires that we impute to CMP the presumptive innocence we also grant to SP and the other practices constitutive of the standard package. Moreover, we lack sufficient reason to believe that CMP is unreliable – a claim that requires, and for which Alston provides, considerable argument. Consequently, we have no reason to believe that those who engage in CMP commit any epistemic improprieties thereby: judged with respect to the general criteria Alston has articulated, CMP passes epistemic muster along with sense perception, introspection, memory, testimony, and other such practices.

It's important not to be misled by Alston's language here: in particular his claim that CMP is innocent until proven guilty. It seems to some that this dictum is a protective strategy that, in effect, *immunizes* CMP from external critique. Thus, for example, Matthew Bagger writes,

> The frequent references to the principle of jurisprudence, "innocent until proven guilty," signal Alston's ... protective intentions. In judicial reasoning we employ this tenet in our system, not because of its a priori necessity, but because we wish to *protect* the accused individual as much as is feasible from mistaken prosecution and punishment.... The scholars who propose that we consider religious perception "innocent until proven guilty" should explain why we should wish to protect religious perception in this manner.[22]

It is by no means difficult to provide the sort of explanation Bagger demands. There is a long history of objecting to religious doxastic practices such as CMP on the grounds that its members can't provide a noncircular justification for those practices. But we find ourselves in the same predicament with respect to sense perception, memory, introspection, inference, and morality. Hence, it would be arbitrary to object to a doxastic practice such as CMP on the grounds that it isn't amenable to noncircular justification. And that is at least part of what the "innocent until proven guilty" metaphor is intended to convey: the "presumptive innocence" claim just means that we ought not object to *any* practice, whether sacred or profane, on the grounds that that practice isn't amenable to noncircular justification. And the other part of Alston's dictum – that a doxastic practice is innocent *until proven guilty* – is expressly intended to endorse the claim that doxastic practices are amenable to external critique. The use of legal metaphor, then, doesn't indicate some intention to protect *religious* doxastic practices from external criticism. Rather, the legal metaphor is of use in getting the points across that (a) we cannot but engage in certain doxastic practices without already having proven their reliability, (b) that this fact ought not count as an objection to any doxastic practice, and (c) that this fact does *not* render any given doxastic practice immune to criticism. Insofar as that is what the innocent until proven guilty metaphor means, I think it entirely defensible.

We can put the point this way. Bagger is correct in claiming that Alston employs the innocent until proven guilty locution with the intention of protecting CMP. But *from what* is he intent on protecting CMP? From the mistaken but all too common objection that CMP lacks positive epistemic status because we can't show that CMP is reliable. Why is that objection a mistake? To invoke another legal dictum, all practices should enjoy *equal protection under the law*: we can provide no noncircular and otherwise adequate justification for *any* of the basic practices in which we engage and should therefore not discriminate against CMP on that very account.

All of this is extremely brief and dogmatic. This is particularly unfortunate since Alston's defense of CMP is very sophisticated and yet, as I hope will become apparent, some advocates of restraint operate with a simplistic, stereotypical, and implicitly skeptical understanding of religious grounds – and mystical perception in particular. I will, however, comment on one feature both of Alston's doxastic practice approach to epistemology and of Alston's defense of CMP, a feature that is essential to an adequate appreciation of CMP's epistemic status and to a satisfactory assessment of epistemic conceptions of public justification.

8.1.3 Autonomy

At the heart of Alston's defense of mystical perception is his defense of the *autonomy* of CMP. Most generally, the claim that a given doxastic practice is autonomous is the claim that internal to that practice are standards of evaluation, types of input and output, procedures for evaluating beliefs, that differ from those proper to other practices. We engage in numerous doxastic practices; there are important and fundamental differences between each of those practices *and those differences are epistemically legitimate*. For example, we base sense perceptual beliefs on very different grounds from those on which we base our memory beliefs, and both of those types of ground differ in important respects from the type of ground on which we rely when forming beliefs about our moods and desires. Thus, we form beliefs about objects in the physical environment on the basis of sensory stimulation – light waves striking retinas, for example – and we form beliefs about our moods, not via sensory stimulation, but by inward concentration. Again, the ways we check sense-perceptual beliefs differ importantly and legitimately from the ways that we check beliefs about our feelings and about mathematical theorems. We would gain nothing of epistemic value were we to require that sense-perceptual beliefs be based on the same type of ground, or be evaluated in light of the same type of checking procedures, that we employ in forming and evaluating mathematical claims, beliefs about our moods, and so on. Treading down that Procrustean path would lead us only to epistemic disaster.

CMP is a beneficiary of this diversity internal to the standard package; that there are considerable differences between the way we form and check M-beliefs and the way we form and check, for example, sense-perceptual beliefs, doesn't thereby provide us with adequate reason to discount the epistemic status of CMP, any more than the considerable differences between the way we check introspective beliefs and sense-perceptual beliefs warrant us in discounting the epistemic status of sense perception. Appreciation of the autonomy of distinct doxastic practices is critical to reaching reasoned conclusions regarding the all-important issue of the adequacy of CMP's overrider system. Recall, briefly, the contrast I drew between SP's and CMP's overrider systems. We expect to be able to provide independent confirmation for ordinary sense-perceptual beliefs: if I claim to see a snark in the woods, and you doubt that I have, we have available resources with which to substantiate my claim. We can both return to the place where I putatively perceived the snark and set about looking for some indication that the snark was in fact in the vicinity. If we find some such indication, my perceptual claim is to some degree corroborated. By contrast, we can provide no such independent confirmation for putative perceptions of God. If God is present to a citizen's consciousness, we have access to no resources by which to determine whether he has in fact perceived God.

Although various critics attempt to discredit CMP on the basis of this difference between CMP and SP, Alston has argued, plausibly by my lights, that such attempts fail. Because God is both transcendent and sovereign, because God is manifest at God's own behest and timing, it isn't reasonable to expect that M-beliefs are amenable to independent corroboration. Because physical objects are enduring objects immersed in a nexus of natural laws, it's reasonable to expect that sense-perceptual beliefs are amenable to such corroboration. Given an adequate understanding of the difference between God and physical objects, we shouldn't expect to be able to evaluate and corroborate M-beliefs in the SP way. But since it's possible that CMP is as reliable as you like even though M-beliefs don't enjoy SP-like confirmation, that lack can hardly count against CMP's epistemic status. Alston concludes, then, that CMP is autonomous vis-à-vis SP, at least with respect to the procedures by which agents check M-beliefs.[23]

The appeal to autonomy in order to neutralize invidious comparisons between SP and CMP raises a critical question: how do we provide principled grounds for the claim that a given doxastic practice is autonomous in some respect? Alston argues as follows. Given our lack of a priori insight into the way we should go about forming and evaluating different sorts of belief, we have little choice but to formulate our epistemic criteria only after we have already acquired quite a bit of information about *subject matter* of the beliefs we wish to evaluate. We acquire an understanding of the subject matter of a given practice by engaging in that practice, and only then are we in a position to determine how we best go about forming and evaluating beliefs about that subject matter. Thus, for example, only by engaging in SP do we learn that physical objects are stable, enduring entities enmeshed in a nexus of natural laws; as a consequence, we learn that we can evaluate beliefs about those entities by determining whether predictions based on those beliefs are accurate. Again, we learn by participating in SP that physical objects aren't sensitive to our wishes regarding those objects; as a consequence, we learn that beliefs based on wish-fulfillment are unreliable.

Parity of treatment requires that we proceed similarly with respect to CMP. We determine whether it's appropriate to expect that CMP enjoys some epistemic desideratum only by consulting the understanding of God developed in that practice. It's by engaging in CMP that we learn that certain features of God render us incapable of perceiving God in the way that we perceive physical objects or of checking M-beliefs in the way that we check sense-perceptual beliefs. In short, the claim that CMP is autonomous in some respect needn't be justifiable by information we acquire independently of that practice so long as it is justifiable by reference to information we acquire by engaging in that practice.

This turn in the argument may raise concerns, once again, about Alston's protective intentions. After all, if it's appropriate for members of CMP to fend off objections to CMP by appealing to the understanding of God's nature and activities internal to CMP, then the very individuals who have a vested interest in CMP's reliability are allowed to trump their critics by gerrymandering the understanding of God internal to CMP in the required respects. Moreover, it is appropriate for members of clearly objectionable doxastic practices to use the same defensive maneuver to fend off objections to their practices by a comparable gerrymandering process. Thus, Dirk-Martin Grube writes,

> An equally clever defender of the existence of Satan could argue along similar lines and claim the existence of special criteria to judge Satan experiences. She could then proceed to invoke the particular nature of the belief in Satan for the purposes of explaining why the postulated Satan experiences have to differ from sense experiences in the way they do. She could conclude that, given the specifics of belief in Satan, the differences between Satan experiences and sense experiences do not indicate the Satan experiences' unreliability.[24]

If appeal to autonomy, and thus to the understanding of the subject matter internal to a given practice, permits Devil worshipers to vindicate their beliefs about the existence and activities of Satan, then something must be wrong with the appeal to autonomy. That Alston's strategy for defending CMP has such epistemically libertine consequences constitutes a reductio of Alston's position. Moreover, these libertine consequences certainly indicate the protective intentions of Alston's appeal to autonomy: any strategy for defending CMP that can also be employed to defend belief in the Devil is a strategy that undermines any effective critical analysis of doxastic practices.

Grube's objection seems to me to avoid the central issue that Alston's appeal to autonomy raises. We cannot but assume that the doxastic practices in the standard package are reliable; each of us is committed to the general reliability of SP, memory, introspection, inference, and testimony. But the practices constitutive of the standard package display considerable *diversity* as regards their epistemic desiderata. Memory differs in important aspects from sense perception, both from introspection, and all three from moral evaluation. If such diversity inhabits the core of our cognitive endowment, if we tolerate considerable autonomy *inside* the standard package, we have no justification for not tolerating autonomy *outside* it as well.

No doubt, allowing for the possibility of autonomous, nonstandard doxastic practices makes epistemic evaluation more complicated than we might wish. It's true that Satanists can appeal to autonomy as effectively as can Christians and those who engage in SP. But that possibility constitutes much less a decisive objection to Alston's position than a complaint about the human condition. Given the human condition, given the plurality of doxastic practices in which we cannot but engage, consistency in judgment requires that we allow for the possibility that the formation of beliefs about Satan properly differs as much from the way that we form beliefs about physical objects as the way we form beliefs about physical objects properly differs from the way we form beliefs about our moods, mathematical feelings, philosophical theories, moral obligations, and the like. To deny the Satanist an argumentative strategy to which we cannot but help ourselves is to commit ourselves either to bad faith or a Procrustean attempt to eliminate autonomy in our core doxastic practices.[25]

My case against epistemic conceptions of public justification depends to a large extent on the claim that both CMP and the secular doxastic practices constitutive of the standard package legitimately exhibit various distinct epistemic desiderata. That appeal to autonomy has two important functions. First, if the justificatory liberal fails to recognize the autonomy of CMP, he may very well conclude that CMP lacks certain epistemic desiderata that it does in fact enjoy. For example, he won't recognize that CMP enjoys those epistemic desiderata because he expects CMP to manifest those desiderata in ways that are appropriate only to very different doxastic practices. But in that case, the justificatory liberal may very well articulate an epistemic conception of public justification that is far too weak to mandate restraint regarding mystical perceptions given the *actual* epistemic desiderata that CMP enjoys.

Second, since the practices constitutive of the standard package exhibit a diverse array of epistemic desiderata, it's important not to require (as is common) that the only sorts of grounds that enjoy public justification are those generated by practices at the upper end of the epistemic spectrum (such as sense perception). Since some of the doxastic practices at the lower end of the epistemic spectrum generate claims essential to healthy political decision making and advocacy, to articulate an epistemic conception of public justification tailored to the upper end of the epistemic spectrum would have intolerable implications for the justificatory liberal – his failure to accord due weight to the autonomy of the practices at the lower end of the epistemic spectrum would require that citizens exercise restraint regarding claims generated by such practices. The problem is this: if, in order to allow citizens to rely on grounds generated by practices at the lower end of the epistemic spectrum (such as moral judgment), the justificatory liberal refrains from privileging practices at the upper end of the epistemic spectrum (such as sense perception), then he won't be able to articulate constraints sufficiently powerful to mandate restraint regarding mystical perception. (More on that in due course.)

8.1.4 Mystical Perception and Public Justification

A final question regarding mystical perception: does anyone really appeal to M-beliefs in deciding which coercive laws merit their support? Is it really plausible to suppose that a citizen in the modern United States will support his favored coercive laws on the basis of a putative perception of God? We might harbor our doubts. But if there aren't any such citizens, or if we can safely relegate them to the lunatic fringe, then why should we expect that using mystical perception as a test case for epistemic conceptions of public justification will reveal anything interesting about the doctrine of restraint? If actual citizens would never dream of appealing to some putative perception of God in deciding whether to support restrictions on abortion, or to oppose capital punishment, or to vote against a legislator unwilling to halt the proliferation of nuclear weapons, what does it matter if a citizen need not exercise restraint regarding his M-beliefs?[26]

The ensuing discussion has important implications for justificatory liberalism even if no citizens rely on M-beliefs as a basis for their favored coercive laws. As I noted above, mystical perception is the sort of religious ground that is most congenial to the justificatory liberal's case: mystical perceptions are considerably more private than are claims to sacred texts, for example.[27] Consequently, if the justificatory liberal can't articulate a conception of public justification that mandates restraint regarding mystical perception, then we have powerful reason to believe that he can't articulate a conception that mandates restraint regarding other sorts of religious grounds, and more particularly, those more commonly employed in political decision making and advocacy.[28]

8.2 A PLETHORA OF EPISTEMIC CONCEPTIONS OF PUBLIC JUSTIFICATION

We are now in a position to articulate and evaluate various epistemic conceptions of public justification. I'll articulate and evaluate eight of the most popular extant conceptions: intelligibility, accessibility, in principle public accessibility, replicability, criticizability, dialogicality, independent confirmability, and provability.[29] I'll show that none of these constraints can be articulated into a defensible conception of public justification.[30]

8.3 INTELLIGIBILITY

Colin Bird has proposed that

(1) A citizen's rationale R counts as a public justification for a given coercive law only if R is publicly intelligible.[31]

Bird's intelligibility constraint is supposed to work as follows. If Elijah supports H.R. 1095 in essential part because he putatively perceived God as commanding him to militate for H. R. 1095, Elijah must be able to identify his grounds for the claim that God so commanded him and he must be able to see why his grounds support the claim that God so commanded him. So, presumably, Elijah must be able to recall having the appropriate experience and to see why his having that experience provides him with reason to believe that God issued the relevant command. This shouldn't be difficult: Elijah will recall God's apparent manifestation to him in just the way he recalls having undergone an ordinary sense-perceptual experience. Elijah's perception of God is intelligible to Elijah because he can identify the experience and see why his having that experience and not some other provides some reason to form the appropriate M-belief.

However, just because Elijah's mystical perception is intelligible *to him*, it doesn't follow that it's intelligible *to anyone else*. Indeed, according to Bird, Elijah's putative perception of God is *not* intelligible to anyone else. Consequently, Elijah's putative perception of God is *publicly* unintelligible. Now what does Bird mean by the claim that Elijah's experience is publicly unintelligible? Apparently, Elijah's experience is unintelligible in the sense that Elijah can't satisfactorily *communicate* with his compatriots about his experience: "the nature of the experience isn't readily communicable to others."[32] And why is Elijah's putative perception of God not readily communicable to others? Because it can't "be unambiguously represented in words."[33] Apparently, Bird argues as follows: a given ground counts as publicly unintelligible if it can't be communicated to others and a ground can't be communicated to others if those who have that experience can't articulate an exhaustive phenomenological description of that experience.[34] The implications of incommunicability are, according to Bird, quite unsettling: if Elijah can't convey to his compatriots an accurate rendering of what it was like to undergo his putative perception of God, his compatriots are in no position "to assess publicly the meaning of the experience."[35] As a consequence of the incommunicability of Elijah's experience, Elijah's compatriots are "uncertain about what kind of evidence would be needed to verify such an experience" and thus whether Elijah's putative perception of God actually supports the M-belief Elijah forms on the basis of that experience.[36] But the least we can require of Elijah's rationale is that his compatriots can identify and understand that rationale adequately enough to determine whether that rationale actually supports the requisite conclusion: a rationale that Elijah's compatriots can't even understand doesn't articulate in *any* meaningful way with his compatriots' respective points of view. As Bird claims, an unintelligible ground is *opaque* to others and thus is immune from meaningful external criticism.

Now if Bird were correct that mystical perceptions are incommunicable, he'd have a *very* strong case for the claim that Elijah's mystical perception doesn't suffice for a public justification. But Bird provides no reason at all to believe that mystical perceptions are incommunicable. And it isn't at all obvious that mystical perceptions *are* incommunicable. If Elijah, having putatively perceived God as commanding him to support H.R. 1095, testifies to Mary by uttering the statement "I perceived God telling me to support H.R. 1095," how is that claim less intelligible than "I perceived my mother telling me to support H.R. 1095?" True enough, it won't be possible for Elijah to provide an exhaustive and explicit phenomenological description of his experience. That is apparently what Bird requires in order for Elijah's experience to count as publicly intelligible. But that requirement is far too demanding: *none* of our experiences are fully describable in explicit terms. That we are unable exhaustively and explicitly to describe a given perceptual experience characterizes *all* perception, as Michael Polanyi argued long ago: I have no idea, for example, how to articulate an "unambiguous representation" of my experience of feeling sand slip through my fingers, or of hearing the whisper of the wind through the trees, or the like. (The same point is even more obvious with respect to our moral convictions – not just those that concern the "meaning of life," but also those complex weighings of disparate moral considerations we cannot but employ in political decision making and advocacy, such as claims about which of the values implicated in the issue of abortion are overriding.) Consequently, it's clear that very few, if any, grounds will count as intelligible (as Bird construes that concept) and thus that to adopt Bird's epistemic constraint on public justification would be to violate the sufficiency condition.

Of course, if Bird *weakens* his understanding of what makes for a communicable experience, if an experience need not be amenable to exhaustive phenomenological description in fully explicit terms, then there seems little reason to believe that Elijah's experience of God is unintelligible. After all, it certainly *seems* that Elijah can communicate to others about his perception of God: again, he can testify to his experience of God's commanding him to support H.R. 1095 in exactly the same way that he can testify to the claim that his mother commanded him to support H.R. 1095. It seems, then, that (1) faces a dilemma: either we adopt Bird's demanding conception of intelligibility, in which case (1) will violate the sufficiency condition, or we weaken Bird's understanding of intelligibility, in which case, we lack reason to believe that mystical perception is unintelligible.

Bird would, I assume, deny that my objection to (1) scratches where he itches: his rather unfortunate appeal to *intelligibility* is merely an entree to a more serious appeal to *external criticism*. "All that is necessary," he claims, for a ground's counting as intelligible "is that others understand clearly the nature of the experience being reported, *so that* everyone is in a position to know what considerations would count against it."[37] It is really because "unintelligible" grounds aren't amenable to "public critical scrutiny," as are the grounds we enjoy in science, mathematics and ordinary sense perception, that they are insufficient for public justification.[38] So, if we are to address the concern that really motivates Bird's claim that mystical perception counts as unintelligible, we must respond to the claim that mystical perceptions aren't amenable to something called "public critical scrutiny." I discuss several such proposals shortly.[39]

8.4 PUBLIC ACCESSIBILITY

The following constraint on what constitutes a public justification is perhaps the most popular epistemic constraint:

(2) A citizen's rationale R counts as a public justification for a given coercive law only if R is publicly accessible.[40]

Unfortunately, popularity is no substitute for consensus: the notion of public accessibility is understood in widely disparate ways and proponents of (2) articulate their favored understanding of public accessibility in widely varying degrees of specificity. That said, public accessibility is *typically* understood to be a species of *possibility*: McCartney's rationale for Amendment 2 counts as publicly accessible only if his compatriots *can* recognize that McCartney's rationale is convincing by employing their own cognitive capacities rather than by having to take McCartney's word on the matter.[41] That is, McCartney's rationale must not only *be* reliable; his compatriots must be able to *see for themselves* that that rationale is sound. Abner Greene's use of the metaphor of a "secret box" to characterize the sense in which religious grounds are inaccessible nicely conveys the intuition driving (2):

> Imagine, for a moment, a group of citizens that has access to a box that contains evidence supporting a certain argument for a particular law. Suppose that group relies in the political process on the contents of that box but denies other citizens access to that box and its contents. We should exclude such shenanigans from politics because some citizens have access to the source of authority backing the law, while others are excluded from that source of authority. . . . Express reference to religious doctrine – understanding religious reference to be to an extrahuman source of normative authority – is like the secret-box model. . . . To be sure, religious reference might be similar to nonreligious philosophical argument and moral reference in many ways. . . . Only religious reference, however, relies on a source of normative authority that is claimed by its proponents to be beyond the scope of human experience and to be based in special relationships that the Believers have with that source of authority and that other citizens might not have.[42]

The party line is that a religious ground such as a mystical perception is publicly inaccessible: a putative mystical perception is publicly inaccessible because, like a rationale hidden in Greene's black box, other citizens can't see for themselves that a putative mystical perception is veridical. Is the party line correct?

As always, the demon is in the details: although the gist of the notion of public accessibility is fairly clear, we cannot determine whether mystical perception is publicly inaccessible until we have a clearly formulated conception of public accessibility before us. Most particularly, it is of central importance that we gain clarity regarding the modal component of the notion of public accessibility: if public accessibility is a species of possibility, and a mystical perception is an inaccessible ground, then what sort of impossibility is involved in the claim that a mystical perception is inaccessible?

We can eliminate certain candidates from the start. Many proponents of the public accessibility criterion understand that concept in *populist* terms.[43] Thus, for example, they claim that some rationale counts as a public justification only if others can endorse that rationale without being rationally required to engage in a drastic revision of their respective evidential sets. On the basis of our prior discussion of populist conceptions of public justification, I'll dismiss populist renderings of the relevant notion of possibility. So, for example, I won't understand public accessibility as a species of *acceptability* as I defined that notion earlier (7.3).

We could cycle through a number of other candidates, but I'll avoid an extensive digression and proceed directly to explicating what I take to be the most promising conception of public accessibility, namely, *in principle* public accessibility. And in order to explicate that conception, I'll contrast it with *actual* public accessibility. Consider the following. Each (normal) human being is endowed with certain cognitive equipment – the standard package – that he shares with his fellow (normal) human beings: each human being can perceive physical objects, understand logical relations, render moral judgments, and the like. But each human being develops that native endowment in various distinctive respects: each of us acquires cognitive skills and epistemic virtues that differ to some extent from those developed by our compatriots. Some citizens, for example, become scientists and in so doing develop the various skills and sensibilities apposite to success in the scientific endeavor, whereas other citizens become carpenters and in so doing develop cognitive skills and epistemic virtues apposite to that endeavor. Pretty obviously, the way a citizen develops his native cognitive capacities is a contingent matter, having to do with his economic circumstances, personal preferences, educational opportunities, cultural environment, and other factors.[44]

With this in mind, consider the following scenario. John never graduated from high school and thus is unable to understand the rationale in support of a scientific theory T that has a direct bearing on a political dispute of obvious importance, such as global warming. Given the course of his personal biography, John finds the mathematical calculations employed by advocates of T totally impenetrable and so he can't determine whether T is correct by employing his cognitive capacities as he's developed them in the course of his life. Of course, John might accept T, and he might even be rationally justified in doing so, if he accepts T on the basis of an appeal to authority. Even so, John won't have accepted T on the basis of his ability to determine, by employing his developed cognitive capacities, that T is compelling; the rationale for T remains impenetrable to him. In this case, T is inaccessible to John in an important sense: T is *actually* inaccessible.

But T is clearly accessible to John *in principle*. The reason John is unable to understand and evaluate the rationale for T has nothing to do with some special insight enjoyed by the initiated; scientific knowledge is generated by people who employ cognitive capacities they share with other normal human beings. The differences between a working scientist and John that explain why the latter cannot grasp a scientific rationale that the former can grasp are contingent ones having to do with access to resources, personal preferences, and the like. If John's circumstances were different, he *could* have developed the capacities necessary to reach his own conclusions on the matter. T is accessible to him, in the sense that he could determine that the rationale for T is probative were his circumstances different, even though he cannot actually determine that the rationale for T is probative by employing his cognitive capacities in their actual state.

Note that although the notion of in principle accessibility is weaker than the notion of actual accessibility, it nevertheless has some teeth. If a citizen is to form his beliefs about a given subject matter *reliably*, he must acquire reliable *information* about that subject matter – otherwise his beliefs are, even if true, only fortuitously so. A citizen's cognitive capacities enable him both to receive and to process information.

But if his capacities enable him to *acquire* reliable information about certain subject matters, they also *constrain* the information to which he has access and thus *limit* the reliable information he can acquire. For example, a citizen who has telepathic powers can acquire reliable information that citizens who lack such powers can't acquire. A citizen who can "read minds" directly and immediately has a cognitive capacity, a means of acquiring information, that (presumably) most of his compatriots lack. Now suppose that there are certain states of mind that are detectable only by telepathy. Then only telepaths can acquire reliable information about those states of mind. Only they can learn about those states of mind; for the rest of us ordinary mortals, reliable information about those states of mind is *impossible* – and since impossible, inaccessible. And not just inaccessible, but inaccessible *in principle*: nontelepathic human beings cannot acquire reliable information about those states of mind given their native cognitive endowment and thus cannot, even in the best of epistemic circumstances, employ their own cognitive capacities to acquire that information.

Given the distinction between actual and in principle accessibility, how should we interpret (2)? Should we understand (2) as requiring actual accessibility: in order for some rationale R to count as a public justification, must a citizen be able to employ his developed cognitive capacities to determine whether R is sound? Or should we understand (8) as requiring accessibility in principle: in order for R to count as a public justification, must it be the case that a citizen *would* have been able to employ his cognitive capacities to determine that R is sound *if* he had developed his native cognitive capacities differently than he actually has?

It seems clear that the justificatory liberal must interpret (2) in the latter way. As I've noted several times, in virtue of the "privileged" status of religious grounds, an adequate conception of public justification must give the result that a citizen ought to withhold support from any coercive law for which he enjoys only a religious rationale. A complementary constraint obtains regarding other sorts of privileged grounds. In particular, certain sorts of grounds are paradigmatically *public* and as a consequence any adequate conception of public justification must permit a citizen to support a coercive law on the basis of a rationale that depends essentially on such grounds. Ordinary sense-perceptual claims count as paradigmatically public grounds: any conception of public justification that forbids a citizen to rely on a rationale that is uneliminably dependent on ordinary sense-perceptual claims thereby counts as inadequate. Reputable scientific theories also count as paradigmatically public grounds.

> The clearest instances of judgments based on publicly accessible reasons are ones based on reasons whose force, rather than being a product of the persons making the judgments, would be acknowledged by any competent and levelheaded observer. That logical deduction and scientific or ordinary empirical inquiry may involve judgments of this kind is fairly straightforward.[45]

But many scientific theories are actually *in*accessible: many citizens will find well-established and reputable scientific theories utterly mystifying and will stand with respect to those theories in much the same epistemic relation as they stand with respect to the reputable prophet who claims to have some special revelation from God. Consequently, we should amend (2) as follows:

(3) A citizen's rationale R counts as a public justification for a given coercive law only if R is publicly accessible in principle.[46]

What should we make of (3)? I see no reason to believe that mystical perception counts as publicly inaccessible in principle. After all, surely it is possible in the relevant sense for *any* (normal) human being to perceive God, just as it is possible that any (normal) human being could have developed his cognitive capacities so that he can determine that the rationale for some complicated scientific theory is probative. It is not that some of us are bound by Kantian categories which blind us to the transcendent whereas others, our categorial veils lifted, are free to traipse about the noumenal realm. Those who claim to perceive God, while willing to admit that others *haven't* perceived God, and while (perhaps) willing to admit that some can't under current conditions perceive God, will resolutely deny that those who haven't perceived God *couldn't* do so were circumstances different. They will no doubt claim that *any* human being has been so created that, so long as his cognitive capacities function properly, he is able to perceive God.

Consider in this regard the difference between telepathy and mystical perception. There is an important sense in which information available only by telepathic means is in principle inaccessible to many citizens: a citizen who claims to "read minds" directly and immediately is committed to the proposition that he has a cognitive capacity, a means of acquiring information, that other human beings lack. Telepathy is inaccessible to ordinary mortals in the same sense as the batlike ability to detect motion through sonar: since we aren't hard-wired to acquire information via sonar, we can't (barring technological innovation) acquire information in that way. Mystical perception is very different from telepathy in that respect. Those who claim to perceive God are not a cognitive elite whose means of acquiring information about the divine simply isn't available to the common mortal. Mystical perception is thoroughly democratic in the relevant sense: just as any citizen enjoys cognitive capacities he could have employed to understand and evaluate the scientific theories that bear on specific coercive laws even though he can't in fact, any citizen can perceive God in that he enjoys cognitive capacities that he can employ to perceive God even though he does not in fact.

8.5 REPLICABILITY

The weakness of the appeal to public accessibility is well exemplified by the problems that afflict Kent Greenawalt's conception of *replicability* (which Greenawalt employs to explicate the notion of public accessibility).[47] Greenawalt understands the concept of replicability as follows. A citizen's claim C counts as replicable only if relevantly similar citizens who find themselves in relevantly similar circumstances would adhere to C: "if we believe that similar external events would cause roughly similar reactions in most people, we cling to an accessible, replicable means for discovering the insight on which we rely."[48] A contrast between mystical perception and sense perception fixes the content of Greenawalt's conception of replicability. Greenawalt mentions St. Paul's conversion experience on the road to Damascus in this regard: even St. Paul wouldn't claim that his own experience was "replicable for other people under similar sets of external circumstances."[49] That is, if there had been a molecule for molecule identical replica of St. Paul – a "Twin Paul" – in exactly the same location at exactly the same time and in exactly the same circumstances in which St. Paul had his vision, Twin Paul wouldn't necessarily have the same experience as St. Paul.[50] Consequently, St. Paul's conversion experience counts as unreplicable.

Matters are different, of course, for sense perception. If I perceive the computer on my desk at a given time, in a given place and in a given set of circumstances, then I would fully expect that, were my simulacrum to find himself so circumstanced, he would have a visual experience exactly similar to my own. When relevantly similar people find themselves in relevantly similar sense-perceptual conditions, they will have relevantly similar sense-perceptual experiences. Hence, sense perception counts as a replicable source of information.

Greenawalt notes that, with respect to replicability, St. Paul's conversion experience differs even from Sally's perception of alien beings who, by the use of sophisticated technology, appear only to her and disappear without leaving any traces detectable by our current state of technology. Although Sally will in fact have a very difficult time getting us to trust her claim that she perceived alien beings – in fact, we should expect that Sally will be unable to provide us with a remotely compelling argument that she has perceived alien beings – we reasonably assume that, *if* we were circumstanced as she claims to have been, we *would* have seen what she saw.[51] Sense perception, even of elusive alien beings, differs from mystical perception with respect to replicability.

Greenawalt's conception of replicability is fairly clear. And it seems that the justificatory liberal might want to put Greenawalt's conception to use in articulating an epistemic conception of public justification. Thus, he might want to defend the following:

(4) A citizen's rationale R counts as a public justification for a given coercive law only if R is replicable.

Is mystical perception unreplicable, as Greenawalt claims? I see no reason to believe so. The crucial question is as follows: why not include God's manifestation to St. Paul in the set of external circumstances we hold constant in determining whether some experience is replicable? If, in determining whether St. Paul's experience is replicable, we assume that God isn't present to Twin Paul, the fact that Twin Paul wouldn't appear to himself to perceive God in relevantly similar circumstances is hardly surprising. Indeed, if Twin Paul did seem to himself to perceive God under those conditions, we would have good reason to regard St. Paul's experience as *delusory*. For in that case, St. Paul would have had the same experience whether or not God was actually present to him – not a very reliable way of forming beliefs! If, on the other hand, we assume that God appears to Twin Paul, then we should expect Twin Paul to perceive God. There is, in short, no reason to deny that mystical perception is replicable in the same sense as is sense perception: so long as we hold *all* of the perceptually relevant factors constant, molecule for molecule identical agents will have exactly similar perceptual experiences. And why shouldn't we hold all perceptually relevant factors constant?

Greenawalt, it seems, denies that we should: he claims that to hold both God's will and other relevant circumstances constant "is not replicability according to ordinary human standards for a broad range of human beings."[52] "Human standards" of replicability, he argues, require that we hold constant only "certain physical and conceptual conditions."[53] But this response begs the question. After all, he will have gerrymandered the concept of replicability such that it is *impossible* for mystical perception to count as replicable; more particularly, he builds into his account of public accessibility an understanding of replicability modeled on, and proper only for, secular practices. But that is precisely the question at issue: on what *principled* basis may we require that citizens exercise restraint regarding M-beliefs but not, say, sense-perceptual beliefs?[54] We can't provide that principled basis by appeal to an understanding of replicability that is gerrymandered so as to get the desired result. After all, why should a participant in CMP accept a conception of replicability if that conception excludes causally relevant factors, whether natural or supernatural, from the set of constants with respect to which we determine whether some source of information is replicable?[55]

This criticism indicates a very important point regarding the notion of replicability. As Greenawalt points out in his discussion of Sally's perception of her elusive alien visitors, we should regard Sally's perception of the elusive aliens as replicable, not because her compatriots are actually in a position to perceive them, and not because her compatriots are actually able to corroborate her claim, but because, *if* they had been in a better position to perceive them than they were in fact, *if* her compatriots had been present with her when her alien visitors manifested themselves to Sally, then her compatriots *would* have been in a position to perceive them using the very same kind of cognitive endowment Sally employed in perceiving the aliens. But if we employ exactly the same test to determine whether a given mystical perception is replicable, it's clear that mystical perception counts as replicable. We can put this objection in the form of a dilemma. Either those factors essential to a veridical perception of God are included in the epistemic desiderata we impute to our compatriots in determining whether they would have perceived God or they are not. If they are, as in the case in which we assume that God is present both to St. Paul and Twin Paul, then we have no good reason to deny that mystical perception is replicable. If they are not, then (4) *arbitrarily* rules out mystical perception. Why arbitrarily? Consider that, if we appropriately deny the replicability of a citizen's perception of God on the basis of the fact that some other citizen to whom God is *not* manifest would *not* appear to perceive God, we must also deny that ordinary perceptual beliefs are replicable. After all, in an exactly parallel fashion, we have no reason to expect that Jack's genuine sensory perception of a given object O would be replicated by Jill in relevantly similar circumstances, save that O is not present to Jill. So a consistent application of the test Greenawalt employs to determine whether mystical perceptions are replicable commits him to the claim that ordinary sense-perceptual claims do not count as replicable. And this implication constitutes a reductio of Greenawalt's replicability criterion. In sum, then, it seems that (4) is either too weak in that it fails to rule mystical perception unreplicable or that, when strengthened, (4) commits the justificatory liberal, on pain of inconsistency, to the claim that neither mystical nor sense perception are replicable sources of information.[56]

8.6 FALLIBILISM AND INERRANCY

Recall for a moment my discussion of the ideal of conscientious engagement: I argued that respect for persons requires a citizen to be willing to learn from her compatriots. I argued further that, since learning from her compatriots requires that a citizen take seriously the possibility that she might be wrong about some coercive law and that her compatriots might be right, respect for other persons requires a citizen to take a *fallibilistic* attitude toward her political commitments (and thus toward any theological claims "directly" related to her political commitments). It might seem, however, that a citizen who engages in certain doxastic practices, including CMP, will refuse to comply with that component of the ideal of conscientious engagement. In particular, it might seem that a citizen who supports a coercive law on the basis of a rationale she derives from a putatively *inerrant* source of information will be unwilling to take seriously the possibility that that rationale is unsound, as was the case, apparently, with the Christian Right activist who informed Clyde Wilcox "in no uncertain terms that a flat tax was biblical policy, and therefore there was no room for discussion."[57] If reliance on putatively inerrant sources is associated with that kind of rigid dogmatism and self-assured close-mindedness, then it would no doubt be much better were a citizen to exercise restraint regarding grounds she derives from inerrant sources.

Daniel Conkle has defended this line of argument. He begins his argument with the claim that each citizen ought to take a fallibilistic position with respect to her political commitments: "Political decisions should be formulated on the basis of a deliberative, dialogic decision-making process, a process that at least permits the possibility that argument or discourse will lead to a change of mind."[58] But some citizens are unwilling or unable to take up that fallibilistic position with respect to their political commitments. He has in mind, most particularly, "religious fundamentalists" who take the Bible to be an inerrant source of information about moral and political matters, although he is clear that his concern also extends to citizens who support their political commitments on the basis of their M-beliefs.[59] According to Conkle, we should regard the "contributions [of fundamentalists] to America's public life ... with caution and skepticism" because fundamentalists are "not willing even to consider the possible truth of contrary positions."[60] Conkle's claim isn't just that some fundamentalists *happen* to regard their political commitments as utterly certain, as would be the case, for example, if fundamentalists were afflicted by a psychological profile – an authoritarian personality – that inhibits them from recognizing their fallibility. Rather the idea is that fundamentalists are *rationally committed* to rejecting fallibilism. Rationally committed in virtue of what? A fundamentalist's rejection of fallibilism with respect to her political commitments is implied by her adherence to the doctrine of biblical inerrancy. Because fundamentalists adhere to the doctrine of biblical inerrancy, they are rationally committed to taking any grounds they derive from the Bible "to be entirely beyond question, reconsideration, or debate."[61]

So Conkle's argument begins with the claim that citizens ought to regard their political commitments as fallible, moves to the claim that citizens who support their favored political commitments on the basis of grounds they derive from inerrant sources are rationally forbidden to take a fallibilistic position with respect to those political commitments, and concludes that citizens should exercise restraint regarding any grounds they derive from putatively inerrant sources. Thus, Conkle appears to accept something like the following constraint on public justification:

(5) A citizen's rationale R counts as a public justification for a given coercive law only if she doesn't regard that coercive law as "beyond question, reconsideration, or debate" and doesn't regard R as "beyond question, reconsideration, or debate."

And Conkle concludes from (5) that a responsible citizen in a liberal democracy ought to exercise restraint regarding any rationale she derives from a putatively inerrant source of information.[62]

I accept (5), but don't accept Conkle's application of (5). Even though CMP counts as an inerrant source of information on Conkle's understanding, a citizen is by no means prohibited from taking up a fallibilistic position regarding her M-beliefs: consequently, a citizen who supports a given coercive law solely on the basis of her M-beliefs need not regard her rationale for that law as beyond question, reconsideration, or debate. Consequently, (5) is too weak to mandate restraint with respect to M-beliefs. Similarly for other putatively inerrant repositories of information, such as the Bible (or some other sacred text): since a citizen needn't regard as inerrant the grounds she derives from what she takes to be an inerrant Bible, (5) doesn't mandate restraint regarding grounds derived from the Bible. (In order to maintain continuity with Conkle's discussion, I will focus on the application of (5) to the Bible and allow the reader to draw the appropriate conclusions regarding CMP.)

How can it be appropriate for a citizen to subject to critical scrutiny a rationale she derives from what she regards as an inerrant source of information? If Bill McCartney accepts the claim that homosexuality is a moral abomination because he believes the Bible expresses this claim, and if McCartney believes that the Bible can't contain any falsehoods, then how can McCartney take seriously the possibility that his conviction about the moral status of homosexuality is false? The answer, it seems to me, is fairly straightforward: there is a distinction between an inerrant *source* of information and a citizen's fallible *apprehension* of that source.[63] If McCartney believes that the Bible is an inerrant source of information, then he is committed to the following conditional: *if* he has interpreted the Bible correctly, *then* homosexuality must indeed be morally wrong. But McCartney can be fully committed to the claim that, although the Bible is inerrant, his ability to divine the claims actually expressed in the Bible is as fallible as you like. (Indeed, commitment to the inerrancy of the Bible is logically consistent with an *extreme skepticism* about the reliability of any particular interpretation of the Bible.) Consequently, even if McCartney regards the Bible as inerrant, and thus assents to the conditional that if God reveals in the Bible that homosexual relations are morally wrong, then homosexual relations are morally wrong, he is by no means rationally committed to the claim that his conviction regarding the moral impropriety of homosexual relations is beyond dispute. Rather, he can freely admit that although he *thinks* homosexual relations are morally wrong, he might be wrong about that, since he might have misunderstood what the Bible really says about homosexuality.

The same point applies to CMP. As a member of CMP, McCartney is committed to the conditional that *if* he has perceived God as informing him that homosexual relations are morally wrong, then homosexual relations are morally wrong. He is, after all, committed to the proposition that God can't utter moral falsehoods and therefore that any moral claim God actually endorses must be true. But he is free to admit that he might have misperceived God as informing him that homosexual relations are morally wrong.

So long as we distinguish between the inerrancy of a source of information and a citizen's fallible apprehension of that source, it's clear that a citizen who relies on a putatively inerrant source of information in supporting her favored coercive laws *need not* regard her rationale for those laws as beyond question, reconsideration, or debate. And not only need she not regard her rationale as beyond question, but she will typically have powerful reason to *affirm* that her rationale might be mistaken. For example, a citizen who engages in the practice of biblical interpretation will undoubtedly have formed a number of false beliefs on the basis of her interpretation of the Bible and thus will have good experiential evidence to believe that, even though God is an infallible moral authority and has inerrantly communicated God's moral convictions in the biblical text, *her* understanding of the Bible can be distorted, self-deceived, myopic, ideological, or the like. Moreover, if she is at all self-reflective and historically conscious, she will be cognizant of the fact that many of her fellow believers have formed false, ideological, corrupt beliefs on the basis of their respective readings of the Bible, and if she exhibits even a minimal degree of humility, she will recognize that she might be affected by the same distorting factors that misled her co-religionists. Finally, if she adheres to a theological tradition (such as the Christian tradition) that asserts that each human being is sinful and that the consequences of sin affect each person's cognitive activities, then she'll have good reason to *expect* that at least some of her interpretations of the Bible are infected by sin. Consequently, she'll be willing to countenance the possibility that, even though the Bible contains no falsehoods, for any given belief *she* forms on the basis of her reading of the Bible, that belief might be false.

It seems, then, that a citizen's affirmation of the fallibility of her theological convictions is entirely consistent with her commitment to the inerrancy of the source of her theological convictions. Consequently, we have no reason to believe that (5) mandates restraint regarding beliefs derived from putatively inerrant sources of information such as CMP or the Bible. That said, nothing I have argued indicates that a citizen who regards the Bible as inerrant will *relish* the fact that the beliefs she derives from the Bible might be false: no doubt fundamentalists are as averse as are most people to reflecting on the possibility that the beliefs that give their lives meaning and purpose are false. And without doubt many citizens will conflate the claim that the Bible is an inerrant source of information with the very different claim that they are infallible interpreters of the Biblical text. But none of this provides any support for the claim that citizens who derive their political commitments from putatively inerrant sources of information are *rationally forbidden* from entertaining the possibility that their political commitments are false. And, so far as I can tell, that's the only claim in the neighborhood of inerrancy that holds out any promise of an epistemic conception of public justification sufficiently powerful to mandate restraint regarding mystical perception.

8.7 EXTERNAL CRITICISM

Although the fallibilism constraint I discussed in the previous section is too weak to mandate restraint regarding mystical perception, a brief reflection on some implications of fallibilism will indicate a strategy the justificatory liberal can pursue to articulate a more powerful and therefore more promising epistemic conception of public justification. A citizen who realizes that the beliefs she forms by engaging in doxastic practice D might be false, and who is also committed to withholding her assent from false beliefs, will have powerful reason to exercise due caution while engaging in D: she'll want to test her beliefs in such a way as to determine whether beliefs that seem true at first blush turn out, after all, to be false, partial, misleading, or the like. As the reader will recall, an overrider system, in Alston's idiolect, just is a set of tests the members of a given doxastic practice can employ to distinguish between apparently true and actually true beliefs. Consequently, a citizen who realizes that the beliefs she forms by engaging in D might be false, and who is also committed to withholding her assent from false beliefs, has powerful reason to ensure that D enjoys an adequate overrider system. In short, given fallibilism, an effective overrider system is a highly desirable epistemic commodity.

The fact that D's having an adequate overrider system is a crucially important epistemic desideratum doesn't guarantee that D enjoys an adequate overrider system. Even more obviously, the fact that having an adequate overrider system is an important epistemic desideratum even for *religious* doxastic practices doesn't guarantee that a given religious doxastic practice enjoys an adequate overrider system. Indeed, many critics of CMP have argued that CMP's overrider system is woefully inadequate and that, as a consequence, we ought to regard CMP with skepticism. Justificatory liberals might want to follow the lead of CMP's critics: although they will want to refrain from skepticism regarding CMP, they might want to focus on CMP's overrider system in attempting to articulate a conception of public justification that will provide principled grounds for the claim that a citizen ought to exercise restraint regarding her M-beliefs. I will discuss one such epistemic conception in this section, namely,

(6) A citizen's rationale R counts as a public justification for a given coercive law only if R is amenable to external criticism.[64]

As applied to CMP, the basic idea animating (6) is as follows: even if a citizen who engages in CMP can readily admit that any given M-belief might be false, and even if CMP enjoys a set of tests and procedures a citizen can employ to evaluate *her* M-beliefs, there are no tests that those who do *not* engage in CMP can employ to evaluate her M-beliefs. The problem isn't that CMP enjoys no tests at all, but that the tests it enjoys are an inside job – available only to those who engage in CMP. Consequently, M-beliefs are immune from meaningful *external criticism* – those who don't engage in CMP have no realistic prospect of providing a citizen who supports a coercive law on the basis of her M-beliefs with reason to believe that her M-beliefs don't provide her with adequate reason to support that law. As Rorty claims regarding religious commitments generally, mystical perception is a "conversation-stopper": if a citizen supports a coercive law on the basis of a putative perception of God, her compatriots will be reduced (if not stunned) to silence since they lack the resources necessary to challenge her claim that she has perceived God in such and such a way.[65] Amy Gutmann and Dennis Thompson echo Rorty's sentiment in a passage worth citing in extenso:

> But the primary reason why [appeals to biblical authority in support of coercive laws] must be rejected as moral reasons [and thus as an appropriate basis for coercive laws] is that they close off any possibility of publicly assessing or interpreting the content of the claims put forward by the authority. It cannot constitute a moral reason to appeal to an authority whose dictates are closed to reasonable interpretation. To argue otherwise would place no limit at all on the claims that could be made in the name of morality. An appeal to authority can certainly count as a reason, but only when its dictates are open to interpretation by publicly acceptable reasons or method of inquiry.[66]

Thesis (6) is a *very* popular constraint on what counts as a public justification – more than a few justificatory liberals regard something like (6) as mandating restraint, not just regarding mystical perception, but regarding religious grounds generally.[67] In some passages, for example, Conkle's advocacy of restraint regarding grounds derived from putatively inerrant sources of information seems motivated by a concern that such grounds will be regarded by believers as utterly certain and *therefore* as immune from external criticism – perhaps it's the immunity from external criticism rather than the rejection of fallibilism that really concerns Conkle. As I noted above, Bird's intelligibility constraint seems to be a circuitous way to require that a prospective public justification be amenable to external criticism: it's really because religious grounds aren't amenable to "public critical scrutiny," rather than because they are unintelligible or incommunicable, that religious grounds are insufficient for public justification.[68] Similarly with many formulations of the public accessibility criterion. Of course, not every appeal to external criticism takes the path (whether intentionally or unintentionally) of indirection: some justificatory liberals argue directly for some version of (6). In this section, I will focus on Thomas Nagel's much-discussed variation on (6).

According to Nagel, a citizen mustn't support any coercive law for which she lacks a "common ground of justification,"[69] where common ground is *not* construed in populist terms.[70] Rather, a citizen's rationale counts as a public justification for a favored coercive law only if it is amenable to external criticism: "public justification in a context of actual disagreement requires ... preparedness to submit one's reasons to the criticism of others, and to find that the exercise of a common critical rationality and consideration of evidence that can be shared will reveal that one is mistaken."[71] I take the statement cited here to be more or less equivalent to (6): in order for a citizen's rationale for some coercive law to count as a public justification, her compatriots must be able to identify and understand that rationale and be able to evaluate that rationale by employing a *common* critical rationality. Nagel endorses an additional constraint on a prospective public justification: "public justification requires ... an expectation that if others who do not share your belief are wrong, there is probably an explanation of that error which is not circular."[72] Both of Nagel's constraints on a prospective public justification are intended to ensure that the political disagreements that will unavoidably characterize a modern pluralistic democracy do "not come down finally to a bare confrontation between incompatible personal points of view."[73] So Nagel seems to endorse the following expanded version of (6):

(6*) A citizen's rationale R counts as a public justification for a given coercive law only if (a) R is evaluable in light of a "common critical rationality," and (b) for any citizen who does not find R compelling, there exists a noncircular explanation as to why she does not find R compelling.

Nagel claims that "conflicts of religious faith fail this test, and most empirical and many moral disagreements do not."[74] Consequently, (6*) requires restraint regarding mystical perceptions.

Although (6*) is considerably more demanding than (5), (6*) is nevertheless too weak to mandate restraint regarding mystical perception. In order to show that (6*) is too weak, I'll show that a citizen's putative mystical perception can satisfy both of the constraints Nagel lays down on a public justification.

Ad (a): Is there any credible reason to believe that a citizen who supports a favored coercive law on the basis of her M-beliefs is immune from criticism by those who don't engage in CMP? That depends entirely on the nature of CMP's overrider system. As I noted above, CMP's overrider system is constituted by a set of *consistency* tests: a citizen who seems to herself to perceive God and forms M-belief M on the basis of that putative perception must determine whether M is consistent (deductively, probabilistically, and abductively) with her other well-grounded convictions. Only if none of a citizen's other well-grounded beliefs constitutes a sufficiently powerful reason to regard M as false does M count as rationally justified, *all things considered*. By contrast, if a citizen's overrider system does contain well-grounded beliefs that provide sufficiently powerful reason to regard M as false, then she ought to withhold support from M – in Alston's idiolect, whatever prima facie justification M enjoys in virtue of its being based on a generally reliable ground, M's prima facie justification is overridden by sufficient evidence to the contrary.

One of the most important tests M must pass is the following: M must be consistent with the understanding of God's nature and activities internal both to CMP and to other religious doxastic practices. Participants in CMP ought to reject any M-belief not "in consonance with the picture of the nature, purposes and doings of God that has been built up in that community."[75] If a citizen apparently perceives God as commanding her to commit acts of torture but the understanding of God internal to CMP indicates that God isn't the sort of being who would utter such a command, then she has powerful reason to conclude that her M-belief is false: whatever prima facie justification that M-belief might enjoy is overridden by its running directly contrary to other well-grounded beliefs about God. Now if the understanding of God internal to CMP and other religious practices plays so important a role in the evaluation of putative mystical perceptions, this might seem to lend some credence to the claim that the tests constitutive of CMP's overrider system are an inside job: those who engage in CMP and associated religious practices enjoy resources to criticize M-beliefs, but those who don't engage in CMP have no such basis and therefore can't employ those tests themselves. Alston's description of CMP's overrider system seems to substantiate the concerns that underlie (6*).

But this appearance is deceptive. First, even if consistency with the understanding of God internal to CMP were the only test for evaluating M-beliefs, it doesn't follow that those who don't engage in CMP can't employ the relevant understanding of God as a basis for leveraging a citizen out of her adherence to a given M-belief. In principle, those who don't engage in CMP can show that a given M-belief is inconsistent with the understanding of God internal to CMP even though they don't regard CMP as a reliable doxastic practice, don't believe that God exists, or believe that God exists but adopt a very different understanding of God's nature and activities. Of course, in order to articulate this kind of criticism, those who don't engage in CMP will have to know something about CMP – they will have to apprise themselves of the understanding of God internal to CMP. And many who don't engage in CMP might regard as a waste the effort required so to apprise themselves. That is as it may be. But we shouldn't confuse the claim that a citizen's M-beliefs are immune from criticism by her compatriots with the very different claim that a citizen's compatriots aren't sufficiently interested in CMP to put themselves in a position to articulate a convincing criticism of her M-beliefs. Mystical perception, as with religion generally, is a conversation *stopper* only for those who don't want to do what it takes to enter into the conversation in a productive manner.

Second, it is not the case that CMP's overrider system is constituted solely by the test that M-beliefs must be consistent with the understanding of God's nature and activities internal to CMP and associated practices. There is another consistency test each M-belief must pass: a citizen's M-beliefs must be consistent with the moral claims contained in her overrider system. Most important for our purposes, a citizen's M-belief M must be consistent with any well-grounded and sufficiently weighty *secular* norm contained in her overrider system. On the understanding of God internal to CMP, God is a morally perfect being. Consequently, members of CMP are committed to the claim that God can't act in a morally inappropriate manner. And if God can't act in a morally inappropriate manner, then any putative perception of God that *seems* to indicate that God acts in a morally inappropriate manner must *not* be veridical. Now suppose that a citizen has powerful secular grounds for a given moral claim C – that torturing innocent persons is morally wrong: suppose she is a convinced Kantian who takes C to be mandated by the universalizability test. In that case, C counts as part of her overrider system and her M-beliefs must be consistent with C. More cautiously, if a citizen has good secular grounds for assenting to C, then she has powerful reason to withhold assent from any putative perception of God in which God seems to violate C.[76]

Thus, for example, assume that Bill McCartney forms his conviction that homosexuality is morally wrong on the basis of his putative perception that God has testified to him that homosexuality is morally wrong. As we saw in the previous section, if McCartney is thinking clearly, he will affirm the conditional: if God has revealed that homosexuality is morally wrong, then homosexuality is morally wrong. But McCartney is free to admit that his putative perception of God might not be veridical. So how does McCartney determine whether his perception of God is veridical? By employing the consistency tests constitutive of CMP's overrider system: any putative perception of God must be consistent with other well-grounded moral claims to which McCartney adheres. Consequently, any citizen who can articulate an objection to the claim that homosexuality is morally wrong articulates an objection that has a direct bearing on McCartney's belief that he has perceived God as testifying to the claim that homosexuality is morally wrong. *If* that objection is compelling, then McCartney *mustn't* have perceived God or must have misinterpreted God's testimony, or the like. Moreover, *any* citizen, whether or not she engages in CMP, whether or not she is religious, can articulate an objection that has a direct bearing on McCartney's conviction that homosexuality is morally wrong. *If* she can articulate an objection that relies solely on secular premises, and *if* that objection is compelling, then McCartney *mustn't* have perceived God or must have misinterpreted God's testimony, or the like. In short, just because any well-grounded moral claim, whether religiously or secularly grounded, counts as a potential defeater for any given M-belief, we have no reason to believe that a citizen who supports a given coercive law on the basis of her M-beliefs alone cannot be convinced by her compatriots that her rationale for that law is thoroughly inadequate. But then it seems that citizens who do not engage in CMP, and indeed who do not engage in any religious doxastic practice, can articulate a convincing criticism of any given M-belief without having to premise her criticism on the understanding of God internal to CMP. And that seems to be just the sort of criticism that (6*) requires.[77]

Since the concern that religious grounds aren't amenable to external criticism is so common a basis for advocating restraint regarding religious grounds, and since there are certain important differences between biblical interpretation and mystical perception, I'll briefly broach the application of (6*) to reliance on interpretations of the Bible as a basis for coercive laws. The structural relation between secular claims and mystical perceptions is exactly the same as the structural relation between secular claims and biblical interpretation: in the latter case, as in the former, secular claims play a substantial role in enabling a citizen to determine whether God has revealed that some moral claim is true.

The role secular claims play in biblical interpretation is as follows. God, as a morally perfect being, cannot act in a morally inappropriate manner, nor can God utter false testimony. Hence, if a citizen has adequate reason to believe that moral claim M is true, then she has prima facie reason to reject any interpretation of the biblical text in which God is understood as testifying to ~M. And this constraint on appropriate interpretations of the biblical texts obtains whether a citizen's reasons for adhering to M are secular or religious: *whatever* her grounds for M, *if* she has good grounds for M, then M counts as a standing defeater for any interpretation of the biblical text according to which God endorses ~M. It seems that a citizen who supports her favored coercive laws solely on the basis of her interpretation of the Bible must be open to purely secular objections to her interpretation of the Bible.

There are, no doubt, some religious citizens who will deny this argument. They will claim that secular considerations ought to have no influence whatsoever in a citizen's interpretation of the Bible. A pertinent example here is the creation/evolution debate: many creationists reject outright the propriety of evaluating God's word in light of modern science and therefore are unwilling to "reinterpret" the first several chapters of Genesis to render that account of creation consistent with what we know on the basis of modern science to be true.

I have no pretensions to neutrality. Consequently, I have no compunction in rejecting such protestations outright: the position that a citizen can interpret the Bible without helping herself to a healthy diet of extra-biblical information is obviously and straightforwardly indefensible. As I see it, the actual practice of biblical interpretation – the actual practice of interpretation by those who deny that secular considerations may play any normative role in Biblical interpretation – belies such explicit affirmations. A simple example should convey why these protestations lack any credibility. *No* interpreter of the Bible prior to, say, the fifteenth century interpreted *any* passage in the Bible consistently with empirical claims we now *know* to be true: for example, no biblical interpreter interpreted claims in the Bible that refer to the movement of the sun consistently with the fact that the earth orbits the sun. Rather, biblical interpreters understood such passages to be consistent with commonly held, plausible but false empirical claims: they regarded as literally true statements in the Bible that seem to indicate that the earth is stationary. To my knowledge, no contemporary interpreter of the Bible interprets those very passages consistently with the claim that the earth is stationary.[78] Even by those who regard the Bible as inerrant, biblical claims that seem to indicate that the earth is stationary are interpreted otherwise: for example, as phenomenological claims – claims regarding how the earth and sun seem to relate from our vantage point. There is one and only one explanation of this sort of move from the literal to the phenomenological: given that the Bible is inerrant, and given that we *know* that the earth isn't stationary, the interpreter concludes that the Bible *cannot* express the claim that the earth is stationary even if it might *seem* to express that claim. She concurs with Galileo's claim that "the holy Bible can never speak untruth – whenever its true meaning is understood. But ... it is very often abstruse, and may say things which are quite different from what its bare words signify."[79] So she casts about for some other interpretation of the relevant statements that will enable her to avoid imputing falsehood to the Bible. Clearly, *everyone*, even the most extreme fundamentalist, takes into consideration well-grounded claims derived from other sources of information in determining which claims the Bible actually expresses.[80] And a similar, although more complicated, story can be told not just regarding the admittedly easy case of terrestrial motion, but also with respect to moral issues such as slavery. (That is, the terrestrial case is easy *now*: it wasn't always regarded as such a cut and dried matter.[81])

Just as, then, commitment to the inerrancy of the Bible is consistent with a thoroughgoing fallibilism, so also is commitment to biblical inerrancy consistent with a citizen's openness to external criticism: *if* a citizen regards some source as inerrant and thus denies that it expresses any false claims, then *any* well-grounded proposition P provides her with reason to deny that that source expresses ~P, irrespective of whether her reasons for assenting to P are secular or religious. Consequently, any citizen, even those who deny, say, that the Bible is inerrant, can engage in meaningful criticism of another citizen's interpretations of the Bible: if McCartney assents to the claim that homosexual activity is morally wrong on the basis of some reading of the Bible, and if McCartney's compatriots can articulate some rationale in support of the claim that homosexual activity is morally appropriate, then McCartney is rationally obliged to take that rationale into consideration in determining how he ought to interpret the Bible.

One final point: (6*) requires not only that a given rationale must be amenable to meaningful external criticism but also that we have the expectation "that the exercise of a common critical rationality and consideration of evidence that can be shared will reveal that one is mistaken."[82] Do we have the expectation that CMP's overrider system is sufficiently powerful as to enable others to detect misperceptions? Here we have to be careful. Some doxastic practices (SP, mathematics) provide us with powerful tests for disconfirming truth claims. Others (morality) provide us with much weaker tests. But we regard each of these practices as productive contributors to political decision making and advocacy, in spite of their varying capacity to track down untruth. So long as CMP's overrider system enjoys tests that are at least as powerful as the tests enjoyed by other practices the justificatory liberal regards as generating beliefs admissible as a basis for coercive laws, then we can't nonarbitrarily exclude M-beliefs from political decision making and advocacy by appeal to (a). I will argue in the next section that that is in fact the case.

Ad (b): The second component of (6*) requires that a citizen who supports a given coercive law on the basis of rationale R is committed to the claim that there exists a noncircular explanation as to why those who reject R are mistaken. Note that this second component does *not* require that a citizen who accepts R must be able to articulate that explanation; rather, he must be committed to the claim that there exists some such explanation: "one may not always have the information necessary to give such an account, but one must believe that there is one, and that the justifiability of one's own belief would survive a full examination of the reasons behind theirs."[83] (Nagel rightly refuses to require that a citizen actually be able to provide a noncircular explanation: that requirement would be far too demanding.) With that clarification in mind, it seems no more difficult for a citizen to believe that there is an explanation as to why his compatriots don't perceive God than it is for him to believe that there is an explanation as to why they don't assent to certain moral claims, such as, for example, Rawls's conviction that the equality of women outweighs the value of human life in the first trimester. I note one possibility: a necessary condition of a citizen's perceiving God requires a willingness on his part to experience God and, perhaps, a certain level or kind of moral virtue. A citizen's failure to perceive God is explicable by the absence of those subjective conditions.[84] Alston writes,

> The most basic point is that God has set certain requirements that must
> be met before He reveals Himself to our experience, at least consistently

and with relative fullness. "Blessed are the pure in heart for they shall see God." Again, the details of this vary, but it is generally acknowledged in the tradition that an excessive preoccupation and concern with worldly goods, certain kinds of immorality – particularly self-centeredness and unconcern with one's fellows – and a mind that is closed to the possibility of communion with God, are all antithetical to an awareness of God. This being the case, and given well-known facts about human predilections, it is the reverse of unexpected that not all people should participate in mystical perception.[85]

Although the kind of explanation offered to explain failure to perceive God will differ from that offered to explain similar lapses in other doxastic practices, mere differences between explananda don't amount to an absence of explanation. CMP, as an autonomous doxastic practice, may employ explanations of error that differ from those we employ in other doxastic practices just as legitimately as the explanation of mathematical errors differs from the way we explain perceptual illusions. To refuse to grant CMP its own explanatory framework would be to refuse to recognize CMP's autonomy. I conclude that although very different from the sort we employ in SP, CMP does offer explanations for misperception.

Nagel claims that such explanations must not be circular. He explicates this constraint in the following way: "The explanation should not come down to the mere assertion that they do not believe the truth (what you believe), but should explain their false belief in terms of errors in their evidence, or identifiable errors in drawing conclusions from it, or in argument, judgment, and so forth."[86] The "moral" explanation of failure to perceive God, or of misperception of God, doesn't amount to the bald assertion that those who disagree with the mystic about the reliability of CMP are wrong. But it is circular in that a citizen's grounds for accepting that kind of explanation depend in part on his acceptance of the general scheme of things internal to CMP. That kind of circularity is innocuous because unavoidable: even in sense perception, we make use of other sense perceptual claims to explain misperceptions in particular cases. As a result of prolonged perceptual contact with the world, we learn that we live in a material environment composed of stable and enduring objects, and that under certain conditions, our access to those objects is less reliable than under other conditions. On the basis of that general understanding of the world, we are able to provide an acceptable explanation of misperceptions. Our explanation of particular misperceptions is parasitic on a general understanding of the world which is itself dependent on a myriad of particular perceptions. If this kind of circularity is acceptable in SP, then such circularity can't be held against CMP. To argue otherwise would be arbitrary.

I conclude that if we accept the basic outlines of Alston's defense of CMP, and in particular, if we accord due weight to the fact that CMP is an autonomous doxastic practice, we have no good reason to deny that mystical perception satisfies (6*).

8.8 INDEPENDENT CONFIRMABILITY

If the constraints on a prospective public justification encoded in (6) and (6*) are too weak to mandate restraint regarding mystical perception, the justificatory liberal can articulate an epistemic conception that requires even more demanding procedures for evaluating putative mystical perceptions. Instead of requiring merely that M-beliefs be amenable to disconfirmation, disqualification, and falsification by others, the justificatory liberal might impose the much more demanding constraint that M-beliefs be amenable to *independent corroboration.* That is, the justificatory liberal might require not just that CMP's overrider system enjoy tests nonparticipants can employ to show that a citizen's M-beliefs are *false,* but also that CMP's overrider system enjoy tests others can employ to show that a citizen's M-beliefs are *true.*

Advocates of restraint are not without allies here. The epistemic correlate of this case has been powerfully argued by Alston's critics.[87] For example, according to Evan Fales, CMP's overrider system is so impoverished, it provides such weak criteria for distinguishing between apparently and actually true beliefs that, *even if* it is highly reliable, epistemically conscientious citizens would refuse to participate in CMP. Fales makes that argument by contrasting SP and CMP's overrider systems. Ever so briefly, here is Fales's argument. Alston argues that both SP and CMP are species of perceptual practice. It's widely granted that a citizen can perceive an object only if he is causally related to that object. But the way in which participants in CMP are causally related to God differs from the way that participants in SP are related to physical objects. And that difference in causal relations between perceiver and God renders CMP's overrider system inadequate. Why?

When we check a given citizen's sense-perceptual beliefs, we assume that, if he did in fact perceive some object, he was causally related to that object in the respects appropriate to his mode of perception. Thus, if he succeeded in seeing the famously elusive snark, light waves must have reflected off that creature's surface, been transmitted through the intervening space, struck his retina, and so on. But we also assume that the snark's presence in the location at which it was putatively spotted has *further* consequences. Not only does the snark reflect light waves, it also makes footprints, defecates, scratches tree trunks, breaks twigs, robs nests, and engages in numerous other activities. As a consequence of its engaging in such variegated behaviors, it enters into or initiates numerous causal chains. That a putatively perceived object is involved in a number of causal chains enables us to detect its presence even when we aren't privy to any light waves reflecting off of its body, that is, when we do not enter into the kind of causal chain the occurrence of which is a necessary condition of the direct visual perception of an object. So, if a citizen claims to have seen a snark, the rest of us check about for the residues of *other* causal chains in which the snark was putatively implicated. In so doing, we hope to *triangulate* its presence and thus to confirm our compatriot's claims.

It seems that the triangulation method partly constitutive of SP's overrider system presupposes that citizens are multiply causally connected to objects in their natural and social environments. According to Fales, a "single, fundamental presupposition ... guides, explains, and justifies" the strategies for checking beliefs constitutive of SP's overrider system:[88] events have *multiple* causal effects to which our respective cognitive endowments are sensitive such that we can, at least in principle, trace back each causal chain to the originating event.

Matters are very different with God. Members of CMP don't presume that God's presentation to a citizen's consciousness generates a series of causal chains any of which his compatriots can trace back to God and by means of which they can provide independent confirmation of his putative perception. Indeed, if CMP is reliable, we expect exactly the opposite.[89] God is directly, immediately manifest to a citizen's consciousness in such a way that God doesn't initiate any causal relations other than those required for God's actual presence. Given the way God has putatively chosen to act, an SP-like overrider system isn't available to members of CMP. Rather, CMP's overrider system is exhausted by the sort of consistency, disqualifying tests discussed in the prior section.

Given this important difference between SP and CMP, Fales's argument proceeds apace. If, given all we know, it's possible that a necessary condition of the reliability of a given perception doesn't obtain, then, in order to know that that perception is reliable, the percipient needs to have independent confirmation that that condition obtains. As I noted above, that a citizen is causally connected to God is a necessary condition of a given mystical perception's reliability. Hence, he needs independent confirmation that he is causally connected to God. But, as a matter of fact, the only way to confirm independently whether a citizen is causally related to some object is to trace back some *other* causal chain to that object. Since that's not possible with mystical perception, he can't know that a given M-belief is reliably formed. Consequently, he shouldn't trust any of the beliefs he forms on the basis of his putative perceptions of God.

I think that the weakness Fales points out in CMP is precisely what makes mystical perception a paradigmatic example of the kind of ground regarding which, according to the justificatory liberal, a citizen ought to exercise restraint. That a citizen's M-beliefs aren't amenable to independent confirmation generates the fear that we can't distinguish between a citizen's subjective urges and genuine divine prompting. Thus, Bird claims that the unintelligibility of mystical experience inhibits those who haven't had perceptual contact with God from determining whether citizens who claim to have perceived God have in fact done so. Perhaps it is not the unintelligibility that bothers him, but the unverifiability he claims is consequent upon the unintelligibility. A similar concern seems to motivate Greenawalt's appeal to replicability: the problem with unreplicable grounds is that others aren't in a position to "credit" those grounds.[90] In spite of defective execution with respect to the details – and sometimes more than just the details – perhaps both would accept something like this:

(7) A citizen's rationale R counts as a public justification for a given coercive law only if R is amenable to independent confirmation.

Unlike many of the other proposals I've canvassed, (7) is sufficiently powerful to mandate restraint regarding mystical perception: because of the way God has putatively chosen to be present to human beings, God doesn't initiate multiple causal chains and thus God's presence isn't subject to the kind of independent corroboration we expect for sense-perceptual beliefs.

What should we make of (7)? First a comment on an argumentative strategy commonly employed by justificatory liberals. As I've noted, a defensible conception of public justification must provide some non-arbitrary distinction between the grounds regarding which a citizen ought to exercise restraint and the grounds regarding which he need not exercise restraint. In order to articulate that distinction, justificatory liberals pursue the entirely legitimate strategy of referring to instances of grounds that obviously fit into one or the other category and using such clear instances as touchstones for formulating the desired conception of public justification. Reference to mystical and sense perception are particularly apropos for this purpose. On the assumption that SP serves as a paradigmatic instance of a practice that generates admissible grounds and that mystical perception serves as a paradigmatic instance of a practice that does not, those justificatory liberals who haven't ruled out mystical perception on even weaker grounds refer diffusely to SP's corroboratory procedures as the feature of SP that differentiates it from mystical perception. This gives the impression that the justificatory liberal is taking a tough line, that standards for a rationale's counting as a public justification are quite onerous. However, once the distinction has been exemplified, the contrast is left behind. Reference to SP's corroboratory procedures recedes into the background, thus making it possible for the justificatory liberal to count as public justifications certain grounds that seem indistinguishable from M-beliefs with respect to their epistemic merits.

That said, what of the merits of (7)? It's as obvious as anything in philosophy can be that we don't and can't confirm our *moral judgments* in the way that we corroborate sense perceptual claims. Consider the following two claims, one perceptual, the other moral:

(A) Franz Stangl, commandant of the Treblinka death camp, colluded in genocide.
(B) Franz Stangl ought not to have colluded in genocide.

We can easily provide independent confirmation for (A): we have pictures of Stangl at Treblinka, numerous eye-witness reports of his many activities there, and his own testimony to that effect. Clearly, Stangl initiated a number of causal chains we can trace back to his presence at Treblinka and, as a consequence, we are able to provide independent confirmation that conclusively establishes (A). Just as clearly, we can't provide anything like that kind of confirmation for (B). (B), after all, is about what *ought* to have been the case: it lays out what should have happened, not what did in fact happen. (B) instructs us that Stangl ought not have put himself in a position to initiate the various causal chains that enable us to establish (A) and thus justifiably to conclude that he violated (B). But what ought to happen (and didn't) enters into no causal relations: if (B) were true, if Stangl had satisfied his obligation to refrain from colluding in genocide, there would have been nothing at all that could have initiated the kind of multiple causal relations that we need in order to provide independent confirmation for (B).[91] In short, since (B) is true irrespective of whether some state of affairs obtains, and since what doesn't actually happen can initiate no causal chains, then, even if (B) is true, we can't expect to provide an SP-like confirmation for (B).

Since there is nothing distinctive about (B), we may generalize: in the very nature of the case, a citizen *cannot* provide the kind of independent confirmation for his moral beliefs that he *can* provide for sense-perceptual beliefs. Moreover, there's no good reason that we should expect him to provide independent confirmation for his moral beliefs: to require SP-like confirmation of moral convictions would be as egregious a violation of *autonomy* as we are likely to find. M-beliefs and moral beliefs are thus similar in a very important respect: the subject matter of our mystical perceptions and moral judgments is such that neither sort of ground is amenable to SP-like confirmation. Just as CMP doesn't enjoy an SP-like overrider system because God doesn't enter into multiple causal relations of the sort associated with our perception of objects in the physical environment, so also our moral doxastic practice doesn't enjoy an SP-like overrider system because the "object" of our moral beliefs doesn't enter into the sort of causal relations associated with sense-perceptual claims.

Since both moral evaluation and mystical perception are legitimately different – *autonomous* – from sense perception with respect to independent confirmation, (9) cannot but involve the justificatory liberal in an indefensible arbitrariness. Since we can't provide independent confirmation for our moral beliefs any more than we can provide independent confirmation for our M-beliefs, it would be arbitrary for the justificatory liberal to mandate restraint regarding M-beliefs on grounds that, by all rights, should also mandate restraint regarding our moral convictions. To recur to a point I made in discussing (6*): the justificatory liberal can't consistently mandate restraint with respect to mystical perception on the ground that CMP's overrider system is inadequate if CMP's overrider system isn't relevantly different from the overrider system of a practice that generates grounds regarding which he doesn't mandate restraint. More simply put, if members of CMP evaluate M-beliefs by employing the same kind of tests they employ to evaluate moral beliefs, and if the justificatory liberal doesn't advocate restraint regarding moral beliefs, then it is utterly arbitrary for him to advocate restraint regarding M-beliefs *on account of CMP's lacking the appropriate tests.*

Of course, even if we cannot provide SP-like corroboration for either mystical perceptions or moral evaluations, perhaps there are some other tests we can employ to evaluate moral judgments that we can't employ to evaluate mystical perceptions. Some such distinction might provide the justificatory liberal with the desired principled basis for mandating restraint regarding mystical perception but not moral judgment.

Here it's impossible to be anything but brief – and therefore, unfortunately, dogmatic.[92] I don't believe that a defensible account of the way we form and evaluate moral judgments will reveal that such judgments are subject to tests any more stringent than those applicable to M-beliefs. In fact, I believe that, at most, moral judgments are subject to disconfirmation via coherence considerations – the same kind of test available for M-beliefs. Here are some unsystematic observations in support of this assertion.

First, it is true that some moral claims satisfy extremely demanding epistemic standards: some *platitudinous* moral claims might very well be necessarily true and even knowable a priori. Indeed, some moral claims seem utterly certain. Thus, W. D. Ross:

> That an act, *qua* fulfilling a promise, or *qua* effecting a just distribution of good, or *qua* returning services rendered, or *qua* promoting the good of others, or *qua* promoting the virtue or insight of the agent, is *prima facie* right, is self-evident; not in the sense that it is evident from the beginning of our lives, or as soon as we attend to the proposition for the first time, but in the sense that when we have reached sufficient mental maturity and have given sufficient attention to the proposition it is evident without any need of proof, or of evidence beyond itself. It is self-evident just as a mathematical axiom, or the validity of a form of inference, is evident. . . . In our confidence that these propositions are true there is involved the same trust in our reason that is involved in our confidence in mathematics; and we should have no justification for

trusting it in the latter sphere and distrusting it in the former. In both cases we are dealing with propositions that cannot be proved, but that just as certainly need no proof.[93]

I'm entirely willing to grant that such claims as Ross mentions are so certain that we don't need to subject them to any tests. Doing so would be pointless anyway: some moral claims are so fundamental to our moral topography that we would immediately reject any consideration that seems to count against them.

But *most* moral claims aren't platitudinous; very few of the moral claims to which we adhere enjoy anywhere near the epistemic standing we ascribe to claims such as that we ought not torture children just to satisfy a whim. More pertinently, very few of the moral judgments on which we rely in political decision making and advocacy will enjoy anywhere near the kind of epistemic status Ross's examples enjoy. Here is one such moral judgment: that in the case of abortion, the equal value of women should outweigh the due respect we ought to accord to human life to the degree that we ought to accord women a right to have an abortion in the first trimester. That claim – that weighing of two platitudinous moral values – is not only not platitudinous, it's eminently debatable. It seems to me no different, at least with respect to its epistemic standing, from the comparable M-belief: that I have perceived God as informing me that in the case of abortion, the equal value of women should outweigh the due respect we ought to accord to human life to the degree that we ought to accord women a right to have an abortion in the first trimester. In both cases, the judgment in question will depend quite heavily on claims about what "seems" to the adherent to be the case, claims whose adherents will have an extremely difficult time justifying to a skeptical audience.

Second, since the moral judgments we must employ in political decision making and advocacy depend so heavily on intuitive judgments about what ought to be the case, it's particularly important that we are able to employ the appropriate tests in order to distinguish between moral truths and moral falsehoods. For example, as Peter Unger has shown in fascinating detail, even some of our most fundamental moral intuitions are skewed by "distortional dispositions" that occlude our awareness of important moral truths.[94] The fact that our intuitive moral judgments are amenable to corruption and distortion in various (systematic) respects renders highly desirable powerful tests for evaluating moral judgments. Unfortunately, the tests we can employ to check moral judgments aren't nearly as powerful as we would like. In the best of all possible worlds, we would be able to provide SP-like corroboration for our intuitive moral judgments. Actually that's not nearly strong enough: in the best of all possible worlds, we would be able to prove our moral commitments with the rigor and with the clarity we are able to provide for theorems in logic and mathematics. But it's only too obvious that we don't live in anything like the best of all possible worlds: the tests we are able to employ to check our moral judgments are considerably weaker than those we employ in sense perception. The tests we can employ to evaluate our moral convictions are consistency tests (the same sort of test we employ to evaluate mystical perceptions).[95]

The method of reflective equilibrium, for example, consists of an elaborate set of consistency tests, requiring the mutual adjustment of particular considered judgments, moral theories and background factual claims. Similarly with respect to perhaps the most popular of the tests we employ to evaluate moral judgments, namely, the test of universalization. Here brevity requires dogmatism: the principle of universalization is a consistency principle that serves as a filter for disqualifying moral claims, but does not enable us to corroborate moral claims. When all is said and done, all the principle of universalization enables us to do is to weed out moral claims; it can't vindicate substantive normative commitments. But such a consistency test nowhere nearly amounts to the confirmatory procedures we employ in SP.[96]

Most moral beliefs and all M-beliefs, then, are similar in the respects (a) that we form them on the basis of intuitive judgments about what "seems" true to us and (b) that we can evaluate such judgments by applying consistency tests which enable us to disconfirm false beliefs. Although moral beliefs, like M-beliefs, are amenable to critical analysis and thus satisfy (6*), I have little hope that the justificatory liberal will articulate some variant of (7) which will enable him to articulate some nonarbitrary basis for mandating restraint regarding M-beliefs but not moral beliefs as well. In short, it seems that the justificatory liberal who endorses (7) in order to mandate restraint regarding M-beliefs but who does not also draw the conclusion that citizens should exercise restraint regarding almost all moral beliefs is guilty of an indefensible arbitrariness.[97]

8.9 PROOF OF RELIABILITY

For completeness sake, I'll mention one final epistemic conception. Perhaps the justificatory liberal will want to advocate restraint regarding mystical perception because many citizens have genuine and reasonable doubts, not so much regarding the checking procedures internal to CMP, but regarding the reliability of CMP as a whole. In order for a rationale constituted in essential part of M-beliefs to count as a public justification, such critics might require that CMP's adherents be able to show that the whole practice of forming M-beliefs – CMP itself – is reliable. Thus, perhaps the following epistemic conception of public justification will achieve the desired result:

(8) A citizen's rationale R counts as a public justification for a given coercive law only if the premises essential to R are generated by a doxastic practice that can be shown to be reliable.[98]

It's often difficult to distinguish between proposals in the (7) family from those in the (8) family, since both can be formulated with the same language. Thus, for example, if the justificatory liberal claims that a citizen's rationale R counts as a public justification only if he can "show" that the premises included in R have been reliably formed, we can understand that constraint as requiring either (a) according to the standards *internal* to some doxastic practice, a citizen has corroboratory evidence for the premises essential to R (e.g., the triangulation method I mentioned earlier) or (b) a citizen has shown that the practice that generates those premises is reliable. The former is a claim about overrider systems, the latter about a whole doxastic practice.

I won't spend much time discussing (8), other than referring the reader to Alston's work on the matter. Alston has provided an exhaustive evaluation and critique of arguments in support of the reliability of SP, and concludes that, when not otherwise defective, arguments in support of SP's reliability are vitiated by an unavoidable epistemic circularity.[99] I find Alston's arguments persuasive. Since we can't provide a noncircular justification for the claim that SP is reliable, and since, of all the practices in which we engage, showing that SP is reliable is our best shot, we have reason to believe that we can't show that any of our basic doxastic practices are amenable to noncircular justification. But that means that (8) is arbitrary: we can't advocate restraint for CMP on the basis of our inability to show that CMP is reliable and refuse to draw the same conclusion with respect to each of the other basic practices in which we engage (SP, introspection, memory, inference, and, most important, morality).

8.10 A GENERAL OBJECTION TO EPISTEMIC CONCEPTIONS OF PUBLIC JUSTIFICATION

The assumption motivating the discussion in this chapter is the following: *if* there is a defensible formulation of the doctrine of restraint, then that formulation will employ an epistemic conception of public justification. Moreover, if there is a defensible epistemic conception of public justification, then that conception must specify some epistemic desideratum that mystical perceptions lack but that the grounds essential to healthy political decision making and advocacy possess. The difficulty is to identify any such desideratum. I've discussed a representative sampling of proposals and have found each defective in some respect or other. There are, no doubt, many other proposals I haven't discussed, but I don't want to wear out my welcome by cycling through another spate of proposals. There is no need to do so in any case, since the discussion up to this point provides sufficient material to articulate a general strategy for undermining any epistemic conceptions I haven't already dismissed. No doubt, articulating a strategy for undermining epistemic conceptions is no proxy for detailed criticism: the epistemic conceptions I haven't addressed will have to be evaluated with due attention paid to each's distinctive features. Nevertheless, it seems to me that articulating such a strategy provides some systematic reason to conclude that there just isn't a defensible epistemic conception of public justification.

As I see it, any justificatory liberal who defends an epistemic conception of public justification faces the following dilemma. Either the justificatory liberal respects the autonomy of CMP or she doesn't respect CMP's autonomy. If the justificatory liberal doesn't respect CMP's autonomy, then she'll have an indefensibly *low* opinion of CMP's epistemic status and will tend to accept an epistemic conception that is too weak to rule out CMP. If, by contrast, the justificatory liberal does respect CMP's autonomy, then she should have a much *higher* opinion of CMP's epistemic status, and must articulate a commensurately more powerful epistemic conception. But in that case she risks *arbitrariness*: it will be very difficult to construct an epistemic conception powerful enough to mandate restraint regarding M-beliefs but weak enough to permit citizens to rely on other kinds of grounds that are essential to healthy political decision making and advocacy. Otherwise put, failure to respect CMP's autonomy correlates with epistemic conceptions too weak to mandate restraint regarding mystical perception, whereas success in respecting CMP's autonomy correlates with epistemic conceptions so strong that consistency requires the justificatory liberal to forbid reliance on grounds essential to healthy political decision making and advocacy. (I have in mind nonplatitudinous moral judgments in particular.)

A brief review of some of the epistemic conceptions I have discussed illustrates the difficulty of navigating safely through this dilemma. Three of the proposals I have discussed are *very* demanding and, if otherwise defensible, would suffice to mandate restraint regarding M-beliefs. But none is defensible: each is sufficiently demanding as to mandate restraint regarding politically essential grounds. Consequently, each can be used as a basis for mandating restraint regarding M-beliefs only if M-beliefs are arbitrarily selected out for special treatment.

(A) Bird's proposal that a rationale must be publicly intelligible (1) is vitiated by an unadulterated arbitrariness: his standards for intelligibility are so *stringent* that he should have concluded that a citizen ought to exercise restraint even with respect to her ordinary sense-perceptual beliefs, not to mention her moral commitments.

(B) If the justificatory liberal requires noncircular justification for CMP (8), her advocacy of restraint is likewise overly demanding-cum-arbitrary: we can't provide any such justification for our basic doxastic practices (including SP, as Alston shows, and no doubt including morality as well).

(C) If the justificatory liberal advocates restraint regarding mystical perception on the grounds that M-beliefs aren't amenable to the sort of independent confirmation available for sense-perceptual beliefs (7), she is open to the charge of arbitrariness in that moral beliefs aren't amenable to independent confirmation either.

The appeal to external criticism – (6) and (6*) – is multiply problematic.

(D) If the justificatory liberal denies that CMP provides explanations for mistaken perceptions of God, say, because we don't explain the failure to perceive physical objects by reference to the moral qualities of the perceiver, the justificatory liberal fails to respect the autonomy of CMP: CMP does enjoy such explanations although they differ from those available in, say, SP. Appreciation of CMP's autonomy reveals that the noncircular explanation of error constraint is too weak to do the necessary exclusionary work.

(E) If the justificatory liberal grants that CMP provides explanations for mistaken M-beliefs, but objects to CMP's explanatory schema on the grounds that that schema circularly presupposes the reliability of CMP, then she adopts far too demanding a constraint. After all, SP's explanatory schema presupposes the reliability of SP as well, and so consistent application of the constraint in question requires restraint regarding sense-perceptual beliefs.

(F) If the justificatory liberal advocates restraint regarding mystical perception in virtue of the fact that M-beliefs aren't amenable to external criticism, and argues that M-beliefs aren't amenable to external criticism because the consistency tests available to members of CMP are so different from the tests available to participants in SP, then she fails to respect CMP's autonomy: external criticism of any given M-belief is possible, although the sort of external criticism differs in appropriate respects from the sort of criticism that can be leveled at sense-perceptual beliefs. So proper appreciation of CMP's autonomy reveals that the constraint in question is too weak to mandate restraint regarding M-beliefs.

(G) If the justificatory liberal respects CMP's autonomy, grants thereby that M-beliefs are amenable to external criticism, and elevates her demands so as to require a more stringent kind of external criticism, then she risks arbitrariness: M-beliefs are vulnerable to just the sort of external criticism as are moral beliefs, such that if the more demanding standard suffices to rule out M-beliefs, it can only nonarbitrarily be ruled to permit reliance on moral beliefs.

Replicability (4) also winds up on the shoals.

(H) If the justificatory liberal determines whether some ground is replicable by whether citizens in relevantly similar physical and conceptual conditions would acquire the same ground, she operates with an understanding of replicability tailored to SP and other "secular" practices, in which case she fails to respect the autonomy of CMP. And in that case, replicability will not enable her to articulate a conception of public justification that is sufficiently powerful to rule out reliance on M-beliefs.

(I) If, by contrast, the justificatory liberal operates with an understanding of replicability that doesn't rule out mystical perception from the start, then she can only arbitrarily mandate restraint regarding M-beliefs but not sense-perceptual beliefs.

The public accessibility – (2) and (3) – constraint fares no better than the alternatives.

(J) If the justificatory liberal requires only that M-beliefs are in principle accessible to citizens, then she has no reason to advocate restraint regarding M-beliefs, as there is no good reason to deny that any normal citizen enjoys the cognitive capacities necessary to perceive God: this proposal is too weak to mandate restraint regarding M-beliefs.

(K) If the justificatory liberal adopts a more demanding conception of accessibility, and so advocates restraint regarding M-beliefs on the grounds that many citizens are unable to employ their developed cognitive faculties to acquire those M-beliefs, then she will be able to advocate restraint regarding M-beliefs only on pain of arbitrariness, since many grounds regarding which she can't reasonably mandate restraint are also actually inaccessible to many citizens.

And, finally, the fallibilism constraint – (5) – has no chance of providing principled grounds for the claim that citizens should exercise restraint regarding M-beliefs.

(L) If the justificatory liberal mandates restraint regarding mystical perception on the grounds that citizens can't take the appropriately fallibilist attitude toward the convictions they form on the basis of their putative perception of God's testifying in favor of some claim, then she is simply confused: members of CMP are perfectly capable of distinguishing between God's infallible judgment and their fallible apprehension of God's infallible judgment.

(M) Perhaps, however, the fallibilism constraint implicitly violates CMP's autonomy in the respect that it imposes on CMP an expectation we legitimately have *only* of a citizen's attitude towards human testimony, that is, that she subject to critical analysis the propositions which she putatively perceives God to endorse. In the nature of the case, divine testimony can't be false and so it makes no sense to require of a citizen that she subject God's moral judgments to critical analysis. But that in no way obviates the need for criticism of *claims* about God's actual testimony. So, when we make due allowance for CMP's autonomy, (5) is too weak to mandate restraint regarding mystical perception.

What's the moral of the story? There is no defensible epistemic conception of public justification. An epistemic conception that mandates restraint regarding mystical perception must accord due weight to the autonomy of CMP. If the justificatory liberal accords due weight to the autonomy of CMP, then she'll be unable to articulate a conception of public justification strong enough to mandate restraint with respect to CMP that doesn't *also* mandate restraint regarding beliefs essential to healthy political decision making and advocacy, and thus that must be arbitrarily exempted from even-handed treatment. Put the other way around, if the justificatory liberal appreciates adequately the diverse ways in which we properly form and evaluate beliefs, more particularly, if she appreciates the legitimately distinctive ways in which members of CMP form and evaluate M-beliefs, then she will be unable to identify some epistemic desideratum (a) that CMP really lacks and so in virtue of which citizens should exercise restraint regarding M-beliefs, but (b) that is possessed by all of the beliefs essential to healthy political decision making and discourse.

This strategy for undermining epistemic conceptions of public justification differs from a complimentary approach powerfully articulated by Larry Alexander.[100] With respect to our conclusions, both Alexander and I attempt to show (a) that the best case for restraint regarding religious belief presupposes epistemic claims regarding those beliefs and (b) that those claims are indefensible. Alexander attempts to establish that conclusion by focusing attention on the *similarities* between the way citizens form religious and secular beliefs. Thus, for example, Alexander paints a portrait of Ann, an ordinary citizen who forms beliefs about secular matters in pretty much the same way that she forms beliefs about religious matters, that is, by relying heavily on testimony and coherence considerations. The point of his portrait of Ann is "to show how continuous Ann's religious epistemology is with her epistemology in general, and how all of her beliefs, criteria of evidence, and methods of reasoning cohere."[101] Alexander's complaint is that requiring citizens to abstain from relying on M-beliefs and other religious claims is arbitrary – there isn't a relevant difference between religious and secular doxastic practices such that the former should but the latter shouldn't be excluded from political decision making and advocacy.

I think this argument, by and large, succeeds. Nevertheless, I think that Alexander's strategy obscures an important point about the category of "secular belief" – that there is a quite wide variation with respect both to the overall epistemic status of, and the evidential criteria, grounds, and checking procedures internal to, distinct secular doxastic practices. The secular practices with which religious practices are unified are themselves a mixed bag; they are, as I have probably stated more often than I should, *autonomous* in various respects. Put somewhat paradoxically, religious practices are "unified" or "continuous" with secular practices in being, like secular practices, distinctive, idiosyncratic, and autonomous in various respects.

Why is this important? Because of a perennial temptation to privilege the upper end of the spectrum of secular practices when distinguishing between religious and secular practices and, on the basis of a fictitious homogeneity among secular practices, advocating restraint regarding the former but not the latter.[102] It is particularly important to focus on the diversity internal to the secular when discussing restraint regarding CMP since some of the most powerful objections to the claim that CMP enjoys positive epistemic status hinge on invidious comparisons between CMP and SP (which I assume to be one of the more reliable secular practices). Whatever their merit as arguments against CMP's reliability, such invidious comparisons can aid the case for restraint only if its advocates obscure the differences between SP and other secular practices. I fear that, by stressing the similarities between religious and secular practices, Alexander's mode of argumentation is incapable of cutting through the fog which obscures recognition of differences among the secular.[103]

A more circuitous way of undermining restraint would, perhaps, be more effective in establishing the conclusion for which both Alexander and I argue: those who reject restraint regarding religious beliefs must show

(A) that the doxastic practices the justificatory liberal is willing to allow citizens to employ in formulating their grounds for their favored coercive laws exhibit a diverse array of epistemic desiderata;

(B) that some of those practices (SP, mathematics) exhibit a large number of important epistemic desiderata, and thus fall on the high end of the epistemic spectrum;

(C) that some of those doxastic practices (morality) exhibit a comparatively lesser number of important epistemic desiderata and thus fall on the low end of the epistemic continuum;

(D) that religious doxastic practices (mystical perception) enjoy important epistemic desiderata even if the way that they exemplify those desiderata differ from the way that many secular doxastic practices exemplify those desiderata;

(E) that some religious doxastic practices (mystical perception) exemplify a set of epistemic desiderata that renders arbitrary any attempt to mandate restraint regarding the deliverances of those religious doxastic practices without also mandating restraint regarding the deliverances of the secular doxastic practices at the low end of the epistemic spectrum (morality).

This strategy is more complicated than Alexander's straightforward attempt to show continuity between religious and secular doxastic practices, but I think that this way of making the case appeals, most particularly, to those (a) for whom the differences between, for example, the way we check sense-perceptual beliefs and the way we check moral beliefs and M-beliefs are glaring and important and (b) for whom the differences between the way we check M-beliefs and the way we check moral beliefs are inconsequential.

CHAPTER 9

A THEISTIC CASE FOR RESTRAINT

9.0 INTRODUCTION

The argument I articulated in the prior chapter is a consistency argument, one of the central components of which is the following claim: any epistemic conception of public justification that is sufficiently powerful to mandate restraint with respect to mystical perception is, when applied consistently, also sufficiently powerful to mandate restraint with respect to all but the most platitudinous moral convictions. Although I intend that central claim to apply to religious commitments generally (notwithstanding my focus on mystical perceptions), certain kinds of religious commitment are more directly relevant to our topic than are others. In particular, any religious grounds that serve as a basis for moral claims, such as Bill McCartney's conviction that the Bible portrays homosexual relations as a moral abomination, play so prominent a role in political advocacy and decision making that they merit special attention.[1]

In order to sharpen the focus on religious grounds that serve as a basis for moral claims, I briefly reformulate my consistency argument against epistemic conceptions of public justification so that it applies directly to religiously grounded moral claims. There is no compelling reason to believe that *secularly* grounded moral claims necessarily or generally enjoy an epistemic status superior to *religiously* grounded moral claims. The most plausible analysis of their epistemic virtues and vices is that religiously and secularly grounded moral claims enjoy a roughly comparable selection of epistemic desiderata. But that the epistemic status of secular and religious norms is roughly comparable implies that *whatever* epistemic conception the justificatory liberal affirms, she can mandate restraint regarding religious norms but not secular norms only on pain of arbitrariness. If the epistemic conception she affirms is comparatively weak, such that secular norms satisfy that conception, then so do religious norms; if the epistemic conception she adopts is comparatively demanding, such that religious norms fail to satisfy that conception, so also do secular norms. In short, no matter which epistemic conception the justificatory liberal adopts, religiously and secularly grounded norms deserve identical treatment.[2] And since the justificatory liberal can't afford to advocate restraint regarding secularly grounded moral claims, neither can she afford to advocate restraint regarding religiously grounded moral claims.

The challenge this consistency argument poses to the justificatory liberal is that of discovering some relevant difference between religious and secular norms in virtue of which it is appropriate to mandate restraint regarding the former but not the latter. There are any number of strategies the justificatory liberal might take in order to identify some such difference. I will articulate and evaluate a strategy I find particularly intriguing: a *theistic case for restraint*. That theistic case addresses the challenge posed to the justificatory liberal by drawing on various claims at the heart of traditional theism in order to show that theists have good reason to expect secular corroboration for religiously grounded moral *truths*, and thus that theists have adequate grounds to doubt religiously grounded moral *claims* for which they can't discern secular corroboration.[3] And, of course, if theists have good reason to doubt secularly uncorroborated religious norms, they should refrain from supporting any coercive law solely on the basis of such norms. By contrast, theists lack adequate grounds to expect that secularly grounded moral truths will enjoy independent corroboration (of any sort); consequently, theists have no reason to doubt *un*corroborated secular moral claims and thus need not exercise restraint regarding secularly grounded moral claims. So although it *seems* arbitrary to require restraint regarding uncorroborated religious norms but not to require restraint regarding uncorroborated secular norms, that appearance is illusory: the relevant difference that warrants separate treatment of religiously and secularly grounded norms is *expectability* – theists reasonably expect to discover independent corroboration for religiously grounded moral truths but not for secularly grounded moral truths. The theistic case, if sound, constitutes a decisive response to (what I take to be) a very powerful objection to the justificatory liberal's project.[4]

I will argue that the theistic case for restraint is unsound. But that isn't all I intend to accomplish in this chapter. My discussion of the theistic case will provide an opportunity to explain further why religious citizens have entirely credible and creditable grounds for rejecting the doctrine of restraint. More particularly, my discussion of the theistic case will enable me to adumbrate further the "strains of commitment" argument against the doctrine of restraint I developed in 5.3. My discussion will show that there is a realistic prospect that a theistic citizen enjoys dispositive religious reasons to support a given coercive law but that she lacks the kind of secular corroboration (and therefore public justification) required by the doctrine of restraint. Consequently, if she commits herself to restraint, she commits herself to a policy that might require her to disobey God, a prospect that renders the doctrine of restraint religiously unacceptable.

9.1 A THEISTIC CASE FOR RESTRAINT

A good deal of what follows is my attempt to articulate in more detail an argument others have presented in an impressionistic way. Thus, for example, Robert Audi writes,

> If we assume a broadly Western theism, we can take God to be omniscient, omnipotent, and omnibenevolent. Might we not, then (at least given this set of divine attributes), expect God to structure us free rational beings and the world of our experience so that there is a (humanly accessible) secular path to the discovery of moral truths, at least to those far-reaching ones needed for the kind of civilized life we can assume God would wish us to live? ... If the freedom preserved by the religious ambiguity of the world is so valuable, should we not expect God to provide for access to rational standards, discoverable by secular inquiry, for the proper exercise of that freedom, as opposed to its abuse or waste in immoral, wrong-headed or ignorant behavior? If God cares enough about us not to compel us toward theism but instead to allow our free choice or rejection of it, would it not seem that we would be equipped with standards for the use of our freedom in the ways appropriate to God's creatures? ... If these considerations from philosophical theology ... are sound, then civic virtue on the part of the religious should embody a commitment to *theo-ethical equilibrium* – a rational integration between religious deliverances and insights and, on the other hand, secular ethical considerations. ... Given the conception of God as omniscient, omnipotent and omnibenevolent, the possibility of theo-ethical equilibrium is to be expected, and a mature,

conscientious theist who cannot reach it should be reluctant or unwilling
to support coercive laws or public policies on a religious basis that cannot
be placed in that equilibrium.[5]

Michael Perry argues in similar vein:

> But even for religious believers – in particular, for religious believers,
> whether Christian or not, who accept what has been the dominant
> Christian understanding of the relation between "revelation" and "rea-
> son" – any religious argument about the requirements of human well-
> being should be a highly suspect basis of political choice if no persuasive
> secular argument reaches the same conclusion about the requirements
> of human well-being as the religious argument. Given the demonstrated
> ubiquitous human propensity to be mistaken and even to deceive oneself
> about what God has revealed, the absence of a persuasive secular argu-
> ment in support of a claim about the requirements of human well-being
> fairly supports a presumption that the claim is probably false, that it is
> probably the defective yield of that demonstrated human propensity. At
> least, it fairly supports a presumption that the claim is an inappropriate
> ground of political choice, especially coercive political choice.[6]

I find both Perry's and Audi's arguments suggestive. Audi seems to
me to be correct in claiming that a citizen's having "secular access"
to moral knowledge is an important good and that we may therefore expect that God will make provision for that access. Similarly with
Perry's claim that a very influential strain of theistic reflection on the
relations between faith and reason posits considerable overlap between
moral claims discoverable via secular reflection and those discoverable
via revelation. And both of those claims are directly relevant to the issue
of restraint: if God will ensure that citizens will have secular access to
moral truths, and if we can have confidence that faith and reason will
overlap to a considerable extent, shouldn't theists *doubt* any religiously
grounded moral claim for which they can't acquire the expected secular
corroboration?

Although highly suggestive, I find Audi and Perry's arguments difficult to evaluate unless formulated more explicitly. My intention is to
develop their insights in more detail.[7] I will divide my explication of
that argument into two parts. In the first part [(1)–(6)], I rely heavily
on claims about God's nature in order to show that, if theism is true,
human beings must have secular access to moral truths. This part of
the argument is reminiscent of various formulations of the problem

of evil. Whereas the proponent of the argument from evil claims that, given God's moral perfection, omniscience, and omnipotence, we shouldn't expect there to be any evil, so much evil, or certain types of evil, the proponent of this theistic case for restraint claims that, given God's moral perfection, omniscience, and omnipotence, we should expect human beings to have access to a great good: moral knowledge. Moreover – and importantly for our purposes – human beings must have *secular* access to moral knowledge: since religious sources of moral knowledge enjoy only limited distribution, the access to moral knowledge guaranteed by God mustn't depend uneliminably on religious sources of information. In the second part of the argument [(7)–(9)], I turn to the issue of restraint proper and provide an argument in support of the claim that citizens ought to exercise restraint regarding secularly uncorroborated religious norms. Because it is likely that religiously grounded moral truths enjoy secular corroboration, theists who can discern no secular corroboration for a given religiously grounded moral claim ought not be confident enough in that claim to impose it on their fellow citizens.

9.1.1 Secular Access: In Principle, Weak and Strong

The first claim we need to establish is that God will provide some sort of secular access to moral knowledge, as well as some analysis of what it means for God to provide secular access. That's what I try to do in this section. Let's begin on reasonably safe ground.

(1) *God wants each person to discharge his moral obligations.*

(1) follows from the claim that God is morally perfect. A necessary condition of an agent A's counting as morally perfect is, not just that A discharges A's moral obligations, and not just that A wants to discharge A's moral obligations, but also that A wants other agents to discharge their moral obligations. That is why, were we to learn that A is entirely indifferent as to whether or not others tell the truth, oppress the poor, torture the innocent, remain faithful to friends and spouse, that would in and of itself provide us with adequate grounds for denying that A is morally perfect.

(2) *In order for a person to discharge his moral obligations (over the long term), he needs to know what his obligations are.*

Suppose that some person, "Adam," unreflectively, effortlessly, and flawlessly acts as he ought to act. Whenever Adam acts, he performs the action he ought to have performed even though he isn't aware that he ought to perform that action; thus Adam doesn't govern his actions, first, by determining which course of action he ought to pursue and then, second, by acting in accord with his determination. Adam is what we might call a *paradisal* moral agent, one who naturally, without reflection, hesitation, or resistance from contrary inclination, acts in accord with the moral law.

If human beings were paradisal moral agents, (2) would be false: it wouldn't have been the case that discharging our moral obligations requires that we have adequate grounds for moral truths. Unfortunately, actual human persons don't find themselves in the state Adam is fortunate enough to inhabit. We aren't paradisal moral agents: we act wrongly on a regular basis, are often ignorant of what we ought to do, and our ignorance is one of the factors that inhibits us from discharging our obligations. More generally, although a person with no moral sense to speak of might in fact perform the appropriate action on a given occasion, he is at best lucky and we know that, over the long term, he is unlikely to be so fortunate. For post-paradisal human persons, then, consistent, long-term adherence to the moral law requires that we know what our moral obligations are and can govern our actions in light of our knowledge of those obligations.

(3) *Since God wants each person to discharge his moral obligations, and since discharging his moral obligations requires that a person know what his obligations are, God wants each person to have moral knowledge.*[8]

The dictum that "One who wills the end wills the means to the end" applies as straightforwardly to God as it does to ordinary human beings. If God wants each person to discharge his obligations, and if knowing what his obligations are is an unavoidable condition of a person's discharging those obligations (over the long term), then God also wants each person to know what his obligations are.

(4) *Since God wants each person to have moral knowledge, and since God can ensure that each person has access to moral knowledge, God has set things up so that each person has access to moral knowledge.*

On the traditional theistic understanding, God has created the world and all that is in it; in particular, God has created human beings and has provided us with various important characteristics. In addition to opposable thumbs and the ability to walk upright, God has provided humans with various cognitive capacities: sense perception, introspection, memory, inference. Those capacities enable us to acquire knowledge of important sorts – about the physical world, about the past, about other people and their states of mind, and about God. In addition, because God wants us to have access to moral knowledge, and because God has it within God's power to provide us with access to moral knowledge, God has provided us with cognitive capacities that enable us to acquire moral knowledge.[9]

We might think that (4) should actually read: since God wants each person to have moral knowledge, and since God can ensure that each person has moral knowledge, God has set things up so that each of us actually enjoys the requisite moral knowledge. After all, just as it was in God's power to create us so that we, like Adam, naturally discharge our obligations, so also was it within God's power to create us so that we have infallible and intuitive knowledge of our moral obligations. Indeed, God could have created us in such a way that our capacity to discern moral truth surpasses our capacity to discern mathematical truths: just as we know that $2 + 2 = 4$ just on reflection, so also we could have been made so that we know that we should give of our excess to *this* person on *this* occasion just on considering the proposition. In such a case, God would have created us, not just so that we have *access* to moral knowledge, but also so that we are in fact *guaranteed* to have moral knowledge. Why, then, is (4) formulated in the weaker "accessibility" way?

In the first place, to adopt the stronger conclusion would be to accept a conclusion we know to be false: many people adhere to moral claims we know to be false; hence, it can't be the case that God's goodness and omnipotence guarantees moral knowledge. To conclude from the considerations I have adduced that each person actually has moral knowledge would be just as absurd as to conclude that, because God is omnipotent, omniscient, and morally perfect, no evil exists.[10]

In the second place, theists will want to explain a given person's lack of moral knowledge in something like the same way they often explain the existence of evil – by the ill use or the misuse of the ability freely to deploy cognitive capacities. Appeal to human freedom plays an important role in explaining why God provides us only with access to moral knowledge rather than guarantees us moral knowledge. How so? One of the most important moral choices a person makes is whether he is interested in determining what he ought to do. The decision to pursue knowledge regarding how we ought to act is itself a moral choice of great importance. To guarantee moral knowledge would circumscribe the operation of human freedom in that very important area. Hence, God provides us only with access to the moral truth.

(5) *Since God has set things up so that each person has access to moral knowledge, each person must have access to adequate secular grounds for the requisite moral truths.*

Why does the fact that God has ensured that each person has access to moral knowledge entail that each person has *secular* access? The answer hinges on the limited distribution of all religious sources of knowledge. Suppose that the Bible is God's revelation and that it contains all the moral truths a person needs to know in order to act appropriately. In having authored the biblical text and in having ensured its preservation over the ages, God will have arranged human affairs in such a way that those who can acquire copies of the Bible and who can understand the Bible will be able to acquire the moral knowledge they need to act in a morally appropriate manner. In a fairly mundane sense of *access*, God's authoring the Bible and God's having ensured its preservation over the ages ensures that those who can acquire copies of the Bible have access to the moral truths they need to discharge their moral obligations: by employing their developed cognitive capacities, those who can acquire copies of the Bible can employ the information contained in their cognitive environment to identify their moral obligations.

But it isn't the case that each person has the relevant sort of access to the Bible. To be sure, each person has access *in principle* to the moral truths encoded in the Bible: each person enjoys cognitive capacities that enable him to realize that the Bible is divinely inspired, and thus each person enjoys cognitive capacities that enable him to realize that the Bible counts as a reliable source of information about his moral obligations. But some human beings can't lay hands on the Bible no matter how assiduously they attempt to do so. Whether or not a citizen has a realistic prospect of acquiring a copy of the Bible is a function of the vicissitudes of temporal and spatial location; consequently, unlike in principle accessibility, the sort of access we have to the Bible is *population-specific.*[11] (Of course, God could have ensured that the biblical text was universally distributed, but God hasn't done so.) We can generalize this empirical point: there are some people who have a realistic prospect of acquiring *no* sacred texts that it's plausible to suppose contain the moral truths they need to know in order to discharge their moral obligations. We can generalize even further: there are some people who have a realistic prospect of engaging in no religious practices of belief-formation which it's plausible to suppose contains the information they need to discharge their moral obligations. Simply put, *all* religious sources of information about moral truths are population-specific; there are *no* religious sources of information about moral truths which each person has a realistic prospect of employing.

We have every reason to suppose that God's desire that each person enjoys moral knowledge extends to people so circumstanced: God wants those persons who can't acquire population-specific religious sources of information about moral truths to discharge their obligations. Hence, God wants them to be able to acquire the information they need in order to identify their moral obligations. Hence, we have good reason to believe that God provides them with nonreligious access to the moral truth: somehow or other, those persons who can't acquire copies of the Bible must be able to acquire the moral knowledge they need in order to discharge their moral obligations. So if the case for (5) is roughly correct, then citizens can acquire moral knowledge without having to rely on religious grounds. Or put the other way around: if the case for (5) is roughly correct, then citizens can acquire moral knowledge by relying solely on secular grounds (by rational reflection, intuition, conscience, or whatever).

(6) *Since each human being has access to adequate secular grounds for moral truths, then religiously grounded moral truths will likely be corroborable by adequate secular grounds.*

Suppose that the Bible reports God as condemning avarice; citizens who can acquire copies of the Bible can come to know that it is morally wrong for them to pursue monetary wealth without limitation. If (5) is correct, there must also be secular paths to that truth available to such citizens. Assuming that secular sources of moral knowledge aren't population-specific in the way that religious sources of knowledge are, religious citizens who believe that avarice is wrong on religious grounds can *also* acquire adequate secular grounds for that claim. That is, persons who can acquire copies of the Bible must *also* have access to secular grounds for the moral truths contained in the Bible, just as persons who can't acquire copies of the Bible have access to secular grounds for the moral truths contained in the Bible. Since there is nothing particularly special about the moral impropriety of avarice, we may generalize from that moral truth to all moral truths: no matter which moral claims a given person accepts on religious grounds, he has good theistic reason to believe that, if those moral claims are *true*, then he also has access to adequate secular grounds for those claims.

Up to this point in my explication of the theistic case, I've employed the notion of secular access loosely. But we know from the prior discussion of public justification that the concept of accessibility can be understood in disparate and contradictory ways. Consequently, it is essential that we clarify the understanding of accessibility implicit in my explication of the theistic case.

As I noted earlier, the concepts of accessibility and possibility are internally related: a citizen has access to some bit of information only if it is possible for him to employ his cognitive faculties in such a way as to acquire that bit of information. And the notion of access I've employed in my explication of the theistic case incorporates that in principle accessibility constraint: given that what it is possible for a person to know is constrained by the cognitive capacities with which he is endowed, a person enjoys access to moral knowledge only if his cognitive capacities enable him to acquire that moral knowledge.

Although a person's having the appropriate cognitive capacities is necessary for him to enjoy moral knowledge, having the appropriate cognitive capacities is by no means sufficient for its being possible (in the sense required by the theistic case for restraint) for him to acquire moral knowledge. Clearly, the theistic case for restraint implies that a citizen has more than just in principle access to the moral knowledge he needs to discharge his moral obligations: in addition to having the required information receptor and processor (cognitive capacity), a person must be able to employ his cognitive capacities to good effect, namely, to acquire moral knowledge. And in order for a citizen to be able to acquire moral knowledge, he needs to be able to acquire the relevant information. And that requires that he find himself ensconced in a cognitive environment that contains the relevant information. In other words, for God to provide us with the relevant sort of access to moral knowledge, God must create *us* with the requisite capacities and place us in an *environment* containing the relevant information. And of course the sources of that information must be *secular* in nature.

Let's call the following *weak* secular access: a person has weak secular access to moral knowledge if and only if he enjoys the requisite cognitive capacities and is situated in an environment that contains secular sources of information that are sufficiently rich as to enable him reliably to identify his moral obligations.

Weak secular access is still too weak. After all, the claim that God's moral perfection, omniscience, and omnipotence ensure weak secular access to moral knowledge is entirely consistent with the claim that a person's prospects for acquiring moral knowledge are quite dim. That a person has the capacity to acquire moral knowledge, and that he is in an environment that contains the information required for moral knowledge, provides no indication at all whether, for example, the required information is extraordinarily difficult to come by. If the information *is* extraordinarily difficult to acquire, then it is possible that only a small moral elite has a realistic prospect of acquiring moral knowledge. In that case, it might very well be the case that a person who conscientiously and assiduously attempts to acquire moral knowledge will be highly unlikely to succeed in his endeavor. But that is exactly what (6) disallows.

Hence, we should understand the theistic case as showing that each citizen enjoys a very demanding sort of secular access to moral knowledge: the theistic case seems to entail that each citizen enjoys what I'll call *strong* secular access to moral knowledge. On the strong understanding of accessibility, God will ensure that each citizen enjoys the appropriate cognitive capacities, that each citizen is situated in a cognitive environment that contains the required information about his moral obligations, and that that information isn't inordinately difficult to acquire. Given that God will ensure that these conditions obtain, theists should expect that a citizen who genuinely and sincerely attempts to acquire moral knowledge will likely succeed in doing so even if he relies solely on secular considerations. Thus, according to the strong understanding of accessibility, if a person has access to moral knowledge, it is not only *possible* for him to acquire moral knowledge given his noetic endowment and the information available in his environment, but it is also *likely* that he will acquire moral knowledge given a good faith effort to discover the truth.

If we adopt the strong understanding, what does the first part of the theistic argument look like? In brief, the argument is as follows. God's moral perfection, omniscience, and omnipotence ensure that God will create the world in such a way that each person will be able to discharge his obligations. Creating the world in that way requires that God provide each person with strong secular access to moral knowledge, which amounts to the claim that God (a) endows each person with the cognitive capacities necessary to receive and process information required for moral knowledge, (b) fashions an environment that contains the information required for moral knowledge, and (c) ensures that that information isn't inordinately difficult to come by. Since each religious source of moral knowledge enjoys only limited distribution, it would be inordinately difficult – in many cases, physically impossible – for many persons to learn about their obligations by consulting such a religious source. Hence, God must ensure that we have a reasonable chance of acquiring moral knowledge without having to rely on religious sources of information. That is, God must provide us with a good chance of acquiring plausible secular grounds for our moral obligations.[12]

9.1.2 Restraint

The argument I've developed in the prior section employs theistic premises to substantiate the conclusion that a cognitively competent person who genuinely and sincerely attempts to acquire secular corroboration for her favored religious norms will be likely to succeed in that endeavor. If sound, that argument has crucially important implications for the topic of restraint, and I will attempt to draw out some of the most salient of those implications in this section.

(7) *Since religiously grounded moral truths will likely be corroborable by secular grounds, then theists are rationally obliged to doubt religiously grounded moral claims for which they lack adequate secular grounds.*

The argument for (7) hinges on a familiar type of inference. The structure of that type of inference is as follows: if I have good reason to believe that A is likely to occur only in the presence of B, and I apparently perceive A but can't after the appropriate investigation discover signs of B, then I should, ceteris paribus, doubt that I actually perceived A. Suppose I have good reason to believe that the occurrence of *As* is almost always correlated with the occurrence of *Bs*: I know that the legendary but elusive snark leaves in its path markings of a distinctive and easily recognizable sort. And suppose that I have moderately good evidence that a snark was in the vicinity in the recent past: I apparently saw the snark in all its furtive glory in broad daylight and in normal perceptual conditions, my eyesight is excellent and I know what to look for. In order to check my conviction regarding the snark's presence, I scour the area for signs of its activity: I attempt to discover the distinctive markings with which I know that genuine snark sightings are correlated. If I discover the appropriate markings, I will have powerful corroboration for my apparent perception of the snark. But if I fail to discover the requisite markings, not only have I failed to verify my conviction, but I reasonably *doubt* the veridicality of what I took to be a snark sighting.

If (6) is correct, then failure to acquire secular corroboration for a religiously grounded moral claim C should have the same implication for our confidence in C that failure to perceive distinctive snark-markings should have for our confidence in the claim that we have perceived a snark. Because it is *likely* that we will discover secular corroboration for a given religiously grounded moral *truth* if we engage in the appropriate investigation, our failure to discover the expected secular corroboration provides us with reason to *doubt* C.[13] Suppose that Bill McCartney genuinely attempts to, but can't discover, any secular corroboration for the claim that homosexual relations are an abomination to God: he can discern no plausible argument that contains only secular premises that provide what he regards as adequate support for the claim that homosexual relations are morally inappropriate. What should he conclude? Well, if the first part of the theistic argument is correct, he should *expect* to discover an adequate secular rationale for his belief that homosexual relations are morally inappropriate: if homosexual relations really are sinful, then he should expect to discover secular corroboration for that claim. Since he can't discover any such rationale, he now has evidence *against* the claim that homosexual relations are morally inappropriate. Since the "signs" that indicate the "presence" of a moral truth are missing, he is rationally obliged to doubt the claim that homosexual relations are morally abominable.

(8) *It is disrespectful for a citizen to support a coercive law on the basis of moral claims they have good reason to doubt.*

The case for (8) rests on my argument in support of the claim that a citizen who respects her compatriots will adhere to the ideal of conscientious engagement. More particularly, the case for (8) rests on one component of that ideal – that a citizen ought to withhold support from any coercive law for which she cannot articulate a sufficiently powerful rational justification. A citizen who adheres to some religiously grounded norm for which she can't discern a plausible secular rationale has a standing defeater to that norm: unless she can discern some such secular rationale, then, given (7), she has good reason to believe that her religious norm is false, that is, she isn't rationally justified in adhering to that norm. And of course, if she isn't rationally justified in adhering to some religious norm, then she ought not support any coercive law solely on the basis of that norm.[14]

(9) *Hence, it is disrespectful for citizens to support coercive policies based on religiously grounded moral claims for which they lack adequate secular grounds.*

Given that God has set matters up so that we have secular access to moral knowledge, and given that having secular access to moral knowledge ensures that people who conscientiously pursue secular corroboration for religiously grounded moral truths will likely succeed in that endeavor, we should doubt religiously grounded moral claims for which we lack secular justification. And since it's disrespectful for us to coerce our fellow citizens to obey a law for which we lack the appropriate degree of rational justification, religious citizens have good reason to restrain themselves from supporting coercive policies solely on the basis of religious norms for which they lack secular corroboration. To gloss Brian Barry, no secularly uncorroborated religious norm "can justifiably be held with a degree of confidence that warrants its imposition on those who reject it."[15]

9.2 IS SECULAR CORROBORATION TO BE EXPECTED?

The claim that religiously grounded moral truths are likely to be corroborable by secular grounds is the linchpin of the theistic case for restraint. If secular corroboration is not to be expected, then we have no reason to doubt uncorroborated religious norms; and if the theistic case doesn't show that citizens ought to doubt uncorroborated religious norms, then we lack reason to exercise restraint with respect to those norms. In short, if (6) is false, the theistic case is unsalvageable. And I think that theists have good reason to reject (6).

9.2.1 Clarification of Secular Access

In order to identify what's wrong with (6), we need to identify one of (6)'s crucial assumptions. It's important to realize that (6) isn't equivalent to the claim that, because human agents have secular access to moral knowledge, then there are likely *to be* corroboratory secular grounds for a given religiously grounded moral truth. That is, (6) is not a claim regarding the *existence* of adequate secular grounds for moral truths. Rather, (6) is a claim regarding the likelihood of a citizen's *discovering* corroboratory secular grounds. We can imagine circumstances in which there is in fact secular corroboration for a given religiously grounded moral truth, but in which a citizen doesn't have any way of acquiring that corroboration, and thus in which she is unlikely to succeed in her pursuit of secular corroboration. The theistic case purports to show that God ensures that citizens won't find themselves in that situation: God's moral perfection, omniscience, and omnipotence ensure that citizens will find themselves in a strong secular position to discover the moral truths they need to discharge their moral obligations.

So (6) is a claim about the success citizens may expect to have in a particular pursuit. To be sure, (6) presupposes that there are in fact adequate secular grounds for religiously grounded moral truths: if it were *not* the case that for a given religiously grounded moral truth T, there exists a corroboratory secular rationale for T, then we wouldn't expect even conscientious and cognitively competent citizens to be able to discover secular corroboration for T. But (6) might be false even if that presupposition is true.

(6) presupposes something further: that citizens who pursue secular corroboration go about their task *in the appropriate manner*. Thus, for example, we can expect that a citizen will succeed in discovering secular justification for a given true religious norm only if she sincerely pursues secular justification. Insincere citizens will tend not to investigate a matter as thoroughly as they should, and thus, even if they can concoct a secular rationale for some moral truth, will not be likely to have arrived at an *adequate* or even *plausible* secular rationale for that moral truth. The theistic case for restraint provides us with no reason to believe that a citizen who insincerely pursues secular corroboration is likely to discover that corroboration.

Much more important than a sincerity condition is an *epistemic* condition on success: citizens who conscientiously pursue secular corroboration will likely enjoy success in their pursuit only if they employ their cognitive capacities in an epistemically appropriate manner. Surely a citizen who sincerely pursues secular corroboration, but who, out of a misguided mistrust of rational argumentation, refuses to consider objections to her moral convictions, isn't likely to discover adequate secular corroboration for the religiously grounded moral truths to which she adheres. Again, if a citizen is unable or unwilling to govern her beliefs in light of the appropriate canons of inference, we have no reason to expect that she'll discover the secular corroboration she pursues. We shouldn't expect her to succeed in discovering an adequate secular rationale, not because of some defect in her cognitive situation that lies outside of her control – God will take care of that! – but because of her failure to pursue secular corroboration in accord with the canons of rationality.

In short, then, the theistic case for (6) assumes that God has constructed a citizen's cognitive situation in such a way that if only she employs her cognitive faculties in the appropriate manner, she can expect to discover an adequate secular justification for the religiously grounded moral truths to which she adheres. Premise (6) thus presupposes a division of labor: God establishes the conditions of a citizen's situation that remain invariant in relation to her own cognitive activities, and citizens employ their cognitive faculties sincerely and rationally. If both partners accomplish their appointed task, we should expect citizens to succeed in their pursuit of secular corroboration.

9.2.2 Secular Access in Epistemically Hostile Conditions

Once we recognize that the likelihood of a citizen's acquiring secular corroboration depends on whether she rationally deploys her cognitive capacities, it's apparent that she might find herself so situated that, *no matter how sincerely and reasonably she deploys her cognitive capacities*, it isn't likely that she'll be able to acquire secular corroboration for some of the religiously grounded moral truths to which she adheres. In fact, it seems that a citizen might be so unfortunately circumstanced that no matter how competently she employs her cognitive faculties, no matter how assiduously she adheres to the procedural canons of rationality, it's *highly unlikely* that she'll discern an adequate secular rationale for some of the religiously grounded moral truths to which she adheres.

Consequently, the theistic case doesn't constitute compelling reason for a general policy of doubting secularly uncorroborated religious norms.

My argument in support of these claims is fairly simple. (1) Whether it's rationally appropriate for a citizen to assent to a given claim depends in uneliminable part on the testimony of other citizens. (2) The testimony of *other* citizens can be so skewed as to render it unlikely that a citizen who pursues secular corroboration for a particular moral truth will succeed in that pursuit, no matter how assiduously *she* adheres to the canons of rationality. (3) The prospect that a citizen's failure to discern secular corroboration for her religiously grounded norms is a consequence of the misuse or ill-use of God-given cognitive capacities and not of the falsehood of those norms entitles her to refrain from doubting uncorroborated religious norms.

Ad (1): Recall my brief discussion of the concept of rational justification (3.2.1). As I noted in that discussion, whether a citizen is rationally justified in adhering to a given claim depends not only on the manner in which he evaluates that claim, but also on the cognitive commitments on which he cannot but rely when evaluating that claim. To recall a pertinent example, that Socrates rationally assented to a Ptolemaic theory of the solar system depended not only on the "procedures" he employed in evaluating that theory, but also on the contents of his evidential set – more particularly, the *background beliefs* he employed to evaluate the Ptolemaic theory. Because the background beliefs on which moderns rely are very different from those on which Socrates relied, it is irrational for us to accept the Ptolemaic theory. That difference is explicable not (necessarily) by differences between the manner in which moderns and Socrates govern beliefs, but by the very different background beliefs moderns and Socrates employ to evaluate theories of the solar system.

That difference in background beliefs, moreover, is a consequence of relevant differences between our and Socrates' respective *cognitive environments*. What does that mean? Most of the convictions to which we adhere are dependent for their justification on the *testimony* of others – on our taking something to be true on the say-so of others. The point is a familiar one: although I've never directly perceived the Aurora Borealis, I've talked with those who have, or have seen a television show in which a scene of the appropriate sort is labeled "Aurora Borealis," or the like. I have arrived at most of my convictions not by (direct) acquaintance of the first sort but by (indirect) acquaintance of the second. A less familiar, though just as plausible, claim is that human agents are in no cognitive position to circumvent testimony: any attempt we might make to show that our reliance on the testimony of others is reliable is itself unavoidably dependent on our reliance on the unchecked testimony of others.[16]

From these claims about rationality and testimony, it follows that what is rational for a citizen to believe depends in crucial but unelim-inable part on the testimony of others. We form most of our beliefs, and also most of our background beliefs, by depending on the unchecked trustworthiness of others and it's by relying on those beliefs that we're able to arrive at a rational evaluation of other beliefs. To refer again to Socrates: I assume that the "procedure" by which he acquired his (by hypothesis) rational belief in the Ptolemaic theory was roughly the same as that by which moderns rationally reject the Ptolemaic theory – by reliance on the testimony of what we take to be competent authori-ties. The content of what those authorities attest to determines, in large part, which theory of the solar system we are rationally justified in affirming.

Ad (2): That the rationality of assenting to a given claim is unavoid-ably dependent on our unchecked acceptance of the testimony of other citizens renders possible a state of affairs in which a given citizen doesn't have a realistic prospect of acquiring adequate secular corroboration for a moral truth she accepts on religious grounds even though she governs her beliefs in an appropriately rational manner.[17] Fully rational citizens can stand with respect to particular moral truths in structurally the same epistemic relation that Socrates stood with respect to the claim that the earth revolves around the sun.

Thus, consider a claim at the center of our moral universe: that all human beings are equally valuable. Surely it's possible that a citizen who conscientiously attempts to determine whether all human beings are equally valuable finds herself so circumstanced that it isn't rational for her to accept that claim. Thus, we might suppose that she's been raised in a society that consistently degrades members of the female gender: the dominant institutions of her society discriminate against women, so that few attain positions of power and prestige; the hege-monic ideology of her society valorizes "masculine" virtues; children, particularly female children, are socialized to believe that women are inherently inferior to men, one consequence of which is that the vis-ceral reactions (intuitions) inculcated into members of that society mili-tate against the prospect of women holding authority over or criticizing men; the uniform and unambiguous testimony of the morally wise (of both genders) underwrites the prejudice that women are inherently inferior to, and thus of less value than, men. In short, we can imagine a situation in which most of a society's resources for molding the convictions and subjective experiences of its members are directed in such a way that they render implausible (what we confidently and rationally take to be) a moral truth. A citizen ensconced in such a cognitive environment would quite reasonably conclude that those of her own gender are of less value than her male counterparts. Indeed, she might even support public policies in accordance with that conviction, such as the refusal to extend the franchise to women. (I take it that some women have found, and do find, themselves in such a situation.)

How is this possible? How could it be the case that people created by a morally perfect, omniscient, and omnipotent being can find themselves in such a desperate epistemic condition with respect to so important a matter? Recall that the theistic case assumes a division of labor between God, who ensures that a person's epistemic environment is conducive to her success in discerning secular corroboration, and particular persons, who employ their cognitive faculties in an appropriate manner. If my argument up to this point is correct, part of a citizen's cognitive environment is itself constituted by the epistemic activity of other citizens. A citizen acquires the background beliefs on which she cannot but rely in evaluating specific claims by relying on the unchecked authority of other, putatively competent, agents. But, just as it's possible for *her* to pursue secular corroboration for her religiously grounded norms insincerely or unreasonably, so also is it possible for the citizens from whom she acquires her background beliefs insincerely and unreasonably to commit to moral falsehoods, to pass those falsehoods off as truths, and, most importantly, to inculcate their moral prejudices into members of succeeding generations.

God could, of course, interfere regularly in human cognitive affairs, such that God ensures that citizens who adhere to false or poorly grounded moral claims don't testify to those claims. But I take it that this kind of interference is unacceptable: it would be improper for God to inflict citizens with amnesia regarding their false moral beliefs when attempting to inculcate those falsehoods in their children, or otherwise to obstruct the ordinary processes of socialization, enculturation, or testimony. If this is the case, then it isn't *entirely* up to God to ensure that a citizen's cognitive environment is such that she has a realistic chance of acquiring secular corroboration for a given religiously grounded moral truth. In particular, it isn't up to God to ensure that that part of a citizen's cognitive environment that depends on the testimony of other people is such that she has a realistic prospect of acquiring secular corroboration for a given religiously grounded moral truth. Whether *that* part of her cognitive environment is conducive to the acquisition of secular corroboration is up to other people – frail, fractious, fallible persons who are afflicted with varying degrees of self-deception, hostility to the truth, and pride. In short, the division of labor (6) presupposes breaks down: what a citizen's cognitive environment is like – whether it's such that it affords her the realistic prospect of acquiring adequate secular corroboration – is as much up to human beings as to God.

The conclusion we should draw from this is clear: even if we stipulate of a particular person that she sincerely and rationally attempts to determine whether there is an adequate secular rationale for a given moral truth, we cannot idealize her out of dependence on the unchecked testimony of others – and in particular their testimony with regard to moral claims. But then, even if a given citizen assiduously collects evidence, reflects on that evidence, converses about that evidence with her compatriots, it's possible that as a result of other citizens' misuse or ill-use of their cognitive faculties, her evaluation of a given moral truth will be so skewed by the false testimony on which she relies that she'll inevitably fail to discover an adequate secular rationale for that moral truth. In short, given the dependence of succeeding generations on the testimony of their forebears, members of a given generation can, through no fault of their own, find themselves so circumstanced that a sincere and rational evaluation of the available secular evidence is likely to result in acceptance of moral falsehoods.[18]

Perhaps some reflection on the (misleading connotations of the) concept of a "secular ground" will render more plausible my rationale for (2). There seems to me to be a danger of construing a secular ground as a ground generated by cognitive capacities that are hardwired into each human being – sense perception, introspection, and so on. By contrast, a religious ground connotes a ground a citizen acquires in some special way: by some set of parochial practices she acquires as a matter of happenstance (or more sympathetically, by divine grace) – mystical perception, religious authority. In short, "secular" connotes "natural" and "universal," whereas religious connotes "supernatural" and "particular." And it's a short step from the double pairing of the secular with universality and the religious with particularity to an evaluative conclusion: that the secular is more reliable and trustworthy than the religious and indeed that the religious stands in need of the support of the secular.

But these associations are misleading. We don't generate any beliefs just by employing our native cognitive capacities. Rather, our cognitive capacities – our hardwiring – is always developed in various specific respects. They run on "software" and are useless without it. How do we acquire that software? Who programs us? In large part, we are programmed by being socialized into a determinate culture. Consequently, when we form some secular ground, we do so by relying, inevitably and unavoidably, on the particular cultural contents we enjoy as a consequence of our maturation in a particular historical time and specific cultural space. Secular grounds, then, are cultural grounds, grounds we find plausible, in large part, because we have been socialized into one culture and not another. And of course this point is just as applicable to secularly grounded moral claims as it is to other secular claims.

Once we construe the notion of the secular in this way, we have ample reason to be wary of (6). Why? To counsel a citizen to doubt religious grounds for which she can't discern adequate secular corroboration is to counsel her to doubt religious grounds for which she can't discern corroboratory support by relying on the secular component of the culture into which she has been socialized. But however much culture molds its members, it is nevertheless the product of human activity: although the convictions, emotions, and aspirations of each citizen are profoundly affected by the culture into which she is socialized, the nature and character of each culture is a function of an incredibly complex set of actions performed by many individuals over extended periods of time. As a consequence, any given culture is vulnerable to corruption, manipulation, or distortion, and the components thereof are therefore worthy of a healthy suspicion. As a further consequence, religious citizens will be quite wary of privileging secular-cum-cultural norms in the way envisioned by the advocate of the theistic case for restraint: they will be aware that the secular component of their cultural heritage might very well be morally misleading and will therefore be unwilling to grant that secular component veto power over their religiously grounded moral commitments.

Recent history bears ample testimony to the possibility of culturally induced blindness to crucially important moral truths. In particular, the dismal record of Christians in Nazi Germany provides a salutary lesson in the dangers of according undue weight to secular moral commitments. Brief mention of the central thesis of Daniel Goldhagen's recent (and extremely controversial) *Hitler's Willing Executioners* will help to convey that lesson.[19]

Goldhagen proposes to analyze German culture as an anthropologist analyzes a primitive society: by assuming that German society might very well adopt a set of moral and metaphysical commitments deeply at variance with our own. What he (putatively) discovers is that German culture prior to and including the Nazi period was corrupt – systematically so – given that it was imbued with "an almost universally held conceptualization of the Jews ... which constituted what can be called an 'eliminationist' ideology, namely the belief that Jewish influence, by nature destructive, must be eliminated irrevocably from society."[20] Given the pervasiveness of this eliminationist ideology, "during the Nazi period, and even long before, most Germans could no more emerge with cognitive models foreign to their society ... than they could speak fluent Romanian without ever having been exposed to it."[21] That racist ideology was, in short, the "common sense" of German political culture.[22] As a consequence, Goldhagen argues, the many racist policies pursued by the Nazi state (and its willing collaborators) enjoyed a rather straightforward rationality: "just as people today accept that the earth revolves around the sun, and once accepted that the sun revolves around the earth, so too have many people [Germans in particular] accepted culturally ubiquitous images of Jews" such that Jews posed so great a threat to the German *Volk* that the preservation of that *Volk* required the extermination of the Jews.[23]

Although Goldhagen's characterization of German culture strikes me (and many others in a better position to know) as considerably overdrawn, it makes the useful point: that German culture was deeply anti-Semitic, that German anti-Semitism was as much secular as religious, and thus that a citizen who happened to assent on religious grounds to the claim that Jewish people are fully human but who attempted to discern a plausible secular rationale for that claim might very well fail to do so.[24] Disastrously, many German Christians were willing to doubt even theological convictions central to the Christian tradition given that they ran counter to the prevailing anti-Semitic ethos: some denied that Jesus Christ was Jewish,[25] incorporated National Socialist conceptions of race into their doctrine of creation, denied that baptism was efficacious for Jews, reconstructed their characterization of Jesus Christ – from "a cowardly sufferer" to "a fighting Christ" – to render it attractive to Storm Troopers, adopted a "criterion of Jewishness as a means to decide what to teach from the New Testament and how to understand it,"[26] rejected the Old Testament as part of the canon, and so on. The result? "A mutant, racialized Christianity, divested of unGerman 'Jewish' elements, and purged of humanitarian sentimentality, that is, sin, guilt and pity."[27] Given this funereal chapter in recent history, it seems eminently sensible that Christians (and theists generally) should be wary of according presumptive weight to the "secular" elements of their culture.[28]

Ad (3): If the argument up to this point is correct, a citizen who pursues secular corroboration for a religiously grounded moral claim C can fail for two basic reasons: he can fail to discern an adequate secular rationale for C because C is false (the case envisioned by the advocate of the theistic case for restraint), or C is true, but his cognitive environment inhibits him from discerning a secular justification for C. In the first case, the policy of restraint gets the right result: there is no secular justification for a given religiously grounded norm because that norm is false. In the second case, the policy of restraint gets the wrong result: the moral claim is true and there is, we may assume, an adequate secular justification for that truth, but the citizen in question is in no position to acquire that justification.

These are the possibilities, but how likely is it that the latter possibility is actualized in a given case? I don't believe that there is a determinate answer to this question. Whether it's likely that other citizens have employed their cognitive capacities appropriately depends on what those citizens decide to do. What the other citizens on whose testimony a given citizen relies decide to do will vary across both historical time and social space. Sometimes the secular claims on which a citizen relies to determine the moral truth will be in good working order; sometimes they won't. If this is the case, it seems that it's reasonable for a religious citizen to conclude that in particular cases, his failure to discern secular evidence indicates more about the poor state of his secular evidence than it does about the falsehood of a moral claim he accepts solely on religious grounds. Please note that I don't claim that he should *always* conclude in favor of his religious evidence, just as I don't claim that he should *always* conclude that his failure to discern secular evidence counts against a given religious norm. The truth is somewhere in that murky territory between the extremes – a territory in which the articulation of hard and fast rules is more likely to lead astray than to guide one to the truth, namely, theistic citizens should expect that *some* but not *all* of their religiously grounded moral norms will enjoy secular corroboration.

Even if there is no determinate answer to the likelihood question, there is some firm ground in sight. It seems entirely appropriate for a religious citizen to reject the doctrine of restraint given the prospect that the secular evidence to which he has access is so botched up that it provides him with unreliable access to the moral truth. Recall my characterization of a common sort of theistic commitment: as involving an overriding and totalizing obligation to obey God. (See 5.3.) Given the more than merely logical possibility that he will, through no epistemic fault of his own, lack secular justification for a particular religiously grounded moral truth, and given that he takes himself to have an overriding and totalizing commitment to obey God, a theist can in good conscience refuse to commit himself to refrain from supporting coercive policies for which he lacks secular corroboration. The strains of a commitment to exercise restraint are too demanding for religious citizens for whom obedience to God is an overriding obligation.

9.2.3 Five Objections

There are any number of objections the advocate of the theistic case for restraint might want to press regarding my criticism of (6). I'll address five.

First Objection. There is an easy way to resurrect (6), one which promises to make short work of my objection. As I noted, (6) presupposes that the citizens who pursue secular corroboration govern their beliefs in an epistemically appropriate manner. I cashed that presupposition out by claiming that the citizens who pursue secular corroboration are *rational*, by which I mean that they adhere faithfully to various procedural constraints on the way they form and evaluate their beliefs – they assiduously pursue evidence relevant to the claim at issue, they do their level best to identify and address the relevant objections to their favored claims, and so on. But there are other, more demanding standards of epistemic evaluation the advocate of the theistic case for restraint might employ to cash out the argument. For example, taking a cue from our prior discussion of populist conceptions of public justification, he might claim that God will ensure that *adequately informed*, rational agents are likely to acquire secular corroboration. And surely, adequately informed, rational agents won't be misled by skewed normative testimony, and thus will be likely to succeed in their pursuit of secular corroboration. In short, (6) is true if interpreted in light of a more demanding epistemic standard than rationality.

This tack won't work for a familiar reason. Suppose we interpret (6) as suggested: a citizen who finds himself in such idealized circumstances has good reason to doubt any religiously grounded moral claim for which he lacks secular corroboration. But that citizens in such ideal epistemic circumstances have reason to doubt uncorroborated religious norms doesn't imply that citizens in less than ideal circumstances have reason to doubt uncorroborated religious norms. After all, the citizens who know that *they* aren't adequately informed have no a priori reason to rule out the possibility that, having discerned no secular justification for a given moral belief, the proper explanation of their failure is that their secular access to the moral truth is distorted by their less than ideally informed state. It seems that, if the advocate of the theistic case strengthens his expectations of the citizens who exercise restraint, then (6) is plausible, but (7) is false: just because citizens who find themselves in epistemically idealized circumstances have reason to doubt religiously grounded moral claims for which they lack secular corroboration, citizens who aren't so fortunately circumstanced – the citizens who actually inhabit a liberal democracy and who are expected to exercise restraint – lack reason to doubt secularly uncorroborated religious norms.

Second Objection. The claim that citizens who sincerely and rationally pursue a secular justification for a given moral truth might find themselves entrenched in a testimonial environment that skews their secular access to the moral truth, thus requiring correction by religious sources of moral knowledge, depends upon a contestable doctrine of sin, one which will be unacceptable to most theists. Most theists believe that God wouldn't allow citizens to sink to such a level that they lose their ability to act in accord with the moral law. Only those at the margins of the dominant theistic traditions believe that human persons are so depraved as to lack secular knowledge as to how they ought to act.

The argument I have presented doesn't depend on any such commitment to the doctrine of total depravity. All it presumes is that a citizen can find himself in such a situation that he can't discern an adequate secular justification for some of the moral truths he accepts on religious grounds. My objection presupposes only that human agents are fallible, not utterly depraved or devoid of moral insight. Here a distinction between a *collective* and a *distributive* interpretation of (6) might be helpful. On the collective interpretation, (6) entails that a high proportion of the set of religiously grounded moral truths to which a citizen assents are such that he will discern secular corroboration for those truths. The collective interpretation is consistent with its being highly unlikely that a citizen will discern secular corroboration for a *subset* of the religiously grounded moral truths to which he assents. On the distributive interpretation, (6) entails that it's likely that an agent is able to discern secular corroboration for *each* religiously grounded moral truth to which he assents. I take it to be fairly obvious that the theistic case requires the distributive interpretation: in order to justify the claim that citizens should exercise restraint regarding *each* uncorroborated religious norm, it must be the case that it's likely that a rational and sincere citizen is able to discern secular corroboration for *each* religiously grounded moral truth.

The objection I have presented in this section is directed at (6) as understood in the distributive sense, but I have provided no reason to doubt (6) as interpreted in the more radical collective sense. Thus, I have argued that a citizen can find himself in such epistemically hostile conditions that he'll be unlikely to discern an adequate secular justification for *particular* religiously grounded moral truths. But even if I am correct about that, it doesn't follow that a citizen has the realistic prospect of being so unfortunately circumstanced that he is unlikely to discern secular corroboration for many or most of his religiously grounded moral truths, much less all such truths. For purposes of my criticism of (6), I can afford to be agnostic about the likelihood of that state of affairs.

Third Objection. Perhaps my criticism of (6) assumes that human fallibility can obstruct a citizen's secular access to moral truth, but doesn't recognize that human fallibility can also render unreliable a citizen's religious access to the moral truth. If I did recognize that human sinfulness and fallibility affect religious sources of knowledge, I wouldn't be so willing to allow citizens to rely solely on religiously grounded moral claims when they support coercive policies.

My criticism of (6) doesn't arbitrarily exclude religious sources of moral knowledge from the effects of fallibility and sinfulness. Both religious and secular sources of moral knowledge can mislead. In some cases, it will be wise for a citizen to rely on secular grounds for moral knowledge, even though his religious sources give a different result: in those cases, the religious sources on which he relies are, he believes, misleading. But why assume that the effects of fallibility and sinfulness are limited to the religious realm? All my criticism of (6) presupposes is that in some cases, a citizen's religious doxastic practices provide him with better access to a given moral truth than do the secular considerations to which he has access.

Fourth Objection. What is an example of a moral truth for which actual citizens can't discern an adequate secular rationale? We might be skeptical that citizens really find themselves in the kind of epistemically hostile conditions that, I have claimed, might occlude secular access to important moral truths. Robert Audi expresses that sort of skepticism in the following passage:

> In addition to differing with Wolterstorff on the likely and extensive alignment between religious and secular reasons, I would ask for examples of cases in which, first, no such overlap can be found and, second, the law or policy in question is supported *only* by religious reasons yet is still one that informed, reflective citizens would wish to defend as appropriate for a religiously and otherwise pluralistic democracy. I am inclined to think that there are few if any such cases.[29]

First, a general point about Audi's challenge: in principle, a citizen might find himself ensconced in epistemic conditions which are hostile to *any* given moral truth. Whether a given citizen is able to discern a plausible secular justification for some moral truth is dependent in crucial part on the contents of his evidential set, and the contents of different citizens' evidential sets vary widely. Consequently, we can't determine whether a citizen is in a strong position to discern a plausible secular rationale for a given moral truth without having a great deal of information about the contents of his evidential set. And acquiring that information will, in turn, require us to acquire a great deal of information about his cognitive environment: most particularly, the authorities on whose testimony he relies. In virtue of these considerations, there just is no general answer to Audi's challenge: any citizen might find himself so circumstanced as to be unable to discern a plausible secular rationale for any given religiously grounded moral truth to which he adheres. This is my main, and most important, reply to Audi's challenge.

Nevertheless, this reply might seem unhelpfully abstract to some: can't we tell a plausible story about specific people in the contemporary American scene who find themselves ensconced in the sort of hostile conditions I have described in this chapter? The following seems plausible. Epistemically responsible and conscientious citizens can be, and some no doubt are, convinced that homosexual relations are morally inappropriate solely on religious grounds – say, on the basis of their interpretation of the Bible.[30] But they might very well find themselves unable to articulate a plausible secular rationale in support of the claim that homosexual relations are morally inappropriate: I myself believe that there is no plausible secular rationale in support of the claim that homosexuality is morally inappropriate (or related claims about sexual relations, such as that polygamy is morally inappropriate). In light of these judgments, I'm inclined to think that current debates over the legal status of homosexual relations (both about the legal status of same-sex marriages and about, say, housing discrimination against homosexual citizens) exemplify particularly clearly the kind of dispute to which the discussion in this book is most directly applicable: it is highly likely that some citizens are rationally justified in adhering on religious grounds to the claim that homosexual relations are morally inappropriate, and it seems equally likely that they cannot discern a plausible secular rationale for that claim.[31]

Fifth Objection. Even if we grant that a citizen who lacks secular corroboration for a religiously grounded norm need not *doubt* that norm, wouldn't it be *wise* for him to wait for secular corroboration? After all, he will be much more confident that a given religious norm is true if he does enjoy secular corroboration than if he doesn't enjoy secular corroboration. And shouldn't the legitimate aversion his compatriots have toward coercion counsel a citizen to withhold support from a given coercive law until he can articulate a rationale for that law that satisfies a more demanding epistemic standard?

It seems plausible to suppose that the deep aversion a citizen's compatriots have toward coercion counsels him to support only those coercive laws he's rationally justified in supporting to a sufficiently high degree (where sufficiency will inevitably remain vague). But it will almost always be possible for a citizen to do more by way of acquiring further evidence for his favored coercive laws. So even when he enjoys a "high" degree of rational justification for a given coercive law, he'll almost always be able to put himself in a position where he can acquire a rationale that satisfies an even more demanding standard. But at some point or other, he's going to have to end his pursuit of rational justification and decide whether to support or reject a given coercive law. Given the constraints of time and energy, it must be permissible for a citizen to support a coercive law on a basis that it is possible for him to improve through further reflection. And so it seems that as long as a citizen who supports a given coercive law solely on the basis of some uncorroborated religious norm enjoys a *sufficiently high* degree of rational justification for that law, practical wisdom doesn't counsel that he satisfy the *most demanding* standard. And there's every reason to believe that a citizen who has only a religious rationale might enjoy a sufficiently high degree of rational justification.

9.3 SHOULD RATIONAL CITIZENS DOUBT UNCORROBORATED RELIGIOUS NORMS?

Suppose that my objection to (6) is not probative; suppose, moreover, that the theistic case provides adequate support for (6). Thus, suppose that, for each religiously grounded moral truth to which a citizen assents, it's likely that she will be able to discern secular corroboration for that moral truth. I believe that we should nevertheless reject (7). Thus, even if citizens who rationally and sincerely pursue secular corroboration for their religiously grounded moral truths *should* expect to discover such corroboration, it doesn't follow that they should doubt secularly uncorroborated norms. That is what I will attempt to show in this section.

I'll do so in two steps. First, I argue that the role a particular uncorroborated norm plays in what I'll call an agent's "moral vision" can render it *rationally justifiable* for her to persist in adhering to that norm, at least so long as her moral vision enjoys general secular corroboration (9.3.1) and (9.3.2). Second, I argue that, in addition to its being rationally justifiable for a citizen not to moderate her confidence in such secularly uncorroborated religious norms, it is *religiously desirable* in certain circumstances that she refuse to moderate her confidence (9.3.3).

9.3.1 Moral Visions

What is a moral vision? A moral vision is not a collection of disconnected moral injunctions; rather, it's a more or less systematic account of what is good and bad for human beings, an account that involves claims about human nature, the function of human beings in the cosmos, the obligations of human beings given their nature and role, and the like.[32] Thus, a moral vision provides not just a laundry list of the obligations to which we should adhere, but also a systematic and internally articulated explanation as to why we should adhere to those obligations, why those obligations enable human agents to flourish, the relative importance of different obligations, and so on.

Many theists place great value on the construction of a moral vision. There are a number of reasons why that is the case. I will mention two.

(1) As I noted previously, theists believe that they have an overriding obligation to obey God. Unfortunately, the theist faces an important practical barrier to discharging that obligation. Theists typically form their religious convictions by relying on a variety of belief-forming practices (interpretations of sacred texts, religious experience, tradition, moral reflection). Those practices provide bits of information of a partial, prima facie contradictory, and antecedently unsystematized nature. Only by discerning order in the welter of partial and conflicting moral outputs of her doxastic practices do those practices provide a citizen with the cognitive means necessary for effective moral action. Thus, the unsystematic and partial nature of the moral guidance she receives from the various practices in which she engages imposes on the theist a synthetic task: she ought to do the best she can to integrate the convictions generated by her disparate doxastic practices into a coherent moral vision.

(2) As I also noted previously, theists typically regard their obligation to obey God as totalizing – as applicable to all manner of settings. This kind of totalizing commitment to God often outstrips the theists' occurrent cognitive resources: for many of the problems she faces, she will lack any direct knowledge of God's commands. Consider any moral-political issue of recent provenance, such as nuclear deterrence, in vitro fertilization, or genetic engineering. It's safe to assume that the religious belief-forming practices in which a given agent, Lauren, engages don't address any of those issues directly: neither the Bible, nor tradition, nor religious experience will provide her with direct moral guidance on those issues. Nevertheless, that Lauren lacks direct moral guidance on any of those issues doesn't obviate her totalizing obligation to obey God. In order to discharge that obligation, then, she must have some reliable way of discovering God's intentions with respect to those matters.

Constructing a moral vision enables her to do that: her moral vision provides guidance for situations in which she lacks explicit knowledge of God's commands. In constructing a moral vision, Lauren extends moral knowledge that is clearly applicable in certain circumstances to contexts in which that knowledge isn't clearly applicable. The pattern is fairly familiar: from the biblical claim that all members of the human species are created in the image of God, Christians draw inferences regarding issues the Bible does not directly address, or which it addresses with unclarity, such as racism, slavery, sexism, or abortion. From the biblical claim that God has created the natural world and given human beings stewardship of that world, theists reject vivisection and despoliation of the environment.[33]

9.3.2 Why It's Rational to Dismiss Counterevidence

A moral vision, then, is the product of a synthesis of particular moral and metaphysical claims into a broad moral framework, a mutual adjustment of apparently conflicting claims, a reinterpretation and extension of particular moral claims, and so on. The product is, ideally, a richly articulated complex of beliefs that provides the theist with accurate knowledge as to how God wants her to act and thus that provides her with reliable moral guidance. Given this account of what constitutes a moral vision and why a theist might value having a moral vision, we can explain why she might rationally reject (7): it's neither rationally obligatory nor religiously appropriate for theists to doubt each religious norm for which she can discern no secular corroboration.

Suppose Lauren has long been convinced that the Bible is divinely inspired. Given that conviction, she has, as stands to reason, attempted to immerse herself in the world contained within that text in order better to understand her own world and in order to discharge her moral obligations. As a consequence of many years of reflection on, discussion of, and action guided by, the moral and metaphysical claims expressed in the Bible, Lauren has reconstructed what she takes to be a compelling understanding of the nature of humankind and, more particularly, the requirements of human flourishing. Because she believes that her divinely imposed obligation to contribute to her fellow citizens' flourishing is overriding, Lauren does her level best to act in accord with the understanding of the moral vision internal to the biblical text.[34]

Suppose further that Lauren has consistently and over the years attempted to articulate a secular rationale for each of the coercive laws she has supported on the basis of the biblical moral vision: she has assiduously pursued, as she should, what Audi has called theo-ethical equilibrium: "a rational integration between religious deliverances and insights and, on the other hand, secular ethical considerations."[35] And suppose that she has been marvelously successful in discovering secular corroboration for the policies that she believes are mandated by her religious commitments: for every coercive law Lauren believes is mandated by the biblical moral vision, Lauren discovers a compelling secular rationale for that law. As a consequence of the consistent secular corroboration of her biblically derived moral vision, Lauren is justifiably confident that the moral vision she has discerned in the biblical text is a reliable moral guide. Given that each time she supports a particular coercive law on the basis of the fact that it is mandated by the moral vision internal to the biblical text, she subsequently discovers a secular rationale for that very law, Lauren reasonably concludes that the moral vision itself enjoys secular corroboration.

But what if it turns out that some claim partly constitutive of the moral vision of the Bible lacks secular corroboration? What should Lauren do if she believes that the biblical text forbids homosexual marriages but discovers that a secular rationale she once thought warranted a prohibition on homosexual marriages is in fact woefully inadequate? Given Lauren's continuing success in establishing equilibrium between her religiously and secularly grounded moral commitments, it's entirely reasonable for Lauren to commit herself to the reliability of her moral vision as a whole. Lauren has powerful inductive evidence for the claim that her moral vision provides her with reliable access to the moral truth. To be sure, that her moral vision supports a moral claim for which she can't discover a plausible secular rationale generates something of a crisis. Given her theistic understanding of the human condition, she'll expect to discover a secular rationale for the claim that homosexual marriages are sinful, if it is in fact the case that such marriages are sinful. That she can discover no such rationale constitutes counterevidence against the claim that homosexual marriages are sinful. (Recall that we are assuming for purposes of argument that (6) is true.)

Nevertheless, rather than inferring from the fact that she can now discover no secular corroboration for her religiously justified ban on homosexual marriages that her moral vision is doubtful in this instance,

Lauren may rationally infer from the fact that her moral vision has been so reliable a moral guide in the past that she should continue to trust her moral vision in this case as well, in spite of the absence of a corroborating secular rationale. It might be rational for Lauren to explain away her inability to discover secular corroboration for her belief that homosexual marriages are sinful. It might be entirely rational for her to regard that gap as anomalous, inexplicable, or incomprehensible without being rationally compelled to doubt her uncorroborated religious norms.

That a person can rationally categorize counterevidence as anomalous, and in so doing explain it away, is a commonplace of the philosophy of science, one made popular by Thomas Kuhn and Michael Polanyi. As both Kuhn and Polanyi argued, a scientist faced with what appears to be counterevidence to an otherwise powerful and empirically adequate theory isn't necessarily rationally compelled to quit the theory. That those who persisted in their commitment to the Copernican theory of the solar system could provide no fully adequate response to the objection that, if the earth was actually moving, objects resting on the earth should fly right off, doesn't indicate any irrationality on their part. The power and fruitfulness of the new theory was compelling enough to warrant many decades of patient forbearance until Newton resolved that problem.

Just as a scientist can rationally persist in her commitment to claims partly constitutive of a fruitful scientific paradigm in spite of her inability to answer objections to each of those claims, a theist can rationally persist in her commitment to norms partly constitutive of a fruitful moral vision in spite of her inability to answer objections to each of those norms. And just as those who accept a given theory in the teeth of counterevidence nevertheless can rationally act on their conviction that that theory is true, as by requesting and expending scarce resources to vindicate that theory, so also can theists who accept a given moral vision in spite of the lack of the expected secular corroboration rationally act on their conviction that their moral vision is reliable, as by supporting coercive policies that depend on uncorroborated norms internal to that vision. Because their moral vision provides them with reliable guidance generally, they may reasonably be loath not to act on that guidance even when its dictates are subject to counterevidence in particular cases.

Note that nothing I have said absolves dogmatic religious agents of their indifference to counterevidence. I claim only that agents *need not* doubt religiously grounded moral claims for which they lack secular corroboration. All I claim is that a lack of secular corroboration does not suffice to render a given religious norm doubtful – and that is all I need in order to show that (7) is false. But that a lack of secular corroboration does not of itself require agents to doubt uncorroborated religious norms does not entail that a lack of secular corroboration counts for nothing. In some cases, a lack of secular corroboration will tip the scales against a given religious norm such that a citizen should doubt that norm and thus should restrain herself from supporting coercive policies on the basis of that norm. Whether the lack of secular corroboration has this consequence in a given case depends on a variety of factors that vary from citizen to citizen, for example, how much other evidence a citizen has for a given uncorroborated religious norm, how important that norm is to the moral vision of which it is a constituent. That variation undermines the blanket claim that citizens should doubt uncorroborated religious norms and thus that they should exercise restraint regarding uncorroborated religious norms.

Here is another way of putting my point. The theistic case for restraint grants veto power to a lack of secular corroboration: a religious norm that lacks secular corroboration is ipso facto doubtful. I deny that a lack of secular corroboration has veto power; rather, it counts as *one sort* of counterevidence which must be weighed with other sorts of counterevidence and against any positive evidence for an uncorroborated claim. An important source of positive support for uncorroborated religious norms that I've attempted to identify is the support a norm acquires in virtue of its being an important constituent in a fruitful moral vision. And the fact that a given norm enjoys that sort of positive support can suffice to outweigh the counterevidence constituted by her failure to acquire the expected secular corroboration.

9.3.3 Loyalty to God and the Strains of Commitment

I take my argument in the prior section to show that theistic citizens are *permitted* by the canons of rationality not to doubt secularly uncorroborated religious norms. But that a citizen is rationally permitted to refrain from doubting secularly uncorroborated religious norms doesn't imply that it's a good thing for her so to refrain. I'll now explain why theistic citizens have good religious reason to be loath to moderate their confidence in, and thus exercise restraint with respect to, uncorroborated religious norms.

My argument in support of the claim that it's rational for theists not to doubt uncorroborated religious norms draws on putative similarities between the way in which a rational citizen properly evaluates counterevidence to her moral vision and the way that she properly evaluates counterevidence to scientific theories. But there's a disanalogy between a scientific theory and a typical theistic moral vision, one which supports the claim that it's good and desirable (from a theistic point of view) that theistic citizens are willing to discount their failure to discern secular corroboration. In brief, the disanalogy is that the content of a scientific theory doesn't predict that scientists will discover counterevidence to that theory, whereas the content of a (common sort of) theistic moral vision does predict that its adherents will encounter counterevidence to that vision. Typically, a theistic moral vision will include claims regarding the limited and distorted grasp citizens have on how they ought to live their lives. Further, a theistic moral vision will (often) involve the claim that religious citizens should expect to find themselves in circumstances in which they must rely on God's guidance when deciding how they ought to act. Thus, theists often believe that having faith in God sometimes involves pursuing a course of action for which they'll have no justification other than (what they take to be) God's command that they pursue that course of action.

What is it about a theistic moral vision that provides a basis for predicting that, in certain cases, God will command citizens to adhere to moral norms for which they can discern no secular corroboration? Here is one possibility: God allows citizens to find themselves in such circumstances because they provide an opportunity to exhibit a citizen's loyalty and devotion to God. A citizen expresses her loyalty to God by her willingness to obey God even when she lacks the reassurance provided by having independent reasons to act as God has commanded. The value of loyalty is sufficiently great that it warrants God's not ensuring that citizens have secular corroboration for each of God's commands.

It might seem that this appeal to the value of loyalty to God is in tension with my claim that a theistic citizen can rationally refuse to moderate her confidence in a given religious norm in spite of her failure to discern the expected secular corroboration. After all, if a citizen can be rationally justified in adhering to secularly uncorroborated religious norms, then how can adherence to such norms test her loyalty to God? The appearance of inconsistency vanishes if we realize that a citizen's loyalty to God can be tested in more ways than by forcing her to choose between her commitment to rationality and her commitment to obeying God. There are any number of commitments a citizen might be tempted to privilege over her loyalty to God: a particularly powerful temptation might be a commitment to act in accord with only those norms the rationale for which she can acquire by relying solely on her own cognitive powers. A citizen might be rationally justified in adhering to and acting upon a given uncorroborated norm, and yet she still might be tempted to reject that norm because she can't discern why that norm is true by relying on her own cognitive efforts.

That a theistic citizen might rationally believe that her failure to discern secular corroboration for a given religiously grounded moral claim provides an opportunity to express her loyalty to God supports the strains of commitment argument against the doctrine of restraint I articulated earlier. A citizen who adheres to a moral vision that is somewhat out of sync with the secular component of her culture may believe that her loyalty to God is being tested: is she willing to obey God only insofar as she enjoys secular insight into God's commands, or is she willing to venture further? Given that there is nothing irrational about a loyalty that explains away counterevidence, and given that loyalty to God renders suspension of disbelief admirable in some circumstances, it's religiously appropriate for citizens to reject the doctrine of restraint on grounds that it constitutes too demanding a strain on their commitment to God.

9.4 CONCLUDING COMMENTS

The strains of commitment argument against the doctrine of restraint that I developed in 5.3 presupposes that there is a realistic prospect that a theist will find herself in certain undesirable circumstances, namely, circumstances in which she enjoys what she regards as a compelling religious rationale for some coercive law but in which she lacks a public justification for that law. That the theist might find herself in such circumstances is what makes the doctrine of restraint religiously unacceptable: if she finds herself so circumstanced, the doctrine of restraint obliges her to withhold her support from that law, and in so doing requires her to disobey what she regards as her most fundamental commitment: to obey God. We might wonder, however, whether a theist should really take that prospect seriously. Indeed, it might seem particularly strange for the theist to bother about finding herself so circumstanced: given her conviction that reality is governed by a morally perfect Benefactor, it might seem that she should expect to find herself in much better conditions as regards her access to the moral truth. At the very least, she should expect to be able to discern a plausible secular rationale for any religiously grounded moral truth to which she assents. The burden of this chapter is to show that theistic commitments have no such implication. Given common theistic convictions regarding human freedom – more particularly, given common theistic convictions regarding the fallible and sinful way in which human beings exercise their freedom – a theist shouldn't be surprised to find herself so situated as to be unable to discern a plausible secular rationale for some of the religiously grounded moral claims she regards as true.

CONCLUDING COMMENTS

The doctrine of restraint is deeply at odds with the norms I think we should associate with the social role of citizen in a liberal democracy. We legitimately expect liberal citizens to decide on and advocate support for their favored political commitments on the basis of their convictions of *conscience*: we should expect our compatriots to support only those coercive laws that they take to be morally appropriate. We legitimately expect liberal citizens to arrive at their convictions of conscience *conscientiously*: otherwise the appeal to conscience can degenerate into intransigent sectarianism. We legitimately expect liberal citizens to be open to the possibility that their moral convictions are false and so to be willing to *learn* from their compatriots. We legitimately expect liberal citizens to do what is within their power to *justify to* their compatriots the claim that some coercive law they conscientiously support is morally appropriate. But at some point, each citizen has to *resolve* what to do: she has to decide which policies merit her support. At that point, at the moment of decision, we should expect citizens to make their respective resolutions on the basis of convictions of conscience – on the basis of what they take to be the relevant moral considerations, whatever those moral considerations happen to be. And we should reject the doctrine of restraint because it is inconsistent with that desideratum: a citizen might lack a public justification for the policies she conscientiously regards as morally appropriate and in that case the doctrine of restraint obliges her to withhold her support from those policies.

Many of the citizens in the United States are theists. Many theists take their religious convictions to bear directly on all manner of political matters. Consequently, many citizens will arrive at their respective convictions of conscience on religious grounds. And some citizens will arrive at some of their respective convictions of conscience on religious grounds *alone*. Convictions of conscience, conscientiously based on religious grounds, even on religious grounds alone, remain convictions of conscience and should be treated accordingly. We should therefore expect religious citizens to employ religiously grounded convictions of conscience to determine which coercive laws merit their support. They shouldn't be discouraged from doing so, much less stigmatized for doing so.

Many object to that kind of reliance on religious convictions. In popular culture, the objection is typically formulated by reference to the supposed impropriety of one person's imposing her "values" on her compatriots: the objector transposes religious convictions into irreducibly subjective preferences and draws the conclusion that such imposition is inappropriate. That sort of objection isn't worth taking seriously: it belongs to the debased and confused chattering that so often poses as public deliberation.

But other objections are worth taking seriously. We have examined a number of them, none of which, I think, are probative. It is not the case, as many justificatory liberals allege, that a citizen's supporting some coercive law solely on the basis of her religious convictions is disrespectful. Nor is it the case that a widespread willingness to support coercive laws solely on the basis of religious grounds has a realistic prospect of generating civil strife. Nor again is it the case that a widespread willingness to support coercive laws solely on religious grounds generates worse consequences, all things considered, than does a widespread refusal to support coercive laws solely on religious grounds. In short, justificatory liberals have articulated no compelling argument in support of the claim that we ought to encode the doctrine of restraint into the social role of citizen in a liberal democracy.

That is not all. Religious citizens have good reason to *reject* the doctrine of restraint. After all, that doctrine is *gratuitously burdensome* to religious citizens: it requires of them a willingness to disobey God and thereby imposes on them a substantial burden for which there is no compelling rationale. Moreover, the doctrine of restraint is *arbitrary*: the justificatory liberal can provide no principled reason to require a citizen to exercise restraint regarding *religious convictions* that doesn't, when consistently applied, have disastrous implications for political decision making and advocacy. About this second point, two facts are relevant. First, religious convictions aren't more controversial than some of the moral claims citizens will unavoidably employ in political decision making and advocacy. Second, religious convictions aren't different in epistemically relevant respects from some of the moral claims citizens will unavoidably employ in political decision making and advocacy. Apparently, religious citizens have more than adequate reason to refuse to exercise restraint regarding their religious commitments.

The implications of this conclusion for my central thesis are direct: each citizen should feel free to support coercive laws on the basis of her religious convictions – even on the basis of her religious convictions alone – so long as she conscientiously regards her religious convictions as providing a sufficient basis for those laws. Of course, she shouldn't *strive* for this state of affairs. Indeed, she should do whatever she feasibly can to avoid putting herself in the condition that she enjoys only a religious rationale for a favored coercive law. But if she does find herself in some such condition, if she has conscientiously arrived at the conclusion, solely on the basis of religious considerations, that some coercive law is morally appropriate, then we should encourage her to support that coercive law and perhaps even admire her for doing so.

The implications of doing so can be – will inevitably be – unsettling. Many convictions of conscience are false, even when conscientiously acquired. Many convictions of conscience based on religious grounds are false, even when conscientiously acquired. And so we can expect that many of the policies citizens support solely on the basis of religious grounds will be misguided, foolhardy, or muddleheaded. So long as we allow ordinary people a modicum of influence over the coercive power the state is authorized to employ, some of the laws the state is empowered to enforce will be rash and unjust. So be it. For to that prospect, there is no morally defensible alternative.

NOTES

Chapter One

1. Amendment 2 reads as follows: "No Protected Status Based on Homosexual, Lesbian, or Bisexual Orientation. Neither the State of Colorado, through any of its branches or departments, nor any of its agencies, political subdivisions, municipalities or school districts, shall enact, adopt or enforce any statute, regulation, ordinance or policy whereby homosexual, lesbian or bisexual orientation, conduct, practices or relationships shall constitute or otherwise be the basis of or entitle any person or class of persons to have or claim any minority status, quota preferences, protected status or claim of discrimination. This Section of the Constitution shall be in all respects self-executing."

2. "But there is no doubting the matter: the question of homosexuality reveals two genuinely different moral camps in America, ones that disagree profoundly about the fundamental nature of what they are contesting." Alan Wolfe, "Civil Religion Revisited: Quiet Faith in Middle-Class America," *Obligations of Citizenship and Demands of Faith*, Nancy Rosenblum, ed. (Princeton, NJ: Princeton University Press, 2000), p. 62. Throughout this book, I'll focus on the political scene in the United States.

3. Those who oppose homosexual rights often regard the state's attempt to coerce them into refraining from housing discrimination as particularly objectionable. "Most heterosexuals find same-gender sex to be both abhorrent and threatening. Such sex is considered by many to be the most glaring indicator of moral and social decay. While heterosexuals may be content to leave gay persons alone, they resist being told that they cannot avoid their company in the workplace or when renting housing. Thus, antidiscrimination statutes are seen as extremely coercive, dictating the behavior of heterosexuals against their will in an area that is emotionally charged." James W. Button, Barbara A. Rienzo, and Kenneth D. Wald, *Private Lives, Public Conflicts: Battles over Gay Rights in American Communities* (Washington, DC: CQ Press, 1997), p. 13.

334

4. I'll assume, without argument, that each citizen has an obligation to employ her modicum of power and influence over state action in a morally responsible manner and thus that a responsible citizen won't decide whether to support or oppose a given law solely by reference to her own interests. A responsible citizen won't, I take it, consult only her own interests in exercising the power available to her (as a voter in a referendum, for example), but will attempt to use her power justly, to further the common good, and so on.

5. Lisa Keen and Suzanne Goldberg, *Strangers to the Law* (Ann Arbor: University of Michigan Press, 1998), pp. 8–10. It's no exaggeration to claim that religious citizens, particularly white evangelicals, black evangelicals, and Catholics, constitute "the primary contestants against gay rights" in recent disputes over the legal status of homosexuality in the United States. See Button, Rienzo, and Wald, *Private Lives, Public Conflicts*, p. 177.

6. Lisa Keen and Suzanne Goldberg, *Strangers to the Law*, p. 7.

7. Lisa Keen and Suzanne Goldberg, *Strangers to the Law*, p. 13.

8. *New York Times*, May 24, 1992, Sec. 1, p. 31. McCartney is here alluding to Leviticus 18:22: "You shall not lie with a male as one lies with a female; it is an abomination." According to one insider, the press conference at which McCartney first publicly expressed his support for Amendment 2 was crucial in jump-starting Colorado for Family Values' otherwise moribund petition drive. See Stephen Bransford, *Gay Rights vs. Colorado and the United States: The Inside Story of Amendment 2* (Cascade, CO: Sardis Press, 1994), pp. 54–55.

9. See John West, *The Politics of Revelation and Reason* (Lawrence: University Press of Kansas, 1996), pp. 88–97. According to West, evangelical reformers were instrumental in forging "a public consensus against dueling, which produced new state laws outlawing duelists from public office." *The Politics of Revelation and Reason*, p. 207.

10. The postal law of 1810 required, among other things, "all postmasters to open their office to the public on every day that the mail arrived, and to deliver 'on demand' any item being held in their office on every day of the week." According to Lyman Beecher, the issue raised by the postal law was "perhaps the most important that ever was, or ever will be submitted for national consideration." Beecher, with many of his contemporaries, articulated explicitly theological considerations for repealing that law. Thus, according to Richard R. John, "For the Presbyterian general assembly, the import of the new law was clear. Now that Congress had taken upon itself the regulation of personal behavior, it too had an obligation to abide by 'those principles of truth and equity revealed in the Scriptures.' Thus, it saw nothing improper in rebuking Congress for its neglect of the Fourth Commandment. Freely citing the Bible in support of its position, it berated Congress for its cruelty not only toward postmasters and mail contractors but also toward the thousands of horses forced to labor seven days a week. Ought not, it thundered, the righteous man be

merciful to his beast? The very form of the petition reinforced its message. Modeled after a biblical jeremiad, it warned Congress that, should it fail to repent, it risked drawing down upon 'our nation' the 'divine displeasure.'" All citations from Richard R. John, "Taking Sabbatarianism Seriously: The Postal System, the Sabbath and the Transformation of American Political Culture," *The Journal of the Early Republic* 10 (Winter 1990): 522, 517, 529–30. See also Robert Abzug, *Cosmos Crumbling: American Reform and the Religious Imagination* (Oxford: Oxford University Press, 1994), pp. 105–116; and John West, *The Politics of Revelation and Reason*, pp. 137–70, particularly pp. 140–48.

11. See John West, *The Politics of Revelation and Reason*, pp. 171–206. Georgia's expropriation of Cherokee land resulted in the "trail of tears," in which 500–2000 Cherokees died *en route* from Georgia to Oklahoma.

12. The Republican Party platform of 1856 declared that it was "both the right and the imperative of Congress to prohibit in the territories those twin relics of barbarism – Polygamy and Slavery." Charles A. Cannon, "The Awesome Power of Sex: The Polemical Campaign against Mormon Polygamy," *Pacific Historical Review* 53 (February, 1974): 62.

13. Here is a representative sample from a prominent abolitionist from the early nineteenth century, George Bourne: "But the BOOK unequivocally declares, that to enslave a man is the highest kind of theft; to purloin children is the compound of all robbery, as it steals a Father's joy, a Mother's tenderness, a Brother's delight, and a Sister's affection; to excruciate a female by stripes or by violation is the height of barbarity; to divest a man of his rational characteristics is the most diabolical impiety; ... and to prolong human existence in agony, the mind bereft of all consolation and the body of needful support is a concatenation of crime indescribable. ... The BOOK condemns this turpitude as the most atrocious criminality: and no man can momentarily admit, that unerring rectitude sanctions a system of iniquity. Whether we advert to the motives, the objects, or the results of slavery, it is totally incompatible with Christianity." John W. Christie and Dwight L. Dumond, *George Bourne and the Book and Slavery Irreconcilable* (Wilmington, DE: The Historical Society of Delaware, 1969), pp. 171–72. As Christie and Dumond argue, William Lloyd Garrison, one of the most well known of the abolitionists, was greatly influenced by Bourne's case for the immediate criminalization of slavery.

14. See Eugene Genovese, *A Consuming Fire: The Fall of the Confederacy in the Mind of the White Christian South* (Athens: University of Georgia Press, 1998).

15. Responding to the Supreme Court's decision in *Reynolds v. the United States*, which upheld the 1862 Morrill Anti-bigamy Act, the president of the Mormon Church, John Taylor, insisted that "polygamy is a divine institution. It has been handed down direct from God. The United States cannot abolish it. No nation on earth can prevent it, nor all the nations on the earth combined. I defy the United States. I will obey God." Quoted in Richard S. Wagoner, *Mormon Polygamy: A History* (Salt Lake City, UT: Signature Books, 1986), p. 114.

16. See John Noonan, *The Lustre of Our Country: The American Experience of Religious Freedom* (Berkeley: University of California Press, 1998), pp. 252–54.

17. Quoted in Allen Hertzke, "Assessment of the Mainline Churches since 1945," *The Role of Religion in the Making of Public Policy*, James E. Wood, Jr., and Derek Davis, eds. (Waco, TX: J. M. Dawson Institute of Church-State Studies, 1991), p. 50. Not everyone was as enthusiastic as Humphrey regarding the support the Civil Rights Act received from churches. Humphrey's colleague from Georgia, Richard Russell, "commented that in supporting civil rights 'men of the cloth' had applied a 'philosophy of coercion' similar to the 'doctrine that dictated the acts of Torquemada in the infamous days of the Inquisition.'" James F. Findlay, "Religion and Politics in the Sixties: The Churches and the Civil Rights Act of 1964," *The Journal of American History* 77 (June, 1990): 66. As we'll see, the association of politically active religion with religious persecution and other civil dysfunctions isn't limited to the rough and tumble of nonacademic political debate.

18. "Finally, in the early and mid-1960s the Word and the Movement assumed an organic relationship not unlike that described in the Book of Acts, where the Word of God is said to have embodied its own community and momentum. What the Book of Acts claims for the earliest Christian preaching could be said of King and his colleagues in Alabama, Mississippi, and Georgia: 'So mightily grew the word of God and prevailed.' The action in the streets and King's preaching became expressions of one another. Historians may 'freeze' the Civil Rights Movement and isolate individual rhetorical performances that appear to be turning points or significant moments, but it is the *ceaseless* activity of biblical interpretation and preaching carried out by King and his colleagues that sustained the Movement as a whole and invested it with transcendent meaning. Under his leadership the quest for equality and justice became a Word-of-God movement." Richard Lischer, *The Preacher King: Martin Luther King and the Word that Moved America* (Oxford: Oxford University Press, 1995), pp. 219–20.

19. The Constitution of Utah (Article 3) prohibits polygamy in the following language: "Perfect toleration of religious sentiment is guaranteed. No inhabitant of this state shall ever be molested in person or property on account of his or her mode of religious worship; but polygamous or plural marriages are forever prohibited." Irwin Altman and Joseph Ginat, *Polygamous Families in Contemporary Society* (Cambridge: Cambridge University Press, 1996), p. 46.

20. Michael Kelly, "A Liberal Win, Thanks to the Churches," *Washington Post* (October 20, 1999): A29.

21. For a balanced treatment of the Christian Right, see Clyde Wilcox, *Onward Christian Soldiers?* (Boulder, CO: Westview Press, 1996).

22. Alan Wolfe, "Civil Religion Revisited," p. 36.

23. Max Weber, "Science as a Vocation," *From Max Weber*, H. H. Gerth and C. Wright Mills, eds. (Oxford: Oxford University Press, 1946), p. 155.

24. This is a common way to frame the issue. See, for example, Kent Greenawalt, *Religious Convictions and Political Choice* (Oxford: Oxford University Press, 1988), p. 4; Nicholas Wolterstorff, "The Role of Religion in Decision and Discussion of Political Issues," in Robert Audi and Nicholas Wolterstorff, *Religion in the Public Square: The Place of Religious Convictions in Political Debate* (Lanham, MD: Rowman and Littlefield Publishers, 1997), pp. 67f.

25. The distinction between a citizen's acting within her rights and a citizen's acting in a morally criticizable manner is helpfully emphasized in Robert Audi's *Religious Commitment and Secular Reason* (Cambridge: Cambridge University Press, 2000), pp. 84ff.

26. Of course, Amendment 2 might very well *be* detrimental to the common good; I'm assuming that McCartney conscientiously and rationally believed otherwise.

27. A brief note about my way of putting these two questions. It's implausible to believe that McCartney supported Amendment 2 on the basis of some rationale constituted *solely* by religious premises; it's rather more likely that he supported Amendment 2 on the basis of a rationale that depends *essentially* on religious premises. That is, it's likely that his rationale for Amendment 2 was constituted by both religious and secular premises, but that his secular premises would not, considered independently of his religious premises, constitute adequate reason to support Amendment 2. Nevertheless, the somewhat misleading language I've adopted is considerably less clumsy than the more accurate alternative.

28. In 6.0, I'll address one argument to the conclusion that citizens shouldn't rely at all on their religious convictions to support their favored policies, that, since the intrusion of religion into the political sphere is so divisive and disruptive, religious citizens should completely evacuate their religious convictions from political decision making and advocacy.

29. I realize that this passing judgment is controversial – that's an understatement! Since, however, it isn't my intention to evaluate arguments for criminalizing or discouraging same-sex relations, I'll let this judgment stand undefended.

30. Many deny that religious citizens can, or do, regard as fallible the positions they support on the basis of their religious commitments. Some religious citizens no doubt satisfy that characterization; perhaps McCartney satisfies that characterization. But he doesn't need to. Or so I shall argue in 8.0.

31. Notice that I've formulated my thesis so that it applies not to laws generally but to coercive laws. I explain this narrowing of my focus in 3.0.

32. Of course, what one thinks of McCartney's reasons for supporting Amendment 2 is another matter. The issue I'm interested in addressing is not, "Is such and such a reason sufficient to warrant support for such and such a law?" or "Is such and such a law good, right and salutary?" but "On the basis of what sorts of consideration may we decide that such and such a law is good, right and salutary?" So we might believe that McCartney's reasons are unconvincing and Amendment 2 a poorly conceived idea, but

also believe that the sorts of reasons (religious ones) on the basis of which he supported Amendment 2 play an appropriate and even salutary role in liberal politics even when unsupplemented by secular reasons.

This raises a more general point: in no way should the fact that I *exemplify* the sort of activity my central thesis endorses by reference to socially conservative Christianity be understood to imply an *endorsement* of socially conservative Christianity. As I see it, my central thesis applies across the board: to socially liberal Christians as well as to socially conservative Christians, to socially liberal members of non-Christian traditions as well as to members of socially conservative non-Christian traditions. In fact, my central thesis has *no* determinate implications for specific political commitments, as it bears solely on the reasons a citizen may employ as a basis for her favored political commitments.

33. I am being deliberately noncommittal here as regards the sort of rationale a citizen should pursue. Clearly, a secular rationale, even a plausible one, need not be widely convincing, even though a widely convincing rationale will almost always, under conditions of pluralism, be secular. At this preliminary point in the discussion, I need not broach this issue, which will receive due attention in the sequel.

34. I have taken this term from Gerald Gaus, who coined it in his *Justificatory Liberalism* (Cambridge: Cambridge University Press, 1996). I should warn the reader, however, that my use of that term is quite a bit broader than Gaus's. Gaus distinguishes his position, "justificatory liberalism," from "political liberalism," the position Gaus associates most closely with Rawls. By contrast, I use "justificatory liberalism" to include Rawls's "political liberalism" as well as views that bear important similarities to Rawls's position, such as Gaus's. In spite of many significant differences, I regard the commonalities between Rawls's political liberalism and Gaus's justificatory liberalism as far more important than those differences, particularly with respect to the implication of their positions for the proper role of religious convictions in politics.

35. There are, of course, any number of adequate specifications of the substantive commitments adherence to which is a necessary condition of adherence to liberalism. For one among many, see Isaiah Berlin, *Four Essays on Liberty* (Oxford: Oxford University Press, 1969), p. 165.

36. This bald claim requires a number of significant qualifications, which I discuss in 3.0.

37. I am assuming, for the sake of illustration, that McCartney does not supplement the claim that homosexuality is an abomination to God with a nonreligious rationale.

38. Gaus does not mention McCartney in particular; he defends the claim that "sectarians" who support laws that criminalize or discourage homosexual relations solely on the basis of their parochial religious convictions "browbeat" their compatriots. *Justificatory Liberalism*, p. 163.

39. I address this concern most directly in 9.0.

40. I should note that justificatory liberals are compelled to take this tack only if what I'll call populist conceptions of public justification are inadequate, as I will argue they are. See 7.0 and 8.0.

41. Justificatory liberals ordinarily deny that they are committed to skepticism regarding religion; that is, they deny that the constraints they propose to impose on religious citizens entail either that religious convictions are false or that religious convictions lack rational justification. (See, for example, Robert Audi, "Liberal Democracy and the Place of Religion in Politics," in Robert Audi and Nicholas Wolterstorff, *Religion in the Public Square*, p. 53.) Unfortunately, their actual commitments often belie such official pronouncements. Thus, for example, when Stephen Macedo claims that "political arrangements are often sustained by power, religious conviction, interest, preference, and sheer inertia, rather than by reasoned reflection," one gets the distinct impression that political arrangements sustained by religious convictions are ipso facto not sustained by reasoned reflection, and, indeed, that religious conviction is incompatible with reasoned reflection. (*Liberal Virtues: Citizenship, Virtue and Community in Liberal Constitutionalism* [Oxford: Clarendon Press, 1990], p. 12.) When Thomas Nagel claims that religious convictions fit into the category of "purely personal" and "subjective," it is hard to avoid the impression that he is committed to skepticism about religious convictions. ("Moral Conflict and Political Legitimacy," *Philosophy and Public Affairs* 16 (1987): 232–34.) Bruce Ackerman's treatment of religious belief seems predicated on a highly prejudicial understanding of religious commitment. It seems that Ackerman resolves religious commitment into belief in ghosts and other disembodied spirits; consequently, it is hard to imagine anyone endorsing Ackerman's position on the proper role of religious convictions in politics if that person is willing to countenance the possibility that citizens might enjoy credible grounds for their religious commitments. (See, for example, *Social Justice in the Liberal State* [New Haven, CT: Yale University Press, 1980], p. 127.) When Amy Gutmann and Dennis Thompson assert that an appeal to the Bible in support of some policy does not count as a moral appeal because such appeals to authority "close off any possibility of publicly assessing or interpreting the content of the claims put forward by the authority," it seems that they are committed to the claim that beliefs based on divine revelation lack a crucially important epistemic desideratum, namely, interpersonal criticizability. (See "Moral Conflict and Political Consensus," *Ethics* 101 [October, 1990]: 70.) Similarly for Abner Greene's claim that religious claims ought not serve as a basis for coercive laws on the grounds that any religious basis is not relevantly different from an appeal to evidence locked in a "secret box" to which only some citizens have a key. (See "Uncommon Ground," *The George Washington Law Review* 62/4 [April, 1994]: 659.) Similarly again for Theodore Blumoff's equation of religious language with a language of the "I can see it but you can't" sort. (See "Disdain for the Lessons of History," *Capitol University Law Review* 20 [1991]: 184, fn. 103.) None of this bodes well for the epistemic status of religious convictions.

See also Kai Nielson, "Liberal Reasonability," *Dialogue* 37/4 (Fall, 1998): 739–59.

42. I am relying here on the familiar distinction between a concept and a conception, that is, between an idea and its more detailed specifications.

43. I'm painting with a very broad brush here; an adequate treatment of this point would require numerous qualifications. For example, even on a classically foundationalist conception of rationality, it's arguable that at least some religious beliefs pass rational muster, even if most do not. Of course, not many nonreligious beliefs pass rational muster on a classically foundationalist model, either.

44. I articulate the main outlines of Alston's doxastic practice approach to epistemology in 8.1.

45. The claim that the "rationalization" of modern culture gives rise to the disenchantment-cum-secularization of modern culture is a commonplace among those who accept some version of the theory of secularization. See for example, Steve Bruce, *Choice and Religion* (Oxford: Oxford University Press, 2000), pp. 3–29; Jurgen Habermas, *The Theory of Communicative Action: Reason and the Rationalization of Society* (Boston, MA: Beacon Press, 1984), passim.

46. John West argues that the evangelical Reformers of the early nineteenth century were convinced that they "did not have to argue solely in terms of the Bible because they believed that the morality it inculcates is also the morality prescribed by reason." *The Politics of Revelation and Reason*, p. 147. I see little reason to believe that the situation has changed in the meantime, even for evangelicals and fundamentalists.

47. Thus, Gerald Gaus: "Liberal politics has both a moral and an epistemological basis. Liberal politics requires, first, that citizens recognize their moral commitment to justify their demands to each another, and second, that citizens understand what is involved in such justification." *Justificatory Liberalism*, p. 292. Charles Larmore makes a similar claim: "In general, political principles are precisely those that we believe may be enforced – imposed by coercion – if need be. The idea that such principles must be rationally acceptable to those who are to be subject to them rests on a moral view about the conditions under which norms may be backed up by force. This underlying moral commitment is that no one should be made by force to comply with a norm of action when it is not possible for him to recognize through reason the validity of that norm." "The Foundations of Modern Democracy: Reflections on Jurgen Habermas," *The Morals of Modernity* (Cambridge: Cambridge University Press, 1996), p. 220.

Chapter Two

1. The claim that religion declines in modernity is a commonplace of modern social science. As Wallis and Bruce write, "Whatever the differences in their approach to religion, Marx, Durkheim and Weber all foresaw a major decline in its role in the modern world. Religion's ability to provide

a single, integrated and generally held conception of meaning had been fatally eroded by the emergence of a plurality of life experiences, deriving from widely differing relationships to a rapidly changing social order, by the increasingly rationalistic organization of an industrialized, mass market economy, and by more universalistic conceptions of citizenship." Ray Wallis and Steve Bruce, "Religion: The British Contribution," *British Journal of Sociology* 40 (1989): 493. See also Bryan Turner, *Religion and Social Theory*, 2nd ed. (London: Sage Publications, 1991), p. xvi.

2. Peter Berger, "The Desecularization of the World: A Global Overview," *The Desecularization of the World: Resurgent Religion and World Politics*, Peter Berger, ed. (Washington, DC: Ethics and Public Policy Center, 1999), p. 2. For a succinct telling of the story, see Steve Bruce, *Choice and Religion*, pp. 8ff.

3. Jon Butler, *Awash in a Sea of Faith: Christianizing the American People* (Cambridge, MA: Harvard University Press, 1990), p. 2. Roger Finke and Rodney Stark have argued for the same conclusion: "What we do find to be the master trend of American religious history is a long, slow, and consistent increase in religious participation from 1776 [roughly, after disestablishment] to 1926 – with the rate inching up slightly after 1926 and then hovering near 60 percent." *The Churching of America: Winners and Losers in Our Religious Economy* (New Brunswick, NJ: Rutgers University Press, 1992), p. 274. See also Callum G. Brown, "A Revisionist Approach to Religious Change," *Religion and Modernization*, Steve Bruce, ed. (Oxford: Clarendon Press, 1992), pp. 36, 46f.

4. Epicycles and deferents were ad hoc devices employed by pre-Copernican astronomers to render their model of planetary motion consistent with the observed facts. The secularization theorist's most important epicycle is to argue that even though a much higher percentage of Americans participate in religious institutions than was previously the case, the nature of their religious participation is itself highly secularized. In this respect, Americans differ from Europeans, by and large: Europeans manifest their secularity by absenting themselves from church, whereas Americans express their secularity by attending church – albeit a highly secularized church. Thus Bryan Wilson: "Few observers doubt [!] that the actual content of what goes on in the major churches in Britain is very much more 'religious' than what occurs in American churches; in America secularizing processes appear to have occurred *within* the church, so that although religious institutions persist, their specifically religious character has become steadily attenuated." *Religion in Sociological Perspective* (Oxford: Oxford University Press, 1982), p. 152. See also Peter Berger, *The Sacred Canopy: Elements of a Sociological Theory of Religion* (Garden City, NY: Anchor Books, 1969), p. 108.

5. "Pluralism and Religious Vitality," *Religion and Modernization*, p. 185.

6. As Michael Perry notes, the central topic of this book assumes its importance against the background of widespread religious commitment: "If few Americans were religious believers, the issue of the proper role of religion in politics would probably be marginal to American politics, because religion

would be marginal to American politics. But most Americans are religious believers. Indeed, the citizenry of the United States is one of the most religious – perhaps even the most religious – citizenries of the world's advanced industrial democracies." *Religion in Politics: Constitutional and Moral Perspectives* (Oxford: Oxford University Press, 1997), p. 3. To which we should add the following rider: if Americans were taken with privatized religiosity, or if we had good reason to believe that religion has no future in a liberal democracy, the issue of the proper role of religious convictions in politics would probably be marginal to American politics.

7. *Religion in the Modern World: From Cathedral to Cults* (Oxford: Oxford University Press, 1996), p. 234.

8. *Religion and Social Theory*, p. 196.

9. See, for example, William Marshall, "The Other Side of Religion," *Hastings Law Journal* 44 (April, 1993): 843–63; Lawrence Solum, "Faith and Justice," *DePaul Law Review* 39 (1990): 1096–97; Theodore Blumoff, "Disdain for the Lessons of History," passim. Very often the assumption is that pluralism poses a threat to *conservative* kinds of religion, as in the following assertion by Stephen Macedo:

> A differentiated society thus serves the cause of freedom and promotes moral laxity as well as a certain kind of individualism. All this is exactly what fundamentalists object to. In such an environment, Vicki Frost [a parent of children compelled to participate in a reading program she found objectionable on various religious grounds] will have a hard time teaching her children that the "totality" of truth is found in the Christian Bible. Many forms of discipline will be hard to sustain in the differentiated society, which indirectly fosters distinctive forms of personality, culture and even religious beliefs. ("Liberal Civic Education and Religious Fundamentalism," pp. 478–79.)

10. This is a bit too cheery: pluralism does not benefit all types of religion. I will lay out some of the necessary qualifications in due order.

11. The claim the citizens with "genuine" religious commitments – those willing to "let God be God" – are antipathetic to religious freedom is a central theme of Stanley Fish's "Why We Can't All Just Get Along," *First Things* 60 (February, 1996): 18–26.

12. *Political Liberalism* (New York: Columbia University Press, 1993), p. 58.

13. *Political Liberalism*, pp. 54–8. Amy Gutmann and Dennis Thompson articulate an account of the sources of moral disagreement that comports with Rawls's account. See *Democracy and Disagreement* (Cambridge, MA: The Belknap Press, 1996), pp. 18–26. See also Charles Larmore, "Pluralism and Reasonable Disagreement," *The Morals of Modernity*, pp. 152–74, esp. 167–71; Joshua Cohen, "Moral Pluralism and Political Consensus," *The Good Polity*, David Copp, Jean Hampton, and John E. Roemer, eds. (Cambridge: Cambridge University Press, 1993), pp. 281–82. Ian Markham discusses the genesis of pluralism from a theological perspective in *Plurality and Christian Ethics*, rev. ed. (Chapaqua, NY: Seven Bridges Press, 1999), pp. 130–43.

14. *Political Liberalism*, pp. 56–57.
15. *Political Liberalism*, p. 55.
16. *Political Liberalism*, pp. xviii; 37.
17. Charles Larmore, "Political Liberalism," *The Morals of Modernity*, p. 122. See also Charles Larmore, "The Moral Basis of Liberalism," *Journal of Philosophy* 96/12 (December, 1999): 600.
18. *The Churching of America*, p. 18. In addition, as Rawls argues, a political society can unite in affirming one religion, philosophical doctrine, or conception of the good *only if* it employs coercion to repress divergent views: "In the society of the Middle Ages, more or less united in affirming the Catholic faith, the Inquisition was not an accident; its suppression of heresy was needed to preserve that shared religious belief." *Political Liberalism*, p. 37. This claim is echoed by Stark and Finke: "Thus, no single religious organization can achieve monopoly through voluntary assent – religious monopolies rest upon coercion." *Acts of Faith: Explaining the Human Side of Religion* (Berkeley: University of California Press, 2000), p. 199.
19. I should note that Rawls's explanation as to why liberalism generates pluralism is only part of a complete explanation. Another significant component of the explanation will, no doubt, incorporate Roger Finke and Rodney Stark's market-oriented explanation. They write:

> The "natural" state of religious economies is one in which a variety of religious groups successfully caters to the special needs and interests of specific market segments. This variety arises because of the inherent inability of a single product to satisfy very divergent tastes. Or, to note the specific features of religious firms and products, pluralism arises because of the inability of a single religious organization to be at once worldly and otherworldly, strict and permissive, exclusive and inclusive, while the market will always contain distinct consumer segments with strong preferences on each of these aspects of faith. This occurs because of "normal" variations in the human condition such as social class, age, gender, health, life experiences, and socialization.

Roger Finke and Rodney Stark, *The Churching of America*, p. 18. See also Rodney Stark and Laurence R. Iannaccone, "A Supply-Side Reinterpretation of the 'Secularization' of Europe," *Journal for the Scientific Study of Religion* 33 (1994): 233; Rodney Stark and Roger Finke, *Acts of Faith*, pp. 193–217.
20. Suggested but not developed by Berger in *The Sacred Canopy*, p. 47.
21. Peter Laslett, *The World We Have Lost: Further Explored*, 3rd ed. (New York: Charles Scribner's Sons, 1984), p. 71.
22. Steve Bruce, *Choice and Religion*, p. 20.
23. Jon Butler, *Awash in a Sea of Faith*, pp. 14–15. Note, by contrast, David Martin's observation that "buildings can be viewed as declarations of cultural war," as illustrated by the resistance to "mosques being built in the *centre* of Bradford or temples erected in key areas of North Dallas." *Does Christianity Cause War?* (Oxford: Oxford University Press, 1997), p. 72.

24. Those familiar with Berger's work will realize how heavily my thought experiment depends on his approach to the sociology of religion.

25. Peter Berger, Brigitte Berger and Hansfried Kellner, *The Homeless Mind: Modernization and Consciousness* (New York: Vintage Books, 1973), p. 81. Virtually the same claim is defended by Steve Bruce: "This is the cancer of choice. To the extent that we are free to choose our religion, religion cannot have the power and authority necessary to make it more than a private leisure activity. Far from creating a world in which religion can thrive, diversity and competition undermine the plausibility of religion. The crucial question for the possibility of religious revival is this: can we forget our individual autonomy? I do not think so. We have been expelled from that particular Garden of Eden and there is no possibility of return." *Choice and Religion*, p. 186.

26. For a fascinating critique of this interpretation of European history, see Rodney Stark and Laurence Iannaccone, "A Supply-Side Reinterpretation of the 'Secularization' of Europe."

27. See, for example, *The Sacred Canopy*, pp. 151–52.

28. Rodney Stark and Roger Finke, *Acts of Faith*, p. 222.

29. This way of conceiving of the relation between pluralism and secularization is consistent with Mark Chaves's claim that the theory of secularization predicts a decline in religious authority, not religion in general. See "Secularization as Declining Religious Authority," *Social Forces* 72 (March, 1994): 752, 754, 759. See also David Yamane, "Secularization on Trial: In Defense of a Neosecularization Paradigm," *Journal for the Scientific Study of Religion* 36 (1997): 113f.

30. See Steve Bruce, *Choice and Religion*, p. 9.

31. *The Sacred Canopy*, p. 130. I've interpreted the claim that pluralism generates secularization in a way that comports, or at least appears to comport, with Mark Chaves's suggestion that we abandon "religion as secularization's object, replacing it with religious authority." "Secularization as Declining Religious Authority," p. 754. Insofar as an agent's adherence to a given religious tradition is justified by reference to her preferences, we should expect the appeal to that tradition to lack a certain sort of authority.

32. In fact, Berger has recently recanted his support for the theory of secularization. "There has been the proposition, which in an earlier part of my own life I supported, that modernization causes secularization. I think that we can say that the data ... falsifies that proposition. Period. It has to be thrown out. I have thrown it out. It's wrong. Because if that were a generally tenable theory, the United States is an important enough case where you have to decide it has been falsified." Cited in "The Story of an Encounter," *Unsecular America*, Richard John Neuhaus, ed. (Grand Rapids, MI: William B. Eerdmans, 1986), pp. 84–85. Others, however, continue to accept the very arguments Berger now disavows. See, for example, Steve Bruce, *Religion in the Modern World*, pp. 43–47; Steve Bruce, *Choice and Religion*, passim.

33. Smith is neither the first nor the only critic of the theory of secularization to make the point that pluralism encourages religious vitality. For example, Rodney Stark and Roger Finke have made that case from the perspective of rational choice theory. The historian, Callum G. Brown, defends the same point; see "A Revisionist Approach to Religious Change," pp. 37f. I focus on Smith's argument, however, since his claim that pluralism encourages the vitality of politically active but normatively distinctive religious subcultures articulates exceptionally well with the concerns that motivate much of the discussion of the proper role of religious convictions in politics.

34. *American Evangelicalism: Embattled and Thriving* (Chicago, IL: University of Chicago Press, 1998), pp. 90f.

35. Charles Taylor, whom Smith cites, has argued powerfully for some such conception of personhood and identity. Taylor writes,

> The claim is that living within ... strongly qualified horizons is constitutive of human agency, that stepping outside these limits would be tantamount to stepping outside what we would recognize as integral, that is, undamaged, human personality. Perhaps the best way to see this is to focus on the issue that we usually describe today as the question of identity. We speak of it in these terms because the question is often spontaneously phrased by people in the form: Who am I? But this can't necessarily be answered by giving name and genealogy. What does answer this question for us is an understanding of what is of crucial importance to us. To know who I am is a species of knowing where I stand. My identity is defined by the commitments and identifications which provide the frame or horizon within which I can try to determine from case to case what is good, or valuable, or what ought to be done, or what I endorse or oppose. In other words, it is the horizon within which I am capable of taking a stand."

    Sources of the Self (Cambridge, MA: Harvard University Press, 1989), p. 27. See also the first several essays in *Human Agency and Language* (Cambridge: Cambridge University Press, 1985).

36. *American Evangelicalism*, p. 90, italics omitted. Berger shares Smith's assumption that humans have an innate drive for meaning.

37. This approach to religion is also foundational to Stark and Finke's application of rational choice theory to religion. See *Acts of Faith*, p. 35.

38. To take a familiar analogy: a game cannot exist without rules that determine how the game is to be played, who may play that game, under what conditions they may play that game, and so on. The rules of a game make possible the existence of that game. So, just as there are no footballs without the "constitutive" rules of the game of football (there are only pigskins filled with air), so also are there no football players, no associations of football players, no football teams without the requisite constitutive rules.

39. Of course, the phenomenon of community construction by means of boundary setting is not unique to religious social groups: one is a Southerner, for example, in virtue of the way one speaks, the food one eats, and so on. *American Evangelicalism*, p. 93.

40. *American Evangelicalism*, p. 105.

41. *American Evangelicalism,* p. 105. It is helpful to note, as Smith does, that reference groups are not tied to geographical proximity. Given the requisite technology, a person's reference group can be scattered quite widely.
42. *Liberal Virtues,* p. 226.
43. "Why We Can't All Just Get Along," p. 20.
44. For a very different, although complementary, argument in support of this claim, see Rodney Stark and Roger Finke, *Acts of Faith,* pp. 193–217.
45. *American Evangelicalism,* p. 115.
46. Perhaps the following claim is also true: since a religious market that lacks pluralism provides inadequate resources for intergroup friction and conflict, a religious market that lacks pluralism has a tendency to undermine the cohesion of and commitment to religious groups. That claim isn't entailed by, but comports well with, Smith's claim that pluralism provides rich resources for conflict and thus invigorates religious groups.
47. *American Evangelicalism,* p. 118.
48. *American Evangelicalism,* pp. 118–19. From their very different, but complementary theoretical perspective, Finke and Stark also claim that "degree of tension" with the cultural environment is crucial to religious vitality. See *The Churching of America,* pp. 40, 148, 150, 237–38.
49. Smith measures the strength of a given religious group by six indices: whether members (1) faithfully adhere to essential doctrines, (2) regard their faith commitment as vitally important, (3) are confident in their religious beliefs, (4) participate regularly in church activities, (5) are committed to the mission of the group, and (6) enjoy high rates of member retention. On the basis of extensive polling and interviews, Smith claims that those who identify themselves as evangelicals score consistently higher according to these indicators than do those who identify themselves as fundamentalists, mainline Christians, or liberals. *American Evangelicalism,* pp. 20–66.
50. *American Evangelicalism,* pp. 148–49.
51. *American Evangelicalism,* pp. 145–47.
52. *American Evangelicalism,* p. 150. Evangelical theologian Carl Henry expresses the evangelical attitude of engaged confrontation in the following way: "The Evangelical Christian challenges the current normative mode of American politics. He does so in a manner different than the radical Anabaptist tradition, which rejects direct political participation and encourages negative criticism. While Evangelicals emphasize the church's distinctive community witness within society, they also advocate direct political participation." "Making Political Decisions: An Evangelical Perspective," *Piety and Politics: Evangelicals and Fundamentalists Confront the World,* Richard John Neuhaus and Michael Cromartie, eds. (Washington, DC: Ethics and Public Policy Center, 1987), p. 101.
53. *Public Religions in the Modern World* (Chicago, IL: University of Chicago Press, 1994), pp. 7, 19–39, 211.
54. *Public Religions in the Modern World,* pp. 20–25.
55. *Public Religions in the Modern World,* p. 20.
56. *Public Religions in the Modern World,* pp. 35–39.

57. Smith's criticism of the theory of secularization thus comports with Casanova's conclusions on the matter: "The central thesis of the present study is that we are witnessing a 'deprivatization' of religion in the modern world. By deprivatization I mean the fact that religious traditions throughout the world are refusing to accept the marginal and privatized role which theories of modernity as well as theories of secularization had reserved for them. . . . [R]eligious institutions and organizations refuse to restrict themselves to the pastoral care of individual souls and continue to raise questions about the interconnections of private and public morality and to challenge the claims of . . . states and markets . . . to be exempt from extraneous normative considerations." *Public Religions in the Modern World*, p. 5.

58. Again, Smith's critique of the theory of secularization is consistent with Casanova's conclusions. Casanova writes, "Concerning the first thesis, that of secularization as differentiation, it is a central claim of this study that this remains the valid core of the theory of secularization. The differentiation and emancipation of the secular spheres from religious institutions and norms remains a general modern structural trend." *Public Religions in the Modern World*, p. 212; see also pp. 6, 40.

59. *Public Religions in the Modern World*, p. 214. If Casanova is correct, the fact that there was never a formally established religion in the United States, unlike the situation in Europe, is central to any adequate explanation of the pervasive religiosity of Americans and equally pervasive secularity of Europeans. "What America never had was an absolutist state and its ecclesiastical counterpart, a caesaropapist state church. This is what truly distinguishes American and European Protestantism. . . . It was the caesaropapist embrace of throne and altar under absolutism that perhaps more than anything else determined the decline of church religion in Europe. . . . One may say that it was the very attempt to preserve and prolong Christendom in every nation-state and thus to resist modern functional differentiation that nearly destroyed the churches in Europe." *Public Religions in the Modern World*, p. 29.

60. *The Churching of America*, p. 39; *Acts of Faith*, pp. 218–58.

61. See R. Stephen Warner, "Work in Progress toward a New Paradigm for the Sociological Study of Religion in the United States," *American Journal of Sociology* 98/5 (March, 1993): 1044–93.

62. Gary North, a leading Christian Reconstructionist, writes: "The long-term goal of Christians in politics should be to gain exclusive control over the franchise. Those who refuse to submit publicly to the eternal sanctions of God by submitting to His Church's public marks of the covenant – baptism and holy communion – must be denied citizenship, just as they were in ancient Israel." *Political Polytheism: The Myth of Pluralism* (Tyler, TX: Institute for Christian Economics, 1989), p. 87.

63. *Christian America?: What Evangelicals Really Want* (Berkeley: University of California Press, 2000), p. 26, italics removed. Smith comments: "A . . . striking implication of this definition is the importance it places on religious pluralism and toleration. When evangelicals think of 'Christian America'

this way, they are not laying the discursive groundwork for the legitimation of Christian social domination. If anything, they are tapping a historical tradition of freedom and choice that reinforces the value of religious pluralism and liberty." *Christian America?* p. 26.

64. *Christian America?* p. 27, italics removed.
65. *Christian America?* p. 29. Smith comments: "A careful reading of our interview discussions reveals that many interviewees defined 'Christian nation' in terms of representative government and the balance of powers. A Bible Fellowship man from Pennsylvania, for example, claimed that 'The idea of having a balanced government with the three branches – the executive, legislative, and judicial – that original theory was something that was derived from a scriptural passage.'" *Christian America?* p. 29.
66. *Christian America?* p. 30, italics removed.
67. *Christian America?* p. 32.
68. *Christian America?* p. 35.
69. *Christian America?* p. 37.
70. That is the conclusion Smith draws from his research: "Most of these evangelicals, then, appear to be baptizing the American system of government with Christian legitimacy rather than seeking to reconstruct American government according to specific and exclusionary Christian principles – whatever those might be." *Christian America?* p. 30. Clyde Wilcox reaches comparable conclusions regarding the Christian Right (not surprisingly, given that evangelicals are a crucially important constituency of Christian Right institutions): "Those who most fear the Christian Right wonder if its elites could ever seize power and control American politics, perhaps someday ruling by force as the Nazis did in Germany. Such fears are almost certainly unfounded. Most leaders of the Christian Right are committed to the democratic process and strongly supportive of the American political system. Although some Christian Right activists would like to restrict the civil liberties of their political opponents, only a few isolated extremists would abolish elections and seek to rule by force [Christian Reconstructionists].... This means that liberals' worst nightmares of an American theocracy are probably just nightmares." *Onward Christian Soldiers?* pp. 141–42. See also Alan Wolfe, "Civil Religion Revisited," pp. 56–57.
71. Religious traditions that encourage their adherents to bring their religious commitments into the political sphere are, in short, "likely to persist over generations and to gain a sizable body of adherents in a more or less just constitutional regime." John Rawls, *Political Liberalism*, p. 15.

Chapter Three

1. The reader should note that this description of justificatory liberalism applies to citizens and to coercive laws; I explain, if not justify, that way of characterizing justificatory liberalism in 3.1. I should also note that not all justificatory liberals derive their restrictions on religion by appealing

to a broader constraint on public justification. (Robert Audi, for example, explicitly denies that the strictures he imposes on religious convictions in political decision making and advocacy depend for their legitimacy on an appeal to public justification. See *Religious Commitment and Secular Reason*, p. 68.)

2. There is virtual unanimity among justificatory liberals on the claim that the exercise of power in a pluralistic democracy generates the central problem that justificatory liberals aspire to resolve. See, for example, John Rawls, *Political Liberalism*, p. 136; Lawrence Solum, "Faith and Justice," p. 1088; Charles Larmore, "Political Liberalism," p. 122; Charles Larmore, *Patterns of Moral Complexity* (Cambridge: Cambridge University Press, 1987), pp. xii–xiii, 43; Charles Larmore, "The Moral Basis of Liberalism," p. 607; Paul Weithman, "Religion and the Liberalism of Reasoned Respect," *Religion and Contemporary Liberalism*, Paul Weithman, ed. (Notre Dame, IN: University of Notre Dame Press, 1997), p. 5. Critics have also noted the importance of cultural pluralism to the justificatory liberal as well. See, for example, Joseph Raz, "Facing Diversity," *Philosophy and Public Affairs* 10/1 (Winter, 1990): 3; Michael Perry, *Love and Power* (Oxford: Oxford University Press, 1991), p. 8. Note that the claim that justificatory liberals aspire to resolve problems generated by pluralism does not entail the claim that justificatory liberals are ambivalent or antipathetic to pluralism. One can be entirely enthusiastic about pluralism while recognizing that it generates problems requiring resolution.

3. *Justice as Impartiality* (Oxford: Oxford University Press, 1995), p. 111.

4. Thus Amy Gutmann and Dennis Thompson: "Having good reason as individuals to believe that a policy is just does not mean that collectively as citizens we have sufficient justification to legislate on the basis of those reasons. The moral authority of collective judgments about policy depends in part on the moral quality of the process by which citizens collectively reach those results." *Democracy and Disagreement*, p. 4.

5. Stephen Macedo, "The Politics of Justification," *Political Theory* 18 (1990): 295. John Rawls expresses the same aspiration: "Citizens realize that they cannot reach agreement or even approach mutual understanding on the basis of their irreconcilable comprehensive doctrines. In view of this, they need to consider what kinds of reasons they may reasonably give one another when fundamental political questions are at stake." "The Idea of Public Reason Revisited," *The University of Chicago Law Review* 64/3 (Summer, 1997): 766. Bruce Ackerman does as well: "Just as you and I try to stick to the point when we are building a car or worshiping god, so too liberal citizens must exercise a similar kind of self-control when engaging in liberal politics – joining together neither to build a better Buick nor to save men's souls, but to solve the conflicts of social life on terms that all participants may find reasonable." "Why Dialogue?" *Journal of Philosophy* 86/1 (January 1989): 20. See also John Rawls, *Political Liberalism*, pp. 138f.; Amy Gutmann and Dennis Thompson, "Moral Conflict and Political Consensus,"

pp. 64f.; Amy Gutmann and Dennis Thompson, *Democracy and Disagreement*, pp. 25–26; Charles Larmore, *Patterns of Moral Complexity*, p. 75.

6. *Liberal Virtues*, pp. 40–41.
7. "Political Liberalism," *The Morals of Modernity*, p. 125.
8. *Democracy and Disagreement*, p. 50.
9. As George Sher points out, there is virtual unanimity on this claim, both among justificatory liberals and their critics. *Beyond Neutrality: Perfectionism and Politics* (Cambridge: Cambridge University Press, 1997), p. 23. On the distinction between constraints on reasons for political decisions and political decisions themselves, see Charles Larmore, *Patterns of Moral Complexity*, p. 44 and Peter de Marneffe, "Liberalism, Liberty, and Neutrality," *Philosophy and Public Affairs* 19/3 (1990): 253f.
10. "The Idea of Public Reason Revisited," p. 795. The passage I have cited concludes with the qualification that the idea of public reason, or public justification as I will call it, concerns only "fundamental political questions," by which Rawls means matters of basic justice and constitutional matters. ("The Idea of Public Reason Revisited," p. 795.) I will not, in the ensuing discussion, restrict the scope of laws and policies for which a citizen requires a public justification to just fundamental political questions.
11. "Political Liberalism," *The Morals of Modernity*, p. 137.
12. *A Theory of Justice* (Cambridge, MA: The Belknap Press, 1971), pp. 337–38.
13. *Liberal Virtues*, p. 249. See also p. 47.
14. "The Liberalism of Reasoned Respect," p. 6.
15. "The Place of Religious Argument in a Free and Democratic Society," *San Diego Law Review* 30 (Fall, 1993): 701.
16. "Faith and Justice," p. 1095. For other endorsements of the claim that respect requires public justification, see Gerald Gaus, *Justificatory Liberalism*, p. 182; Kai Nielson, "Liberal Reasonability," p. 750; Colin Bird, "Mutual Respect and Neutral Justification," *Ethics* 107 (October, 1996), passim; Amy Gutmann and Dennis Thompson, *Democracy and Disagreement*, pp. 39f.
17. I should note that although many of the points I make about citizens can be applied readily to legislators and judges as well, caution should be exercised in the application. After all, it is perfectly reasonable to suppose that different obligations attend different social roles, so that what we may appropriately expect of citizens is forbidden to legislators or judges (and vice versa). That said, I don't believe that it would be wise or practicable to require citizens and legislators to decide which laws merit their support in fundamentally different ways. I think that Kent Greenawalt is correct that a "sharp discontinuity" would create "unfortunate tension." *Private Consciences and Public Reasons* (Oxford: Oxford University Press, 1995), p. 151. See also Kent Greenawalt, *Religious Convictions and Political Choice*, pp. 10–11; Jeremy Waldron, "Religious Contributions in Public Deliberation," *San Diego Law Review* 30 (1993): 827f.; Michael Perry, *Religion in Politics*, pp. 130–31, fn. 41.

18. See, for example, Paul Weithman, "Rawlsian Liberalism and the Privatization of Religion," *Journal of Religious Ethics* 22 (1994): 14; Amy Gutmann and Dennis Thompson, *Democracy and Disagreement*, p. 91; Lawrence Solum, "Constructing an Ideal of Public Reason," *San Diego Law Review* 30 (1993): 737; Stephen Macedo, "Transformative Constitutionalism and the Case of Religion," *Political Theory* 26/1 (February, 1998): 71; John Rawls, "The Idea of Public Reason Revisited," p. 769.
19. *Religious Commitment and Secular Reason*, p. 85.
20. *Religious Commitment and Secular Reason*, p. 92.
21. See Philip Quinn, "Political Liberalisms and Their Exclusion of the Religious," *Proceedings and Addresses of the American Philosophical Society* 69/2 (1995): 37.
22. See H. L. A. Hart, *Law, Liberty, and Morality* (Stanford, CA: Stanford University Press, 1963), p. 21; Robert Merrihew Adams, *Finite and Infinite Goods* (Oxford: Oxford University Press, 1999), p. 326. Punishment can take various forms, most notably the infliction of physical pain, forcible confinement, or levying financial penalties.
23. John Rawls and Charles Larmore, among others, have defended this claim. See John Rawls, *Political Liberalism*, pp. xlvi, 214–15, 227–30; Charles Larmore, "Political Liberalism," p. 126. Amy Gutmann and Dennis Thompson have defended the broader claim (*Democracy and Disagreement*, pp. 50, 377, fn. 44), as has Lawrence Solum, "Constructing an Ideal of Public Reason," pp. 738–39. I should note that Rawls's reason for limiting the scope of the public justification constraint seems to be that doing so gives the case for public justification its best chance of success, not because there is some deep or principled distinction between coercive laws and laws that bear on constitutional matters.
24. "Constructing an Ideal of Public Reason," p. 738.
25. There are other plausible arguments against the claim that citizens should exercise restraint only regarding fundamental matters. Kent Greenawalt, for example, rejects that position on the basis that the distinction between fundamental and derivative matters is too blurred for the citizens and legislators who are supposed to exercise restraint to employ that distinction effectively. See *Private Consciences and Public Reasons*, pp. 106–20.
26. This seems particularly apparent if we grant, as I believe, that there is no morally relevant difference between getting the state to do something and stopping the state from doing something in the sense that state *action* need not be any more or any less morally objectionable than state *inaction*. The state's failure to protect Jewish people from pogroms can be just as morally objectionable as is the state's active discrimination against Jewish people.
27. Consider in this regard Bruce Ackerman's claim: "*If* there is anything distinctive about liberalism, it must be in the *kinds of reasons* liberals rely on to legitimate their claims to scarce resources. Nazis are not liberals because there is *something* about the reasons they give in support of their claims that is inconsistent with the organizing principles of liberal power talk." *Social*

Justice and the Liberal State, p. 7. As I see it, the most crucial difference between mere liberalism and Nazism has *nothing* to do with the reasons on the basis of which Nazis and liberals support their characteristic policies, and *everything* to do with the sorts of policies they support. The defining characteristic of Nazism – *mere* Nazism – is its commitment to various racist policies, nationalism, authoritarianism, militarism, and the like. By contrast, the defining characteristic of liberalism – *mere* liberalism – is its commitment to the very freedoms Nazis are unwilling to support. Of course, liberals are free also to require that the substantive commitments that distinguish the liberal from the Nazi are amenable to a certain sort of rationale – a public justification. In that case they are not mere but justificatory liberals. But the same basic move is open to the Nazi: as a conceptual matter, there is such a thing as *justificatory Nazism*, just as there is such a thing as justificatory communism, socialism, and the like.

28. I take no stand on the understanding of religious freedom a citizen ought to adopt: I take there to be reasonable differences of opinion among good liberal citizens both on what constitutes religious freedom and about the implications of that right for specific issues. Of course, I *am* committed to the claim that a citizen who supports his favored coercive laws solely on the basis of his religious commitments doesn't violate his compatriots' right to religious freedom – he isn't imposing his religious commitments on them in a way that violates their religious freedom. And I take it to be clear that he doesn't: that a citizen (or a majority of citizens) supports, say, a flat tax solely on religious grounds does not transmute that flat tax into a religious imposition. Given that, on any reasonable understanding of the matter, the state appropriately taxes its citizens – given that taxation falls under the legitimate jurisdiction of the state – support for a flat tax solely on religious grounds doesn't count as a violation of religious freedom.

29. George Sher makes this point effectively in *Beyond Neutrality*, pp. 5–7.

30. I'll argue for this constraint and for several others in 4.0.

31. John Stuart Mill, *On Liberty* (New York: Penguin Books, 1974), p. 68.

32. Thus, Kent Greenawalt claims that "to support prohibition in a liberal society, one must be able to point to some genuine damage to individuals or society (or other entities)" and at the same time rejects, at least in some cases, the sorts of strictures on religious grounds I have imputed to justificatory liberals. (*Religious Convictions and Political Choice*, p. 94.) As I read him, Greenawalt argues that a citizen is permitted to rely solely on her religious convictions in political decision making but she is not so permitted in political advocacy.

33. Thus in the following passage, Jerry Falwell articulates an argument that has obvious implications for the legal status of homosexuality, that clearly satisfies the principle of harm, but that doesn't constitute a public justification.

> The rise and fall of nations confirm to the Scripture. . . . Psalm 9:17 admonishes "The wicked shall be turned into hell, and all the nations that forget

God." America will be no exception. If she forgets God, she too will face His wrath and judgment like every other nation in the history of humanity. But we have the promise of Psalm 33:12, which declares "Blessed is the nation whose [God] is the Lord." When a nation's ways please the Lord, that nation is blessed with supernatural help.

Cited in Clyde Wilcox, *Onward Christian Soldiers?* p. 17. Falwell's association of moral uprightness with divine blessing for a nation and of moral corruption with divine punishment of a nation is clearly applicable to a wide variety of political disputes, such as abortion, economic justice, racial justice, and welfare policy.

34. My attempt to explicate the concept of public justification by contrasting it with the concept of rational justification might seem a fruitlessly obfuscatory exercise. After all, the concept of rational justification is paradigmatically protean: there are few concepts that have been construed, used, and abused in as many different ways as that of rational justification. Consequently, it might seem pointless to explicate the notion of public justification by contrasting it with something so obscure. While I have a great deal of sympathy for this objection, and might be better off employing a different concept, such as entitlement, warrant, or reliability, I persist in thinking that the notion of rational justification has a stable and useful core. That core is constituted by the two components I mention, all too briefly, in the text, namely, formation of belief in the appropriate manner and adequacy of reason for belief as judged from some particular perspective.

35. I refer in what follows to the rationality of *beliefs* but the application to support for *laws* is direct.

36. "In part" because a necessary condition of a citizen's having formed beliefs rationally is that she has formed her beliefs in the appropriate manner. So the rational justification of Jack's theistic commitments don't depend just on the contents of his evidential set – perhaps Jack's evidential set ought to have been different as a consequence of his having an obligation to adhere to procedures he has in fact neglected such that his theistic commitments would seem irrational as judged from what his evidential set ought to have been.

37. See William Alston, "Concepts of Epistemic Justification," in *Epistemic Justification: Essays in the Theory of Knowledge* (Ithaca, NY: Cornell University Press, 1989), pp. 82–83; "Level Confusions in Epistemology," *Epistemic Justification*, p. 166; "Justification and Knowledge," *Epistemic Justification*, p. 180; "An Internalist Externalism," *Epistemic Justification*, p. 235.

38. "The Idea of Public Reason Revisited," p. 786. In this section, I have tended to explicate the concept of public justification in populist terms, as I believe that a populist conception of public justification comports most naturally with the justificatory liberal's commitment to respect. See 7.0.

39. Amy Gutmann and Dennis Thompson, *Democracy and Disagreement*, p. 85.

40. On this point, see Gerald Gaus, *Justificatory Liberalism*, pp. 147–48.

41. Of course, soundness is also necessary neither for rationality nor public justification.

42. Such a rationale would "articulate" with others' points of view in a vanishingly weak sense: a citizen's compatriots *can* regard her rationale as convincing in that there is some possible world in which each of her compatriots would regard that rationale as convincing, even though they have no reason in the actual world to regard that rationale as convincing.

43. "Liberal Democracy and the Place of Religion in Politics," p. 16. A recent essay by Charles Larmore also exemplifies the confusion between pursuing public justification and exercising restraint. At one point, Larmore claims that the "moral core of liberal thought" is the commitment *"to seek* principles that can be the object of reasonable disagreement" among citizens of diverse points of view. ("The Moral Basis of Liberalism," p. 602, my emphasis.) The moral core of liberal thought is here characterized as a commitment to pursuing public justification. But several pages later Larmore switches to the doctrine of restraint. He writes: "It is this coercive character of political principles which we have in mind, when we hold with the assurance that we do ... that such principles must be the object of reasonable agreement. Our belief is that *only so* can the use of force to implement these principles be justified." ("The Moral Basis of Liberalism," p. 607, my emphasis.) A bit later, Larmore claims that "thus, to respect another person as an end is to *require* that coercive or political principles be as justifiable to that person as they presumably are to us." ("The Moral Basis of Liberalism," p. 608, my emphasis.) In these last two passages, Larmore claims that a given political principle is legitimate *only if* that principle is the object of reasonable agreement – and thus that citizens *should not* support political principles that are not the object of reasonable agreement. The first passage has to do with pursuing public justification, the second two with exercising restraint. Shortly after the third passage I have cited, Larmore reverts to the language of pursuing public justification: "On the contrary, the idea of respect is what directs us to *seek* the principles of our political life in the area of reasonable agreement." ("The Moral Basis of Liberalism," p. 608, my emphasis.)

    For other instances of a failure to distinguish between the obligation to pursue public justification and the obligation to exercise restraint, see Stephen Macedo, "Introduction," *Deliberative Politics: Essays on Democracy and Disagreement*, Stephen Macedo, ed. (Oxford: Oxford University Press, 1999), pp. 7–8; Stephen Macedo, "Liberal Civic Education and Religious Fundamentalism," pp. 477f.

44. "Liberal Democracy and the Place of Religion in Politics," p. 16, my italics.

45. As with Audi, John Rawls is particularly explicit on this point. He writes: "Suppose, then, that different combinations of values, or the same values weighted differently, tend to predominate in a particular fundamental case. Everyone appeals to political values but agreement is lacking and more than marginal differences persist. Should this happen, as it often

does, some may say that public reason fails to resolve the question, in which case citizens may legitimately invoke principles appealing to non-political values to resolve it in a way they find satisfactory. ... The ideal of public reason urges us not to do this in cases of constitutional essentials and matters of basic justice. Close agreement is rarely achieved and abandoning public reason whenever disagreement occurs in balancing values is in effect to abandon it altogether." *Political Liberalism*, pp. 240–41. See also Gerald Gaus, *Justificatory Liberalism*, pp. 182–84.

46. The distinction I have in mind is similar to that between the putative obligation to "prove that God exists" and the putative obligation not to believe in God if such proof is not in the offing. An agent can be fully committed to proving that God exists but reasonably refuse to cease believing in God because she doesn't enjoy that sort of evidence for her conviction that God exists. Now perhaps it is the case that those who can't prove that God exists should cease believing in God, but that conclusion cannot be reached simply by showing that theists have an obligation to do what they can to prove that God exists.

47. I assume that abstaining from supporting coercive policies isn't a realistic option.

48. *Justificatory Liberalism*, p. 162. Gaus's claim is false if he uses "justify" as an aspirational rather than a success term. For this important distinction, which complicates and complements the distinction under discussion, see 5.2.1.

49. I understand "theism" as belief in "God" where "God" denotes an omnipotent, omniscient, morally perfect person. Of course, this understanding of "religious ground" presupposes a substantive definition of religion, one that defines "religious" as "theistic." That is not an accident. Throughout this book, I focus on theistic religions, which seems appropriate to our topic, given that only theistic religions currently play an important political role in the United States.

50. The category of "secular ground" is the complement of "religious ground": a secular ground is any ground that lacks religious content. Paradigmatic secular grounds are, for example, a putative perception of a bird on a tree, the claim that each person has a right to own private property, the testimony of an authority in economics that lowering the capital gains tax increases investment in the stock market. Note that secularity is insufficient for publicity: some secular grounds are so idiosyncratic or controversial that they are utterly unconvincing to the members of the public and so don't constitute a public justification. Nevertheless, given conditions of pervasive religious pluralism, every public justification is constituted solely by secular grounds. So secularity is necessary but not sufficient for publicity.

51. The Poverty Reduction Act authorizes, among other things, cancellation of debts owed the United States by forty-five of the poorest countries for various loans and credits owed the United States.

52. See Kent Greenawalt, *Private Consciences and Public Reasons*, p. 63; Robert Audi, "The Separation of Church and State and the Obligations of Citizenship," *Philosophy and Public Affairs* 18/3 (1989): 279, 287f., 293; Lawrence Solum, "Constructing an Ideal of Public Reason," pp. 739ff.

53. Elijah's support for C constitutes what Robert Audi has called "mixed obligational overdetermination," which "occurs when there are both sufficient religious reasons *and* secular reasons for a kind of conduct." ("Liberal Democracy and the Place of Religion in Politics," p. 13. See also *Religious Commitment and Secular Reason*, p. 120.) Note that my assumption here is that the secular ground on the basis of which Elijah accepts C – the intuitive plausibility of C – persists in spite of his rejection of T. Elijah's secular grounds for C must remain constant in spite of changes in his religious convictions in order for him to accept C on secular grounds. By contrast, Elijah wouldn't have secular grounds for C in the following circumstances: he accepts C on the basis of T, rather than on secular grounds, but would, *as a consequence* of his rejection of T, acquire secular grounds for C. Although Elijah would, in that circumstance, continue to accept C even though he doesn't accept T (or any other theological claim), he doesn't do so on the basis of grounds that persist in spite of changes to his theological commitments, and thus doesn't support C on the basis of secular grounds prior to his rejection of T. My thanks to Terence Cuneo for raising this point.

54. Greenawalt explicitly notes the counterfactual component of reliance on religious convictions: "If a person knows he would oppose a law proscribing homosexual acts but for their scriptural condemnation, he is patently relying on religious conviction when he supports that law." (*Religious Convictions and Political Choice*, p. 36.) Suppose that Elijah regards C as intuitively plausible, would continue to regard C as intuitively plausible even in the absence of theological support, but doesn't believe that C is, by itself, sufficiently compelling to warrant supporting H. R. 1095. And suppose that he supplements C with theological claims that, together with C, are sufficiently compelling to warrant supporting H. R. 1095. Does Elijah support the Poverty Reduction Act on the basis of his religious convictions *alone*? As I have formulated the issue, he has: because his nonreligious grounds aren't by themselves sufficient to support H. R. 1095, Elijah supports that law on the basis of his religious convictions alone. I realize that the terminology I've decided to use is misleading: in this case, Elijah clearly doesn't support the proposed law on the basis of his religious convictions *alone*. More accurate would be the claim that his support for that law depends *essentially* on his religious convictions. Unfortunately, the more accurate terminology is more cumbersome, so I will have to ask the reader to bear in mind the limitation of my way of formulating the issue.

55. "The Role of Religion in Decision and Discussion of Political Issues," p. 73.

56. "Moral Conflict and Political Consensus," p. 65.

57. "Gag Rules of the Politics of Omission," *Constitutionalism and Democracy*, Jon Elster and Rune Slagstad, eds. (Cambridge: Cambridge University Press, 1988), p. 23.

58. See, for example, John Rawls, *Political Liberalism*, p. 220; Gerald Gaus, *Justificatory Liberalism*, pp. 142, 162–63; Thomas Nagel, "Moral Conflict and Political Legitimacy," p. 232; Lawrence Solum, "Faith and Justice," p. 1093; Lawrence Solum, "Constructing an Ideal of Public Reason," p. 731; Stephen Macedo, *Liberal Virtues*, pp. 52f.; Joshua Cohen, "Moral Pluralism and Political Consensus," p. 286; Colin Bird, "Mutual Respect and Neutral Justification," pp. 66, 72ff.; Amy Gutmann and Dennis Thompson, *Deliberative Democracy*, p. 56.

59. See Robert Audi, "Liberal Democracy and the Place of Religion in Politics," p. 13.

60. On the claim that justificatory liberalism privatizes religious belief, see, for example, Michael Sandel, *Democracy and Its Discontents* (Boston, MA: Harvard University Press, 1996), pp. 18f.; Roger Trigg, *Rationality and Religion* (Oxford: Blackwell, 1998), p. 16; Frederick Gedicks, "The Religious, the Secular and the Antithetical," *Capitol University Law Review* (1975): 113–145; Daniel Conkle, "Secular Fundamentalism, Religious Fundamentalism, and the Search for Truth in Contemporary America," *Journal of Law and Religion* 12/2 (1995–96): 345, 353–58. Abner Greene attributes this view (falsely, I believe) to Rawls: "Common ground can and should be found, argues Rawls, through public reason that proceeds through an overlapping consensus of comprehensive doctrines.... All normative doctrines – religious, philosophical, and moral – must accept this common ground of public reason and the concomitant silencing of sectarian views in lawmaking." "Uncommon Ground," p. 647.

61. Richard Rorty, "Religion as a Conversation-Stopper," *Common Knowledge* 3/1 (1994): 2.

62. "Wolterstorff on Religion, Politics, and the Liberal State," in Robert Audi and Nicholas Wolterstorff, *Religion in the Public Square*, p. 138. See also John Rawls, *Political Liberalism*, pp. li–lii; John Rawls, "The Idea of Public Reason Revisited," pp. 784ff; Paul Weithman, "Rawlsian Liberalism and the Privatization of Religion," pp. 3–28; Lawrence Solum, "Inclusive Public Reason," *Pacific Philosophical Quarterly* 75 (1994): 227; Lawrence Solum, "Constructing an Ideal of Public Reason," pp. 747–49; Robert Audi, "Liberal Democracy and the Place of Religion in Politics," pp. 50f. Robert Audi, "The Place of Religious Argument in a Free and Democratic Society," p. 694.

Chapter Four

1. I fear that I argue in some detail for conclusions that might strike many as obviously true. But overcompensation is warranted, in my opinion, because many of the extant attempts to articulate the argument from respect are insufficiently precise – they often amount to little more than an

expression of the "intuition" that respect requires something or other by way of restraint or public justification.

2. Stephen Darwall, "Two Kinds of Respect," *Ethics* 88/1 (October, 1977): 39. Darwall's distinction between appraisal and recognition respect is similar to Larmore's distinction between respect for beliefs and respect for persons as articulated in the latter's *Patterns of Moral Complexity*, pp. 59–66.

3. Stephen Darwall, "Two Kinds of Respect," p. 45.

4. Many justificatory liberals endorse this claim. Thus, Jeremy Waldron claims that liberals are committed to the "requirement that all aspects of the social world should either be made acceptable or be capable of being made acceptable to every last individual." "Theoretical Foundations of Liberalism," *Liberal Rights: Collected Papers 1981–1991* (Cambridge: Cambridge University Press, 1993), pp. 36–37. Gerald Gaus is equally clear on this point: "To publicly justify a principle is to show that each and every member of the public has conclusive reason to embrace it." *Justificatory Liberalism*, p. 209. So is Bruce Ackerman: "Like his contractarian comrade, the liberal is also dissatisfied with a utilitarian philosophy that makes an individual's rights depend upon the shifting preferences of his peers. Even if there were only a single person who questioned the legitimacy of his power position; even if the overwhelming majority passionately desired to suppress the questioner; the questioner's right to an answer remains fundamental in liberal theory. To silence this single dissenter would require the dominant coalition to declare that it has the right to treat the dissenter as merely a plaything for their own desires. Such a declaration breaks the dialogic bond that binds all citizens together to form a liberal state." *Social Justice and the Liberal State*, p. 340. See also Joshua Cohen, "Procedure and Substance in Deliberative Democracy," *Democracy and Difference*, Seyla Benhabib, ed. (Princeton, NJ: Princeton University Press, 1996), pp. 100, 102; Charles Larmore, "The Foundations of Modern Democracy," *The Morals of Modernity*, p. 220; Thomas Nagel, *Equality and Partiality* (New York: Oxford University Press, 1991), pp. 8, 33–40; John Rawls, *Political Liberalism*, pp. xlvi, 137, 217; John Rawls, "The Domain of the Political and Overlapping Consensus," *The Good Polity*, pp. 254ff.; and John Rawls, "The Idea of Public Reason Revisited," p. 770. Some justificatory liberals reject the unanimity requirement; for example, Lawrence Solum, "Novel Public Reasons," *Loyola of Los Angeles Law Review* 29 (1996): 1478.

5. A complementary point. The quality of a person's beliefs can vary in just the same way that the quality of a person's character traits can vary: some people's beliefs deserve our appraisal respect, some do not. Since a citizen ought to respect each of her compatriots, the sort of respect a citizen owes to them doesn't consist in her positive evaluation of, much less agreement with, their convictions. In the relevant sense of the notion of respect, a citizen can be thoroughly disgusted by her compatriots' convictions, or regard them as trivial or superficial, and nevertheless be committed to respecting her compatriots fully. In short, a citizen ought to respect *each* of her compatriots, not because she credits each one's character or beliefs, but,

if need be, *in spite of* each one's character or beliefs. See Charles Larmore, *Patterns of Moral Complexity*, p. 64.

6. Stephen Darwall, "Two Kinds of Respect," p. 40.

7. I have no intention of articulating a complete conception of personhood or of identifying necessary and sufficient conditions for personhood. I'm interested only in picking out a few relevant components about persons that serve my purposes.

8. Although what constitutes personhood is, to put it mildly, a contested topic, I think that we can characterize that notion in a sufficiently nonpartisan way to identify an understanding of the notion of respect for persons that is not unduly parochial. In the following account, I rely heavily on Charles Taylor's philosophical anthropology, although I haven't incorporated the more controverted elements of his account, for example, his claim that there is an internal relation between personhood and "strong evaluation."

9. To be clear, it is mattering itself that imposes moral constraints on us but mattering in combination with certain moral platitudes that bear on mattering, for example that we ought not gratuitously frustrate another person's cares and concerns.

10. See Charles Taylor, "Self-Interpreting Animals," *Human Agency and Language*, p. 60.

11. On the distinction between higher and lower level desires and commitments and the relation between that distinction and the concept of person, see Charles Taylor, "What Is Human Agency?" *Human Agency and Language*, pp. 15–44.

12. Understood thus, the fact about her fellow citizens to which a citizen ought to accord due weight is closely related to their autonomy, so long as autonomy is modestly "conceived of as a second-order capacity of persons to reflect critically upon their first-order preferences, desires, wishes, and so forth and the capacity to accept or attempt to change these in light of higher-order preferences and values," rather than the ability to reflect critically on first-order preferences, desires, wishes, and so forth in complete independence of other people, tradition, and so on. Gerald Dworkin, *The Theory and Practice of Autonomy* (Cambridge: Cambridge University Press, 1988), p. 20. See Charles Larmore, *Patterns of Moral Complexity*, p. 63.

13. Although I don't regard these two claims as particularly controversial, I'll articulate the argument in more detail than might seem necessary, as doing so will be helpful in setting up the later discussion of the relation between respect for persons, public justification, and restraint.

14. *Finite and Infinite Goods*, pp. 327–28, 335.

15. I take this claim to be at the heart of "mere" liberalism; nothing is original or excessively provocative here. Although I have reservations about some of his arguments, see Michael Perry's discussion of why we ought to be extremely reticent in coercing our compatriots in *Love and Power*, pp. 128–36. In addition to respect for our compatriots, compassion, the value of community and friendship, and self-interest should motivate us to practice what Perry calls "ecumenical political tolerance," that is, to make

judgments regarding right and wrong, moral and immoral, good from evil, "and sometimes to make them publicly, perhaps in the course of or as a conclusion to ecumenical political dialogue, but to refrain from coercing others on the basis of the judgments, especially to refrain from using the apparatus of the state to coerce others." *Love and Power*, p. 129.

16. *Love and Power*, p. 135.

17. I take the argument in this section to answer a question forcefully put by Nicholas Wolterstorff, who writes:

> Once again, then, it is obvious that the role of citizen involves restraints on the legislation advocated. But what is the rationale for *epistemological* restraints on the decisions and debates of citizens? That is, why should epistemological restraints be laid on a person *when the legislation advocated by that person does not violate the restraints on content* [that is, are not illiberal]? What difference does it make what reasons citizens use in making their decisions and conducting their debates, if the positions they advocate do not violate the Idea of liberal democracy?

"The Role of Religion in Decision and Discussion of Political Issues," p. 77. I take it that Brutus fails adequately to respect his compatriots just in virtue of his willingness to flaunt the canons of rationality when deciding which coercive laws to support. (I don't think Wolterstorff would disagree, but statements such as the one cited here might be read as a denial that Brutus violates the moral norms properly associated with the role of citizen.) Of course, it's quite another matter to infer from the claim that each citizen ought to withhold his support from coercive laws for which he lacks *rational justification* the further claim that each citizen ought to withhold his support from coercive laws for which he enjoys only a *religious rationale*. It's the latter claim Wolterstorff is most interested in denying, an aim with which I am entirely sympathetic.

18. I take it that the relation between the obligation to pursue rational justification and the obligation not to support any law for which one can't discern a rational justification is structurally the same as that between the obligation to pursue public justification and the obligation to exercise restraint. With respect to both sets of obligations, the first member of the set doesn't entail the second, whereas the second does entail the first.

19. Two brief notes about this point. First, I don't assume that Elijah's willingness to articulate a rationale for a favored coercive law by itself ameliorates his compatriots' distress: in fact, Elijah's articulation of a rationale could easily exacerbate his compatriots' distress if his rationale is particularly offensive. Rather, Elijah's articulation of a rationale ameliorates his compatriots' distress if he makes it clear *why* he addresses his compatriots, namely, because he accords significant value to the fact that his compatriots are agents. Second, mitigation isn't compensation: the fact that Elijah articulates a rationale for a favored coercive law is highly unlikely to "outweigh" the distress generated by his support for that coercive law, particularly if his compatriots regard that law as quite objectionable.

20. *Liberal Purposes: Goods, Virtues, and Diversity in the Liberal State* (Cambridge: Cambridge University Press, 1991), p. 109.
21. Two points about this claim. First, it seems clear that the range of conceptions of public justification available to the justificatory liberal are constrained by the arguments she regards as providing support for the claim that a citizen ought to adhere to the principle of pursuit and doctrine of restraint: an argument to the conclusion that respect requires a citizen to pursue a rationale that her compatriots *actually accept* will provide no support for a conception of public justification according to which a public justification is a rationale that contains premises citizens *would* accept *if* they were fully rational and adequately informed. Second, although some conceptions of public justification are ruled out by the justificatory liberal's arguments in support of the claim that a citizen ought to adhere to the principle of pursuit and doctrine of restraint, it seems clear that there are a number of alternative conceptions that can satisfy a given argument, and that, within that range of acceptable conceptions, some conceptions are preferable to others.
22. See Chapter 7.
23. Lowering his expectations to this level might move Elijah out of the "populist" camp and into the "epistemic" camp: sometimes the notion of in principle accessibility is understood in populist terms and sometimes it seems to indicate a purely epistemic property of a given rationale. I do not dispute the claim that the version of the argument from respect I've articulated in this chapter can be satisfied by nonpopulist conceptions of public justification. Again, for more on this, see Part III.
24. Thus, for example, Bruce Brower writes: "Principles meet the *publicity constraint* whenever they are justifiable by public reasons. This constraint requires more than that principles be justifiable to everyone. That requirement could be met by theories that permit individuals to have different self-interested reasons for accepting the same principle. An appeal to public reason is stronger: it requires that agents have reasons all would accept, not only that they all have reasons for a conclusion all would accept." "The Limits of Public Reason," *Journal of Philosophy* 91/1 (January, 1994): 5. To adopt this conception of public justification is not only not entailed by my argument for the claim that citizens should pursue public justification, but also renders an extremely demanding constraint utterly utopian. (Hence, it should come as no surprise that Brower ends up considerably weakening the publicity constraint.)
25. This *disjunctive* conception of public justification is endorsed by Gerald Gaus: "We can think, then, of a public justification as a set of arguments for a proposal; sometimes the set may contain only one argument, at other times it may contain several." *Justificatory Liberalism*, p. 146.
26. On this point, see Gerald Gaus, *Justificatory Liberalism*, p. 139.
27. More precisely, it strikes me as preferable that Elijah regard as sound both his religious rationale and at least one widely convincing argument for each coercive law he supports.

28. A brief word to dispel the air of unreality that might seem to emanate from this discussion of what might seem to be a thoroughly unrealistic constraint: pretty clearly, no one is able to consult all of the citizens in the United States whose judgment merits her admiration. As with each of the constraints I discuss in this chapter, what the constraint under discussion actually requires in a given case must be limited by considerations of resources, both temporal and material.

29. The notion of remoteness is incurably vague, and I won't even attempt to render it more precise.

30. As I noted in 2.0, citizens are not falsificationists regarding the claims constitutive of their moral identity, and it seems highly undesirable to require that they become falsificationists in order to be good liberal citizens.

31. *Religion in Politics*, p. 64.

32. *Pluralism: Against the Demand for Consensus* (Oxford: Clarendon Press, 1993), p. 163.

33. Nicholas Rescher, *Pluralism*, p. 164.

Chapter Five

1. Robert Audi is clear about the intuitive pull of the doctrine of restraint, at least as relevant to religious convictions. He writes, "For any of us who are religious, the prospect that we might be coerced by preferences based on some other religion is generally loathsome. Few have a similar reaction to coercion plausibly imposed for purposes of maintaining law and order or public health or a minimum level of education. Liberalism is in part a response to the intuitive difference nearly everyone feels in such cases." "Wolterstorff on Religion and Politics," p. 134.

2. I'm not claiming that the justificatory liberal is wrong to exemplify the refusal to exercise restraint by reference to folks like McCartney, Falwell, and Robertson. In order to indicate the importance of the justificatory liberal's position on the proper role of religious convictions in political decision making and advocacy, it's appropriate to refer to specific dangers that that position is intended to combat. Nevertheless, taking that tack risks occluding the central issue at stake: if the justificatory liberal regularly refers to citizens who are defective in a variety of respects that have nothing in particular to do with their violation of the doctrine of restraint, she risks confusing the problems associated with a refusal to exercise restraint and those associated with irrelevant factors.

3. See, for example, Harlan Beckley, "A Christian Affirmation of Rawls, Part I," pp. 210, 215; Joshua Cohen, "Moral Pluralism and Political Consensus," p. 286; Richard Rorty, "In Defense of Minimalist Liberalism," *Debating Democracy's Discontent: Essays on American Politics, Law, and Public Philosophy*, Anita L. Allen and Milton C. Regan, eds. (Oxford: Oxford University Press, 1998), p. 119; Ronald Dworkin, "Neutrality, Equality and Liberalism," *Liberalism Reconsidered*, Douglas MacLean and Claudia Mills, eds. (Totowa, NJ: Rowman and Allanheld, 1993), p. 1; Amy Gutmann and Dennis

Thompson, *Democracy and Disagreement*, p. 56; Ted Jelen, "In Defense of Religious Minimalism," *A Wall of Separation: Debating the Public Role of Religion* (Lanham, MD: Rowman and Littlefield, 1998), passim; Norman Daniels, "Reflective Equilibrium and Justice as Political," *Justice and Justification: Reflective Equilibrium in Theory and Practice* (Cambridge: Cambridge University Press, 1996), p. 167; Stephen Macedo, "Liberal Civic Education and Religious Fundamentalism," passim.

4. There is discussion in the literature of what Joshua Cohen has called "rationalist" versions of fundamentalism. ("Moral Pluralism and Political Consensus," p. 286.) In Cohen's discussion, rationalist fundamentalists are committed to providing nonsectarian reasons to accept their sectarian sources of knowledge – as when the apologist attempts to show that the Bible is reliable by appeal to purely historical arguments, and then, having shown on historical grounds that the Bible is reliable, the apologist takes the Bible as a source of moral authority and thus as a source of knowledge on which to rely when deciding which policies to support. Since, however, almost nobody but those already convinced that the Bible is reliable believe that those arguments are compelling, it's hard to take that tack as a serious attempt to provide a public justification. I have in mind a very different possibility: not a citizen who pursues public justification for religious claims that she then employs to justify a particular law, but a citizen who supports a given law solely on religious grounds but endeavors to provide a public justification that isn't "routed through" her religious commitments.

5. A brief note about this example. Given the various conceptions of public justification, it's difficult to construct an example of a citizen who lacks a public justification for a given law on every rendering of the concept of public justification. So different examples have to be constructed for different conceptions of public justification – a task I have no intention of pursuing at this point. Assume that the conception of public justification I employ here is one tied very closely to the actual convictions of the members of the public. That is, in the language I adopt in Part III, I am assuming a "populist" conception of public justification.

6. Of course, whether a given factor has a role to play in eliciting our differential reactions to the propriety of McCartney and Elijah's manner of supporting their respective policies will vary from person to person. I simply lay out a few possibilities.

7. As I will make clear later in this chapter, McCartney's inflammatory rhetoric constitutes an unwillingness to accommodate his compatriots and counts as disrespectful.

8. Solum articulates additional arguments in support of the doctrine of restraint, but those arguments make no appeal to the notion of respect. Since I'm interested only in the argument from respect, at least at this point, I ignore those additional arguments.

9. "Faith and Justice," pp. 1092–93. Solum articulates essentially the same argument elsewhere. Thus, he writes, "This argument begins with the premise that there is an ideal of full respect for fellow citizens as free and

equal. This ideal expresses the notion that one ought to treat one's fellow citizens as possessing an equal human reason that grounds their capacity to exercise their freedom. Treating one's fellows as reasonable in this sense requires that one gives them reasons when acting in a way that affects them; one such action might be voting on the coercive use of state power. The full requirements of this ideal include: (1) that I give fellow citizens reasons that they could accept as reasonable (i.e., I give them public reasons); (2) that I do not give them reasons that they could not accept as reasonable (i.e., I give them only public reasons); and (3) that I disclose to them all of the reasons that are the basis for my position (i.e., I make full disclosure)." "Inclusive Public Reason," p. 227. For reasons I won't discuss, Solum argues that we should relax the requirements of the ideal of full respect by dropping (2), thus arguing that respect requires only the inclusive version of the doctrine of restraint I have attributed to justificatory liberalism. (See 3.4.4.)

10. Solum's explicit claim is that a citizen who supports a policy on the basis of publicly *in*accessible reasons thereby *dis*respects her compatriots; more briefly, *lack* of public justification is sufficient for *dis*respect. This claim is logically equivalent to the claim that a necessary condition of respect is public justification.

11. In Solum's case, a citizen provides a public justification for a given law just in case she articulates publicly accessible reasons for that law; otherwise put, Solum's *conception* of public justification requires a citizen to articulate *publicly accessible reasons* for her favored coercive laws. I do not dispute Solum's conception of public justification at this point, although I believe that it is inadequate. I turn to that question in Part III.

12. Note that, in the cited passage, Solum does not explicitly distinguish between a citizen who supports her favored coercive laws on the basis of her religious beliefs and one who supports her favored laws on the basis of her religious beliefs alone. But Solum does accept that distinction and, at least for citizens if not for judges, advocates the inclusive position that a citizen may support her favored coercive laws on the basis of her religious beliefs as long as she enjoys a complementary public justification for those laws. (See "Inclusive Public Reason," passim.) My exposition of Solum's argument assumes this point.

13. Examples of the use of "public justification" as a success term are legion; here is a sample. "Our theory of deliberative democracy expresses a set of principles that prescribe fair terms of cooperation. The most important principle is reciprocity, which says that citizens owe one another justifications for the laws they collectively enact." Amy Gutmann and Dennis Thompson, "Reply to Critics," *Deliberative Politics*, Stephen Macedo, ed., p. 244. "Liberal citizens must give reasons for their political demands, not just state preferences or make threats. Moreover, these reasons must be 'public' reasons, in the sense that they are capable of persuading people of different faiths or nationalities. Hence, it is not enough to invoke scripture or tradition." Will Kymlicka and Wayne Norman, "Return of the

Citizen," *Ethics* 104 (January, 1994): 366. "The aim, rather, is to suggest that the most basic political rights and institutions should be justified in terms of reasons and arguments that can be shared with reasonable people whose religious and other ultimate commitments differ. Religious beliefs are, on this account, regarded as no different than secular ideals of life as a whole. Neither Protestant fundamentalism nor Dewey's secular humanism are proper grounds for determining basic rights and constitutional principles." Stephen Macedo, "Liberal Civic Education and Religious Fundamentalism," p. 475.

14. My thanks to Philip Quinn and Terence Cuneo for valuable discussion of this point.

15. As I noted in 3.1, Larmore claims that the basic commitments of the liberal state – constitutional matters and matters of basic justice – ought to be publicly justifiable, but relaxes that constraint for less basic matters. I ignore this important qualification in my discussion, but nothing of significance, so far as I can tell, hangs on my ignoring that qualification.

16. *Patterns of Moral Complexity*, p. 64.

17. "Political Liberalism," p. 137. See also Charles Larmore, "The Moral Basis of Liberalism," pp. 607ff. Thomas Nagel makes essentially the same point: "When we force people to serve an end that they cannot share, and that we cannot justify to them in objective terms, it is a particularly serious violation of the Kantian requirement that we treat humanity not merely as a means, but also as an end. The justification of coercion must meet especially stringent standards." "Moral Conflict and Political Legitimacy," p. 238.

18. "Political Liberalism," p. 135.

19. I hesitate between the claim that it is possible that there is insufficient common ground to resolve the dispute over abortion and that it is likely for the following reason. Whether there is in fact common ground depends upon the content of large numbers of citizens' evidential sets. No one can decide that question by arm-chair reflection; in order to arrive at a definitive conclusion on the matter, we need to have a great deal of information about the states of mind of large numbers of people. Nevertheless, the persistent disagreement among the few who publicly articulate their convictions on the matter provides us with some reason to regard resolution as unlikely.

20. *Patterns of Moral Complexity*, p. 67.

21. *Patterns of Moral Complexity*, p. 67.

22. *Patterns of Moral Complexity*, p. 67.

23. *Patterns of Moral Complexity*, p. 68.

24. *Democracy and Disagreement*, pp. 84–85. "If citizens seek what we call an economy of moral disagreement, they will search for significant points of convergence between their own moral understandings and those of citizens whose positions, taken in their more comprehensive forms, they reject. They will seek the rationale for a law or public policy that minimizes rejection of the position they reject." (Amy Gutmann and Dennis Thompson,

"Reply to Critics," p. 261.) Gutmann and Thompson specify some important differences between their understanding of the economy of moral disagreement and Larmore's (see *Democracy and Disagreement*, p. 377, fn. 43), but the similarities are a great deal more apparent and important than the differences.

25. *Patterns of Moral Complexity*, p. 46.
26. *Justificatory Liberalism*, p. 122.
27. *Justificatory Liberalism*, p. 122.
28. *Justificatory Liberalism*, p. 124.
29. "For Betty to make moral demands on Alf when she knows they cannot be justified to him is to browbeat him." *Justificatory Liberalism*, p. 156.
30. *Justificatory Liberalism*, p. 129.
31. Gaus isn't alone in articulating this argument. James Sterba endorses basically the same argument: "Presumably, if the imposition of the majority will on the minority is to be fair, it must be possible to morally blame the minority for failing to accept that imposition. If that weren't the case, then the minority could justifiably resist that imposition, and the will of the majority would lack moral legitimacy. But if the imposition of the will of the majority is to be fair, there must, then, be sufficient reasons accessible to the minority, religious or otherwise, to morally require it to accept that imposition. For a group cannot be morally required to do something if they cannot come to know *and* so come justifiably to believe that they are so required. So fairness here requires that there be reasons accessible to a minority that are sufficient to require the acceptance of the will of the majority by that minority." "Reconciling Public Reason and Religious Values," *Social Theory and Practice* 25/1 (Spring, 1999): 8.
32. "Liberal Democracy and the Place of Religion in Politics," p. 25.
33. Audi applies the role reversal test to the issue of the role of religious convictions in political decision making and advocacy, although he does not connect that test to the norm of respect, in *Religious Commitment and Secular Reason*, p. 202.
34. "Wolterstorff on Religion and Politics," p. 141.
35. *Religious Commitment and Secular Reason*, p. 201. See also "Wolterstorff on Religion and Politics," p. 134.
36. "Liberal Democracy and the Place of Religion in Politics," p. 28. Audi formulates his role-reversal argument later in the same essay (p. 51) as follows: "What I may not do without adequate secular reason . . . is advocate or support *coercive* laws or public policies on this or other matters that concern me. That, too, is a kind of restraint I would wish to be observed by members of other religious groups who would want to coerce my behavior in the direction of their preferred standards."
37. *Moral Thinking: Its Levels, Method and Point* (Oxford: Oxford University Press, 1981), pp. 24–64.
38. I hesitate to claim that I would feel *resentment* because there is a close relationship between resentment and blameworthiness: I resent others for performing some action only if I'm willing to blame them for performing

that action. And I feel no inclination at all to blame a citizen for supporting a coercive law if she is rationally justified to a sufficiently high degree in regarding that law as morally appropriate, pursues public justification for that law, is sufficiently accommodating, and so on. Nevertheless, it seems to me that if a law is sufficiently objectionable, I can resent being subject to that law even if I don't blame those who support that law. Thus, for example, it would be appropriate for a slave to feel resentment regarding his condition as a consequence of the sheer injustice of that condition even if he thought that his owner didn't know any better.

39. Audi has suggested, in conversation, that his argument doesn't have this weakness, that it doesn't depend on the contingent reactions of just any citizens. Rather, his role-reversal test is supposed to apply to fully rational and adequately informed citizens: would fully rational and adequately informed citizens be willing to endorse a general policy permitting their compatriots to support coercive laws solely on religious grounds? But it seems likely to me that this move will ultimately turn out to beg the central question at issue: the manner in which we construe "full rationality" and "adequate information" will mirror our position on the merits of the doctrine of restraint. For substantiation of this suspicion, see 7.5.

40. *Political Liberalism*, p. 137.

41. *Political Liberalism*, pp. 217–18.

42. *Political Liberalism*, p. lv; see also pp. 240f.

43. Perry writes: "The question why a majority of citizens (we're talking about a democracy, after all) should abandon the coercive political choice they believe they should otherwise make just because, in their view, no premise that other citizens could (reasonably) accept supports the choice [the duty of civility] *is* the question why a majority of citizens may exercise political power over a citizen only if a premise or premises that they believe the citizen (understood as free and equal) could accept supports the majority's doing so [the liberal principle of legitimacy]." *Religion in Politics*, p. 58.

44. *Political Liberalism*, p. 225.

45. *A Theory of Justice*, pp. 175ff.

46. *A Theory of Justice*, p. 176.

47. *A Theory of Justice*, p. 176.

48. *A Theory of Justice*, p. 175.

49. *A Theory of Justice*, p. 176.

50. *A Theory of Justice*, p. 177.

51. See Brian Barry, *Justice as Impartiality*, p. 65.

52. True, the argument would be ad hominem, but since many justificatory liberals are taken with Rawls's machinery, perhaps the argument will have broad appeal. That said, it seems possible to articulate the argument without essential dependence on Rawls's machinery.

53. *Political Liberalism*, p. 213.

54. Quoted in Kenneth Wald, *Religion and Politics in the United States*, 3rd ed. (Washington, DC: Congressional Quarterly Press, 1997), p. 64.

55. "The Role of Religion in Decision and Discussion of Political Issues," p. 105.

56. See 2.4.1.
57. Michael Perry, *Morality, Politics and Law* (Oxford: Oxford University Press, 1988), pp. 181–82.
58. More cautiously, since there is no doubt some better alternative than the ideal of conscientious engagement: the parties in the original position will choose the ideal of conscientious engagement rather than the liberal principle of legitimacy when faced with a choice between only those two.
59. *A Theory of Justice*, p. 177.
60. *Understanding Rawls: A Reconstruction and Critique of* A Theory of Justice (Princeton: Princeton University Press, 1977), p. 127.
61. Norman Daniels, "Reflective Equilibrium and Justice as Political," p. 167.
62. "Reflective Equilibrium and Justice as Political," p. 167.
63. This response to my strains of commitment argument, it seems to me, exemplifies an unfortunately common tendency among those inclined to invoke the notion of reasonableness, namely, a tendency "to slide from the status of trivial to that of tendentious without any intervening argument, as the theorist quietly introduces her cherished opinions as to whether this or that seems reasonable." Richard Arneson, "The Priority of the Right over the Good Rides Again," *Ethics* 108 (October, 1997): 172. The treacherous nature of the appeal to "reasonableness" is commonly noted in the literature; Arneson's treatment of that subject in the essay just cited is a representative and trenchant formulation of that criticism. See also Paul Campos, "Secular Fundamentalism," *Columbia Law Review* 94 (1994): 1814–27. See as well Stanley Fish's "Mutual Respect as a Device of Conclusion," pp. 88–101, wherein Fish articulates what is, by my way of thinking, a convincing critique of the aforementioned tendency in Gutmann and Thompson's *Democracy and Disagreement*. This point will be important in the ensuing discussion of Rawls's conception of public reason in Chapter 7.
64. I have nothing but anecdotal evidence for this assertion.
65. Stephen Macedo, "Liberal Civic Education and Religious Fundamentalism," p. 482.
66. Stephen Macedo, "Liberal Civic Education and Religious Fundamentalism," p. 480.
67. I know of no theorist who denies the claim that it is a good and desirable thing for citizens to cooperate with one another by trying to articulate a public justification for their favored coercive laws. However, I have seen that view *attributed* to critics of justificatory liberalism. For example, Paul Weithman makes the following claim: "Even the weak requirement seems plausible only if Rawls assumes the desirability and possibility of a society in which citizens cooperate on the basis of their common reasonability. But it is just these assumptions that Wolterstorff, like Quinn, calls into question." ("The Liberalism of Reasoned Respect," p. 21.) As I read them, neither Wolterstorff nor Quinn denies the *desirability* of cooperation on the basis of common reasonability. They deny its *possibility* (in most cases) and therefore deny the desirability of *thinking* that we can cooperate on the

basis of common reasonability when we can't. This is, of course, consistent with the claim that such cooperation would be desirable if it were possible and that such cooperation is desirable in those rare instances when it is possible.

Chapter Six

1. "In Defense of Minimalist Liberalism," p. 119.
2. Some religious authorities regarded Hitler's invasion of Russia as a crusade akin to that perpetrated by the Teutonic Knights (whose slogan in the bloody Wendish crusade of 1147 was "baptism or extermination" and for whom baptism was a "token of subjection") in an earlier Germanic drive to the east. (Geoffrey Barraclough, *The Origins of Modern Germany* [New York: W. W. Norton, 1984], pp. 252, 268.) Thus John Toland: "The Pope's attitude toward [Hitler's invasion of Russia] was not at all vague. While taking no definite stand on the German invasion, he made it clear that he backed the Nazi fight against Bolshevism, describing it as 'high-minded gallantry in defense of the foundations of Christian culture.' A number of German bishops, predictably, openly supported the attack. One called it a 'European crusade,' a mission similar to that of the Teutonic Knights. He exhorted all Catholics to fight for 'a victory that will allow Europe to breathe freely again and will promise all nations a new future.'" *Adolf Hitler* (New York: Anchor Books, 1976), pp. 674–75.
3. I understand the claim that a citizen ought to privatize her religious convictions as equivalent to the *exclusive* version of the doctrine of restraint, namely, the claim that a citizen ought not adhere to a coercive law on the basis of her religious convictions. The exclusive version of the doctrine of restraint is distinct from the *inclusive* version, – the claim that a citizen ought not adhere to a coercive law *solely* on the basis of her religious convictions. I focus on the exclusive version because I think that both of the historical-consequentialist arguments I discuss are more plausible when read as vindicating that version of the doctrine of restraint.
4. I take this label from David Martin, *Does Christianity Cause War?* p. 7. I should note that the version of the argument from Bosnia I address is somewhat different from the version Martin addresses. Martin's target is the association of *religiosity* with civil strife, whereas my target is the association of a refusal to privatize religion with civil strife. Nevertheless, much of what Martin says is directly relevant to the version of the argument from Bosnia that I address.
5. "Disdain for the lessons of history" is the title of an essay by Theodore Blumoff, in which Blumoff criticizes Michael Perry for advocating an increased openness to religious argumentation in liberal politics.
6. "Notes on the Culture Struggle: Dr. King in the Law Schools," *First Things* (November, 1990): 9. Glendon continues: "All too frequently, what is implied is that religion and particular communities are *presumptively* intolerant and socially divisive." Notice that in the cited passage, Glendon mentions

two sorts of undesirable consequences that putatively result from admixing religion and politics, that is, civil strife and social division. Although there is no doubt not a clear and unambiguous distinction between those sorts of consequences, I find them significantly different, both with respect to their moral undesirability and with respect to the likelihood of their occurrence, such that it is helpful to treat them as constituting two different arguments for privatization.

7. "Political Liberalism: Religion and Public Reason," *Religion and Values in Public Life* 3/4 (Summer, 1995): 4.
8. "The Other Side of Religion," p. 859.
9. "Disdain for the Lessons of History," p. 185.
10. *Religious Commitment and Secular Reason*, p. 103.
11. "Religion and Liberal Democracy," *University of Chicago Law Review* 59 (1992): 197–98.
12. "Faith and Justice," p. 1096. The refusal to privatize religion is connected to strife in Charles Larmore, "Political Liberalism," p. 151; Robert Audi, "The Separation of Church and State and the Obligations of Citizenship," p. 296; Suzanna Sherry, "The Sleep of Reason," *Georgetown Law Journal* 84 (1996): 479f. Stephen Holmes, "Gag Rules or the Politics of Omission," pp. 23–25, 43–50. Richard Rorty outstrips other advocates of the argument from Bosnia by endorsing the claim that the very survival of liberal democracy depends on privatizing religion: "Contemporary liberal philosophers think that we shall not be able to keep a democratic political community going unless the religious believers remain willing to trade privatization for a guarantee of religious liberty." "Religion as a Conversation Stopper," p. 3.
13. There are alternative formulations that seem to me to capture the basic intention of the argument from Bosnia equally well. But this formulation seems sufficient for our purposes.
14. As I see the matter, nothing of ultimate significance depends on this move: my objections to the argument from Bosnia don't depend on my interpreting that argument as providing support for the exclusive version of the doctrine of restraint.
15. Lawrence Solum, "Faith and Justice," p. 1096.
16. Robert Audi, *Religious Commitment and Secular Reason*, 103.
17. "Political Liberalism: Religion and Public Reason," p. 4.
18. Stephen Holmes, "Gag Rules or the Politics of Omission," pp. 19–58.
19. Ideologically driven hand-waving to boot. According to David Martin, arguably the United Kingdom's preeminent sociologist of religion, the association of religion and conflict – Martin focuses on the commonplace that "religion causes war" – has a "surface plausibility" in virtue of its status as "a trope in an established narrative." (*Does Christianity Cause War?* p. 26.) Notwithstanding its surface plausibility, that association, says Martin, is a vast and ideologically driven oversimplification:

> The selection of religion as the source of evil needs itself to be analyzed as a cultural trope residually derived from the massive conflict in European

culture . . . over the role of religion during the past two centuries. The ideologies of secular establishment have promoted the idea so successfully that Christians have internalized it and asked forgiveness for it when, in terms of a serious contribution to a debate, it is a vast oversimplification.

Does Christianity Cause War? p. 20. Martin's book on religion and conflict is useful reading for those inclined to take the argument from Bosnia seriously.

20. The empirical argument is going to be a lot harder to pull off than one might initially expect. The issue as to what counts as a religiously generated conflict significantly complicates the matter and has been helpfully discussed by Martin in *Does Christianity Cause War?* Among many points Martin makes, the following is particularly important. Just because religion is implicated, *somehow or other*, in some conflict, it doesn't follow that religion plays a *causal* role in generating that conflict. In particular, according to Martin, it's often the case that religion serves as a *symbolic marker* that differentiates between warring factions without being a cause of conflict itself. Combatants can engage, and do engage, in conflict for reasons that have little to do with disagreements over religious commitments even though they distinguish themselves from their enemies in religious terms and legitimate their conflict on religious grounds. Martin writes: "The role of symbolic markers of identity often leads to combatants 'naming' themselves in these symbolic terms, and offering their identity cards as reasons for their mutual antagonism. They may well name each other and abuse each other in terms of rival identities, for example, 'the unspeakable Hun'. But the First World War did not *come about* because of the unspeakable Hunnishness of the Germans." (*Does Christianity Cause War?* p. 28.)

Due in part to the fact that religion can be implicated in a given conflict without playing a causal role in generating that conflict, and due as well to other complexities, Martin concludes that the empirical basis for the association of religion and conflict is not nearly as rich as one might think were one to attend only to the received wisdom of popular culture. Indeed, if Martin is correct, "Since the seventeenth century the involvement of religion in wars has been largely as one marker of national identity, though a major one. In the eighteenth century the wars between 'Protestant' England and 'Catholic' France were not *about* religion." (*Does Christianity Cause War?* p. 104.) According to Martin, religion plays this symbolic role in recent conflicts between Orthodox, Catholic, and Muslim in the former Yugoslavia. Religion no more plays a role in *generating* that conflict than do other symbolic markers, such as language. Religion, as with language, functions as a means by which combatants identify one another, berate and dehumanize one another, but is not in any appreciable sense a cause of conflict. As Martin sardonically comments, "Nobody need suppose that the razing of Catholic churches in Krajina from 1991 to 1995 had anything whatever to do with a disagreement over the *filioque* clause in the Creed." (*Does Christianity Cause War?* p. 72.)

21. I don't suggest that the coercive imposition of religion is *likely* to result in strife and conflict; rather, I speculate that, *if and when* religion plays a role in generating conflict, it typically does so when the state employs coercion for religious ends. So, my suggestion is consistent with the claim that, in most cases, coercion for religious ends is met with submission, subterfuge, avoidance, self-deception, and so on.

22. *A Letter Concerning Toleration*, James Tully, ed. (Indianapolis, IN: Hackett, 1983), p. 55.

23. *A Letter Concerning Toleration*, p. 33. See also pp. 51f. Mack Holt's *The French Wars of Religion: 1562–1629* (Cambridge: Cambridge University Press, 1995), a central thesis of which is that religion does play a causal role in generating the series of civil wars that wracked France in the late sixteenth and early seventeenth century, corroborates Locke's account. On the purely anecdotal level, the following passage indicates the sort of phenomenon to which Locke refers: "And although much of the manifesto [of the Catholic League] concerned political issues such as the call for a general reduction in taxation, it was above all a harsh criticism of Henry III and Catherine de Medici for having tolerated and legally recognized Protestantism in the various edicts of pacification. And that the League planned to use their aristocratic arms and Spanish money to assure their goals was made very clear in the oath all members were required to swear: 'We have all solemnly sworn and promised to use force and take up arms to the end that the holy church of God may be restored to its dignity and [reunited in] the true and holy Catholic religion.'" *The French Wars of Religion*, p. 124.

24. *A Letter Concerning Toleration*, p. 55.

25. Of course, that lack of awareness might very well be a function of my own lack of experience and unfamiliarity with the relevant literature. If so, I await correction.

26. Although the effective protection of the right to religious freedom is an essential component of the process of differentiation characteristic of modern societies, it is by no means the only component of that process of differentiation. Other aspects include the progressive laicization of the government, the distinction between sedition and heresy, the refusal to establish religion, and others. Given, as it is plausible to suppose, that other aspects of the process of differentiation also inhibit religious disagreements from escalating into religious conflict, it is clear that *many* of the features of a modern society inhibit religious disagreement from escalating into religious conflict.

27. John Noonan, *The Lustre of Our Country*, p. 2.

28. *Religion in Politics*, p. 12.

29. This is the central thesis of Rodney Stark's rational choice approach to religion, which I don't completely endorse, but which seems to have more than a grain of truth.

30. Robert Audi suggests some such correlation: "Granted, a non-religious source of conviction can also be felt to be infallible, and it may also be non-public. But not every non-public source of views and preferences poses the authority problem raised by many religions, or the special threat to

religious freedom that can arise from certain kinds of unconstrained religious convictions." *Religious Commitment and Secular Reason*, p. 69.

31. Not only is it possible for a citizen to refuse to privatize religion and yet to affirm religious freedom, it is possible for her to *privatize* religion and yet to *reject* religious freedom. That is, it's possible to articulate a purely secular rationale for denying religious freedom. After all, a fairly common argument in early modern society against the right to freedom of religion was entirely secular in nature. Many of those who rejected Locke's call for toleration did so on the authority of a commonly held assumption, namely, that agreement in fundamentals – particularly matters of faith – was a necessary condition of social order. In order to ensure social stability, and in particular, obedience to legitimate state authority, uniformity of religion – and not necessarily any particular religion – was essential. Since diversity of opinion was widely regarded as inimical to social order, and since the state has the means of stamping out diversity of opinion, critics of toleration were more than capable of articulating an entirely nonreligious justification of refusing to accord citizens freedom of religion. See, for example, Christopher Hill, "The Necessity of Religion," *The Collected Essays of Christopher Hill: Religion and Politics in 17ᵗʰ Century England* (Amherst: The University of Massachusetts Press, 1986), pp. 11–18; Derek Hirst, *Authority and Conflict: England, 1603–1658* (Cambridge, MA: Harvard University Press, 1986), p. 226.

32. Thus, it is false that religious freedom entails that religious citizens cannot "win" in the sense that they cannot employ their religious convictions to shape the state's actions. Stanley Fish writes: "One knows what [Michael McConnell] means: without the public/private split religion will not be protected from state action; were the state not barred from interfering with the free exercise of religion, that freedom might disappear. But of course the freedom thus gained is the freedom to be ineffectual. . . . What is not allowed under the public private distinction is the freedom to *win*, the freedom not to be separate from the state, but to inform and shape its every action." "Why We Can't All Just Get Along," p. 23. As I see it, religious citizens who voluntarily refrain from trying to "win" *certain* battles – to get the state to employ its coercive power to compel religious practices of one sort or another – thereby accept a political framework in which they are free from righteous stigma when they attempt to win *other* battles, such as matters of justice and the common good.

33. *Law, Liberty, and Morality*, p. 63.

34. "The Political Balance of the Religion Clauses," *Yale Law Journal* 102 (May, 1993): 1630.

35. *Religious Convictions and Political Choice*, p. 219. Greenawalt expresses similar concerns regarding the public airing by legislators of religious arguments for coercive policies in *Private Consciences and Public Reasons*, p. 157. See also Greenawalt's "Grounds for Political Judgment," *San Diego Law Review* 30 (1993): 675.

36. "Disdain for the Lessons of History," p. 181.

37. "Liberal Democracy and the Place of Religion in Politics," p. 32. See also John Rawls, *Political Liberalism*, p. 129; Ted Jelen, "In Defense of Religious Minimalism," pp. 27–33; Mark Tushnet, "The Limits of the Involvement of Religion in the Body Politic," *The Role of Religion in the Making of Public Policy*, p. 213.
38. Thus, according to Abner Greene, "the reason for excluding certain types of argument from justifying law is the exclusionary and polarizing effect that a sectarian argument can have." "Uncommon Ground," p. 658, fn. 81.
39. As with the argument from Bosnia, I regard the argument from divisiveness as most plausibly construed as supporting a thoroughgoing privatization of religion: interpreted in what I take to be the most natural way, it supports the conclusion that a citizen may not support her favored coercive laws on the basis of her religious convictions, irrespective of any other reasons she might have for those laws. And so, as I did in the prior section, I use "privatize" and "exercise restraint" interchangeably. I should note, however, that not all of those sympathetic to the argument from divisiveness draw an exclusivist conclusion – Audi for example, explicitly draws only the inclusive conclusion. I modify my objection to fit Audi's version of the argument from divisiveness in "Religion and Liberal Democracy," in *The Blackwell Guide to Social and Political Philosophy*, Robert Simon, ed., forthcoming.
40. James Farmer, Program Director for the SCLC, later remarked regarding the Freedom Rides of 1960–61: "We planned the Freedom Rides with the specific intention of creating a crisis. We were counting on the bigots in the South to do our work for us. We figured that the government would have to respond if we created a situation that was headline news all over the world, and affected the nation's image abroad. An international crisis, that was our strategy." Quoted in David Garrow, *Bearing the Cross: Martin Luther King and the Southern Christian Leadership Conference* (New York: William Morrow, 1986), p. 156. Apparently, opponents of institutionalized racism engaged in what they knew would be extremely divisive activity with the intention of forcing the federal government to intervene. So the division generated by the Freedom Rides was regarded by the Freedom Riders as not nearly serious enough to "outweigh" the morally desirable intervention the Freedom Rides would, they hoped, initiate.
41. Ted Jelen's version of the argument from divisiveness seems to me of this sort. See "In Defense of Religious Minimalism," pp. 27–33.
42. *Religion in Politics*, p. 45. Perry argues, further, that appeal to religious claims in political advocacy can be much less sectarian, and thus much less divisive, than appeal to secular claims. *Religion in Politics*, p. 48.
43. I have to say that, in some cases, justificatory liberals who make use of the argument from divisiveness often seem to take the less complicated path to the desired conclusion: they show that refusing to privatize religion is "divisive" and let matters stand at that.
44. John Noonan, *The Lustre of Our Country*, p. 250.
45. John Noonan, *The Lustre of Our Country*, p. 250.

46. *The Culture of Disbelief* (New York: Anchor Books, 1993), p. 37. From a very different theoretical perspective than Carter's, Jacques Ellul has articulated an analysis of modernity that provides powerful support for this objection. For a concise statement of that analysis, see Jacques Ellul, "Epilogue," *Jacques Ellul: Interpretive Essays* (Chicago: University of Illinois Press, 1981), pp. 291–308.
47. *The Political Illusion* (New York: Vintage Books, 1972), p. 222.
48. In appreciating this objection to the argument from divisiveness, recall that that argument forbids citizens not only from employing their religious commitments as a basis for *supporting* coercive laws but also as a basis for *rejecting* coercive laws. Were a citizen to privatize her religious convictions she would be forbidden not only to employ her religious convictions as a basis for imposing her favored coercive laws on her compatriots but also as a basis for stopping her compatriots from imposing their convictions on others (and herself).
49. Sociologists are not, of course, alone in their recognition of the legitimating function of religion: time and again, politicians have remarked upon the utility of religion in securing obedience to the state. Examples are legion, although few have been so forthright as the first Stuart King of England: "King James upon the conference at Hampton Court did absolutely con-clude, 'No bishops, no king, no nobility'; which as you see hath lately fallen out according to his prediction. It is the church which supports the state, it is religion which strengthens the government; shake the one, and you overthrow the other. Nothing is so deeply rooted in the hearts of men as re-ligion, nothing so powerful to direct their actions; and if once the hearts of the people be doubtful in religion, all other relations fail, and you shall find nothing but mutinies and sedition. Thus the church and the state do mu-tually support and give assistance to each other; and if one of them change, the other can have no sure foundation." Bishop Godfrey Goodman, cited in Christopher Hill, "The Protestant Nation," *The Collected Papers of Christopher Hill*, p. 21.
50. *Religion and Social Theory*, p. 109. Peter Berger also accepts the claim that religion has played an overwhelmingly cohesive role: "Religion has been the historically most widespread and effective instrumentality of legitima-tion. All legitimation maintains socially defined reality. Religion legitimates so effectively because it relates the precarious reality constructions of em-pirical societies with ultimate reality." *The Sacred Canopy*, p. 32.
51. See Christian Smith, "Correcting a Curious Neglect, or Bringing Religion Back In," *Disruptive Religion: The Force of Faith in Social Movement Activism*, Christian Smith, ed. (London: Routledge, 1996), p. 7. Smith is by no means alone in noting the disruptive side of religion. Among the classics of sociology, Karl Mannheim's *Ideology and Utopia* emphasizes the capacity of religion to delegitimate the existing social-political order.
52. Rodney Stark and Roger Finke, *Acts of Faith*, p. 32.
53. *Religion in Politics*, p. 44.
54. *Religion in Politics*, p. 45.

55. Even the exclusive understanding of the doctrine of restraint, here under discussion, imposes constraints *only* on political decision making and advocacy.
56. Recall that in this chapter I take the claim that a citizen should privatize his religious convictions to be equivalent to the exclusive version of the doctrine of restraint. Consequently, claims I have earlier established regarding the inclusive version of the doctrine of restraint – such as that it's distinct from the principle of pursuit – apply forthwith to the privatization claim.
57. The following case seems to me to represent a typical reaction of theists to the prospect of disobedience to God: "In 1934 a care worker wrote to the Bishop of Limburg outlining how her duties enmeshed her in the Law for the Prevention of Hereditarily Diseased Progeny. She could not collaborate with what she described as 'such violent interference with God's right as creator and the personal rights of individuals, not to speak of the consequences for them, especially psychological, which can be anticipated.' The idea of doing anything against the will of God literally terrified her 'innermost soul.'" Michael Burleigh, *The Third Reich: A New History* (New York: Hill and Wang, 2000), p. 364.

Concluding Comments on Part Two

1. Michael Perry, *Love and Power*, p. 47.
2. *Religious Commitment and Secular Reason*, p. 123.
3. "Liberal Civic Education and Religious Fundamentalism," p. 495.
4. Thus Mark Tushnet: "The distinction between principle and prudence should be emphasized. The fundamental question is not whether, as a matter of prudent judgment in a religiously pluralist society, those who hold particular religious views ought to cast their argument in secular terms. Even an outsider can say that the answer to that question is clearly, 'Yes, most of the time,' for only such a course is likely to be successful overall." "The Limits of the Involvement of Religion in the Body Politic," p. 213.
5. Michael Perry, *Love and Power*, p. 125.

Introduction to Part Three

1. A brief clarification of my use of "conception of public justification" in this chapter and the next: strictly speaking, a citizen adheres only to the doctrine of restraint and not to a conception of public justification. After all, a conception of public justification neither enjoins nor forbids a citizen to do anything at all; it merely demarcates one sort of rationale from another. Since, however, we are surveying various conceptions of public justification *in order to* integrate them into the doctrine of restraint, I'll assume that a given conception of public justification has already been so integrated and evaluate that conception on that basis.

Chapter Seven

1. "The public" is a technical term that refers to a particular characterization of the target group with respect to which, on a particular conception of public justification, some rationale counts or doesn't count as a public justification. It is roughly equivalent to what Marilyn Friedman, in her discussion of Rawls's conception of public justification, has called the "legitimation pool": "the pool of persons whose endorsement would confirm the legitimacy of Rawls' political liberalism." "John Rawls and the Political Coercion of Unreasonable People," *The Idea of Political Liberalism: Essays on Rawls*, Victoria Davion and Clark Wolff, eds. (Lanham, MD: Rowman and Littlefield, 2000), p. 16.

2. I have borrowed the term "populism" from Gerald Gaus, *Justificatory Liberalism*, pp. 130f.

3. "Facing Diversity," p. 46.

4. A citizen's rationale is essentially dependent on religious considerations if removing all religious considerations from that rationale would render it either unsound or implausible.

5. Perhaps the model of neutral dialogue Charles Larmore articulates in *Patterns of Moral Complexity* and "Political Liberalism" commits him to some variant of (4) – at least for constitutional matters and matters of basic justice. Given Larmore's understanding of what counts as rational discourse, namely, retreating to common ground relative to p when disagreement regarding p is intractable, and given that any discourse regarding matters of basic justice and constitutional matters often involves many millions of citizens, it seems that a rational resolution of such disputes in modern, pluralistic democracies is possible only if there are sets of premises that have two features – (a) they are in fact acceptable to the millions of citizens who have a say on the policy under discussion and (b) they are determinate enough to provide guidance on the policy under discussion.

6. Populist conceptions also articulate exceptionally well with both the argument from Bosnia and the argument from divisiveness; I leave it to the reader to make the requisite connections.

7. See Thomas Hill, *Respect, Pluralism and Justice: Kantian Perspectives* (Oxford: Oxford University Press, 2000), p. 79.

8. Bruce Ackerman, "Why Dialogue?" p. 19.

9. Bruce Ackerman, "Why Dialogue?" p. 18.

10. There are some religious claims that many, perhaps even most, citizens in the United States accept; it is possible that most citizens accept some version of McCartney's claim that homosexuality is an abomination to God (particularly, if we formulate that claim somewhat more judiciously, for example, by employing such antiseptic terminology as "abnormal"). But no religious claims garner the actual assent of all rational citizens: given the burdens of judgment, there will always be *some* dissenters.

11. Gerald Gaus notes: "The first challenge confronting 'justificatory liberalism' is, then, to show that these basic liberties are indeed victoriously

justified; if this cannot be shown, it is unclear whether what I have called 'justificatory liberalism' is, in a substantive sense, really liberal at all." *Justificatory Liberalism*, p. 160.

12. Rawls expresses a similar condition (in his distinctive idiom) as follows: "Another essential feature of public reason is that its political conceptions should be complete. This means that each conception should express principles, standards and ideals, along with guidelines of inquiry, such that the values specified by it can be suitably ordered or otherwise united so that those values alone give a reasonable answer to all, or to nearly all, questions involving constitutional essentials and matters of basic justice. . . . The significance of completeness lies in the fact that unless a political conception is complete, it is not an adequate framework of thought in the light of which the discussion of fundamental political questions can be carried out." "The Idea of Public Reason Revisited," p. 777. See also *Political Liberalism*, pp. 225, 244.

13. This is, of course, an *empirical* claim and consequently requires for its justification an appropriate experiential basis. I have no idea how to go about providing that experiential basis; I rely on the very same appeal to anecdotal experience, common sense, and testimony commonly employed in support of the claim that, for example, there is irremediable disagreement regarding any and all religious grounds, or that there is no consensus in the United States regarding conceptions of the good, or that there are no comprehensive doctrines that enjoy the assent of all reasonable people.

14. This is a familiar point. See for example, Jeremy Waldron, "Religious Contributions in Public Deliberation," p. 840; William Galston, *Liberal Purposes*, pp. 102–05, 143, 154–62; Michael Perry, "Religious Arguments in Public Political Debate," pp. 1451f.; Philip Quinn, "Political Liberalisms and Their Exclusion of the Religious," pp. 39–40; Lawrence Solum, "Constructing an Ideal of Public Reason," pp. 743f.

15. Lawrence Solum rightfully brings attention to this point: "The principle of respect for citizens as free and equal does mean that we should give our fellow citizens the sort of reason they *could reasonably accept*. The modal operator 'could' is crucial here. The requirement is not to give reasons that all or most of one's fellow citizens *will* accept; rather the requirement is to give reasons they reasonably *could* accept." "Constructing an Ideal of Public Reason," p. 736.

16. Lawrence Solum, "Novel Public Reasons," p. 1477.

17. Wilcox's description continues: "Perhaps most controversial is the reconstructionists' call for capital punishment to be meted out according to Mosaic law – to those who commit murder, commit adultery, engage in homosexual behavior, act incorrigibly as teenagers, blaspheme, or commit acts of apostasy. [Gary] North has claimed that death by stoning not only is an important part of the Mosaic code but also has certain advantages: Stones are plentiful and cheap, no 'killing blow' can be traced to any individual, and group stone-throwing underscores the community norms being enforced." *Onward Christian Soldiers*? pp. 124–25.

18. It is, of course, important to bear in mind the distinction between truth and rationality: a citizen can adhere to many wildly false claims but can be perfectly rational in adhering to those wildly false claims.

19. No doubt the comparable claim is true of other liberal commitments: so long as there is a Communist party in the United States, and I suppose we cannot reasonably expect it to wither away any time soon, then the United States will be populated by citizens who rationally (but wrongly) deny that their compatriots have a moral right to own private property, in which case, according to (5), we lack a public justification for the claim that each citizen has a right to private property.

20. See Lawrence Solum, "Novel Public Reasons," p. 1477.

21. As I see it, the universalism of justificatory liberalism is one of its most attractive features.

22. There is a crucial difference between these two claims even if the quantity of citizens who satisfy the relevant set of reasonable conditions is *lower* than the quantity of citizens who adhere to a widely prevailing view.

23. The literature on Rawls's notion of public reason is voluminous, and I will not attempt to address it. One treatment of Rawls, however, merits mention, given that its criticisms articulate nicely with those I develop in this section, namely, Gerald Gaus's *Justificatory Liberalism*.

24. *Political Liberalism*, p. 8.

25. I remind the reader that Rawls formulates his conception of public justification so that it applies solely to constitutional matters and matters of basic justice, not to coercive laws generally. I formulate his position in the broader way in order to maintain a consistent focus throughout my discussion. Nothing in my discussion of Rawls hangs on that, however.

26. Rawls writes, "Reasonable persons . . . are not moved by the general good as such but desire for its own sake a social world in which they, as free and equal, can cooperate with others on terms all can accept. . . . By contrast, people are unreasonable in the same basic aspect when they plan to engage in cooperative schemes but are unwilling to honor, or even to propose, except as a necessary public pretense, any general principles or standards for specifying fair terms of cooperation." *Political Liberalism*, p. 50.

27. Rawls's terminology can be confusing at this point. Rawls claims that, given the burdens of judgment, it's possible that many citizens "reasonably" adhere to different religious commitments, metaphysical positions, and so on. In this claim Rawls means by "reasonable" that different citizens who employ their cognitive capacities competently can nevertheless arrive at different religious commitments, and so on. "Reasonable" as used here is a purely epistemic conception. When, however, Rawls claims that a reasonable citizen recognizes the burdens of judgment and their implications, his understanding of "reasonable" is primarily a moral one: a citizen who is reasonable in this second sense grants that citizens who are reasonable in the first, epistemic, sense can adhere to widely varying religious commitments. On this point, see Jean Hampton, "The Moral Commitments of Liberalism," *The Good Polity*, p. 305.

28. Perhaps more accurate is the claim that citizens will adhere to those claims *insofar* as they are reasonable: after all, citizens who are reasonable in general can be unreasonable in specific cases.

29. *Political Liberalism*, p. xliv.

30. Brian Barry explicates this argument as follows: "Suppose you were to say: 'The reason I should be able to practise my religion but you should not be able to practise yours is that mine is right and yours is wrong.' You would, obviously, reject a claim made in similar terms by somebody else with opposing ideas about what was right and what was wrong. In rejecting that claim, you would be acting reasonably. But then it follows that you cannot reasonably object when others reject your claim." *Justice as Impartiality*, p. 142.

31. As I understand Rawls, that group of commitments is composed, most centrally, of political values embedded in the political culture of an extant liberal democracy. Those political values must be worked up into a unified "political" conception of justice which, when applied in specific cases, provides a citizen with her rationale for her favored political commitments.

32. Something like (7) seems to be entailed by what Rawls calls "the liberal principle of legitimacy," that is, "our exercise of political power is fully proper only when it is exercised in accordance with a constitution the essentials of which all citizens as free and equal may reasonably be expected to endorse in light of principles and ideals acceptable to their common human reason." *Political Liberalism*, p. 137. Many others have followed Rawls in employing the notion of the "reasonable" to articulate a populist conception of public justification. Stephen Macedo, for example, writes: "Citizens are asked to put aside their comprehensive moral and religious conceptions, in the sense that they should acknowledge the political authority and adequacy of reasons that can be shared by reasonable people who disagree about their ultimate ideals." "Liberal Civic Education and Religious Fundamentalism," p. 477. See also Peter de Marneffe, "Liberalism, Liberty and Neutrality," pp. 255f.

33. *Political Liberalism*, p. 152.

34. Thus, Rawls's favored conception of justice as fairness must be articulated and defended on the basis of common ground but need not elicit consensus among even reasonable persons, which, of course, it has not.

35. Amy Gutmann and Dennis Thompson defend a comparable restriction on the composition of the public: "Deliberative reciprocity expresses two related requirements, one primarily moral and the other primarily empirical. When citizens make moral claims in a deliberative democracy, they appeal to reasons or principles that can be shared by fellow citizens who are similarly motivated. The moral reasoning is in this way mutually acceptable. The qualifying phrase 'similarly motivated' indicates that a deliberative perspective does not address people who reject the aim of finding fair terms for social cooperation; it cannot reach those who refuse to press their public claims in terms accessible to their fellow citizens. No moral perspective in politics can reach such people, except one that replicates

their own comprehensive set of beliefs. And since that perspective would entail rejecting entirely the comprehensive beliefs of their rivals, it would not help reduce, let alone resolve, moral disagreements." *Democracy and Disagreement*, p. 55. See also Charles Larmore, *Patterns of Moral Complexity*, p. 60; Kai Nielson, "Liberal Reasonability," pp. 751–52.

36. There is a significant factual disagreement here. Some justificatory liberals claim that there exists the sort of consensus Rawls needs in order for his populist conception to work. For example, Stephen Macedo writes (commenting on Michael Sandel):

> Sandel tries to suggest that there is just as much reasonable disagreement about issues of basic justice as there is about religious truth and other ultimate questions. This seems to me wrong. There does not seem to be any reasonable disagreement about the core meaning of the constitutional basics: the good of basic democratic procedures and core civil liberties. ("Liberal Civic Education and Religious Fundamentalism," p. 495.)

It seems to me that Macedo's judgment is false, that Sandel's position is more plausible. How do we determine who is correct? I assume that Macedo's claim is an *empirical* one, rather than a *definitional* one: that he is making a claim about whether there are citizens who instantiate the property of reasonableness as Rawls conceives it and who affirm "the good of basic democratic procedures and core civil liberties" rather than that he is making the claim that a reasonable person *just is* a person who affirms the good of basic democratic procedures and core civil liberties. The ideal way to establish Macedo's claim is by engaging in an empirical project of herculean magnitude: we engage in extensive psychological evaluation of the citizenry in order to distinguish the reasonable ones from the unreasonable ones, and then see what those reasonable citizens affirm. No one, so far as I know, has done anything like that. So we are thrown back on second best: I'll argue that Rawls's explanation of the reasonable disagreement about conceptions of the good, religious claims, and so on, predicts similarly extensive disagreement about the good of basic democratic procedures and core civil liberties.

37. *Political Liberalism*, pp. 56–57.

38. *Justificatory Liberalism*, p. 293.

39. Some of Rawls's readers have taken his discussion of abortion to constitute an *argument* in support of the position that a woman should have a duly qualified right to have an abortion during her first trimester rather than an *illustration* of his claim that a comprehensive doctrine "runs afoul" of public reason if it cannot support a reasonable balance of political values. Rawls has subsequently clarified that he intended his discussion only to serve only the latter purpose. See *Political Liberalism*, p. lv, fn. 31.

40. Presumably, the notion of "reasonable" employed in Rawls's example is the same moral notion I mentioned earlier: a balance of values is reasonable only if it can serve as a fair basis for social cooperation given the burdens of judgment.

41. *Political Liberalism*, p. 243, fn. 32.
42. *Political Liberalism*, p. 243, fn. 32.
43. *Political Liberalism*, pp. 243–44, fn. 32.
44. *Political Liberalism*, p. 243, fn. 32.
45. *Political Liberalism*, p. 243, fn. 32.
46. *Political Liberalism*, pp. 56–57.
47. There is another obvious source of disagreement. Any given platitude is amenable to any number of alternative and conflicting specifications, and any appeal to a given platitude, in order to do the work required of it, will invariably require recourse to a particular specification.
48. This statement is an elliptical *argument* rather than a *tautology*. I do not assume that the commitment to religious freedom is tautologically built into Rawls's conception of the reasonable, such that, as a matter of definitional fiat, all reasonable citizens assent to the claim that each citizen ought to be accorded the right to religious freedom. Many of Rawls's critics have made that sort of claim: that Rawls construes the notion of the reasonable in such a way what makes for a reasonable citizen *just is* her willingness to assent to central liberal commitments. If commitment to religious freedom were built into the notion of the reasonable then, of course, my point in this section would be moot. But then Rawls's conception of the reasonable would be utterly without interest.
49. Brian Barry, *Justice as Impartiality*, p. 83.
50. The claim that agreement on fundamentals is essential to social order is not a crazy claim (although it is false). Even some modern theorists accept a close cousin: although few accept the claim that social order requires *religious* uniformity, they do accept the claim that social order requires some shared normative commitments. Thus, for example, James Davison Hunter: "Yet absent some common assumptions, some common metaphysical dream of the world, is it possible to think of people as deeply divided as we are living together in relative peace for very long into the future. Where, now, is the *unum*, capable of binding together a *pluribus* that seems ever more fragmented? The central premise of this essay is that in a democratic society the unum cannot be imposed from the top down but must be generated from the bottom up, in the dialectical process of generating new working agreements out of a serious confrontation with our deepest differences." *Before the Shooting Begins: Searching for Democracy in America's Culture War* (New York: The Free Press, 1994), p. 228.
51. *Political Liberalism*, p. 56.
52. *Justice as Impartiality*, p. 167.
53. Brian Barry, Gerald Gaus, and Robert Audi have each defended a position approximating (8). Thus, for example, Robert Audi has defended the following "surrogacy conception of justified coercion": "According to this view, coercing a person, S, for reason R, to perform an action A, in circumstances C, is fully justified if and only if at least the following three conditions hold in C: (a) S morally ought to A in C, for example to abstain from stealing from others (perhaps someone has a right, in the circumstances,

against A that S A – certainly a feature of most cases in which a liberal democracy can reasonably coerce its citizens); (b) if fully rational and adequately informed about the situation, S would see that (a) holds and would, for reason R (say from a sense of how theft creates mistrust and chaos, or for some essentially related reason), perform A, or at least tend to A; (c) A is both an 'important' kind of action (as opposed to breaking a casual promise to meet for lunch at the usual place) and one that may be reasonably believed to affect someone else (and perhaps not of a highly personal kind at all)." "The Place of Religious Argument in a Free and Democratic Society," pp. 688–89.

54. Brian Barry mentions this problem, but so far as I can tell, doesn't solve it. See *Justice as Impartiality*, p. 69.

55. Brian Barry explicates the notion of adequate information as follows: "The remaining stipulation in the specification of a Scanlonian original position [which Barry accepts] is that the people in it are well informed. I take this to mean not only that they know the bare facts about their society but also that they know that other societies do things differently and that their own could feasibly be different in various ways." *Justice as Impartiality*, p. 107. A little later on in Barry's explication of his version of justificatory liberalism, Barry adopts a very different, and *much* more demanding understanding of adequate information: he claims that his version of justificatory liberalism "requires the parties not to have false beliefs." *Justice as Impartiality*, p. 114. It will be pretty clear, I hope, that my objection to the adequate information condition applies just as squarely to Barry's proposals as it does to the version I address in the text.

56. This becomes abundantly clear in Brian Barry's discussion of slavery. He writes: "We often find an elaborate rationalization of the indefensible. Slavery, for example, may be justified by maintaining that it is part of the natural order or by claiming that the people who are enslaved are subhuman and hence outside the protection due to human beings. Since justice as impartiality requires the parties not to have false beliefs, it is hardly surprising that there should be people to whom it is not accessible, given their existing beliefs." *Justice as Impartiality*, p. 114.

57. I assume for the duration of this discussion that McCartney is committed to determining what adequately informed, reasonable, and rational citizens would find acceptable, although I'll drop reference to reasonableness and rationality for the sake of simplicity.

58. God is, McCartney assumes, an omniscient being and so cannot be wrong in God's moral commitments. Hence, to be unaware of a source of information about an omniscient being's moral commitments is to be desperately ignorant.

59. Of course, what's good for the goose is good for the gander: exactly the parallel situation obtains for those who reject McCartney's theological orientation.

60. A comparable point is applicable to the relation between (8) and the arguments from both Bosnia and divisiveness.

61. *Justificatory Liberalism*, p. 129.
62. *Justificatory Liberalism*, p. 140. This passage actually refers to what Gaus calls "open" justification, rather than public justification. But this feature of open justification translates directly to a successful public justification.

Chapter Eight

1. Expressions of that conviction are legion, from various Old Testament texts to Jerry Falwell. For example, John Mason, bemoaning the fact that the Constitution made no mention of God, said in 1793: "Should the citizens of America be as irreligious as her Constitution, . . . we will have reason to tremble, lest the Governor of the universe, who will not be treated with indignity by a people any more than by individuals, overturn from its foundations the fabric we have been rearing, and crush us to atoms in the wreck." Cited in James E. Wood, Jr., "Religion and Public Policy," *The Role of Religion in the Making of Public Policy*, p. 7. Erich Klapproth, objecting to the Kristallnacht pogrom, wrote the following to Hitler, Goring, and Goebbels: "First of all, I, as a Protestant Christian, have no doubt that carrying out and tolerance of such reprisals will evoke the wrath of God against our people and Fatherland, as sure as there is a God in heaven. Just as Israel is cursed and on trial because they were the first who rejected Christ, so surely that same curse will fall upon each and every nation that, by similar deeds, denies Christ in the same way." Cited in Michael Burleigh, *The Third Reich*, p. 332. More recently, Jerry Falwell has expressed the same concern: "The rise and fall of nations confirm to the Scripture. . . . Psalm 9:17 admonishes 'The wicked shall be turned into hell, and all the nations that forget God.' America will be no exception. If she forgets God, she too will face His wrath and judgment like any other nation in the history of humanity." Cited in Clyde Wilcox, *Onward Christian Soldiers?* p. 17. Gary North's 700-page diatribe against pluralism and liberalism is a series of variations on the theme that God imposes what he calls "negative sanctions" on those nations that flaunt God's revealed commands. See *Political Polytheism*, passim.
2. Of course, even if McCartney is fully committed to obeying the doctrine of restraint, his obligation to obey that doctrine doesn't necessarily override all other obligations. Consequently, even if McCartney is committed to obeying the doctrine of restraint, and even if he cannot articulate a public justification for Amendment 2, he might nevertheless reasonably conclude that the consequences of exercising restraint in a given case are so egregious that he ought, all things considered, to refuse to exercise restraint. And if McCartney holds the set of beliefs I have attributed to him, then he will be very likely to refuse to exercise restraint. This indicates a point I haven't emphasized up to this point, namely, that even if a citizen has a moral obligation to exercise restraint, that obligation is prima facie only and thus can be overridden by more weighty considerations.
3. *Justificatory Liberalism*, p. 3.

4. Nicholas Wolterstorff, "The Role of Religion in Decision and Discussion of Political Issues," p. 87.

5. Kent Greenawalt, *Religious Convictions and Political Choice*, p. 23. This point is generally, although not universally, acknowledged in the literature. Thus, Thomas Nagel: "I believe that the demand for agreement, and its priority in these cases over a direct appeal to the truth, must be grounded in something more basic. Though it has to do with epistemology, it is not skepticism but a kind of epistemological restraint: the distinction between what is needed to justify belief and what is needed to justify the employment of political power depends on a higher standard of objectivity, which is ethically based." "Moral Conflict and Political Legitimacy," p. 229. Brian Barry (discussing Rawls, Nagel, and Larmore): "The three lines of argument are similar. All of them turn on the crucial move of distinguishing between what can reasonably be believed and what can reasonably be advanced as the foundation of a society's basic institutions." *Justice as Impartiality*, pp. 187–88.

6. For an influential explication of this approach, see Charles Larmore, *Patterns of Moral Complexity*, pp. 52f. See also Amy Gutmann and Dennis Thompson, "Moral Conflict and Political Consensus," p. 66. Not every justificatory liberal agrees with this. See, for example, Gerald Gaus, *Justificatory Liberalism*, pp. 175f.

7. Consider: what point would there be to the justificatory liberal's resting her case solely on a *theological* rationale most citizens have no reason to accept and many have sufficient reason to reject?

8. Of course, the justificatory liberal is free to argue that religious grounds don't enjoy the *highest* possible epistemic status and that religious grounds don't enjoy *every* epistemic desideratum. Neither of those claims implies skepticism.

9. Alston's position is definitively articulated in *Perceiving God: The Epistemology of Religious Experience* (Ithaca, NY: Cornell University Press, 1991).

10. William Alston, "Perceiving God," *Journal of Philosophy* 83 (1986): 655.

11. *Perceiving God*, p. 1.

12. *Bearing the Cross*, p. 58.

13. *Perceiving God*, p. 193.

14. *Perceiving God*, pp. 146–65; "Belief-Forming Practices and the Social," *Socializing Epistemology*, Frederick Schmitt, ed. (Lanham, MD: Rowman and Littlefield, 1994), pp. 31–32; "A Doxastic Practice Approach to Epistemology," *Knowledge and Skepticism*, Marjorie Clay and Keith Lehrer, eds. (Boulder, CO: Westview Press, 1989), passim; "Taking the Curse Off Language Games: A Realist Account of Doxastic Practices," *Philosophy and the Grammar of Religious Belief*, Timothy Tessin and Mario van der Ruhr, eds. (London: St. Martin's Press, 1995), p. 34.

15. *Perceiving God*, p. 159.

16. That SP enjoys such effective procedures for checking sense-perceptual beliefs is one reason, perhaps the most important reason, that the burdens of judgment don't generate the widespread disagreement regarding

sense-perceptual matters that they generate regarding matters for which we do not enjoy such effective checking procedures, such as morality and religion, psychology and economics.

17. More precisely, although CMP doesn't enjoy the sort of confirmatory procedures that we employ in SP, it does enjoy confirmatory procedures of another sort. What sort? Well, if a citizen putatively perceives God as telling her that murder is wrong and consequently forms the belief that murder is wrong, she can confirm that belief if she can provide independent reason to believe that murder is wrong – perhaps by means of a Kantian argument of some sort.

18. In *Perceiving God*, Alston argues that only socially established practices enjoy presumptive innocence and that idiosyncratic practices require discursive redemption. But he has since dropped entirely the appeal to social establishment. See "Reply to Critics," *Journal of Philosophical Research* 20 (March, 1995): 72.

19. Alston notes a kind of consideration that may bolster a practice's presumptive innocence, what he calls "significant self-support," which plays little role in my argument and hence to which I don't include substantive reference at this point.

20. *Perceiving God*, p. 153.

21. Actually, if Alston failed to add the "until proven guilty" rider, then the *presumptive* aspect of the dictum would lack motivation. After all, if a given practice isn't subject to proof of guilt, then it is impossible to remove the presumption of guilt, in which case we might just as well impute innocence straightaway.

22. "The Miracle of Minimal Foundationalism," *Religious Studies* 29 (1993): 303.

23. For more on the concept of autonomy, and in particular, on criteria for granting autonomy, see Christopher J. Eberle, "The Autonomy and Explanation of Mystical Perception," *Religious Studies* 34 (1998): 299–316; and "God's Nature and the Rationality of Religious Belief," *Faith and Philosophy* 14 (April, 1997): 152–69.

24. Dirk-Martin Grube, "Religious Experience after the Demise of Foundationalism," *Religious Studies* 31 (1995): 41.

25. Perhaps avoiding both the inauthentic and the Procrustean paths paved by the denial of autonomy requires that we risk some degree of epistemic liberality; perhaps we will find ourselves unable to construct fair criticisms of apparently dubious doxastic practices. But allowing for some degree of liberality doesn't imply that "anything goes," that effective external criticism of autonomous doxastic practices is impossibly difficult. That "something goes" for one practice, say astrology, that doesn't "go" for another, say SP, doesn't entail that "anything goes" for SP (or for astrology for that matter).

26. Michael Perry first clued me in to skepticism about the existence of citizens who make political commitments on the basis of their M-beliefs. On surveying others, I have found general, though not unanimous, agreement with his point.

27. This is one reason that even some religious traditions regard mystical perception with skepticism.
28. For more on this objection, see Christopher J. Eberle, "Liberalism and Mysticism," *Journal of Law and Religion* 13/1 (1996–98): 234–38.
29. As I see it, the idealizing conception of public justification I discussed at the conclusion of the prior chapter is an epistemic conception: it can be formulated as the claim that a public justification must have the following highly desirable epistemic desideratum, namely, the property of being acceptable to a fully rational adequately informed citizen. It seems to me, however, more natural to discuss that conception in connection with populist conceptions of public justification – as a natural modification of populist conceptions rather than as an alternative to populist conceptions. Of course, nothing substantive hinges on the location of a given conception in my treatment of justificatory liberalism: whether the idealizing conception I discussed earlier is a modified populist or a straightforwardly epistemic conception, it is still problematic!
30. Given the limits imposed by the reader's patience, I have culled out simple and straightforward formulations from what are often complicated, multifaceted conceptions. Given the complexity of the conceptions I discuss, I make no claim to exegetical exactitude. While I have attempted to get the gist of a given position across, it's impossible to formulate each conception with due respect for each conception's distinctive nuances, qualifications, and so on.
31. Colin Bird, "Mutual Respect and Neutral Justification," pp. 62–96. A whiff of this understanding of what counts as a public justification hangs over Daniel Conkle's discussion of fundamentalism. See, for example, Daniel Conkle, "Different Religions, Different Politics," *Journal of Law and Religion* 10/1 (1993–4): 1–32, where Conkle analogizes fundamentalists to "those who adopt an 'English only' rule for a society that includes people who speak, not English but Spanish."
32. "Mutual Respect and Neutral Justification," p. 73.
33. "Mutual Respect and Neutral Justification," p. 73, fn. 25.
34. It seems that providing some such description is what Bird requires in order for some experience to count as communicable. The italicized sections in the following passage indicate that he has that in mind (although I admit that it is by no means clear exactly how Bird understands the notion of intelligibility): "Religious conversion experiences provide the paradigm example of an opaque experience, but it seems clear that many of the everyday ethical views and convictions held and asserted by modern citizens fall into this category as well, whether they are ostensibly religious or not. For example, a person's ethical views about what constitutes a meaningful life likely result from a prolonged and intensive internal deliberation about the events of his or her life, *and these are likely to be too detailed and comprehensive to be fully communicated to outsiders* (who have their own life experiences to cope with). Alternatively, a person may have formed her views about the point of human life under the influence of particular people with whom

she has had special relationships in which others cannot share or are in no position fully to understand. *Or perhaps the agent simply finds the vocabularies available to him inadequate to convey the full significance and nature of the experience he has had."* "Mutual Respect and Neutral Justification," p. 73 (my emphasis).

35. "Mutual Respect and Neutral Justification," p. 73, fn. 25.
36. "Mutual Respect and Neutral Justification," p. 73.
37. "Mutual Respect and Neutral Justification," p. 72, fn. 23 (my emphasis).
38. "Mutual Respect and Neutral Justification," p. 71.
39. As I see it, Bird uses such phrases as "public critical scrutiny" to refer to a number of importantly distinct phenomena: in particular, to *criticizability*, *independent confirmation*, and *provability*. A ground can be criticizable without being amenable to independent confirmation; the former requires only that we are able to bring considerations *against* some claim and the latter that we are able to provide independent evidence *for* that claim. And provability is different from both criticizability and independent confirmability: provability refers to a doxastic practice *as a unit* and specifies that that doxastic practice can be shown to be reliable on grounds that aren't drawn from that practice (as, for example, Descartes attempts to do when he attempts to provide a rational justification for the claim that sense perception is reliable). I'll discuss each of these epistemic desiderata elsewhere in this chapter.
40. Michael Perry and Kent Greenawalt have both made considerable use of the notion of public accessibility in articulating an account of restraint, although Perry has recanted his endorsement of this constraint. (See Perry's "Religious Morality and Political Choice," pp. 703–727.) Greenawalt claims that citizens and legislators should typically employ publicly accessible grounds in public political discourse, although he believes that, because of the inability of public reason to resolve many important issues, citizens should feel free to rely on their personal, publicly inaccessible grounds in deciding which policies to support. See *Religious Convictions and Political Choice*, pp. 12, 56ff.; "Religious Convictions and Political Choice," pp. 1040–41, 1046; and *Private Consciences and Public Reasons*, pp. 151–64.
41. Here are two representative selections. "Deliberative reciprocity expresses two related requirements, one primarily moral and the other primarily empirical. When citizens make moral claims in a deliberative democracy, they appeal to reasons or principles that can be shared by fellow citizens who are similarly motivated." Amy Gutmann and Dennis Thompson, *Democracy and Disagreement*, p. 55. "The criterion for public reason is not universal prior acceptance. Rather, public reasons are those that *could* be widely shared by those who considered them, and these can be as novel as you like. No prior conditions to the admissibility of an idea into public reason attach, except those which are directly attendant to whether the reason is available." Lawrence Solum, "Novel Public Reasons," p. 1477.
42. "Uncommon Ground," p. 659. Greene picks up the same cudgel in "The Political Balance of the Religion Clauses," pp. 1616ff.

43. For example, Ted Jelen employs a populist notion of public accessibility in his "In Defense of Religious Minimalism," pp. 14–19.
44. We could complicate the distinction between native cognitive capacities and developed capacities by further distinguishing between what we might call *personally* developed cognitive capacities and *socially* developed cognitive capacities. I leave that exercise and its application to this discussion to the reader.
45. Kent Greenawalt, *Religious Convictions and Political Choice*, p. 57.
46. Jeremy Waldron claims that something like (3) is central to liberalism: "The liberal insists that intelligible justifications in social and political life must be available in principle for everyone, for society is to be understood by the individual mind, not by tradition or sense of a community. Its legitimacy and the basis of social obligation must be made out to each individual, for once the mantle of mystery has been lifted, *everybody* is going to want an answer." "Theoretical Foundations of Liberalism," p. 44.
47. On my understanding of justificatory liberalism, Greenawalt is not a justificatory liberal, although he adheres to some of the positions definitive of that position, namely, that a citizen ought not advocate support for a coercive law solely on religious grounds. Nevertheless, Greenawalt's conception of replicability might be employed in the services of justificatory liberalism.
48. *Private Consciences and Public Reasons*, p. 38.
49. *Private Consciences and Public Reasons*, p. 47.
50. I'm not extremely confident of the accuracy of this interpretation. For, in addition to the claim that sense perceptions are replicable, Greenawalt also claims that certain experiences (e.g., witnessing the birth of one's child) can generate publicly accessible normative claims (e.g., having children is a wonderful experience) but that other experiences (e.g., death of a loved one) generate only inaccessible normative claims (e.g., a life of caring is better than a life of withdrawal). His grounds for denying that the latter experience is replicable are as follows: "Modest changes in circumstances might have made the counsel of withdrawal dominant, and I suppose that for some people it does dominate. I do not think any simple set of external circumstances will produce in others what I felt and what I feel I understand." (*Private Consciences and Public Reasons*, pp. 35–36.)

     First, of what relevance is the fact that *simple* circumstances wouldn't produce in others what it no doubt took very *complex* circumstances to produce in me? Second, and more important, we determine whether some ground is replicable by keeping constant *all* of the factors relevant to the production of that ground and then determining whether *other* agents in those circumstances would acquire that ground. Postulating "modest changes in circumstances" throws the whole test out of whack, so long as those circumstances are causally relevant to an agent's having the experience. After all, that John wouldn't perceive the computer on the desk in circumstances similar to those in which Mary had the experience *save that* John wasn't paying attention to his environment hardly counts against the replicability of Mary's perception. Nor should it count against the replicability of John's experience of the death of a loved one that Mary, with different beliefs, values, personal history, and so on wouldn't react as John does to that experience.

51. Thus Greenawalt: "Sally believes that other people of ordinary perception would have seen what she did if they had been there.... Thus, I claim that Sally's perception is, in principle, replicable in a manner that Saul's is not, even if she faces great difficulties persuading others that she observed what she did." *Private Consciences and Public Reasons*, p. 48.
52. *Private Consciences and Public Reasons*, p. 48.
53. *Private Consciences and Public Reasons*, p. 188, fn. 15.
54. If it was permissible to gerrymander the notion of replicability so that religious sources of information can't count as replicable even though clearly they seem to be on a natural understanding of the notion of replicability, then we might as well have ended our analysis with (1) and simply stipulated that a religious ground is insufficient for a public justification.
55. Perhaps Greenawalt would pursue a different response: given that agents have such varied reactions to putative perceptions of God, and given that reasonable people diverge quite sharply in their evaluations of the epistemic merits of mystical perception, it's reasonable to infer that mystical perception isn't replicable. Thus, he writes, "If we consider the reasons for Christian belief, we must quickly realize that many highly intelligent people aware of all of the arguments in favor of such belief find those arguments wholly unconvincing.... This is a pretty strong basis for doubting that the truth of Christianity can be established by publicly accessible reasons." *Religious Convictions and Political Choice*, p. 74. (I'm not quite sure how Greenawalt's account of public accessibility in his earlier work, here quoted, articulates with the more recent work in which he cashes out accessibility as replicability.) The assumption seems to be that a type of ground's being replicable is at least roughly correlated with generalized acceptance or, at least, the absence of widespread dispute. (Colin Bird presents essentially the same argument in "Mutual Respect and Neutral Justification," p. 77.) I deny that assumption. Given the complexity of the influences on a citizen's belief-forming activity, given the burdens of judgment, I think that we should expect exactly the contrary: replicable grounds will elicit as violent an opposition as nonreplicable grounds. Hence, the inference from dissensus to unreplicability is objectionable. Just as the inference from 'Some claim C is true' to 'C will enjoy consensus' is fallacious, so also is the inference from 'Some claim C is replicable' to 'C will enjoy consensus.' See Nicholas Rescher, *Pluralism*, pp. 50f.
56. At the end of this chapter, we'll return to this argument, when I lay out a general objection to epistemic conceptions of public justification.
57. *Onward Christian Soldiers?* p. 151. Perhaps it was the same activist (Wilcox doesn't say) referred to in another encounter Wilcox describes: "One northern Virginia Republican told me that when he appeared at the local caucus to help select Republican candidates for a state legislative race, a Christian

Right activist asked him which candidate he was supporting. When he said
he was supporting the moderate, the activist replied, 'You must not be a
Christian, then.' The moderate Republican, who had taught Sunday school
for many years in a Methodist church, was understandably appalled."
Onward Christian Soldiers? p. 105.

58. "Secular Fundamentalism, Religious Fundamentalism, and the Search for
Truth in Contemporary America," p. 339.

59. Conkle focuses on biblical inerrancy for expository purposes, but is clear
that his position on biblical inerrancy should be extended to "other religious
sources, such as direct revelations or the statements of contemporary religious leaders." "Different Religions, Different Politics," p. 14, fn. 43. Conkle
also claims that secular citizens can be just as dogmatic and close-minded
in their political commitments as are fundamentalists, and that the dogmatism of secular citizens can derive from their commitment to inerrant
sources. This is the burden of Conkle's argument in "Secular Fundamentalism, Religious Fundamentalism, and the Search for Truth in Contemporary
America."

60. "Secular Fundamentalism, Religious Fundamentalism, and the Search for
Truth in Contemporary America," p. 339. "We should be wary of fundamentalist involvement in the political process. Regardless of the substantive
position being advanced, fundamentalist policies violate a core tenet of our
democratic system – that legal policies should be formulated on the basis
of a dialogic decision-making process, a process requiring an openness of
mind that fundamentalism does not allow." "Different Religions, Different
Politics," p. 15.

61. "Religious Purpose, Inerrancy, and the Establishment Clause," p. 10.

62. I should note that Conkle is an advocate of a greater role for religion in
public life in the United States. He believes that the case for greater inclusion can best be made when we discourage citizens from relying on
inerrant sources of information: by excluding the bad, we make room for
the good. Much of what Conkle has to say is consonant with the position for
which I argue – most particularly, my advocacy of the ideal of conscientious
engagement.

63. Conkle acknowledges this distinction, but fails to appreciate its significance
for his argument. (See "Religious Purpose, Inerrancy, and the Establishment Clause," pp. 11–12, fn. 46.) Matters aren't helped when those who
believe in biblical inerrancy fail to make the requisite distinction. Thus,
for example, when David Smolin claims that "the debate about fallibilism
and pluralism is essentially a debate about whether God has clearly and
authoritatively spoken," he conflates the claim that the Bible is inerrant
with the claim that he, David Smolin, is an infallible interpreter of the
Bible. See Smolin's "Regulating Religious Conflict in America: A Response
to Professor Perry," *Iowa Law Review* 76 (1991): 1086.

64. Bruce Brower accepts a variation on (6): according to Brower, "Citizens
who treat each other with equal respect will share a goal of giving public

reasons, and will treat reasons presented in conversation as open to rational criticism." "The Limits of Public Reason," p. 23.

65. "Religion as a Conversation-Stopper," pp. 1–6.
66. "Moral Conflict and Political Consensus," p. 70. See also Gutmann and Thompson's *Democracy and Disagreement*, pp. 52–94; Alan Wolfe, "Civil Religion Reconsidered," p. 62. Much the same position regarding the immunity of religious convictions to external criticism animates Fish's "Why We Can't All Just Get Along." Thus, Fish asserts: "That is what neutrality means in the context of liberalism – a continual pushing away of orthodoxies, of beliefs not open to inquiry and correction – and that is why, in the name of neutrality, religious propositions must either be excluded from the marketplace or admitted only in ceremonial forms." p. 22. See also Fish's "Mission Impossible," *Columbia Law Review* 97/8 (December, 1997): 2279ff.
67. Conceptualizing religion as a "conversation stopper" is apparently quite popular, as it has been employed not only by Rorty but also by Suzanna Sherry ("The Sleep of Reason," p. 476), Kent Greenawalt (*Private Consciences and Public Reasons*, p. 157), Martha Minow ("Political Liberalism: Religion and Public Reason," p. 5), and no doubt many others.
68. "Mutual Respect and Neutral Justification," p. 71.
69. "Moral Conflict and Political Legitimacy," p. 232.
70. "We need a distinction between two kinds of disagreement – one whose grounds make it all right for the majority to use political power in the service of their opinion, and another whose grounds are such that it would be wrong for the majority to do so. For this purpose, we cannot appeal directly to the distinction between reasonable and unreasonable beliefs. It would be an impossibly restrictive condition on political power to say that its exercise may be justified only by appeal to premises that others could not reasonably reject (though less restrictive than the condition that the premises be *actually* accepted by all)." "Moral Conflict and Political Legitimacy," p. 231.
71. "Moral Conflict and Political Legitimacy," p. 232.
72. "Moral Conflict and Political Legitimacy," p. 232.
73. "Moral Conflict and Political Legitimacy," p. 232.
74. "Moral Conflict and Political Legitimacy," p. 232.
75. William Alston, "The Autonomy of Religious Experience," *International Journal for the Philosophy of Religion* 31 (1992): 74.
76. This is a familiar point. See, for example, William Alston, *Perceiving God*, p. 190; Robert M. Adams, *Finite and Infinite Goods*, pp. 256, 284ff., 364; Alvin Plantinga, *Warranted Christian Belief* (Oxford: Oxford University Press, 2000), p. 259.
77. On this point, see Robert Audi, *Religious Commitment and Secular Reason*, pp. 129–30.
78. I rely here, not on my expertise in the discipline of the history of biblical interpretation – which is nonexistent – but on the expertise of colleagues in that field.

79. "Letter to Madame Christina of Lorraine, Grand Duchess of Tuscany, Concerning the Use of Biblical Quotations in Matters of Science," *Discoveries and Opinions of Galileo*, Stillman Drake, trans. (New York: Anchor Books, 1957), p. 181. Later in the same essay, Galileo writes: "From this and other passages the intention of the holy Fathers appears to be (if I am not mistaken) that in questions of nature which are not matters of faith it is first to be considered whether anything is demonstrated beyond doubt or known by sense-experience, or whether such knowledge or proof is possible; if it is, then, being the gift of God, it ought to be applied to find out the true senses of holy Scripture in those passages which superficially seem to declare differently." "Letter to Madame Christina of Lorraine," p. 199. This is basically the position I take in this book.

80. So in spite of my willingness to deny claims one sometimes hears my co-religionists defend, I do believe that those who accept the doctrine of biblical inerrancy can satisfy (6*). Nothing inerrantists actually believe (as judged by their interpretive practice) is inconsistent with allowing their interpretations of the Bible to be influenced by all manner of secular claims they bring to the Bible.

81. See Richard J. Blackwell, *Galileo, Bellarmine and the Bible* (Notre Dame, IN: University of Notre Dame Press, 1991).

82. "Moral Conflict and Political Legitimacy," p. 232.

83. "Moral Conflict and Political Legitimacy," p. 232.

84. *Perceiving God*, pp. 198–99, 268; "The Christian Language Game," *The Autonomy of Religious Belief*, Frederick Crosson, ed. (Notre Dame, IN: University of Notre Dame Press, 1981), p. 156. Kierkegaard expresses the general point in his distinctive idiom: "In the case of a kind of observation in which it is requisite that the observer should be in a specific condition, it naturally follows that if he is not in this condition, he will observe nothing. He may, of course, attempt to deceive by saying that he is in this condition without being so; but when fortunately he himself avers that he is not in this condition, he deceives nobody. Now if Christianity is essentially something objective, it is necessary for the observer to be objective. But if Christianity is essentially something subjective, it is a mistake for the observer to be objective." *Concluding Unscientific Postscript*, David F. Swenson and Walter Lowrie, trans. (Princeton, N J: Princeton University Press, 1941), p. 51. That there are such subjective conditions of apprehending reality is also crucial to MacIntyre's rejection of the "Encyclopaedic" understanding of rationality that has clear affinities to liberal advocacy of restraint. See, for example, *Three Rival Versions of Moral Enquiry* (Notre Dame, IN: University of Notre Dame Press, 1990), pp. 17f., 60.

85. *Perceiving God*, pp. 198–99.

86. "Moral Conflict and Political Legitimacy," p. 232.

87. Alston addresses this objection in *Perceiving God*, pp. 209–222 and "Christian Experience and Christian Belief," *Faith and Rationality: Reason and Belief in God*, Alvin Plantinga and Nicholas Wolterstorff, eds. (Notre Dame, IN: University of Notre Dame Press, 1983), p. 122. For an explication of the

objection, see C. B. Martin, *Religious Belief* (Ithaca, NY: Cornell University Press, 1959), pp. 64–94; Richard Gale, *On the Nature and Existence of God* (Cambridge: Cambridge University Press, 1991), pp. 285–343; Anthony O'Hear, *Experience, Explanation and Faith* (London: Routledge, Kegan and Paul, 1984), pp. 25–55; Michael Levine, "Mystical Experience and Non-Basically Justified Belief," *Religious Studies* 25 (1989): 335–45; Evan Fales, "Mystical Experience as Evidence," *International Journal for the Philosophy of Religion* 40 (August, 1996): 19–46.

88. "Mystical Experience as Evidence," p. 28.
89. See 8.1.
90. Kent Greenawalt, "Grounds for Political Judgment," p. 649.
91. Of course, if Stangl's life had gone better than it did in fact, we might have been in a position independently to confirm that Stangl didn't collude in genocide. But that's a very different matter than confirming (B).
92. In part, dogmatism is unavoidable as a consequence of the fact that the epistemology of moral judgment is in a state of almost complete disrepair.
93. *The Right and the Good* (Indianapolis, IN: Hackett, 1988), pp. 29–30.
94. *Living High and Letting Die: Our Illusion of Innocence* (Oxford: Oxford University Press, 1996), p. 13.
95. Thus, for example, although Unger ferrets out a number of misleading and distorted moral intuitions regarding the obligations of rich to poor, he relies on an ingenious set of thought experiments to expose the inconsistency of those distorted moral intuitions with even deeper and more fundamental moral judgments. Nowhere, so far as I can tell, does he rely on anything but considerations of coherence.
96. This is not, of course, an uncommon claim; many have leveled it.
97. Note that I am not endorsing skepticism with respect to moral claims; exactly the opposite. I find that a modest foundationalism, a position William Alston has developed in various papers, provides a helpful framework for understanding the epistemic status of both M-beliefs and moral beliefs: we form prima facie justified moral and M-beliefs on a corrigible, (sometimes) noninferential basis, and evaluate both kinds of belief by employing consistency tests. See "Two Types of Foundationalism," "Has Foundationalism Been Refuted?" and "What's Wrong with Immediate Knowledge?" William Alston, *Epistemic Justification*, pp. 19–78.
98. Thus, Kent Greenawalt says, "A person is born and raised in a particular religious tradition. She believes that she is fortunate to be within the tradition whose religious understanding most closely approximates truth. But, she does not think there are generally accessible arguments sufficient to persuade those outside the tradition of the validity of its understanding." "Grounds for Political Judgment," p. 650. Here the emphasis is not, as it was in the prior discussion of Greenawalt's position, on the accessibility of the kind of ground employed *in* a given practice, but on the ability of a given citizen to present arguments for the reliability *of* a practice.
99. See William Alston, *The Reliability of Sense Perception* (Ithaca, NY: Cornell University Press, 1993) and *Perceiving God*, pp. 102–45.

100. "Liberalism, Religion, and the Unity of Epistemology," *San Diego Law Review* 30 (Fall, 1993): 763–97.
101. "Liberalism, Religion, and the Unity of Epistemology," p. 769.
102. Unfortunately, examples of this kind of obfuscation litter the literature on the proper role of religion in politics. I have already discussed several examples. Here is another. According to Suzanna Sherry, "The lasting accomplishment of the Enlightenment ... was its development of an epistemological method," a method that involved the "repudiation of 'the millennium of superstition, other-worldliness, mysticism and dogma known as the Middle, or Dark, Ages.'" ("The Sleep of Reason," p. 456.) And exactly what, according to Sherry, constitutes that "epistemological method?" Well, it is by no means clear. Sherry associates that "method" with something called "Reason," which in turn she associates with a number of things, among which are the following: (1) pragmatism; (2) the propriety of certain sorts of questions: for example, "Doesn't that contradict what you said earlier?" "If that's true, wouldn't it follow that?"; (3) the impropriety of certain sorts of claims, for example, "I have faith that this is true regardless of its internal contradictions or its consistency with the evidence"; (4) an avoidance of appeals to power in order to convince. But at the heart of Sherry's characterization of the Enlightenment's epistemological "method" is an appeal to sense-perception and science: "what distinguishes reason from alternative epistemologies is its general reliance on basic logic[!] and the evidence of the senses (augmented by scientific discoveries)." ("The Sleep of Reason," p. 455.) Since it's pretty obvious that the Enlightenment method is *not* distinguished from its competitors (Alvin Plantinga's deeply anti-Enlightenment conception of warrant, for example) by its reliance on basic logic, Sherry's characterization of the distinctiveness of the Enlightenment method amounts to a privileging of sense-perception and science. Having thus privileged the "high end" of the epistemic scale in characterizing the Enlightenment method, Sherry then has no problem categorizing as "nonrational forms of knowledge" religious claims that derive from putative revelations from God. ("The Sleep of Reason," p. 477.) And once she makes that move, she is free to advocate the doctrine of restraint without facing what I take to be the very difficult problem of showing that many of the moral convictions on which citizens cannot but rely when engaging in political decision making and advocacy aren't different in any epistemically relevant respect from religious grounds.
103. I should note that Alexander's argument does contain an appreciation for the point I'm trying to make here (see p. 774, for example), although I don't think it receives the attention it deserves.

Chapter Nine

1. Note that in the last chapter, I used a particular sort of religious ground – mystical perception – as a foil to establish the claim that the justificatory

liberal is unable to articulate a defensible epistemic conception that mandates restraint regarding religious grounds, *whatever* the content of the claims a citizen accepts on the basis of those religious grounds. In this chapter, I focus on claims with a particular content – moral claims – that a citizen accepts on the basis of religious grounds, *whatever* the kind of religious ground, namely, mystical perception, appeal to divine revelation, reliance on religious authority, and so on.

2. It is important to keep in mind the central qualification that there are some moral claims that enjoy perhaps even the highest epistemic standing, for example, that they are as intuitively obvious as the claim that modus ponens is a valid form of argument. My consistency argument does *not* depend on the claim that there are *no* secularly grounded moral claims that enjoy the highest epistemic standard. It *does* depend on the claim that most of the moral claims a citizen employs as a basis for her favored coercive laws do not satisfy the highest epistemic standards: very few (if any) coercive laws are amenable to justification by a rationale that contains only platitudinous moral claims.

3. I distinguish throughout between moral truths and moral claims. A moral claim is either true or false, so that all moral truths are moral claims but not vice versa. If the theistic case is sound, then, if a given religiously grounded moral claim is *true*, we should expect to find secular corroboration for that *claim*. We do not, of course, expect that each religiously grounded moral *claim* will enjoy adequate secular corroboration: in particular, we don't expect to discern secular corroboration for religiously grounded moral claims that are *false*.

4. Notice that the theistic case doesn't get the justificatory liberal *exactly* what she wants: even if the theistic case shows that a citizen ought not support any coercive law solely on the basis of a religious norm for which she lacks secular corroboration, it doesn't follow that she should refrain from supporting a coercive law solely on the basis of a religious norm for which she lacks public justification. By all accounts, a secular ground can be so idiosyncratic and contentious that it doesn't constitute a public justification. Consequently, even if a citizen satisfies the secularity constraint, she needn't satisfy the public justification restraint. Nevertheless, all public justifications are secular and none are religious. So an argument that establishes that a citizen ought to exercise restraint regarding secularly uncorroborated religious norms gets the justificatory liberal at least part of the way to her desired destination.

5. "Liberal Democracy and the Place of Religion in Politics," pp. 18, 21.
6. *Religion in Politics*, p. 75.
7. I should note that, although the theistic case I develop in this essay was suggested by both Perry and Audi, I don't intend to explicate their arguments, so the issue of how well my formulation of the argument captures their intentions is beside the point. The argument I articulate shouldn't be blamed on either.

8. As I will use the term in this essay, "moral knowledge" is roughly synonymous with "reliably formed, true moral beliefs." Thus, an agent who has adequate grounds for a true moral belief has moral knowledge.

9. The sort of accessibility I have in mind here is, at a minimum, in principle accessibility as explicated in the prior chapter. But the notion involved here is also stronger than in principle accessibility, as will be clear shortly.

10. Of course, it is open to the atheologian to articulate a version of the argument from evil that posits some contradiction or unlikelihood between the claim that humans lack moral knowledge and the claim God is morally perfect, omniscient, and omnipotent.

11. The notion of access employed here is different from either of the notions I articulated in the prior chapter, namely, in principle accessibility and actual accessibility. I'll clarify that third notion shortly.

12. I have no clear idea how to explicate the scope of this argument, that is, the extent of the moral knowledge to which the theistic arguments putatively shows that we have strong secular access.

13. I hope it is clear that (7) works only if the antecedent states that religiously grounded moral truths will *likely* enjoy secular corroboration. I hope it is also clear why the theistic case must be formulated in terms of *strong* secular access: only when we formulate (6) in terms of strong secular access may we infer, in (7), that secular corroboration is likely. Merely in principle or weak secular access does not achieve the desired result.

14. If fully explicated, this step in the argument would have to be much more involved than the foregoing indicates: just having a defeater for belief B doesn't render a citizen unjustified in adhering to B. But none of the necessary qualifications illuminate the central issue and so are better left unsaid until later (9.3) when I discuss one such qualification.

15. *Justice as Impartiality*, p. 169.

16. See C. A. J. Coady, *Testimony: A Philosophical Study* (Oxford: Clarendon Books, 1992). We can, of course, check out a given authority's testimony regarding particular claims. Hence, there are no testimonial claims which we can't "in principle" check. But as a matter of realistic and unavoidable fact, whenever we go about checking an authority's claims regarding a particular fact, we rely on a host of other testimonial claims we have no realistic prospect of checking. That each bit of testimony is "in principle" checkable doesn't entail that each bit of testimony is actually checkable. Again, we can check out the reliability of a given authority, not just the particular claims she presses on us. But the "in principle" checkability of particular authorities doesn't translate into the realistic prospect of checking each particular authority: as a matter of realistic and unavoidable fact, whenever we go about checking one authority's credibility, we rely on the credibility of a host of other authorities.

17. I have in mind here primarily the procedural aspects of rationality, namely, engaging in critical discourse with one's compatriots, doing one's best to accumulate reliable and representative evidence, adhering to appropriate canons of inference, and so on.

18. In order to appreciate the nature of my objection to the theistic case for restraint, recall that the theistic case has a structure similar to that of the argument from evil. Whereas the proponent of the argument from evil contends that traditional theistic claims about God's nature are inconsistent with the claim that evil exists, the proponent of the theistic case contends that theistic claims about God's nature render it likely that agents will have access to a great good, namely, secular access to moral knowledge. One venerable response to the problem of evil is to claim that God can create a world in which evil can exist so long as evil is brought about by the misuse of human freedom. It seems to me that the theistic case is vulnerable to something like the same response. It's possible that even ideally rational citizens will find themselves so circumstanced that they are unlikely to acquire secular corroboration for religiously grounded moral truths because others have misused their cognitive capacities.

19. I should make clear from the outset that I by no means endorse Goldhagen's characterization of German culture as pervaded (or nearly so) by an "eliminationist anti-Semitism." It seems to me that Goldhagen far overstates his case and that more nuanced positions, such as that articulated by Christopher Browning, are more plausible. See Browning's *Ordinary Men: Reserve Police Battalion 101 and the Final Solution in Poland* (New York: Harper-Collins, 1998), particularly pp. 191–223. For trenchant and generally convincing criticism of Goldhagen's central claims, see Norman Finkelstein and Ruth Bettina Birn, *A Nation on Trial: The Goldhagen Thesis and Historical Truth* (New York: Henry Holt, 1998). Nevertheless, although Goldhagen overstates his case, even a considerably more refined version of his thesis illustrates the central point: that the "secular component" of a culture can be sufficiently corrupt as to render at least some of its members rationally justified in rejecting important moral truths.

20. *Hitler's Willing Executioners: Ordinary Germans and the Holocaust* (New York: Vintage Books, 1996), p. 48. Goldhagen claims to prescind from moral judgments of the sort expressed in this sentence.

21. *Hitler's Willing Executioners*, p. 34.

22. *Hitler's Willing Executioners*, p. 106.

23. *Hitler's Willing Executioners*, p. 46. Goldhagen writes: "Germans did not merely understand themselves to be carrying out what were considered to be the crazy plans of a criminal madman; rather, they really comprehended why such radical action ... had to be undertaken, why, in order to safeguard the existence of the *Volk*, the extermination of the Jews was to be a German national project." *Hitler's Willing Executioners*, p. 404.

24. In fact, many Germans no doubt thought that "rational" reflection recommends anti-Semitism, agreeing with Hitler that "National Socialism is a cool and highly reasoned approach to reality based on the greatest of scientific knowledge and its spiritual expression." Cited in Michael Burleigh, *The Third Reich*, p. 13.

25. See Susannah Heschel, "When Jesus Was an Aryan," *Betrayal: German Churches and the Holocaust* (Minneapolis, MN: Fortress Press, 1999), pp. 74–78.

26. Doris Bergen, *The Twisted Cross: The German Christian Movement in the Third Reich* (Chapel Hill: University of North Carolina Press, 1996), p. 163. For three case studies on theologians who allowed the prevailing Nazi ethos to alter their theological convictions, see Robert P. Erickson, *Theologians under Hitler: Gerhard Kittel, Paul Althaus and Emanuel Hirsch* (New Haven, CT: Yale University Press, 1986). For a history of the Protestant church under Nazism, see Gloria Barnett, *For the Soul of the People: Protestant Protest under Hitler* (Oxford: Oxford University Press, 1992).
27. Michael Burleigh, *The Third Reich*, p. 14.
28. The point of this reference to the church under Nazism is *not* to deny that theists should dismiss secular considerations altogether. In fact, I have explicitly denied that claim in the prior chapter. The point is merely to indicate why theists have good reason, given their recent history, to be wary of according too much weight to secular moral considerations.
29. "Wolterstorff on Religion and Politics," p. 127.
30. See, for example, Richard Hays, *The Moral Vision of the New Testament* (San Francisco: HarperCollins Publishers, 1996), pp. 379–406.
31. I am well aware that many will deny that a citizen can be rationally justified to a sufficiently high degree, solely on religious grounds, in believing that homosexual relations are morally inappropriate. Michael Perry has powerfully pressed this point in conversation and in unpublished work. But that is a topic for another day, given that my intention is to illustrate the central point of this chapter, not broach substantive arguments regarding homosexuality directly.
32. I take the term "moral vision" from Richard Hays, *The Moral Vision of the New Testament*. That notion is reminiscent of Rawls's "comprehensive doctrine" and the ubiquitous "conception of the good."
33. For a compelling example of the kind of phenomenon I discuss in this paragraph, see Nicholas Wolterstorff, *Until Justice and Peace Embrace* (Grand Rapids, MI: Eerdmans, 1983).
34. In the interests of ease of exposition, I refer to the moral vision encoded in the Bible, although the Bible is only one of the sources from which Lauren will construct her moral vision.
35. "Liberal Democracy and the Place of Religion in Politics," p. 21.

INDEX

Abolitionism, 175–6
Abortion, 6, 123–2, 176, 217–20, 284, 382
Abzug, Robert, 336
Accessibility, 117, 301, 389
 actual, 256–60, 290
 and replicability, 260–3
 in principle, 100, 256–60, 301, 303
 public, 255–60, 290
 secular (weak and strong), 301–5, 398
Ackerman, Bruce, 11, 340, 350, 352–3, 359, 378
Acquiescence, 107–8, 191
Adams, Robert Merrihew, 90, 352, 393
Alexander, Larry, 291–3, 396
Alston, William, 15, 63, **240–52**, 268, 270–1, 276–7, 286, 288, 341, 354, 386, 387, 393, 394–5
Altman, Irwin, 337
Amendment 1, 6
Amendment 2, 3–4, 110–11, 334, 335, 338
Argument from Bosnia, 19, **153–66**, 174, 185–6, 332, 370, 378, 384
Argument from divisiveness, 19, **166–86**, 332, 338, 375, 376, 378, 384
Argument from respect, 19–20, 109–40, 152, 185, 204–5, 229–31, 332, 365
Arneson, Richard, 369
Audi, Robert, 11, 53, 55–6, 68–9, 77, 105, 134–40, 155, 168, 189, 296–7, 320, 325, 338, 340, 355, 357, 358, 363, 367, 368, 371, 373, 375, 383, 393, 397
Autonomy (epistemic), 246–51, 282–3, 291–3
Autonomy (moral), 360

Bagger, Matthew, 245–6
Barnett, Gloria, 400
Barraclough, Goeffrey, 370
Barry, Brian, 50, 143, 307, 368, 381, 383, 384, 386
Beckley, Harlan, 363
Beecher, Lyman, 335
Bergen, Doris, 400
Berger, Brigitte, 345
Berger, Peter, 25, 31, 32–5, 37–40, 342, 344, 345, 346, 376
Bird, Colin, 252–5, 269, 280, 288, 351, 358, 388, 389, 391
Birn, Ruth Bettina, 399
Blackwell, Richard J., 394
Blumoff, Theodore, 155, 168, 182, 340, 343, 370
Bourne, George, 336
Bransford, Stephen, 335
Brower, Bruce, 362, 392–3
Brown, Callum G., 342, 346
Browning, Christopher, 399
Bruce, Steve, 24–5, 341, 342, 344, 345
Burdens of judgment, 27–8, 215–17, 219–20, 222, 378, 380, 386–7
Burleigh, Michael, 377, 385, 399, 400
Butler, Jon, 24, 342, 344
Button, James W., 334, 335

Campos, Paul, 369
Cannon, Charles, 336
Carter, Stephen, 177, 376
Casanova, José, 43–5, 348
Chaves, Mark, 345
Christian America, 45–6, 348–9
Christian Mystical Practice, 242, 245–6, 263, 265–6, 287–91
 autonomy of, 246–51, 277, 287–8

Christian Mystical Practice (*cont.*)
overrider system, 268, 270–3, 276,
278–80
Christian reconstructionism, 45, 208–9,
212–13, 223, 235, 348, 349, 379
Christian Right, 6, 176–7, 263–4, 349
Christie, John, 336
Citizenship, 7–10, 82, 105, 156, 183–4,
331–3
Civil Rights Movement, 5, 175
Coady, C. A. J., 398
Cohen, Joshua, 343, 358, 359, 363
Conkle, Daniel, 264–5, 269, 358, 388,
391
Consensus, 107–8, 191, 214, 382
Creationism, 274
Cuneo, Terence, 357, 366

Daniels, Norman, 364, 369
Darwall, Stephen, 84–5, 359, 360
de Marneffe, Peter, 351, 381
Differentiation, 43–5, 167, 348, 373
Doctrine of restraint, 10, 18, **68–71**,
75–6, 82, 109–110, 114, 118–20,
124, 125–6, 150–1, 181–2, **187–92**,
195, 237–8, 251, 287, 329, 331–3,
355, 370, 377, 385
Doxastic practice approach to
epistemology, 15, 240–52
Dueling, 5
Dumond, Dwight L., 336
Dworkin, Gerald, 360
Dworkin, Ronald, 363

Eberle, Christopher J., 375, 387, 388
Ecumenical political dialogue, 189
Ellul, Jacques, 177, 376
Erickson, Robert P., 400
Evangelicalism, 42, 44–6, 111, 341, 347,
348–9
External criticism, 100, 244–6, 267–8

Fales, Evan, 278–9, 395
Fallibilism, 102, 242, 263–7, 319–20,
338, 392
Falwell, Jerry, 353, 385
Farmer, James, 375
Findlay, James F., 337
Finke, Roger, 28, 45, 342, 344, 345, 346,
347, 376
Finkelstein, Norman, 399
Fish, Stanley, 40, 343, 369, 374, 393
Friedman, Marilyn, 378
Foundationalism, 15, 100, 341, 395
Fundamentalism, 42, 111, 148–50,
264–6, 341, 343, 364, 392

Gale, Richard, 395
Galileo, 275, 394
Galston, William, 97–9, 104, 379
Garrison, William Lloyd, 336
Garrow, David, 241, 375
Gaus, Gerald, 11, 12, 70, 128–34, 216,
230–2, 236, 339, 340, 351, 354, 356,
358, 359, 362, 367, 378, 380, 383,
385, 386
Gedicks, Frederick, 358
Genovese, Eugene, 336
Ginat, Joseph, 337
Glendon, Mary Ann, 154, 370–1
Goldberg, Suzanne, 335
Goldhagen, Daniel, 315, 399
Greenawalt, Kent, 167, 260–3, 280,
338, 351, 353, 357, 374, 386, 389,
390, 391, 393, 393, 395
Greene, Abner, 167, 255, 340, 358, 375,
389
Grube, Dirk-Martin, 249–50, 387
Gutmann, Amy, 11, 52, 73, 127, 269,
340, 343, 350, 351, 352, 354, 358,
363, 365, 366, 369, 381, 386, 389,
393

Habermas, Jurgen, 341
Hampton, Jean, 380
Hare, R. M., 138
Hart, H. L. A., 166, 352
Hays, Richard, 400
Henry, Carl, 347
Hertzke, Allen, 337
Heschel, Susannah, 399
Hill, Christopher, 374
Hill, Thomas, 378
Hirst, Derek, 374
Holmes, Stephen, 74, 371
Holt, Mack, 373
Homosexuality, 3, 9, 15, 111, 130–1,
225, 234, 265–6, 272–3, 321, 334,
338, 353
Hunter, James Davison, 383

Iannoccone, Laurence R., 344, 345
Ideal of conscientious engagement,
19–20, 82, 84, **104–8**, 112, 140,
146–8, 164, 180–1, 184, 188, 191–2,
263, 306–7, 369
Inerrancy, 263–7
Intelligibility, 252–5

Jelen, Ted, 364, 375, 390
John, Richard R., 335–6
Justificatory liberalism, 11–13, **48–78**,
339

and public justification, 11, 48, 51–2,
195–7
and religion, 12, **71–8**, 196
and respect, 11, 81, 84, 109–110,
109–151
central commitments of, 54, 58,
187
distinguished from mere liberalism,
11, 59–61
epistemic assumptions of, 14–16,
196–7, 237–9, 287, 341, 386
not committed to religious
skepticism, 237–8

Keen, Lisa, 335
Kellner, Hansfried, 345
Kelly, Michael, 337
Kierkegaard, Soren, 394
King, Jr., Martin Luther, 5, 145, 241–2,
337
Klapproth, Eric, 385
Kuhn, Thomas, 326
Kymlicka, Will, 365

Larmore, Charles, 11, 28, 51–2, 98,
120–8, 340, 343, 344, 350, 352,
355, 359, 360, 366, 367, 371, 378,
382, 386
Laslett, Peter, 344
Levine, Michael, 395
Liberal principle of legitimacy, 140–3,
381
Liberation theology, 112
Lischer, Richard, 337
Locke, John, 160–61

Macedo, Stephen, 40, 50–1, 53, 189,
340, 343, 350, 352, 355, 358, 364,
366, 369, 382
MacIntyre, Alasdair, 394
Manifestation beliefs, 241
Mannheim, Karl, 376
Markham, Ian, 343
Marshall, William, 154, 343
Martin, C. B., 395
Martin, David, 344, 370, 371–2
Mason, John, 385
Mere Liberalism, 11, 59–61, 188, 353,
360
Mill, John Stuart, 353
Minow, Martha, 154, 393
Moral identity, 35–7, 146–8, 177–8, 346,
363
Moral platitudes, 206, 217–220, 283–4,
397
Moral vision, 322–9

Morrill Anti-bigamy Act, 336
Mystical perception, 21, **240–93**

Nagel, Thomas, 11, 269–78, 340, 358,
359, 366, 386
Nielson, Kai, 340, 351, 382
Noonan, John, 162, 175, 337, 373,
375
Norman, Wayne, 365
North, Gary, 348, 385

O'Hear, Anthony, 395
Original position, 142–3
Overrider systems, 242–3, 268, 270–3,
278–80

Paradisal moral agents, 299
Perry, Michael, 91, 104, 141, 146, 162,
171, 179–80, 189, 297, 342, 350,
351, 360, 368, 369, 375, 377, 379,
387, 389, 397, 400
Plantinga, Alvin, 393, 396
Pluralism (cultural), 18, 24–47, 214–17,
346, 347, 350
and religious freedom, 26–7, 43–7
engenders religious doubt, 31–5,
37–40
vivifies religion, 41–4
Polanyi, Michael, 326
Polygamy, 5, 95, 122, 175, 336, 337
Principle of harm, 60, 188–9, 353
Principle of pursuit, 10, 18, **68–71**, 75-6,
82, 99, 111, 114, 118–20, 125–6,
150–1, 181–2, 189, 355
Privatization of religion, 26, 33, 44,
76–8, 144–5, 153–86, 348, 370, 371,
374, 375, 377,
Prohibition, 175
Public justification, 11, 14, 51–2, 63–8,
73–4, **195–293**, 377
and respect, 109–151, 189–90
and scientific theories, 258–9
concept versus conception of, 66–8,
99–100, 196, 238, 341
contrasted with rational justification,
63–6, 88, 198, 350
contrasted with religious
justifications, 73–4, 196, 205, 397
core concept of, 198–200
enumerative conceptions of, 201
epistemic conceptions of, 14–16, 21,
67–8, 196–7, **237–93**, 362, 388
exclusionary role of, 196, 208, 225,
227, 229, 289
idealizing conceptions of, 199–200,
222–33, 388

Public justification (*cont.*)
  populist conceptions of, 20–1, 67–8,
    100, 196, **200–22**, 229–31, 340, 362,
    364, 388
  providing versus pursuing, 118–20,
    356, 365–66

Quinn, Philip, 352, 366, 369, 379

Rational choice theory, 346
Rationality, 15, 61–6, 121–2, 310–12,
    354
  and respect for persons, 88–94
  and testimony, 310–11
  as a constraint on public justification,
    202–3
  contrasted with public justification,
    63–6, 88, 198
  person-relative nature of, 62,198
  state versus activity of rational
    justification, 63–4

Rawls, John, 11, 25, 27–8, 52, 52–3, 65,
    140–50, 191, **211–22**, 344, 349, 350,
    351, 352, 355, 358, 359, 368, 375,
    379, 380, 382, 383
Raz, Joseph, 200, 350
Reasonableness, 212–22, 369, 380, 382,
    383
  and religious freedom, 220–2
  and theism, 148–50
  defined, 149, 212
  as a constraint on public justification,
    212, 381

Religious freedom, 13, 18, 26–9, 59,
    153, 161–3, 209, 212–13, 220–2,
    235, 353, 374
Religious grounds (reasons), 71–3,
    270–8, 291–3, 313–14, 356
Religious legitimation (of the state), 46,
    178–9, 349 376
Religious liberalism, 42
Religious norms, 294–6, 377
  as conversation-stoppers, 269, 393
  as overriding and totalizing, 145,
    183, 317, 323

Religious sectarianism, 187,190–1
Religious wars, 27, 152, 156–6, 371,
    372, 373
Rescher, Nicholas, 107–8, 363, 391
Respect for persons, 11, 19–20, 52–4,
    81–3, **84–140**, 229–31, 359–60, 361
Rienzo, Barbara A., 334, 335

Rorty, Richard, 77, 152, 268, 358, 363,
    371, 393
Russell, Richard, 337

Sandel, Michael, 358, 382
Secular grounds (reasons), 21, 72–3,
    270–8, 291–3, 313–14, 339, 356
Secularization, theory of, 6, 18, 23–7,
    29–45, 341, 342, 345, 348
Sense perception, 242–3, 258, 260–2,
    277–8, 278–81, 386–7, 396
Sher, George, 351, 353
Sherry, Suzanna, 371, 393, 396
Skepticism, 237–8, 239, 268, 340–1, 386
Slavery, 5, 175–6, 212–13, 336
Smith, Christian, 27, 35–46, 169, 346,
    347, 348, 349, 376
Smolin, David, 392
Social harmony, problem of, 49–51,
    106–7, 190, 350
Solum, Lawrence, 11, 53, 56, 116–20,
    155, 343, 350, 352, 358, 359, 364,
    365, 371, 379, 380, 389
Stark, Rodney, 28, 45, 342, 344, 345,
    346, 347, 373, 376
Sterba, James, 367
Strains of commitment, 140–50, 317,
    329
Subcultural identity theory, 35–43
Sufficiency condition, **205–7**, 209,
    215–16, 220, 222, 254
Sullivan, Kathleen,155

Taylor, Charles, 346, 360
Taylor, John, 336
Telepathy, 258–60
Thomson, Dennis, 52, 73, 127, 269,
    340, 343, 350, 351, 352, 354, 358,
    364, 365, 366, 369, 381, 386, 389,
    393
Toland, John, 370
Trigg, Roger, 358
Turner, Bryan, 26, 178, 342
Tushnet, Mark, 375, 377

Unger, Peter, 284, 395

Veil of ignorance, 142–3

Wald, Kanneth D., 334, 335, 368
Waldron, Jeremy, 351, 359, 379, 390
Wagoner, Richard S., 336
Wallis, Ray, 342
Warner, R. Stephen, 348
Weber, Max, 337

Weithman, Paul, 53, 350, 352, 358, 369
West, John, 335, 336, 340
Wilcox, Clyde, 208, 263, 337, 349, 354, 379, 385, 391
Wilson, Bryan, 342

Wolfe, Alan, 334, 349, 393
Wolff, Robert Paul, 148
Wolterstorff, Nicholas, 73, 145, 237, 338, 361, 369, 386, 400

Yamane, David, 345